Reinsurance Arbitrations

Kyriaki Noussia

Reinsurance Arbitrations

Springer

Kyriaki Noussia
Athens
Greece

ISBN 978-3-642-45145-4 ISBN 978-3-642-45146-1 (eBook)
DOI 10.1007/978-3-642-45146-1
Springer Heidelberg New York Dordrecht London

Library of Congress Control Number: 2014930749

Printed on acid-free paper

Springer is part of Springer Science+Business Media (www.springer.com)

To Prof. Dr. Ioannis K. Rokas

Preface

Business and society nowadays are in profound upheaval. Major changes occur on a constant basis, following events such as the 2008 credit crunch. Reinsurance is a vitally important sector of economy, which has undergone major changes in the past years. In spite of the currently ongoing financial upheaval, reinsurance has maintained its strong position in the insurance and reinsurance market and industry as well as in the world economic arena.

Due to various factors, arbitration is often the preferred approach for resolving reinsurance and other complex commercial business disputes. For this reason, most reinsurance contracts, especially reinsurance treaties, contain an arbitration clause requiring that disputes arising under the contract be resolved by arbitration.

But why is arbitration preferred? To name but a few reasons, firstly arbitration has been the traditional method of dispute resolution for reinsurance disputes for many decades. Secondly, insurance and reinsurance companies would rather have their disputes resolved by a panel of industry-related experts who will decide disputes based on industry custom and practice. Thirdly, traditional reinsurance arbitration clauses relieve the arbitrators from following the strict rules of law and specifically require the arbitrators to consider the reinsurance contract as an honourable engagement rather than a strict legal obligation. In addition, reinsurance arbitrations are also private, confidential proceedings that are not open to public or competitor scrutiny.

During the course of my research in the past years it became, too often, obvious that this was a book which was needed to be written. Notwithstanding the fact that the topic has been touched upon numerous times—albeit not comprehensively—the absence of any extended analysis of reinsurance arbitrations, for the benefit of both the worlds of legal academia and practice, was both notable and remarkable. Having said that, it needs also to be stated that it has been a highly rewarding subject to research and to analyse, and one which I hope will appeal more to others as a result of my effort to present it as a useful and important action. The challenge, as I saw it, was to produce a book which would, on the one hand, inform and interest legal academics yet, and on the other hand, provide a user-friendly, practical resource for busy arbitration practitioners. Though maintaining the balance between a scholarly work and a practitioner text has at times proved delicate, the desired result—in my view always—has been achieved to a great extent. Along the way, this exercise has operated as a powerful practical demonstration of a point which many might acknowledge as a matter of theory, but is far too seldom put into practice, i.e. that each of the two worlds can benefit enormously from the wisdom and experience of the other.

The current monograph explores in-depth reinsurance arbitrations and issues that arise within their conduct. Before embarking on an in-depth analysis of reinsurance arbitrations, the history of reinsurance and the main features, aspects and functions of the reinsurance contract, with regard to its formation, interpretation and the arbitration agreement within it, are being discussed. The analysis of reinsurance arbitrations involves also a discussion of various issues, such as the reinsurance arbitration clause and the rules of its construction, the commencement and procedure of reinsurance arbitration, and the multiple issues to be discussed therein, as well as the reinsurance arbitration award and enforcement issues. Following the above, a critical discussion of the status of reinsurance arbitrations is conducted and general conclusions are being drawn.

Athens, Greece Kyriaki Noussia
October 2013

Acknowledgements

I have incurred many debts along the way of completing the current work.

I would like to thank the Alexander von Humboldt Foundation (AvH) for awarding me an AvH Research Fellowship (2007–2010) during which I mainly researched and wrote the previous monograph on the topic of confidentiality in arbitration, and I also developed the idea and conducted part of the initial and basic research for this monograph.

Special thanks are also owed to the German Academic Exchange Service (DAAD) for awarding me a small period research grant in 2011, which also enabled me to research a major part of the current monograph.

I am also indebted to the University of Hamburg, Faculty of Law, Institute of Procedural and Private Law and the Max Planck Institute of Comparative and Private International Law in Hamburg, for repeatedly awarding me a Max Planck Society Research Scholarship (2011–2013) and hosting me as a reader as well as for all of the research assistance provided. In this respect special thanks are owed to Frau Elke Halsen Raffel of the Max Planck Institute of Comparative and Private International Law in Hamburg.

I have significantly benefited from the numerous discussions I have had with Prof. Dr. Ioannis Rokas. His guidance has been crucially helpful and this book is dedicated to him as a means of acknowledgement of the above. At the same time, I owe a big intellectual debt to Prof. Rob Merkin not least for suggesting, in the first place, i.e. some years ago, that someone needed to undertake this project. Other jurists (academic and/or practising) have allowed me to profit from their support and intellectual rigour. It is, therefore, a pleasure to thank *inter alia* Prof. Dr. Ulrich Magnus RiOLG, Prof. Martin Schauer, Mr Andreas Schwarz and Mr Robert Hird. Talks with practitioners at various reinsurance companies (Hannover Re, Munich Re, Swiss Re, Zurich Re, Scor) have also significantly enhanced this work and enriched it with an indispensable practitioners' flair. Again, special thanks are owed to all of the people who provided me with valuable feedback, in this respect.

The current work was also research-wise enriched—alongside other research—during my stay as a Fulbright (Greece) Visiting Scholar at Columbia Law School, USA (2013). I wholeheartedly thank the Fulbright (Greece) Foundation for awarding me the academic Visiting Scholar Fellowship and status during the academic year 2012–2013. In addition, I owe a big debt to the Stavros Niarchos Foundation for acting as a sponsor. Within Columbia Law School, special thanks are owed to Prof. George Bermann for his valuable insight. Whilst in NY, USA, I have also been able to talk and exchange views with arbitrators and lawyers acting as counsels in reinsurance arbitrations. Special thanks are therefore owed to all of the people who I have met and discussed with in this respect.

My publishers, Springer Verlag, and most notably Dr. Brigitte Reschke have been a great source of help and support all the way, as ever, and I also wish to acknowledge them hereby.

On a personal tone, I would like to thank once again my family for their support over the years.

Responsibility for any lapses is, of course, entirely mine.

The law stands as on October 12, 2013.

Athens, Greece
October 2013

Kyriaki Noussia

Abbreviations

ADR	Alternative Dispute Resolution
AIDA	Association Internationale de Droit des Assurances
ARIAS	AIDA Reinsurance and Insurance Arbitration Society
BGB	Bürgerliches Gesetzbuch
CPR	Civil Procedures Rules
DAC	Departmental Advisory Committee on Arbitration Law
DAS	Deutscher Ausschuss für Schiedsgerichtswesen
DIS	Deutsche Institut für Schiedsgerichtsbarkeit
FAA	Federal Arbitration Act
Fed. R. Civ. P.	Federal Rules of Civil Procedure
FRA	Facultative Reinsurance Agreement
HGB	Handelsgesetzbuch
ICC	International Chamber of Commerce
LIRMA	London Insurance and Reinsurance Market Association
LUA	Lloyd's Underwriters' Association
OLG	Oberlandesgericht
UNCITRAL	United Nations Commission on International Trade Law
VCTL	Vienna New York Convention on the Law of Treaties
VVG	Versicherungsvertragsgesetz
ZPO	Zivilprozessordnung

Contents

Introduction 1
1.1 General 1
1.2 Reinsurance Aspects and History 3
1.2.1 Reinsurance Treaties 3
1.2.2 The History of Reinsurance 5
1.3 Reinsurance Relationship 14
1.3.1 General 14
1.3.2 Modern Times 14
1.3.3 The Use of Arbitration in Reinsurance 15
1.3.4 Choice of Forum: Litigation Versus Arbitration 20
1.4 Aims, Outline and Scope 34
1.4.1 General 34
1.4.2 Aims 34
1.4.3 Background Justification 35
1.4.4 Research Purpose 35
1.4.5 General Outline 35
1.4.6 Detailed Outline 36
References 36

The Reinsurance Contract 39
2.1 Formation of Contracts 39
2.1.1 The Role of Industry, Custom and Practice 39
2.1.2 The Procedure 40
2.1.3 Identification of the Contract 41
2.1.4 The Contract Terms 44
2.2 Rules of Construction 47
2.2.1 The Role of Industry Custom and Practice 47
2.2.2 Interpretation and Construction 48
References 72

The Need for Reinsurance Arbitration: The Legal Framework 73
3.1 General Introductory Remarks on Arbitration in Reinsurance 73
3.2 The Legal Framework in England 75
3.2.1 Scope of the Arbitration Act 1996 76
3.3 Reinsurance in the USA 81
3.3.1 General 81
3.3.2 The Legal Framework in the USA 84
3.4 Reinsurance in Germany and Arbitration Within It 101
3.4.1 Statistical and Anecdotal Evidence 102
3.4.2 An Empirical Evaluation 104
3.4.3 Party Neutrality 105
3.4.4 Arbitral Law and Environment 105
3.4.5 Substantive Law 105
3.4.6 Expertise and Infrastructure 106
3.4.7 Convenience 106
3.4.8 Language 107
3.4.9 Confidentiality 107
3.4.10 The Practice of Arbitration in Germany 107
3.4.11 Arbitrating in Germany in Practice 113
3.5 Overall Conclusions 120
References 121

The Reinsurance Arbitration Clause 123
4.1 Introductory Remarks 123
4.1.1 The Arbitration Clause 124
4.2 The Everlasting Struggle: Arbitration or Litigation? 130
4.2.1 Procedural Difficulties in Arbitration 133
4.2.2 Arbitration: The Quick Result 133
4.2.3 The Advantages of Expert Knowledge 134
4.2.4 Where Avoidance of Precedent Is Preferred 135
4.2.5 The Relative Costs of Litigation and Arbitration 135
4.2.6 Joining Third Parties to the Proceedings 135
4.2.7 The Flexibility of Arbitration 136
4.3 The Arbitration Procedure 137
4.3.1 Does the Arbitration Agreement Cover the Dispute? 138
4.3.2 Provisions with Ambiguous Scope 139
4.4 Considering the Obligation to Arbitrate 140
4.4.1 The Agreement to Arbitrate 140
4.4.2 Scope of the Agreement to Arbitrate 141
4.4.3 Arbitrability 146
4.4.4 Intent to Arbitrate 148
4.4.5 The Arbitration Notice 152

4.4.6 Response to the Arbitration Notice 153
4.4.7 Demanding Arbitration 153
4.4.8 Avoiding Arbitration 155
4.4.9 Lack of a Written Agreement to Arbitrate 156
4.4.10 The Dispute Is Not Arbitrable 156
4.4.11 Fraud 157
4.4.12 Waiver of the Right to Arbitrate 157
4.4.13 Multiple Parties and Multiple Actions 159
4.4.14 Service of a Demand for Arbitration 161
4.4.15 Selection of Arbitrator 161
4.4.16 Challenging an Arbitrator: The Position Under the FAA 172
4.4.17 Removal or Resignation of Arbitrators 173
4.5 Jurisdiction of Courts 190
4.5.1 Choice of Law in Reinsurance Arbitration Disputes 191
4.5.2 The Law Governing the Agreement to Submit the Dispute to Arbitration 191
4.5.3 The Law Governing the Reference to Arbitration 193
4.6 Conclusions 197
References 200

The Reinsurance Arbitration Proceedings 201
5.1 Procedure at the Hearing 201
5.1.1 Ensuring Procedural Justice in Arbitrations 203
5.1.2 General Duty of Arbitrators 204
5.1.3 Powers of the Court 204
5.1.4 Enforcement of Peremptory Orders 204
5.1.5 Injunctions and Similar Orders 205
5.1.6 Determination of Preliminary Points of Law 205
5.1.7 Staying Court Proceedings 206
5.1.8 "Domestic" and "Non-domestic" Arbitration Agreements . . 207
5.1.9 Arbitration and the Service of Suit Clause 208
5.1.10 Pre-answer Security 209
5.1.11 Organisational Meeting 210
5.1.12 Hearing 211
5.1.13 Post-hearing Issues 211
5.1.14 Enforceability of the Arbitration Agreement 211
5.1.15 Enforcing a Reinsurance Arbitration Provision 214
5.2 Salient Differences Between the U.S. and English Arbitration Systems 224
5.3 Consolidation of Arbitration Proceedings 224
5.4 Critique 226
5.5 Existing Panel Approach 236
5.5.1 Critique 238

5.6 Discovery . . . 238
5.6.1 Contractual Limitations Are Enforceable . . . 239
5.6.2 Discovery Under the FAA . . . 239
5.6.3 Non-party Discovery . . . 240
5.6.4 Other Discovery Issues . . . 244
5.7 Confidentiality . . . 246
5.8 Summary Adjudication . . . 259
5.9 Hold Harmless Agreements . . . 260
5.10 The Honorable Engagement Clause . . . 261
5.11 Conclusions . . . 262
References . . . 262

The Reinsurance Arbitration Award . . . 265
6.1 The Reinsurance Arbitration Award . . . 265
6.1.1 The Arbitration Award . . . 265
6.1.2 Formalities . . . 266
6.1.3 Effect of a Valid Award . . . 267
6.1.4 Enforcement . . . 269
6.1.5 Confidentiality of Awards . . . 276
6.1.6 Enforceability of Reinsurance Arbitral Awards: The US Approach . . . 278
6.2 Reinsurance Arbitrations and the Issue of the Application of Strict Rules of Law . . . 294
6.2.1 Relevant Jurisprudence of the Court of Appeal . . . 296
6.3 The Effect of an Arbitration Award on a Subsequent Arbitration Between Different Parties . . . 302
6.4 The Facts and Arbitral Holding in *Lincoln National Life Insurance Co v Sun Life Assurance Co of Canada* . . . 303
6.4.1 *The Cigna* Award . . . 304
6.4.2 Were the Arbitrators in the *Lincoln* Arbitration Bound by the Award in Cigna? . . . 304
6.4.3 Previous Cases on the Effect of an Earlier Award on Subsequent Arbitration Between Different Parties . . . 305
6.5 Conclusions . . . 315
References . . . 316

Discussion . . . 317
7.1 General Remarks . . . 317
7.2 Overall Conclusions in Relation to Arbitration . . . 319
7.2.1 An Overview . . . 319
7.2.2 General Observations in Relation to Reinsurance Arbitrations . . . 319
7.3 More Specific Observations: Critique . . . 322
References . . . 325

Table of Cases 327
A. England 327
B. USA 329
C. Germany 332

Table of Statutes 333
A. International 333
B. England 333
C. USA 334
D. Germany 334

About the Author 335

Index 337

Introduction

Reinsurance contracts traditionally have been considered "gentlemen's agreements." In modern times, reinsurance contracts have moved away from the handshake agreements of yesterday and focus more on the realities of the bottom line. Reinsurance contracts often, if not always, especially reinsurance treaties, contain an arbitration clause. Hence, should a dispute arise, it will be resolved by resort to arbitration. Reinsurance arbitration differs markedly from commercial arbitration in other industries. Even if one forgets for a moment that the traditional reinsurance relationship is the reason why arbitrations occur in the reinsurance industry, and perhaps offers the greatest advantage for using arbitration, there also other numerous advantages to using arbitration alongside some disadvantages. Still, arbitration remains the preferred dispute resolution method in reinsurance.

1.1 General

Reinsurance is a transaction in which an insurance company (the primary insurer or reinsured) cedes all or part of a risk of loss to another insurance company (the reinsurer). In return for agreeing to indemnify the reinsured for losses that may occur, the reinsurer receives premiums from the reinsured.[1] Reinsurance contracts often, if not always, especially reinsurance treaties, contain an arbitration clause. Hence, should a dispute arise, it will be resolved by resort to arbitration.

Many people ask, what is the difference between litigation and arbitration today anyway? Commercial arbitration, especially reinsurance arbitration, has become complex, costly, and time consuming. Fundamentally, there is no difference

[1] This practice is not limited to a primary insurance company and a reinsurer. It is commonplace for a reinsurer to turn around and retrocede risk to another reinsurer. In that transaction, the reinsurer is known as the retrocedent, and the insurance company assuming the risk of loss is the retrocessionaire; McDonald (2001), p. 328.

K. Noussia, *Reinsurance Arbitrations*, DOI 10.1007/978-3-642-45146-1_1,

between litigation and arbitration because in each proceeding, a neutral third party decides the dispute between the parties and issues a binding decision. Procedurally, however, there are dramatic differences. Arbitration is a consensual dispute resolution mechanism generally founded on a contract provision that requires all disputes to be resolved by arbitration instead of litigation. Because it is generally a contract right, courts enforce arbitration clauses.[2]

Perhaps, the biggest difference between litigation and arbitration is the decider of the dispute. In court, of course, it is a state-court judge who is appointed. In arbitration, the decider is an arbitrator or a panel of arbitrators, who are private citizens being paid by the parties to resolve the dispute. In reinsurance, the practice has been to have a panel of three arbitrators often—but not always—chosen from either active or former executive officers of insurance or reinsurance companies. In other words, industry "experts" act as the arbitrators in reinsurance disputes.

Another big difference is the rules. In court, litigation is governed by either state or federal procedural rules. These rules cover all aspects of the litigation, from commencement through appeals. In commercial arbitration there may or may not be rules. The rules in commercial arbitration may come from arbitral bodies or be formed *ad hoc* by parties.

In reinsurance disputes, the parties may agree to use procedures promulgated over the years by a task force of insurance and reinsurance industry professionals, or may agree to procedures before the arbitration panel that suit both the parties and the arbitrators. Unlike other forms of commercial arbitration, it is rare that a reinsurance arbitration will take place under the auspices of an arbitral organization, or tribunal with rules and procedures that must be followed.

Flexibility of the process is another significant difference between litigation and arbitration. In court, there is very little flexibility as the venue will be the courthouse and the civil procedure rules make clear how the process will unfold. In arbitration, the parties and the arbitrator may find that the arbitration hearing should be held in more than one location or that only briefs and oral argument are necessary to decide the case. Because commercial arbitration is a private, confidential, and consensual procedure, the parties and the arbitrator may adopt unique methods for resolving the dispute.

Undoubtedly, a huge difference between litigation and arbitration is confidentiality, for, in arbitration, the process is private and confidential.

Finally, another major difference is the ability to appeal. In court, the right of appeal exists by statute. In commercial arbitration, generally there is no right of appeal. While there are some ways to challenge an arbitration award, courts construe these grounds narrowly, and it is rare to see an arbitration award vacated.

As stated already, most reinsurance contracts, especially reinsurance treaties, contain an arbitration clause. However, arbitration clauses in reinsurance contracts

---

[2] In the USA a federal policy in favour of arbitration developed many years ago and was made part of the law by Congress when the FAA was enacted. Most states also favour arbitration and have similar laws and court decisions enforcing arbitration clauses; Schiffer (2006).

tend to be very broad. This means that virtually any dispute or disagreement concerning the interpretation or application of any part of the reinsurance contract, including its formation, must be decided by arbitration.

Reinsurance arbitration differs markedly from commercial arbitration in other industries. Reinsurance arbitrations are often controlled by the parties and the arbitrators, not by an arbitral body. Most reinsurance arbitrations traditionally do not require adherence to any particular set of rules.

The predominant reinsurance markets are, traditionally, the English and USA markets. However, Germany is also one of the most important reinsurance markets. More than 40 reinsurers, have their business headquarters in Germany. Altogether, they represent around 27 % of the global reinsurance market. Amidst the German reinsurance companies, are two of the biggest, in size—in terms of premium volumes—worldwide, i.e. Munich Re and Hannover Re. In addition, Swiss Re, Zurich Re and Scor Reinsurance have their business quarters in a territory, where German language is also predominantly spoken, i.e. Switzerland.

One may find the reinsurance industry's preference for arbitration as very unusual in the commercial world. Industry experts offer an amalgamation of reasons for this preference, but the most obvious and intimate, from the standpoint of the reinsurer and the reinsured, are the fact that reinsurance treaties are not commonly plain and typical commercial contracts, the fact that arbitrations are not as adversarial in character and physiology as litigation, the fact that discovery rules are more restrictive and lastly the fact that decisions remain between the parties and are neither published nor count as precedent.

The above constitutes a combination of the reasons that produced the traditional reinsurance relationship. One could say using arbitration was never a conscientious decision by the industry participants; rather, it was simply an extenuation of traditional business practices. Much as the traditional reinsurance relationship, arbitration has come under siege in the era of the "new" reinsurance relationship.

1.2 Reinsurance Aspects and History

1.2.1 Reinsurance Treaties

Reinsurance enables insurers to protect themselves against unexpected events and forms a means of managing potential liability.

In England, the Insurance Companies Act 1982 requires insurers to have adequate reinsurance in place and thus it is common practice in Lloyd's for a broker to arrange reinsurance before seeking subscriptions for a primary policy, so as to make the latter a more attractive proposition.[3]

[3] *General Accident Fire and Life Assurance Corpn v Tanter* (*The* "*Zephyr*") (1985)2 Lloyd's Rep. 529; Lowry and Rawlings (1999), p. 301.

In its simplest form, insurers, having agreed to indemnify the insured against a particular loss, enter into the reinsurance to cover their potential liability under that policy.[4]

Facultative reinsurance is the most basic form of reinsurance business, where the reinsurer chooses or not to accept a particular risk and the reinsured retains a proportion of the risk.[5] In facultative reinsurance, every risk is being considered separately and individually and both insurer and reinsurer have a choice as to whether to enter a reinsurance contract in respect of each risk.[6]

Obligatory or treaty reinsurance is entered into by an agreement usually referred to as a treaty, whereby the reinsured agrees to reinsure primary insurer of a specified class and the reinsurer agrees to accept the business. Both the reinsured and the reinsurer have no choice to deny reinsurance, if the business comes within the class specified in the treaty. Thus, the central distinguishing feature of the treaty method of reinsurance is that the insurer is obliged to cede to the reinsurer such risks, as he has agreed to cede under the treaty and the reinsurer is obliged to accept those risks. It is, as such, the predominant method of reinsurance.[7]

Reinsurance may also be proportional or non-proportional.

In proportional reinsurance, the reinsurers agree, for part of the premium, to take on either an agreed proportion, i.e. a quota share, of all the risks of a particular type or the surplus over a particular amount.[8] The reinsurer has an interest in all the insured's losses as it will pay the proportion of such losses that he has agreed to reinsure, leaving the remainder to be paid by the insurer.[9]

Non-proportional reinsurance covers loss over an agreed amount, divided into excess of loss reinsurance, where the reinsurers are liable for the amount by which individual or aggregated claims on primary policies, exceed an agreed amount and stop loss reinsurance, where the reinsurers are liable above a certain percentage, calculated by the ratio of losses to premium income or as a fixed sum.[10] Thus, in non-proportional reinsurance, the reinsurer is uninterested in any type of loss until it reaches the excess point. For any loss greater than the excess point, the reinsurer pays the part he has insured.[11]

Facultative proportional reinsurance is more frequent than facultative non-proportional reinsurance.[12]

---

[4] Butler and Merkin (1999); Lowry and Rawlings (1999), p. 301.

[5] Lowry and Rawlings (1999), pp. 302–303.

[6] Edelman et al. (2005), pp.11–12.

[7] Edelman et al. (2005), pp. 12–13.

[8] Lowry and Rawlings (1999), pp. 303–304.

[9] Edelman et al. (2005), pp. 9–12.

[10] Lowry and Rawlings (1999), pp. 302–304.

[11] *Balfour v Beaumont* [1982] 2 Lloyd's Rep. 493, 496; Edelman et al. (2005), p. 9.

[12] *Forsokringsakteselskapet Vesta v Butcher* (1989)1 Lloyd's Rep 331, 352; Edelman et al. (2005), pp. 9–12.

Under a proportional treaty the insurer agrees to cede a proportional share of its business within the limits of the treaty and the reinsurer agrees to accept the share. The limits of the treaty can be in relation to the risk, its nature or its amount. However, once agreed the reinsurance is automatic, i.e. the insurer is obliged to cede and the reinsurer is obliged to accept all risks that are within the compass of the treaty.

Proportional reinsurance treaties are either quota share proportional reinsurance treaty or surplus proportional reinsurance treaty. By a quota share proportional reinsurance treaty, insurer and reinsurer are obliged to cede and accept a fixed share of each and every risk within the scope of the treaty.[13] By a surplus proportional reinsurance treaty, the reinsurer agrees to accept the liability above that which the insurer wishes to retain for itself. The insurer decides what sum it wishes to cede to the reinsurer depending on the size and type of risk.[14]

Non-proportional reinsurance treaties are based more on claims than risks, and are categorised as either excess of loss or stop loss non proportional reinsurance treaties. In excess of loss non-proportional reinsurance treaties the reinsurer becomes involved only where the loss on any risks exceeds the deductible and becomes liable for the layer of the loss he has agreed to reinsure. Stop loss non-proportional reinsurance treaties may be excess of loss ratio non-proportional reinsurance treaties, whereby the stop loss excess is expressed as a percentage of loss to premium income, and aggregate excess loss non-proportional reinsurance treaty, whereby the stop loss excess is expressed as a particular sum.[15]

1.2.2 The History of Reinsurance

Reinsurance contracts traditionally have been considered "gentlemen's agreements." Business was done on a handshake with written contracts that were brief and arcane. At the commencement of performance of the contract, the only existing documentation of the transaction generally was a placement slip. A reinsurance placement slip is a model of brevity; its terms are restricted to single paragraphs and incorporate only industry boilerplate terms by reference. For instance, if the formal treaty is to include an arbitration clause, the slip would simply state "arbitration clause." Then a treaty would be generated providing a more formal and detailed documentation of the reinsurance contract. Sometimes a formal treaty may never be generated, the only terms of the reinsurance contract being in the placement slip. Formal treaties often were not much clearer than the placement slips. The treaties usually incorporated antiquated language that rarely was read, or for that matter, legally understood.[16]

---

[13] Edelman et al. (2005), pp. 12–13.

[14] Edelman et al. (2005), p. 13.

[15] Edelman et al. (2005), p. 15.

[16] McDonald (2001), p. 329.

Reinsurance has its origins in marine insurance and in the first centuries of its existence occurred almost exclusively in its wake. Thus, the histories of these two forms of insurance are closely inter-linked. Even in pre-Biblical times, the Babylonians (4000–3000 BC) used to "insure" ships on the basis of loan contracts under which the interest and the loan itself were (re)paid only if the ship arrived safely at its destination. Under these arrangements, the interest on the loan was the insurance premium, whereas the release from the obligation to repay the loan was the insurance benefit. This kind of marine insurance was also practised by the Hindus (600 BC) and the ancient Greeks and Romans. The historical situation towards the end of the Middle Ages formed the backdrop for the evolution of marine insurance: the city-states of the Mediterranean region had developed into important trading centres thanks to the Crusades, while in northern Europe the Hanseatic League was forming. The result was an upswing in European trade. More and bigger cargoes were being transported by sea, so there was a growing need to hedge the value of the transported goods.

By the end of the fourteenth century there were already several insurance policies in force. Documentation has been preserved to this day. It proves that marine insurance was already spreading around the Mediterranean at this time. In the first half of the sixteenth century, marine insurance became even more important as a result of growth in overseas trade. The insurance providers were mainly private bankers and moneychangers, but also merchants trading with insurance on a professional basis. Especially the Italian merchant dynasties such as the "Medici" were involved in insurance deals. The most important insurance centres were Genoa, Florence and Venice. Trade with Flanders and Holland led to the establishment of insurance business in the "Low Countries" ("Pays-Bas"), too. In England, the first insurance contracts were concluded in the early sixteenth century, in Germany (Hamburg) as of the second half of the sixteenth century. The beginnings of reinsurance likewise date back to the fourteenth century. The first known reinsurance contract was concluded in Genoa back in 1370, whereby the direct insurer promised to indemnify the insured if the latter's ship failed to reach the destination port within a certain time and in case the vessel arrived the insurer would be entitled to sell the cargo as salvage, and, in turn, the reinsurer had promised the direct insurer to buy up the entire cargo.[17] This marked the birth of reinsurance, even if this kind of transaction was still rare at first. The more common form of insurance for large risks at this time was coinsurance, in which several insurers share a risk that would be too big for any one of them to take on, on his own. As trade flourished and economies boomed, the demand for reinsurance cover likewise rose. As the limited possibilities of coinsurance became exhausted, reinsurance became more and more important.

In late-seventeenth-century London, prosperous businessmen used to gather in Edward Lloyd's coffee shop to get the latest news. This meeting place became the

[17] Schwepcke (2004), pp. 1–2.

place to go to buy or sell marine insurance. Apart from everyday insurance contracts, reinsurance agreements were also concluded here. By the end of the seventeenth century, reinsurance had arrived in France and the Netherlands, and in the early eighteenth century it finally reached Germany and the rest of England. The first reinsurers were direct insurers.

In 1720, for example, a Rotterdam insurance Company reinsured four ships that had been insured with another direct insurer in London for a voyage to India. The first description of a reinsurance contract is to be found in the "Guidon de la Mer", an authoritative treatise on marine insurance (published in Rouen) written by an anonymous author in the second half of the sixteenth century. This document advises that a risk should be reinsured whenever the direct insurer regrets having concluded the insurance contract. The term "reinsurance" came into use in the mid-eighteenth century but did not originally imply any specific form of transaction. It was not until early in the nineteenth century that the modern concept of a reinsurance contract developed.

The first legal regulations on reinsurance were passed in the Low Countries in 1609. The law expressly declares reinsurance allowable. Louis XIV's "Ordonnances de la Marine", promulgated in 1681 and amended in 1686, are generally considered the model for modern insurance legislation.

In Germany, the first statutory provisions on reinsurance were embodied in the "Hamburger Assekuranz- und Havarie-Ordnung" of 1731. This served as a prototype for insurance legislation in Denmark, Sweden and Prussia and already contained a Provision governing the direct insurer's Obligation to provide the reinsurer with full information. The Prussian "Allgemeine Landesrecht für die Preussischen Staaten" of 1794 contains a first comprehensive code of insurance law, including reinsurance law. Articles 2016–2023, for instance, deal with the permissibility, scope and separate legal entity of the reinsurance contract.

In England, King George II enacted a law in 1746 that severely limited marine reinsurance. This was in response to abusive practices involving reinsurance: direct insurers had been offering reinsurance at prices way below the original premiums. According to this law, reinsurance was permissible only in the case of insolvency or death of the original direct insurer. These restrictions were not lifted again until 1864. But even such severe constraints could not curtail the development of reinsurance: the direct insurers' need and desire to diversify their risks were too strong.

In the eighteenth century, the marine underwriting at Edward Lloyd's coffee house, the Act of the Parliament of 1745 and the constitution of Lloyd's as a society in 1811 helped the prosper of reinsurance. In the nineteenth and early twentieth centuries, two important features, i.e. the formation of independent reinsurance companies in continental Europe and the growth of non-marine reinsurance at Lloyd's, contributed to the further development of the reinsurance market.

In particular industrialisation and urban expansion in the nineteenth century, led to a growing demand for non-marine insurance, particularly fire insurance. The need for reinsurance capacity, at that time, was at first met by the insurance companies writing direct business, acting like the merchants that preceded them, accepting as reinsurers risks from other insurance companies. The earliest known reinsurance treaty was a reciprocal fire treaty between "La nationale compagnie d' assurance" of Paris and the "Compagnie des proprietaires reunis" of Brussels, dating from 1821. In Germany, the first statutory provisions on reinsurance were embodied in the "Hamburger Assekuranz- und Havarie-Ordnung" of 1731. This served as a prototype for insurance legislation in Denmark, Sweden and Prussia and already contained a Provision governing the direct insurer's Obligation to provide the reinsurer with full information. The Prussian "Allgemeine Landesrecht für die Preussischen Staaten" of 1794 contains a first comprehensive code of insurance law, including reinsurance law. Also, a number of German companies formed subsidiaries in order to write fire reinsurance: the first truly independent reinsurance company was the Kölnische Rückversicherungs-Gesellschaft ("Cologne Re"), founded in Cologne in 1843. In 1863, the Swizerische Rückversicherungs-Gesellschaft ("Swiss Re") was founded in Zurich. In 1880, the Munchener Rückversicherungs-Gesellschaft ("Munich Re") was founded in Munich. In England, King George II enacted a law in 1746 that severely limited marine reinsurance. This was in response to abusive practices involving reinsurance: direct insurers had been offering reinsurance at prices way below the original premiums. According to this law, reinsurance was permissible only in the case of insolvency or death of the original direct insurer. These restrictions were not lifted again until 1864. But even such severe constraints, could not curtail the development of reinsurance: the direct insurers' need and desire to diversify their risks were too strong.[18] The first professional reinsurance company in England i.e. the "Reinsurance Company Ltd" was incorporated in 1867. Although the term "reinsurance" came into use in the mid-eighteenth century it did not originally imply any specific form of transaction and was not until early in the nineteenth century that the modern concept of a reinsurance contract developed.

In the nineteenth century, two factors played a significant role in the growth of Lloyd's, i.e. the introduction of the syndicate and, secondly, the move into non-marine underwriting, where Lloyd's proved to have a competitive edge over the more conservative companies.[19]

Notwithstanding the above developments, in the twentieth century, moreover, the profound social, political and economic changes that occurred and the globalisation of the world economy and the world market, all lead to the globalisation of the reinsurance market.[20] Not least, in an effort to cope with new challenges, the business of alternative risk transfer was created to encompass reinsurance and financial or capital market features.[21]

---

[18] Schwepcke (2004), pp. 1–2.

[19] O'Niell and Woloniecki (1998), pp. 31–32.

[20] O'Niell and Woloniecki (1998), pp. 27–34.

[21] Geiger (2000), pp. 50–51.

1.2.2.1 The Emergence of Professional Reinsurance

In the early days of reinsurance, there were various forms of reinsurance cover: in England and the USA, especially, domestic direct insurance companies reinsured each other. At about the same time, insurance companies all over the world started to look for reinsurance cover in other countries. This was not always easy for German insurance companies, who feared losing their reinsurance cover in the event of a war. To respond to their needs, the first professional reinsurance companies in Germany were founded. For similar reasons, insurers in other countries with global interests endeavoured to become as self-supporting as possible. Although commerce between (re)insurers in different political spheres of interest was possible and indeed was practised in individual cases, it still remained the exception.[22]

1.2.2.2 The Industrial Revolution: The Heyday of Reinsurance

Trail-blazing inventions in transport (steamships, railways) created risks requiring insurance in new dimensions. Without a sophisticated system of direct insurance and reinsurance, it would not have been possible to cover all these new risks. This fact, too, fostered the establishment of the first professional reinsurers. Initially these were subsidiaries of direct insurers.

The first reinsurance subsidiary was set up by a marine insurer: the "Niederrheinische Güter-Assekuranz-Gesellschaft" in Wesel, a mutual insurance company that converted to a joint stock company in 1842. In 1853, the "Aachener Rückversicherungsgesellschaft" was founded as a subsidiary of the "Aachener und Münchner Feuer-Versicherungsgesellschaft" which, since being bought out by the US Employers' reinsurance corporation, now belongs to GE Frankona Re. The world's first stand-alone reinsurance company, the "Kölnische Rückversicherungs-Gesellschaft" was founded as a joint stock company in 1843 in response to the "Great Fire of Hamburg" in 1842. A majority shareholding of the US reinsurance company General Re since 1994, the company operated under the name of General-Cologne Re for a few years as of 2000 and now calls itself GenRe. Both companies have belonged to the Berkshire Hathaway group for some years now. In other countries, the evolution of the reinsurance sector could not keep up with the pace set in Germany. The first specialised reinsurance company founded in any other country was the "Schweizerische Rückversicherungsgesellschaft", or else "Schweizer Rück" for short, established in Zürich in 1863. The company was formed from a merger between the "Allgemeine Versicherungsgesellschaft Helvetia" in St Gallen, the "Schweizerische Kreditanstalt" and the "Basler Handelsbank". Since the Swiss market offered only limited business opportunities, "Schweizer

[22] Schwepcke (2004), pp. 3–4.

Rück" (Swiss Re) soon began to establish business relationships abroad. In the following years, further professional reinsurers emerged in France and Austria.

In the UK and the US, professional reinsurance companies did not emerge until after 1900. However, most of the demand for reinsurance in these markets was already being satisfied above all by Lloyd's, the insurance exchange that had evolved out of Edward Lloyd's coffee shop, and the so-called "fringe market". This consisted mainly of branch offices of local direct insurers set up "on the fringe of Lloyd's".[23]

1.2.2.3 From the Imperialism Era to Modern Times

1.2.2.3.1 The Imperial Age

The imperial age was marked by steady growth in world trade and aspirations to autarchy on the part of the powers involved in global politics. The insurance industry could not avoid being caught up in this development. Exchanging goods and services between spheres of interest was a risky business. It happened, but nobody wanted to have to rely on it. The (re)insurance industry in Central Europe was geared towards the continent, and especially towards the East. British markets serviced the entire Empire and the English-language regions of North America. France had its own colonies as its market.

In 1871, Lloyd's achieved recognition as a Corporation ("Corporation of Lloyd's"). In many ways, the coffee-shop meeting place had evolved into a unique institution that, even today, can claim to be a global player in many fields (not just reinsurance). Lloyd's is an association of independent insurers, until recently limited to private persons that contract insurance deals of all kinds by means of an exchange system. The London "fringe market" around Lloyd's likewise flourished during the colonial period. London commanded a leading role, both in the English-speaking world and also in certain lines of business, especially in marine insurance. In this global context, it was often necessary to offer reinsurance. By the late 1870s there were already 15 professional reinsurers in Germany.

In 1880 the "Münchner Rückversicherungsgesellschaft", "Münchner Rück" for short, was founded. The company's declared aim was to engage in international reinsurance business. The company opened up a branch office in London as early as in 1890, and shortly afterwards a major office in New York. Münchner Rück (Munich Re) was also involved in setting up a number of direct insurers such as Allianz Aktiengesellschaft in 1890.

In 1886, the "Badische Rück- und Mitversicherungsgesellschaft" was set up in Mannheim. After relocating to Frankfurt in 1907, the company was renamed "Frankona Rück- und Mitversicherungsgesellschaft". It was acquired by the Employers Reinsurance Company in 1995 and today operates under the name of

[23] Schwepcke (2004), p. 4.

GE Frankona Re. In 1911, the Bayerische Hypotheken- und Wechselbank founded the "Bayerische Rückversicherungsbank" as a co-subsidiary alongside the "Bayerische Versicherungsbank". Following the sale of the "Bayerische Versicherungsbank" to Allianz, also Münchner Rück (Munich Re) and Schweizer Rück (Swiss Re) bought a majority share in the Bayerische Rückversicherungsbank in 1924. Previously only a captive reinsurer for Bayerische Versicherungsbank, the "Bayerische Rück" that emerged from this deal started writing reinsurance business of all kinds. Renamed Swiss Re Germany in 2001, the company is today responsible for the Swiss Re's group's business in the markets of Central, Northern and Eastern Europe.[24]

1.2.2.3.2 The World Wars Era

Even before the outbreak of the First World War, reinsurance was already highly international. Germany was the leader on the world market (with the exception of marine insurance). There was an international role division into "provider countries" such as Germany, Switzerland, Russia and the UK (mainly through the London market) and "demand countries" such as France, Italy, Belgium and the USA. During the First World War, cross-border activities had to be discontinued as a result of bans imposed in some countries. This led to a re-orientation of the reinsurance market, in particular the German reinsurers lost their Eastern European markets. When the peace treaties were eventually signed, such reinsurance contracts as were still in existence were dissolved and wound up. However, since the legal restrictions and bans seriously impaired economic development, they were soon repealed. In the years following the First World War, the reinsurance companies had to cope with inflation and the global economic crisis. Once inflation had been brought back under control in Germany, a short-lived reconstruction phase followed as of 1923, only to be brought to an end again in 1929 by the depression accompanied by high unemployment. During this time, a large number of insurance companies collapsed. The USA were a very late arrival on the reinsurance stage. Though the USA had already been the world's largest direct insurance market in the nineteenth century, US insurers had either reinsured each other or had sought all of their reinsurance cover in Europe. "Employers Re", the first US reinsurance Company, was not founded until 1908. Its original name, "Employers Indemnity Exchange", was changed to "Employers Reinsurance Corporation" in 1928. "General Re" followed in 1921. The Second World War again split the international insurance market into two camps. Only the reinsurance companies in neutral countries were able to maintain their business relationships with the two warring sides. This benefited Switzerland especially, but also Spain, Portugal and Sweden. Often companies from the warring nations broke off their business relationships

---

[24] Schwepcke (2004), p. 4.

with companies in hostile countries. But there are also many examples of international business relationships having survived those turbulent times.[25]

In the wake of the Second World War, several factors acted against the reinsurers: the shortage of insurable property as a result of the destruction caused by the war, high mortality rates, and rampant inflation. A particular problem for German insurers was that the Allied Control Council Act No. 47 of March 1947 did not allow them to establish reinsurance relationships with other countries. This applied both to reinsurers and to direct insurers. Many reinsurance contracts had to be annulled. The Act was relaxed in 1949 and eventually repealed in 1950, mainly due to economic considerations: it had become apparent that German insurers and reinsurers would not be able to cope with large-scale losses on their own. Together with the repeal of this Act, the 1948 currency reform and the ensuing economic recovery formed the basis for the reconstruction of the German insurance industry. The German reinsurers also had other difficulties to contend with during the post-war period: they had lost their Eastern European markets completely, and they had to regain the confidence of foreign insurers. As of about 1953, international business had again attained pre-war levels and rose steadily from then on. The turmoil of the post-war period reinforced and intensified cooperation between direct insurers and reinsurers in the domestic market. In 1966, the "Feuerschadenverband Rheinisch-Westfälischer Zechen" in Bochum, a mine operators' fire insurance mutual, founded the "Aktiengesellschaft für Transport und Rückversicherung". Following rapid expansion on the international reinsurance markets, the Company merged with the "Haftpflichtverband der deutschen Industrie V. a. G." (HDI) in 1970; in 1976 it was renamed "Hannover Rückversicherungs Aktiengesellschaft". For many decades after 1945, the London market was able to defend its position as the world's largest insurance and reinsurance centre, thanks largely to Lloyd's. In the US, many direct insurers founded independently operating reinsurance departments in the years following 1945, some of which were later spun off into separate companies.[26]

1.2.2.3.3 The Move to the Modern Times Era

In recent years, reinsurance contracts have moved away from the handshake agreements of yesterday and focus more on the realities of the bottom line. While most of the industry's historic customs and practices remain-for example, slip agreements and antiquated language, the relationship between the parties has changed fundamentally. No longer is it the norm for parties to work out their differences in the boardroom. It is the exception. Indeed, the reinsurance industry has seen an increase in formal reinsurance disputes, whether in the form of arbitration or litigation.

---

[25] Schwepcke (2004), pp. 4–6.

[26] Schwepcke (2004), pp. 4–6.

Several views have been offered to explain this fundamental shift, but two main reasons emerge.

First is the notorious soft property and casualty market of 1979–1984, a period that brought an influx of new entrants to the market, attracted by the cash flows available. Because of their relative inexperience, many of the new reinsurers did not charge enough in premiums for the risk protection they were offering. The flood of inexperienced players, record low prices, and new long-tail loss exposures—for instance, asbestos—caused extraordinary underwriting losses that logically lead to a dispute explosion.[27]

The second reason for the drastic change is the globalization of the reinsurance industry. The rapid advancement in computer and electronic technologies has shrunk the marketplace and given the reinsurance market a more international perspective. The traditional network of familiar faces has become a plethora of faces both new and old. The new entrants do not always play by the "old" rules, forcing old participants to move away from their traditional way of doing business in an effort to stay competitive. Essentially, the new entrants are applying their traditional ways of doing business to the reinsurance industry, reshaping the way reinsurance transactions are conducted.

The "in with the new and out with the old" phenomena has left little room for procedures to become ingrained in the minds of anyone. There may no longer be customary practices in the reinsurance industry. Customs are created only when they become so ingrained in the minds of customers that they are considered requirements of doing business. One casualty of this shift appears to be arbitration.[28]

1.2.2.3.4 The Present Day: Internationality and Critical Size

Capacity bottlenecks have always been the mother of invention in the insurance industry, leading to the emergence of new risk carriers. To this day mutual insurance companies provide convincing evidence of this in the direct insurance context. Such companies are set up at locations with interesting tax environments. Nowadays these are above all Bermuda, the Caribbean islands, Switzerland, the Channel Isles and Luxemburg. In reinsurance, too, the market forces typically respond in the following pattern:

- A capacity shortage is recognised as an opportunity to earn money
- Non-insurable risks are made insurable via the formation of SPV companies on a mutual basis.[29]

---

[27] McDonald (2001), p. 330.
[28] McDonald (2001), p. 330.
[29] Schwepcke (2004), pp. 4–6.

1.3 Reinsurance Relationship

1.3.1 General

Reinsurance business initially was done on a handshake with written contracts that were brief and arcane. At the commencement of performance of the contract, the only existing documentation of the transaction generally was a placement slip, mainly a model of brevity, for, its terms are restricted to single paragraphs and incorporate only industry boilerplate terms by reference.[30] Often, even the formal treaty, generated after the conclusion of the placement slip, would not be much clearer than the latter.[31] Reinsurance business was negotiated among closely knit groups that maintained long-term relationships, so that all the parties to the reinsurance agreement intimately understood the custom and practice of the industry. Because all sides were interested in maintaining amicable relations, if and when a dispute arose, it usually would be handled with an eye to maintaining the relationship. This eliminated much of the need for a carefully constructed commercial contract. Resolution of claims was subsumed into the over-all, usually profitable, relationship of the reinsurer and reinsured. This practice allowed the relationship between the parties to remain congenial, and it also enabled its continuation. It is no wonder that the traditional reinsurance relationship has often been compared to that of a marriage.[32]

1.3.2 Modern Times

In recent years, reinsurance contracts focus more on the realities of the bottom line. While most of the industry's historic customs and practices remain, nevertheless,

---

[30] For instance, if the formal treaty is to include an arbitration clause, the slip would simply state "arbitration clause." Then a treaty would be generated providing a more formal and detailed documentation of the reinsurance contract. Sometimes a formal treaty may never be generated, the only terms of the reinsurance contract being in the placement slip; McDonald (2001), p. 328.

[31] The treaties usually incorporated antiquated language that rarely was read, or for that matter, legally understood. A typical example of the traditional relationship is found in an anecdote told by a gray-haired reinsurance executive, perhaps in contemplation of the "good old days." He remarked: "[A]fter a treaty had been executed in those days, the superior threw it in the bottom drawer and it remained there for the duration of the treaty relationship. If a question was raised by the reinsured company about the treaty, as unlikely as that was, an amicable discussion would have followed and an agreement would have been reached without either party consulting the treaty. If the treaty had to be removed from the drawer, that suggested a major schism in the reinsurance relationship, even if the immediate questions were ultimately resolved"; Strain (1997), p. 568; McDonald (2001), p. 329.

[32] Cohen et al. (1994), pp. 602–603; *Compagnie de Reassurance d'Ile de France v New England Reins. Corp.*, 825 F.Supp. 370, 383 (D. Mass. 1993); McDonald (2001), p. 329.

the relationship between the parties has changed fundamentally. No longer is it the norm for parties to work out their differences in the boardroom, but more the exception. Indeed, the reinsurance industry has seen an increase in formal reinsurance disputes, whether in the form of arbitration or litigation.

1.3.3 The Use of Arbitration in Reinsurance

Even if one forgets for a moment that the traditional reinsurance relationship is the reason why arbitrations occur in the reinsurance industry, and perhaps offers the greatest advantage for using arbitration, there still are numerous independent advantages to using arbitration. But there also are certain disadvantages to using arbitration over the judicial system.

1.3.3.1 The Legal Framework for Reinsurance ADR: The Case for Arbitration

Unusually for a piece of English legislation, the Arbitration Act 1996 contains a number of statements of general principle. Section 1 reflects an explanatory memorandum which accompanied the Bill (which subsequently became the Arbitration Act 1996) when it was introduced in December 1995.

The memorandum stressed the importance of party autonomy. The majority of the provisions of the Arbitration Act 1996 apply where the "seat of the arbitration" is in England and Wales, or in Northern Ireland: section 2(1); a number of its provisions, however, apply even if the seat is outside England, Wales or Northern Ireland, or if the seat of the arbitration has yet to be designated or determined for example section 7 (separability of arbitration agreement), sections 9–11 (stay of all proceedings) and section 66 (enforcement of arbitral awards). Similarly, the powers of the court under section 43 (securing the attendance of witnesses) and section 44 (general powers exercisable in support of arbitral proceedings) apply if the seat is outside England, Wales or Northern Ireland, or if the seat of the arbitration has yet to be designated or determined, although the court has, in such circumstances a discretion to refuse to exercise any such powers.

1.3.3.2 ARIAS

ARIAS, the Insurance and Reinsurance Arbitration Society, is a society with branches in the USA, the UK and France. The Society has been established under the aegis of AIDA (Association Internationale de Droit des Assurances). Arising from the relatively recent growth of disputes in the world-wide insurance and reinsurance markets, it became apparent that there existed a need for a body to encourage current and retired market practitioners to become part of a panel of independent arbitrators who suitably trained in arbitration procedures. This became the prime objective of ARIAS. Additionally, and in general, ARIAS aims to promote and assist in the development of insurance and reinsurance dispute resolution through arbitration, and to make this more responsive to the needs of the industry worldwide. ARIAS, aims to facilitate dispute resolution wherever required.

1.3.3.3 The ARIAS UK Arbitration Rules

ARIAS, is always prepared to act as an appointing body. Herein below, we will examine the arbitration rules drawn up by ARIAS UK.

With regards to the commencement of the arbitration proceedings, the person wishing to commence an arbitration (the claimant) must send to the other party (the respondent) a written notice of arbitration.[33] This must contain, the full name and correspondence address of the claimant and name and contact person or reference to which all communications are to be addressed; if appropriate, the full text of the arbitration clause under which the arbitration clause is commenced together with identification of the contractual document or documents in which the arbitration clause is contained (under which, the arbitration arises, if different) specifying the period and type of insurance and reinsurance cover provided; a brief outline of the nature of the dispute referred to arbitration and specifying the type of relief sought; if the reference is to a sole arbitrator, the name and address of the person or persons the claimant considers would be an appropriate arbitrator; if the reference calls for party appointed arbitrators, the name and address of the arbitrator appointed by the claimant.[34] The arbitration is deemed to have commenced on the date the respondent receives the notice of arbitration.[35]

The respondent is required, within 14 days of receipt of the notice of arbitration, to send a response.[36] The response should contain the following particulars: (a) if the reference is to a sole arbitrator, it should contain an agreement to or counter-proposals concerning the appointment of a sole arbitrator, including the name and address of any proposed arbitrator, (b) if the reference is to a three person tribunal with party-appointed arbitrators: the name and address of the arbitrator appointed by the respondent and (c) a brief statement of the nature of any counterclaims to be referred to the arbitration. If the respondent fails to send a response, he is not precluded from denying the claim or asserting any counter-claim at a later stage.[37]

With regards to the appointment of the arbitral tribunal, the parties are free to agree on the number and qualification of the arbitrators.[38] If there is no agreement

[33] Rule 4.1 of the 1997 ARIAS UK Rules.

[34] Rules 4.1.1–4.1.5 of the 1997 ARIAS UK Rules.

[35] Rule 4.21 of the 1997 ARIAS UK Rules.

[36] Rule 5.1 of the 1997 ARIAS UK Rules.

[37] Rule 5.2 of the 1997 ARIAS UK Rules.

[38] Rule 6.1 of the 1997 ARIAS UK Rules.

as to number, the tribunal will comprise three arbitrators, one appointed by each of the parties and the third appointed by the two party-appointed arbitrators.[39] If there is no agreement as to the qualification of arbitrators, they shall be persons, including those who have retired, with no less than 10 years of experience in insurance or reinsurance within the industry or as lawyers or other professional advisers serving the industry.[40] Where the arbitration agreement provides for: (a) a sole arbitrator, if the parties have not agreed on one within 28 days, then upon the application of either party, ARIAS will appoint the arbitrator[41]; (b) party appointed arbitrators, if the respondent fails to appoint an arbitrator within 14 days of the delivery of the notice of arbitration, then upon the application of the claimant, ARIAS will appoint an arbitrator for the respondent[42]; (c) two party-appointed arbitrators to appoint a third, they shall do so as soon as practicable and, in any event, within 28 days,[43] and may consult with those appointing them with regards to the identity of the third[44]; if they are unable to agree after 28 days, then upon the application of either party, ARIAS will appoint the third, who will be a third arbitrator, not an umpire.[45] If, after appointment, any arbitrator dies, is unable to act or is removed from the reference, ARIAS will—in default of reappointment within 14 days—upon the request of either part or the remaining member of the arbitral tribunal, appoint a substitute arbitrator.[46]

With regards to the arbitral procedure, the parties are free, under the ARIAS Rules, to agree upon any procedure for the conduct of the arbitration. In default of agreement, the arbitral tribunal has the widest discretion permitted under the law governing the arbitral procedure to make orders and get directions.[47] The seat is deemed to be London, unless the parties agree otherwise.[48] The award issued, irrespective of where signed or delivered, is deemed issued at the seat of the arbitration.[49] The parties may agree that the tribunal make their award on the basis of documents alone,[50] but, in the absence of any such agreements, both parties have the right to be heard before the tribunal and to be represented by lawyers. Also, both parties are entitled to question any witness who appears at the hearing[51] and all meetings and hearings are private and confidential to the parties.[52]

---

[39] Rule 6.2 of the 1997 ARIAS UK Rules.
[40] Rule 6.4 of the 1997 ARIAS UK Rules.
[41] Rule 6.4 of the 1997 ARIAS UK Rules.
[42] Rule 6.5 of the 1997 ARIAS UK Rules.
[43] Rule 6.6 of the 1997 ARIAS UK Rules.
[44] Rule 6.7 of the 1997 ARIAS UK Rules.
[45] Rule 6.9 of the 1997 ARIAS UK Rules.
[46] Rule 6.12 of the 1997 ARIAS UK Rules.
[47] Rule 9.1 of the 1997 ARIAS UK Rules.
[48] Rule 10.1 of the 1997 ARIAS UK Rules.
[49] Rule 10.2 of the 1997 ARIAS UK Rules.
[50] Rule 11.4 of the 1997 ARIAS UK Rules.
[51] Rule 12.2 of the 1997 ARIAS UK Rules.
[52] Rule 11.5 of the 1997 ARIAS UK Rules.

With regards to the powers of the arbitral tribunal, the ARIAS Rules confer the following powers on the tribunal: (a) to determine the applicable law; (b) to order rectification of any contract solely in order to correct mistakes which the tribunal determines where made by both parties in expressing their true intentions when drawing up the contract; (c) to allow claims, counter-claims or cross-claims, defences or replies to be amended; (d) to order the production of any document relevant to the matters in dispute; (e) to order the inspection of one party of the books and records of the other party; (f) to require suitable undertakings from the parties that the documentation and evidence produced will remain confidential; (g) to determine the costs of the arbitration; (h) to dispense with the strict rules of evidence; (i) to limit both expert testimony and witnesses of fact, on the grounds of number, duplication and relevance; (j) to place such reliance as it sees fit on the written evidence of any witness, if such witness is not present at the hearing; (k) to order the exchange of the statements of any witness of fact or expert witness, written statements of issues or written submissions prior to the arbitration hearing; (l) to order security for the costs of the award; (m) to order security for the costs of the arbitration; (n) to rule on objection as to its own jurisdiction including those relating to the existence, validity or scope of the arbitration agreement; (o) to declare contracts null and void *ab initio*; (p) to rule on the validity and enforceability of the totality of the agreement between the parties; (q) to proceed at any application or at the hearing in the absence of one party; (r) to proceed with a hearing where there has been a failure or refusal to comply with orders of the tribunal and to take whatever steps it considers necessary to ensure compliance with its orders and directions; (s) to order the payment of simple interest; (t) to make interim, monetary or declaratory awards.

The ARIAS Rules expressly provide that the tribunal shall not have additional equitable powers unless such powers have been specifically conferred upon it by the parties in writing[53] and, in particular, the tribunal shall not have the power to order or award[54]: the posting of security for the sums in dispute—save in the case of an award enforcing a contractual obligation; the payment of exemplary, punitive, multiple or other non-contractual damages; save in a case of rectification of a mistake made by the parties, the alteration or amendment of agreed contractual terms; injunctive relief.

With regards to the arbitration award, it should be in writing, in the language of the arbitration and, unless otherwise agreed, must state reasons.[55] It is valid, if signed by a sole arbitrator, or, in the case of tribunal of three, by any two arbitrators.[56] Where the parties settle a case, the tribunal may, at their request,

[53] Rule 14.1 of the 1997 ARIAS UK Rules.

[54] Rule 14.2 of the 1997 ARIAS UK Rules.

[55] Rule 16.2 of the 1997 ARIAS UK Rules.

[56] Rule 16.3 of the 1997 ARIAS UK Rules.

make a consent award.[57] Within 28 days of the publication of the award, the tribunal—on its own initiative or on the application of either party—may correct an award so as to remove any clerical mistake or error arising from an accidental slip or omission or clarify or remove any ambiguity in the award[58]; or make an additional award in respect of any matter, including interest or costs, which was presented to the tribunal but omitted from the award.[59]

With regards to "honourable engagement" clauses and the power of arbitrators to depart from law, such clauses are not uncommon in reinsurance contracts and raise questions, such as, whether the clause shows that the parties did not intend to create legally enforceable obligations, or whether the clause is sufficiently certain to give rise to legally enforceable obligations, or whether the clause is contrary to public policy.[60]

The question of whether the clause shows that the parties did not intend to create legally enforceable obligations, was raised in *Home Insurance Co v Administratia Asigurarilor De Stat*,[61] where the relevant part of the arbitration clause provided that the award of the arbitrators or the umpire would be final and binding upon all parties without appeal and that the reinsurance treaty would be interpreted as an honourable engagement rather than as a legal obligation and that the award would be made with a view to effecting the general purpose of this treaty rather than in accordance with a literal interpretation of its language. The defendant reinsurers argued that the agreement was binding in honour only and not in law. It was held that the clause did create a legally binding agreement to arbitrate and to abide by an award, and if and in so far as the arbitration clause went further than the law permits, it could be struck out in whole or in part without affecting the validity of the reinsurance treaty.

The question of whether the clause is sufficiently certain to give rise to legally enforceable obligations, or whether the clause is contrary to public policy, may arise where the arbitrators are directed to apply the usages and customs of the reinsurance market, as opposed to rules of law. The difficulty which such a clause poses is that there must be some objective criteria upon which the arbitrators can base their decision. If they ignore rules of law altogether and apply subjective views of market custom, such a clause may also be open to attack as being contrary to public policy.

In *Orion Compania Espanola de Seguros v Belford Maatschappij Voor Algemene Verzekringeen*[62] it was held that a clause which required arbitrators to

---

[57] Rule 16.10 of the 1997 ARIAS UK Rules.

[58] Rule 16.11.1 of the 1997 ARIAS UK Rules.

[59] Rule 16.11.2 of the 1997 ARIAS UK Rules.

[60] O'Niell and Woloniecki (1998), pp. 639–647.

[61] *Home Insurance Co v Administratia Asigurarilor De Stat* [1983]2 Lloyd's Rep. 674.

[62] *Orion Compania Espanola de Seguros v Belford Maatschappij Voor Algemene Verzekringeen* [1962]2 Lloyd's Rep. 257.

decide according to an equitable rather than a strictly legal interpretation of the terms of the relevant contract, was invalid and should be given no effect.

However, in *Eagle Star Insurance Co. Ltd v Yuval Insurance Co. Ltd*,[63] it was held that there was nothing in public policy to make the clause in question void; that the clause seemed entirely reasonable, not ousting the jurisdiction of the courts but only technicalities and strict constructions, something which not only equity did in the old days, but also arbitrators would do under such a clause, in the current context, nowadays.[64]

1.3.4 Choice of Forum: Litigation Versus Arbitration

The reinsurance community has historically selected arbitration over litigation, not least because arbitration generally provides more expert, expeditious, cost effective and confidential awards. Although reinsurance disputes have historically been resolved behind closed doors, mounting pressures on the industry—such as asbestos and environmental liability, huge jury verdicts, and insurance insolvencies, to name a few—have prompted more litigious behaviour and, therefore, to a certain extent, it is argued that reinsurance disputes have spilled out of arbitration in the courtroom. Court battles over, a party's efforts to compel arbitration, the scope of arbitrable claims, umpire selection, challenges to arbitrators and actions to vacate awards have proliferated, arguably undermining some of the chief benefits of arbitration: efficiency, privacy and confidentiality and speed. Arbitration, nevertheless, retains these advantages of expert adjudication, neutrality and enforceability, which are particularly important in an international industry featuring specialised terminology, custom and practice. Litigation and arbitration, each carry distinct advantages and disadvantages.[65]

1.3.4.1 Preference for Arbitration

The reinsurance industry's preference for arbitration is very unusual in the rest of the commercial world. Industry experts offer an amalgamation of reasons for this preference, but the most obvious and intimate—from the standpoint of the reinsurer and the reinsured—are the following:

First, reinsurance treaties are special commercial contracts, which are usually drafted by knowledgeable lawyers and cover numerous contingencies. Were reinsurance treaties drafted with the same care as most other commercial agreements involving comparable sums, they would be longer and more complex. Since the

---

[63] *Eagle Star Insurance Co. Ltd v Yuval Insurance Co. Ltd* [1978]1 Lloyd's Rep. 357.

[64] O'Niell and Woloniecki (1998), pp. 639–647.

[65] Thomas and Lyons (2012), pp. 77-16, 77-17.

realities of the reinsurance trade make it impractical to negotiate and draft such complex documents, the parties expect that in the event of disputes, expert arbitrators will fill in the unavoidable blanks using "custom and practice," "intent of the parties" and "honourable undertaking" as guidelines for decision.[66] Moreover, given that arbitration has been the traditional method of dispute resolution for reinsurance disputes for many decades, insurers and reinsurers would rather have their disputes resolved by a panel of industry experts.[67] Traditional reinsurance arbitration clauses relieve the arbitrators from following the strict rules of law, and specifically require the arbitrators to consider the reinsurance contract as an honourable engagement rather than a strict legal obligation. This way, instead of a judge that knows nothing about the industry and who will construe the reinsurance agreement like any commercial contract, reinsurance disputes are determined based on industry business practices by industry experts.[68] Second, arbitrations are much more amicable as a process if compared to litigation, which is an important consideration when the parties are in an on-going relationship despite the current dispute. Third, discovery is more restrictive, thus less extensive and less expensive,[69] and predicated on confidentiality.[70] In effect, the discovery produced most likely will not be considered on the public record, thus, arbitration will almost always be less expensive than litigation.[71] Arbitrations commonly feature limited discovery, relaxed rules of evidence and virtually no appellate review. Arbitrators have only limited authority to compel third parties to participate in the proceedings or furnish discovery.[72] In a segment of an industry in which on-going relationships are important, speed and cost are primary motivators—in determining how a dispute should be resolved—and, although arbitration has its detractors, it is unlikely that litigation will be competing against these two factors any time soon.[73] Fourth, most arbitration decisions remain between the parties, are not published, and have little or no precedential effect.[74] In the English case of *Insurance Company v Lloyd's Syndicate*,[75] where there was no leading arbitration clause, it was held that there was no market custom that would automatically entitle the reinsured to disclose an arbitration award to the following market without the consent of the leading underwriter, and that the scope of the qualification of the duty of confidentiality was to be implied as a matter of business efficacy.[76] Fifth,

---

[66] McDonald (2001), p. 330.

[67] Who will decide disputes based on industry custom and practice, the intent of the parties' and the honorable undertaking occurring in reinsurance; McDonald (2001), p. 330; Schiffer (2006).

[68] Schiffer (2006).

[69] McDonald (2001), p. 330.

[70] Schiffer (2006).

[71] McDonald (2001), p. 331.

[72] Thomas and Lyons (2012), p. 77-18.

[73] McDonald (2001), p. 331.

[74] McDonald (2001), p. 330.

[75] *Insurance Company v Lloyd's Syndicate* [1995]1 Lloyd's Rep. 272.

[76] O'Niell and Woloniecki (1998), pp. 632–633.

reinsurance arbitrations offer much flexibility, in terms of procedure. A typical reinsurance arbitration is most of the times, organised, administered, and controlled by the parties and the arbitrators, not by an arbitral body. In other words, no third-party organisation—but only the parties themselves—administers the arbitration. In addition, most reinsurance arbitrations traditionally do not require adherence to any particular set of rules.[77] Thus, in reinsurance arbitrations, it is the parties and the arbitrators who set their own rules, for the arbitration, to be followed.[78] Sixth, a unique, in importance, advantage which arbitration offers, over litigation, is speed, flexibility and efficiency. Parties sometimes prefer arbitration, because it generally provides more efficient, flexible and expeditious dispute resolution than litigation. Expert adjudication, by seasoned industry arbitrators, may reduce the costs of fact discovery and expert discovery, educating a generalist adjudicator, and hearing time, and permits procedures tailored to the individual dispute.[79] Although the time required to complete arbitration may have increased over the past few years, it is still a much faster method of resolving disputes than the court system.[80] Seventh, there is the issue of expert adjudication. Reinsurance arbitration provides adjudication by seasoned industry experts, rather than generalist judges. Reinsurance arbitrations, therefore, can provide business resolution of disputes, tempered by industry custom and practice, rather than strictly legal decisions. Parties may have greater confidence in the ultimate awards rendered by expert adjudicators that the parties themselves selected.[81] Eighth, another advantage of arbitration is the flexibility in arriving at an award. The arbitrators will apply the customs and practices of the industry in fashioning their decision. This is something a court of law may not be able to do, or want to do. Many in the industry feel that an arbitration award has a better chance of reflecting the intent of the parties to the treaty. Where it is still common for business to be done without fully detailed contracts, the flexibility in an arbitration award offers much utility.[82] In addition, parties may prefer arbitration over litigation in the context of international reinsurance disputes as arbitration agreements and awards are generally more easily enforced than court judgments rendered in state courts of a nation. The New York Convention,[83] which has been ratified by more than 140 countries, allows and obliges signatory states to recognise and enforce international commercial arbitration agreements and awards, and requires national courts to refer parties to arbitration, pursuant to a valid arbitration agreement subject to the New York Convention. There is no other corresponding

---

[77] Unlike contracts that require arbitration before a specific arbitral organisation under that organisation's rules, such as, for example, the American Arbitration Association and its Commercial Arbitration Rules; Schiffer (2006).

[78] Schiffer (2006).

[79] Thomas and Lyons (2012), p. 77-17.

[80] McDonald (2001), p. 331.

[81] Thomas and Lyons (2012), pp. 77-17, 77-18.

[82] McDonald (2001), pp. 331–332.

[83] Convention on the Recognition and Enforcement of Foreign Arbitral Awards (New York, 1958).

world-wide treaty relating to forum selection agreements or judgments of a court, and legal rules of enforcement can be cumbersome and expensive.[84] Ninth, another advantage of arbitration is the neutrality it provides coupled with the element of privacy and confidentiality already mentioned above. In international disputes, parties may prefer arbitration to litigation, because it may provide a neutral forum in which to resolve disputes, outside the home country of either party. Moreover, arbitration is in general more private and confidential than litigation. Parties often prefer the greater privacy inherent in arbitration to protect reputations and good will, to foster continuing business relations by resolving disputes behind closed doors and occasionally to permit inconsistent positions unfettered by the rules of preclusion.[85]

All, of the above constitute a combination of reasons that produced the traditional reinsurance relationship. One could say using arbitration was never a conscientious decision by the industry participants; rather, it was simply an extenuation of traditional business practices.[86] Even if one forgets, for a moment, that the traditional reinsurance relationship is the reason why arbitrations occur in the reinsurance industry, and perhaps offers the greatest advantage for using arbitration, there still are numerous independent advantages to using arbitration. But there are also certain disadvantages to using arbitration over the judicial system. The last 15–20 years, whereby there has been a notable dispute explosion, have taken a toll on both the participants and the system, and in the process some possible deficiencies in the way arbitrations resolve a dispute have been exposed.

These disadvantages can be grouped as follows: First, a mostly common cited disadvantage of reinsurance arbitration relates to the finality of the award as no appeals process exists for arbitration proceedings. If a party feels members of an arbitration panel erred in their decision, no peer review is available. Second, another disadvantage is cited to be the lack of precedent in arbitration proceedings. Lack of precedent or uniformity in decisions, becomes clear when one arbitration panel decides the exact issue in an entirely different way than another panel. Some would say that this freedom is in harmony with arbitration's goal of deciding a case based on the customs and practices of the parties to that particular reinsurance treaty. However, even if this is true, the uncertainty can make it difficult for parties to make well-informed business decisions about an existing dispute.[87] Third, although the increasing complexity of reinsurance disputes and the increased amount in moneys, at issue, have blurred some of the distinctions between arbitration and litigation, nonetheless, in weighing the relative merits of either forum, in conclusion there is a lot to be remarked.

[84] Thomas and Lyons (2012), pp. 77-17, 77-18.

[85] Thomas and Lyons (2012), p. 77-17.

[86] McDonald (2001), p. 331.

[87] McDonald (2001), p. 332.

The predominant situation nowadays is that, virtually, all reinsurance disputes are resolved through settlement or arbitration. While the language set forth in the so-called arbitration clauses in most reinsurance treaties appears straightforward, the actual custom, practice and mores of reinsurance arbitrations create traps for the uninitiated.

Indeed, preliminarily, a recurring issue of debate among cedents and reinsurers—is the relative merits of adjudicating disputes through arbitration as compared to court litigation. While this issue has been discussed at length by various commentators, little focus has been placed on the actual practical realities facing the parties.

All too often, this issue of arbitration versus litigation is discussed and analysed in splendid isolation, with little regard being given to the usual set of limitations that exist when a dispute arises. As a practical matter, most reinsurance contracts, whether treaty or facultative, contain arbitration provisions. Therefore, when a dispute arises, cedents and reinsurers are presented with a seeming "fait accompli". Again, much debate is focused on whether arbitration or litigation is the better forum.

However, ideally, this issue should be considered prospectively, i.e. before the parties enter into a contract of reinsurance. Therefore, key points should be reviewed and analysed before the inception of the treaty. Also, treaty reinsurance must be considered as to how it fits with all the title insurers' insurance needs, both on the primary and reinsurance level.

Title insurers must be aware of potential conflicts or contradictions between their treaty reinsurance and risks either within or assumed on a facultative basis. However, many problems unanticipated at the time of the execution of the contract arise years after the contract was executed. The increasing complexity of the disputes and the increased amount in moneys at issue, have blurred some of the distinctions between arbitration and litigation.

Not least, there is one salient feature of arbitration that is largely ignored in weighing the relative merits of either forum, and this is the arbitration's virtual unassailability. There is virtually no recourse for a losing party in arbitration. The standards to overturn arbitration are narrow and circumscribed. No arbitration record is kept, so no record can be referenced in the event of an appeal. The arbitration panel selection process is usually the key to a party's success or failure at arbitration. Again, each side selects its own party arbitrator under most treaties, with the neutral umpire selected in accordance with varying processes, including the drawing of straws and other chance methodologies. The umpire's selection is of key importance, since the recurring trend in arbitration is for each party to regard its own arbitrator as its advocate much akin to that of a designated expert witness in litigation.

One potential pitfall for most title insurer cedents is that the criteria for an arbitrator's selection is often narrow and circumscribed. Many treaties contain clauses that limit an arbitrator's qualifications to active or retired insurance executives or officers of reinsurance companies. As a result, the pool of available arbitrators is often limited. The arbitration pool is dominated by "professional" arbitrators who have not been actively involved as officers and directors for insurance companies for many years. Instead, they have earned their post-retirement living as arbitrators and umpires. Virtually none of them have had any meaningful title insurance experience. For a title insurer involved in arbitration, it will require the education of its own party arbitrator. Further, the title insurer cedent must educate the panel as a whole. The arbitration decision-making process is closed and generally not under any outside scrutiny. The generally established practice, in the USA and in England, for arbitration panels in rendering awards is to not specify the bases for such award. Therefore, an aggrieved party in an arbitration has little or no recourse to overturn an award on appeal.

An example of this concept is reflected in the USA decision of the Ninth Circuit in *Michigan Mutual Insurance Company and Others v Unigard Security Insurance Company*[88] where the reinsurance arbitration award that granted certain retrocessionaires, i.e. the reinsurers of reinsurers, relief beyond what they requested in the underlying arbitration was upheld. The arbitration panel granted rescission to retrocessionaires without requiring them to return the premium to the reinsurer. On appeal, the reinsurers contended that the award was inherently unfair because it gave retrocessionaires more than what they actually requested at arbitration. In its decision, the Ninth Circuit noted the anomaly of the panel's award. It is notable that, in this case, the arbitration award is somewhat surprising because its effect is to put retrocessionaires in a better position in which they would have been had the panel awarded the contract rescission requested by retrocessionaires. Notwithstanding the above remarks, though, we cannot conclude nevertheless that the arbitrator's award was either completely irrational or a manifest disregard of the law.

The decision in *Michigan Mutual Insurance Company and Others v Unigard Security Insurance Company*[89] has also demonstrated that the arbitration clause of the retrocessional agreement gave the panel wide lateral to resolve disputes between the parties. The court in *Michigan Mutual Insurance Company and Others v Unigard Security Insurance Company*[90] also noted that the contract provided that the parties had to submit "any" dispute to arbitration with no limitation placed on the panel. Not least, the decision in *Michigan Mutual Insurance Company and Others v Unigard Security Insurance Company*[91] demonstrates the extent to which a court will go to reaffirm an arbitration award.[92]

---

[88] *Michigan Mutual Insurance Company and Others v Unigard Security Insurance Company*, 44 F.3d 826 (9th Cir. 1995).

[89] *Michigan Mutual Insurance Company and Others v Unigard Security Insurance Company*, 44 F.3d 826 (9th Cir. 1995).

[90] *Michigan Mutual Insurance Company and Others v Unigard Security Insurance Company*, 44 F.3d 826 (9th Cir. 1995).

[91] *Michigan Mutual Insurance Company and Others v Unigard Security Insurance Company*, 44 F.3d 826 (9th Cir. 1995).

[92] The governing standard for an award is that it not be "completely irrational" or be a "manifest disregard of the law". In practice, however, it is virtually impossible to overturn an arbitration award. Further, no real appellate rights exist. For title insurers, this unfamiliar process can cause

It is arguable that parties who wish to eliminate arbitration from reinsurance treaties should be prepared to amend the treaties so that they will more closely resemble other complex commercial contracts outside of the reinsurance industry.

The problem with this suggestion is that even relatively simple reinsurance treaties are usually signed after the coverage period expires, with the parties relying on the placement slip in the interim. Simply put, the reinsurance industry does not facilitate the drafting of complex contracts before performance. This is readily evident by examining how business has always been done. Treaties were never that important historically because they were never relied on or used. The parties knew what was expected of each other and they held to those expectations.

Turning to present, the problem culminates in the fact that parties may no longer bind themselves to the custom and practice of the industry as stringently as they once did. However, the reinsurance transaction of today still leaves little room for the drafting and negotiation of complex contracts prior to performance. This puts the parties in a difficult position. To suggest further drafting and negotiation may risk the entire deal, but not to suggest clarifying certain terms may risk having the agreement enforced according to the intent of the parties. The resulting problem is that a party to a reinsurance deal now has a window of opportunity, depending on the circumstances of how the business transaction was consummated (i.e. if and when a formal treaty is signed), to avoid arbitration. The case law examination shows that this situation has the potential to render well-intended and bargained-for arbitration clauses hanging in the wind.

What then is the solution? Perhaps the simplest is to include a slightly more detailed arbitration clause in the placement slips, perhaps largely boilerplate, familiar to the parties, which leaves room for amendments to be made when the actual treaty is finalized. If a dispute arises before consummation of the treaty, or if the treaty is never drafted and signed, the boilerplate provisions in the placement slip will control. Is such a contract enforceable? It should be no less enforceable than the "arbitration clause" language used to compel arbitration in the cases discussed above, and perhaps such language would have been enough to have justified compelling arbitration in general. Regardless of what safeguard is ultimately used, the point remains that not all participants in the reinsurance industry are playing by the rules established long ago, and in order to see that the intent of any reinsurance transaction is realized, the parties should be careful to take small steps, which will not upset the nature of the transaction, aimed at ensuring the rules are followed.[93]

Unfortunately, in the brave new world of treaty reinsurance, it will become more necessary for title insurers who are willing to increase their capacity to compete in the competitive market-place. The increased value of title risks insured have

great difficulties. The arbitration panel's likely ignorance of title insurance law, in combination with an unfamiliar procedure, may daunt title insurers, whose previous reinsurance experience, if it existed at all, consisted of cordial relationships among fellow title insurers in which disputes were rarely arbitrated; Hosack and Kline (1998), p. 109.

[93] McDonald (2001), p. 338.

followed the general real estate inflation, and therefore the title insurance industry cannot continue to provide this capacity with outside help. Nonetheless, in the reinsurance sector, arbitration continues and will continue to be a preferred dispute resolution method.[94]

1.3.4.2 The Last Decade's Emergence of ADR in Reinsurance Disputes: Pros and Cons

In insurance issues, the potential fields of dispute, as the interests of more than two parties must be considered. Not only the interests of the classic parties—insurers and the insured—are likely to be in dispute, but also those of third parties. Thus, injured or injuring third parties or other insurers, especially re-insurers, often have to be taken into consideration. Moreover, the claims can be directed in different ways, depending on the circumstances.

As a result of the attacks in New York on 11 September 2001, the most expensive non-natural catastrophe for the insurance industry so far,[95] the Deutsche Bank building next to the World Trade Center site (130 Liberty Street) was seriously damaged by falling debris and contaminated with asbestos set free by the collapse of the World Trade Center and by toxic mould which developed in the months afterwards. The building carried insurance policies totalling up to $1.715 billion borne by a consortium of four insurers: Allianz and Chubb Corp. (with 30 % each) and Axa and Zurich Financial Services AG (with 20 % each). According to Deutsche Bank, the building was a 'total loss,' the damage covered by the insurance policies summing up to $1.9 billion.[96] While an agreement in the amount of $525 million proved capable of being settled quickly with Chubb Corp. and Zurich Financial Services AG—in the range of $315 million on the part of Chubb Corp. and $210 million due from Zurich Financial Services AG—nevertheless, negotiations with Allianz and Axa at first failed. Deutsche Bank therefore filed a law suit against the two insurers in the New York City Supreme Court. Allianz and Axa claimed that the building could be salvaged and the losses on the part of Deutsche Bank were lower that those claimed. Deutsche Bank, however, demanded the full policy share of Allianz and Axa (50 % of $1.715 billion, i.e., $858 million) and alleged moreover that, if an agreement lower than the one with the two cooperative insurers were made, i.e., lower than on a total base of $1.05 million, which means an amount of $315 million due from the Allianz and $210 million from Axa, the bank would have to reimburse the difference to Chubb and Zurich.[97] The primary interests of Deutsche Bank were the demolition of the building and a maximum sum of indemnification. Allianz and Axa, on the other hand, wanted to have to pay out as

[94] Hosack and Kline (1998), p. 108.
[95] Neubacher (2004).
[96] Duwe (2009), p. 189.
[97] Duwe (2009), p. 189.

little as possible. Another crucial point might have been the question of liability for possible consequential losses in the case.[98] Over and above the interests of the parties directly involved, the public had to be considered, since the fate of the Deutsche Bank building was crucial for the plans for Ground Zero because the drafts for the memorial on the site of the World Trade Centre included the property and the Port Authority was interested in purchasing it.[99] Thus, a quick settlement was desired, otherwise "the Deutsche Bank property ordeal would stand in the redevelopment of the site".

The law suit filed by Deutsche Bank was dismissed because the insurance contract established jurisdiction on the part of an arbitral tribunal. Another law suit from Deutsche Bank filed against New York City in order to obtain indemnification was dismissed, too.[100]

Due to immense public interest, George E. Pataki, New York State Governor, appointed a mediator: George E. Mitchell, a former U.S. Senator who already had mediated in the Northern Ireland peace process (as 'Chairman of the International Commission on Disarmament and the subsequent Peace negotiations'), an intervention which was readily welcomed by the deadlocked parties. According to Mitchell, mediators do not resolve disputes, it can only be done by the parties. Thus, Mitchell only set time limits for the parties to find solutions—time limits which had to be postponed several times (first to 31 December 2003, then to 31 January 2004, then to 28 February 2004). Nevertheless, the mediator managed to create diligence and a spirit of cooperation in the negotiation process. On 26 February 2004, a final agreement was settled: the insurers covenanted to pay $140 million to Deutsche Bank, it was decided that the building had to be demolished and the 'Lower Manhattan Development Corporation,' a government agency, agreed to purchase the site for $90 million and the costs of cleaning and demolition were capped at $45 million, any costs accrued above that becoming the responsibility of the insurers. The dispute was thereby able to be settled in 4 months. The question of the alleged creation duties to reimburse Chubb Corp. and Zurich Financial Services AG has not been clarified.[101]

Nonetheless, some issues could not be settled by mediation: the question of indemnification for business interruption and for damage to furniture, equipment, etc., was subjected to arbitral proceedings. Thus, it becomes clear from this example that each ADR method has its merits but is not suitable to solve every contentious point. Yet creative combinations of different types of ADR are possible.[102]

A dispute concerning insurance and reinsurance issues connected to the attacks of 9/11 arose between Allianz and the French reinsurer Scor. First, Allianz and

---

[98] Duwe (2009), p. 189.

[99] Duwe (2009), pp. 189–190.

[100] Duwe (2009), pp. 189–190.

[101] Duwe (2009), pp. 189–190.

[102] Duwe (2009), pp. 189–190.

eight other primary insurers were involved in judicial proceedings with Silverstein Properties, the leaseholder of the World Trade Center, arguing particularly about the question of whether there had been one or two attacks on 9/11, the latter meaning an obligation for each of the insurers to pay double the amount of compensation. A federal jury in New York finally agreed with Silverstein in December 2004 that there had been two occurrences, but no judgment was made to determine the actual amount of damages. Scor, Allianz's reinsurer, considered the verdict to be "contrary to the terms of the insurance coverage in force and to the intent of the parties." Thus, Scor was willing to fully support Allianz's efforts to overturn the verdict. However, in May 2007, Allianz and six other primary insurers entered into an agreement with Silverstein Properties about paying out an additional $2 billion. The settlement was supposed to resolve all outstanding claims and to help speed up the redevelopment of the site. Scor, in the wake of this development, announced that I would challenge the Allianz settlement by seeking arbitration. According to Scor, the settlement did not respect the terms and conditions of the certificate of reinsurance between Scor and Allianz, since, as Scor stated, it exceeded the contractual requirements and contained *ex gratia* elements. Pursuant to the terms of the clause set out in the certificate of reinsurance between Allianz and Scor. Scor requested that the case be referred to arbitration in May 2007.[103]

Many of the numerous battles over insurance which were spawned by the destruction of the Twin Towers are still going on today with the arbitrations not having still been decided. Furthermore, the policy to settle agreements without involving the public is characteristic of the reinsurance business: thus, it is doubtful whether the existence of a contingent settlement will ever become known. Time-efficiency, cost-efficiency, confidentiality, and flexibility are just some of the several advantages which favour the application of arbitration in reinsurance disputes.[104]

In the last decade, the European Commission has been especially active in promoting the development of alternative dispute resolution in domestic as well as in cross-border disputes. Two Recommendations[105] adopted by the European Commission have established quality criteria that each ADR scheme should offer to its users. In addition, the Commission's proposal for a European Directive on Mediation in Civil and Commercial Matters[106] was approved by the European Parliament on 21 May 2008. The adoption of the Directive finished a 10-year process and represented a European-level attempt to achieve a higher degree of quality, homogeneity and predictability regarding the mediated resolution of commercial disputes. In order to realise cross-border dispute resolution, the so called FIN-NET was launched by the European Commission in 2001. FIN-NET is a

[103] Duwe (2009), p. 197.

[104] Duwe (2009), p. 197.

[105] European Commission, Commission Recommendation 98/257/EC (1998), p. 31; European Commission, Commission Recommendation 2001/310/EC (2001), p. 56.

[106] Directive 2008/52/EC (2008), p. 3.

financial dispute resolution network in European Economic Area countries of national ADR schemes responsible for handling disputes between consumers and financial services providers, i.e., banks, investment firms, and insurance companies.[107] By the end of 2007, the network linked 46 national ADR schemes. Within FIN-NET, the schemes cooperate to provide consumers with easy access to out-of-court complaint procedures in cross-border cases. If a consumer in one country has a dispute with a financial services provider from another country, FIN-NET members will put the consumer in touch with the relevant ADR scheme and provide the necessary information about it. FIN-NET has proven successful, handling 1,041 cross-border cases in 2007. To improve FIN-NET further, the European Commission has recently launched a public consultation on ADR in the area of financial services.[108] Alternative ADR schemes, such as the ombudsman, mediators or complaint boards do not currently exist in all European Union member states or for all financial services sectors.

Where ADR is available, consumers are often not systematically informed about this possibility. Reflecting these gaps, FIN-NET currently covers only 19 Member States. Bearing in mind the above, several questions arise. Is our legal system still up to date? Should litigation be replaced by alternative dispute resolution? Should we expect a mediation boom? The answer to all these question is 'certainly not.' Although ADR offers certain benefits, it cannot be regarded as a substitute for court proceedings and traditional litigation. It should rather be a supplement to traditional litigation approaches.[109]

The reinsurance industry has undergone material changes, including deterioration of the industry's preference to abide by the customs and practices of the industry and to arbitrate disputes. Given this trend, what can a party wishing to protect its agreement to arbitrate do to guarantee that if and when arbitration is needed, the arbitration agreement can be enforced?

It has been suggested that parties who wish to eliminate arbitration from reinsurance treaties should be prepared to amend the treaties so that they will more closely resemble other complex commercial contracts outside of the reinsurance industry. This is no good solution, as the reinsurance industry is not in practice eager to facilitate the drafting of complex contracts before performance. This is readily evident by examining how business has always been done. Treaties were never that important historically because they were never relied on or used. The parties knew what was expected of each other and they held to those expectations.

The problem today is that parties may no longer bind themselves to the custom and practice of the industry as stringently as they once did. However, the reinsurance transaction of today still leaves little room for the drafting and negotiation of complex contracts prior to performance. This puts the parties in a difficult position. To suggest further drafting and negotiation may risk the entire deal, but not to

[107] http://ec.europa.eu/internal_market/fin-net/index_de.htm.

[108] European Commission (2008), Consultation Document.

[109] Duwe (2009), pp. 197–198.

suggest clarifying certain terms may risk having the agreement enforced according to the intent of the parties.

The resulting problem is that a party to a reinsurance deal now has a window of opportunity, depending on the circumstances of how the business transaction was consummated (that is, if and when a formal treaty is signed), to avoid arbitration. This situation also has the potential to render well-intended and bargained-for arbitration clauses hanging in the wind.

What then is the solution? Perhaps the simplest is to include a slightly more detailed arbitration clause in the placement slips, perhaps largely boilerplate, familiar to the parties, which leaves room for amendments to be made when the actual treaty is finalized. If a dispute arises before consummation of the treaty, or if the treaty is never drafted and signed, the boilerplate provisions in the placement slip will control.

Is such a contract enforceable? It should be no less enforceable than the "arbitration clause" language used to compel arbitration in the cases discussed above. Regardless of what safeguard is ultimately used, the point remains that not all participants in the reinsurance industry are playing by the rules established long ago, and in order to see that the intent of any reinsurance transaction is realized, the parties should be careful to take small steps, which will not upset the nature of the transaction, aimed at ensuring the rules are followed.[110]

1.3.4.3 The Reasons for Opting for Either Arbitration or Litigation

The decisions regarding whether to include an arbitration clause in a contract and what provisions to put in it, as well as whether to take advantage of arbitration once a dispute arises, are not simple.

Arbitration has sometimes been perceived as the solution to every ill or inconvenience attendant to the judicial system. It is not capable of fulfilling the extravagant promises that have been made for it. Because one has to pay for the services of arbitrators and the space in which to conduct the hearing, arbitration is not necessarily cheaper than comparable litigation. Nor is it always quicker. While courts sometimes have backlogs, arbitrators may have full-time jobs, and schedules of their own. In general, the delays attendant on both litigation and arbitration arise primarily from the needs of the parties and their lawyers, rather than the inertia inherent in the court or arbitral systems.

Litigation has the advantages of being determined by judges who are usually familiar with basic principles of law, and of unequivocal *albeit* appealable authority, at least within the jurisdiction where a judgment is rendered. This is not as great an advantage in the international context as it is in the domestic one, due to the hazards of foreign enforcement of judgments. Litigation proceeds, for better or for worse, by preordained rules which, though complicated, have at least a degree of

[110] McDonald (2001), p. 336.

predictability. The authority of the court is not limited by contractual terms, nor is its reach limited to the parties to any agreement. This can be extremely significant.

The popularity of arbitration is not based on its speed or economy, which are somewhat illusory, but upon the hope of the parties to the contract that by employing arbitration they can maintain a degree of control over the intensity of the dispute and the methods used to resolve it, which they perceive to be impossible in the lawyer-dominated field of litigation. The popularity of *ex aequo et bono* clauses, under which an arbitrator is directed to interpret a contract as an "honourable engagement" and to "abstain from following strict rules of law" may be evidence of the hostility the negotiators of these contracts feel towards the intrusion of legal principle into their domain.

Arbitration is perhaps best resorted to under the following circumstances.

First, in connection with routine business, under which the parties expect to have disputes which, while substantial, will not interfere with the business relationship between them. In those circumstances, arbitration sometimes can be carried out in an atmosphere of civility that does not destroy an ongoing business relationship. The parties to such disputes are unlikely to make the kind of destructive allegations of fraud and misconduct that arbitration is ill-suited to deal with anyway. Because of the nature of the relationship that already exists, they are unlikely to need the more extensive discovery of witnesses and documents that may be available in litigation. Perhaps most important, success of either party in this type of relatively minor dispute is not determinative of the survival of the loser. Arbitration, is by definition, "arbitrary." It is entirely possible that arbitration will produce a bad result. However, if the dispute is such that the parties can more easily afford error than stalemate, arbitration is a very logical choice.

A second type of case that lends itself well to arbitration is a dispute in which the decision-maker will need a generally international viewpoint in order to fairly decide the merits of an argument. Parties who feel they have a cosmopolitan relationship requiring such an international view may also conclude that a neutral forum, in which neither party has an undue advantage, is the fairest *situs* for the resolution of any dispute.

A third type of situation that may benefit from a neutral territory arbitration clause is one for which the choice of a particular system of law is very important. It may be possible, by use of an arbitration clause directing decision by an arbitration award not subject to appeal, to avoid expansive interpretations of law that might frustrate the purpose of the contract. The parties might elect neutral forum arbitration (coupled with a suitable choice of law) if there is a possibility that, in the natural forum, the agreement might be challenged under, for instance, the U.K. Insurance Companies Acts prohibition of unauthorized transaction of insurance business, the E.E.C. Article 85(1) prohibition on restrictions on competition, or United States RICO or antitrust legislation.[111]

[111] Milligan-Wbyte and Cannon Veed (1989), p. 125.

1.3.4.4 Considering Mediation

Parties involved in reinsurance mediation should consider well their options and the pros and cons of opting for such an ADR method in resolving their dispute. Even if a party is involved in a reinsurance mediation, because it is compelled to do so by contract, it should be aware of the potential benefits of the process—even if they fall short of an early and satisfactory resolution of the dispute. Even an unsuccessful mediation enables parties to learn more about the other side's case and approach. The best time to embark upon a mediation differs from case to case, however few reinsurance mediations are likely to involve much open constructive dialogue between parties, at least until those parties have some understanding of the extent of evidence in respect of the most salient facts and have formed a considered assessment of the strength of their legal case. Hence, it is often more productive to explore mediation once formally pleaded positions have been articulated and some steps taken to substantiate any factual or expert evidence.

Clearly, the selection of the right mediator is a crucial first step to a successful mediation. In as specialised a market as reinsurance, parties need to have confidence in the mediators understanding of the reinsurance issues at stake and the likely reactions to these of a court or arbitration panel. This usually means drawing on a fairly limited pool with requisite expertise beyond mediation skills.

Also, it is customary for mediators to attempt to record any agreement reached in the form of a settlement agreement or at least in heads of agreement, which may thereafter be made the subject of a more formal and binding agreement. However, those involved with a reinsurance dispute may often have to take into account the effect of any binding agreement upon a number of other interested parties, such as brokers or retrocessionaires.

Those interests are likely to have already been taken into account at a much earlier stage, but care is needed to remember them, especially if eleventh-hour talks or concessions have involved a higher sum or unanticipated element, such as a return of premium, being introduced into settlement deliberations. If no settlement has been reached, but only some new material or facts have come to life in the course of mediation, other parties may be precluded from relying upon these on account of the confidential and without prejudice character of the mediation.

Following the mediation, however, a party may wish to consider whether information has emerged during the mediation process which suggests that other parties have not fully discharged their duties to disclose all relevant documentation. Alternatively, a party may wish to consider what impact any new facts may have upon evidence which has been provided or may yet be provided in such proceedings.[112]

The main attraction of ADR, and specifically mediation, is the prospect of successfully avoiding or foreshortening prolonged, expensive and acrimonious formal legal proceedings to settle disputes.

[112] Barlow Lyde and Gilbert LLP (2009), pp. 861–862.

Although the reinsurance market was one of the sectors most resistant to the adoption of ADR measures, mediation in some form or other—at least as a tool assisting negotiated settlements—is now an everyday feature of reinsurance contract dispute resolution. It has not however usurped and remains most unlikely wholly to usurp the important role played by arbitration or the courts in determining issues of liability in the most contested reinsurance cases, but it will continue to afford an alternative means of parties seeking to resolve reinsurance disputes.[113]

1.4 Aims, Outline and Scope

1.4.1 General

This monograph is on reinsurance arbitrations, from a comparative perspective. Reinsurance arbitrations, arising out of clauses, in reinsurance treaties, opting for arbitrations as the chosen dispute resolution method, will be examined from a comparative perspective and angle. In effect reinsurance arbitrations in the predominant reinsurance markets, i.e. the English and the USA market will be examined. In parallel, as Germany holds an important share of the volume of the reinsurance market, the position as to certain aspects of the arbitral procedure within this market, will also be there assessed.

1.4.2 Aims

The monograph has the following aims: (1) to study, identify and reflect on the main aspects of the reinsurance contract; in particular, to examine the history of reinsurance, the formation of the reinsurance treaty, the rules of construction of reinsurance treaties and their interpretation; (2) to critically discuss and analyse the arbitration agreement clause within such treaties; (3) to study compare and contrast the way in which reinsurance arbitrations are conducted in the different reinsurance markets; (4) to critically discuss and analyse, the advantages and disadvantages of arbitration in reinsurance; (5) to answer the question of the purpose of arbitration and its interplay with reinsurance; (6) to help detect the problems that may, in some cases, impede the flourish of arbitration in reinsurance; (7) to draw conclusions, provide critique, and, in discussing the various aspects and problems entailed within reinsurance arbitrations, to also establish the main trends imposed in law, in terms of arbitration in reinsurance.

[113] Barlow Lyde and Gilbert LLP (2009), pp. 861–862.

1.4.3 Background Justification

England and the USA have, traditionally, been major reinsurance markets, whereby reinsurance treaties concluded also purport for the resolution of disputes arising out of reinsurance contracts by arbitration. This is attributable, amidst other factors, to the fact that organisations, such as ARIAS UK and ARIAS US support the use arbitration as a dispute resolution mechanism for reinsurance disputes, hence also further enhancing the growth of arbitration within the reinsurance world. In addition, Germany has also been established as holding big shares of the global reinsurance market.

Arbitration, in reinsurance, asserts, more than ever nowadays, a pivotal role. This monograph will investigate the way in which reinsurance arbitrations are perceived nowadays, their different aspects and features and their effect on parties, as well as the future prospects for arbitration within reinsurance, in light of the great importance of the former within the latter.

1.4.4 Research Purpose

The currently proposed research and the resulting monograph, concerns reinsurance arbitrations. The purpose is not only to research in a comparative way—in the legal regimes of England and of the USA predominantly[114] and also that of Germany wherever the resources permit a comparative analysis on the issues involved—but also to comment from a legal angle on the different aspects of reinsurance arbitrations and to explore other issues which embody economic-financial features and aspects. The approach to be taken will aim to draw conclusions, regarding the prospect of further flourish of arbitration and the positive or negative role of it within reinsurance.

1.4.5 General Outline

The monograph discusses the main features of reinsurance contracts, the main aspects of arbitrations within reinsurance as well as the *status quo* of the former in terms of its application on the latter, the economic-financial aspects involved within the notion of arbitration in reinsurance, and the question of the purpose of arbitration in reinsurance. It is also hoped to provide some food for thought, via the critical analysis which is being conducted, and it investigates the impact and the results of resorting to arbitration, in reinsurance, as an alternative dispute resolution mechanism, rather than to litigation.

[114] And, to a lesser extent, in Germany and Switzerland.

1.4.6 Detailed Outline

This chapter, attempts to address the aims of the monograph, as well as the background justification and the research purpose of it. Moreover, it touches upon the reinsurance relationship, historically and in modern times. It also touches upon the eminence of the use of alternative dispute resolution methods, i.e. of arbitration, over state court litigation, in reinsurance disputes and upon the reasons for the preference of arbitration in reinsurance. Further on, it discusses the history of reinsurance and the role that arbitration plays within it. It also critically discusses and analyses the main advantages and disadvantages of reinsurance arbitrations as opposed to, but not only, state court litigation. It also attempts to answer the question of the purpose of arbitration and its interplay with reinsurance and to detect the problems that may, in some cases, impede the flourish of arbitration in reinsurance. Finally, it discusses the general and detailed outline of the issues within the present monograph.

Chapter 2, discusses the main features of negotiating and contracting the reinsurance contract, i.e. the main features of the formation of the reinsurance treaty, the rules of construction of reinsurance treaties and their interpretation.

Chapter 3, discusses the need for reinsurance arbitration and the arbitral legal framework in the jurisdictions of England, USA and Germany.

Chapter 4 discusses the notion of the reinsurance arbitration clause. More specifically it analyses the arbitration agreement clause within reinsurance treaties.

Chapter 5 discusses compares and contrasts the way in which reinsurance arbitrations proceedings are conducted in the different reinsurance markets, predominantly those of England and the USA, although, at points parallelisms to the German reinsurance markets are also drawn.

Chapter 6 discusses the reinsurance arbitration award.

Chapter 7 attempts an overall assessment, on the basis of the examined case law and systems whereby reinsurance arbitration is conducted. Not least, it draws conclusions, provides critique, and—in discussing the various aspects and problems entailed within reinsurance arbitrations—also, attempts to establish the main trends imposed in law, in terms of arbitration in reinsurance, and suggest future routes and directions to be followed, as to the position and treatment of arbitration within reinsurance.

References

Barlow Lyde and Gilbert LLP (2009) Reinsurance practice and the law. Informa, London

Butler J, Merkin R (1999) Reinsurance law. Kluwer, Kingston upon Thames

Cohen DF, DeMasi TE, Krauss A (1994) Uberrimae Fidei and reinsurance rescission: does a gentlemen's agreement have a place in today's commercial market. Tort Ins Law J 29(2):602–618

Duwe C (2009) Arbitration and alternative dispute resolution in insurance law—a practitioner's approach. ERA Forum 10:177–198

Edelman C, Burns A, Craig D, Nawbatt A (2005) The law of reinsurance. OUP, Oxford

European Commission (1998) Commission Recommendation 98/257/EC of 30 March 1998 on the principles applicable to the bodies responsible for out-of-court settlement of consumer disputes. OJ L 115 (17 April 1998)

European Commission (2001) Commission Recommendation 2001/310/EC of 4 April 2001 on the principles for out-of-court bodies involved in the consensual resolution of consumer disputes. OJ L 109 (19 April 2001)

European Commission (2008) Consultation document: alternative dispute resolution in the area of financial services. Brussels (11 December 2008)

Geiger H (2000) The comparative law and economics of reinsurance. Nomos Verlag, Baden-Baden, pp 50–51

Hosack J, Kline CJ (1998) Current title insurance issues in the United States. Int Law Rep 6 (4):106–109

Lowry J, Rawlings F (1999) Insurance law: doctrines and principles. Hart, Oxford

McDonald J (2001) Reinsurance arbitration will the new ways cripple arbitration? Def Couns J 68:328–338

Milligan-Wbyte J, Cannon Veed M (1989) Bermudian, English and American reinsurance arbitration law and practice and ADR methods. Tort Ins Law J 25:125

Neubacher (2004) Streit um Hochhaus am Ground Zero nähert sich dem Ende. Börsenzeitung (December 28)

O'Niell PJ, Woloniecki J (1998) The law of reinsurance. Sweet and Maxwell, London

Schiffer LP, Expert Commentary (2006) Reinsurance arbitration – a primer. http://www.irmi.com/Expert/Articles/2006/Schiffer06.aspx. Accessed 1 Oct 2010

Schwepcke A (2004) Reinsurance: principle and state of the art. Verlag Versicherungswirtschaft GmbH, Karlsruhe

Strain RW (1997) Reinsurance: claims management. Strain Publishing Inc, Athens

Thomas JE, Lyons S (eds) (2012) New Appleman on insurance law – library edition, vol 7, Property insurance (chapters 71–79 §§ 71.01–79.06). Lexis Nexis, Los Angeles

The Reinsurance Contract

Reinsurance contracts are formed on the basis of ordinary rules of contract law but are also subject to the usages of this particular trade; for, such usages are of great importance. Reinsurance contracts are in writing. In addition, binders are being used in reinsurance contracts and are fully effective. A typical reinsurance contract is a relatively short and concise document containing the clauses with the names of the parties, the terms, the reinsurance clause, the amount expressed as proportion or excess point and limit and the premium or formula for calculating it. Exclusions also exist and are important, in both proportional and excess loss treaties. Reinsurance may be also subject to implied terms. There is no reason for reinsurance contracts not to be interpreted and construed according to the general rules for contracts; however, the special nature of reinsurance arrangements makes it imperative that arbitral tribunals consider industry custom and practice in interpreting reinsurance contracts. Reinsurance transactions are a matter of "utmost good faith".

2.1 Formation of Contracts

2.1.1 The Role of Industry, Custom and Practice

Even though the amounts at stake involved in reinsurance contracts are in the range of multi-million currency exposures, contractual arrangements in the industry may be very informal. The custom and practice of the industry, thus, can affect both the manner in which reinsurance contracts are created and the content of such contracts. For instance, a reinsurance contract commonly is formed when a reinsurer accepts the terms of a "slip" offered by the cedent or its agent. Such a slip, typically, will contain only the barest details of the parties' contractual relationship.[1] Similarly,

[1] *Quinta Commc'ns v Warrington* (2000) Lloyd's Rep. IR 81.

K. Noussia, *Reinsurance Arbitrations*, DOI 10.1007/978-3-642-45146-1_2,

whether a reinsurance contract is based on a slip or on more formal wording, the custom and practice of the industry may provide a basis for implying terms into the contract.[2]

2.1.2 The Procedure

In the direct-insurance setting, the majority of policies are issued on standard forms, whether developed by industry organisations or individual insurers. This is particularly true in the highly regulated field of consumer insurance. One, however, may encounter manuscripted, i.e. specially drafted, terms in reinsurance contracts, which reflect the sophisticated nature of parties to a reinsurance contract.[3]

When reinsurance was mainly facultative, it was almost always placed by direct negotiation. The insurer would commonly show the reinsurer a proposal and negotiate the amount, premium, and retention.[4] In some instances, the policy itself was shown and the reinsurance would be endorsed on a copy of it. In others, the same form was used, as for the underlying insurance, and this was considered acceptable, even though the subject was described to be the property insured by the underlying policy and some terms might have had to be disregarded as inappropriate to reinsurance.[5]

The formation of a reinsurance contract is governed by the ordinary rules of contract law. As with other commercial contracts, the process is also subject to the usages of this particular trade. Especially in the English market, those usages are of great importance so as to determine when a contract is made and for what. Binders are also used in reinsurance, as in direct insurance, and are fully effective where they contain adequate terms, or the means of settling them, to provide the rudiments of a definite contract.[6]

Usage may make an incomplete binder binding. In *American Eagle Fire Ins. Co. v Eagle Star Ins. Co.*,[7] the trial court took testimony establishing a practice of reinsurance bound open for particulars and not showing the exact amount of insurance, because it was not known at the time, but showing the rates the insurer was willing to pay. It was held, that the evidence showed that it was the custom that

[2] *Reliastar Life Ins. Co. v IOA Re, Inc*, 303 F.3d 874, 881–882 (8th Cir. 2002); Thomas and Lyons (2012), pp. 72–78.

[3] Thomas and Lyons (2012), pp. 72–79.

[4] *Imperial F. Ins. Co. v Home Ins. Co* (1985 CA5 La) 68 F 698; *Fireman's Fund ins. Co. v Aachen & Munich Fire Ins. Co.* (1906) 2 Cal App 690, 84 P 253; *Insurance Co. of North America v Hibernia Ins. Co.* (1891) 140 US 565, 570, 35 L Ed 517, 11 S Ct 909; Staring (1993), § 11:1.

[5] *Jackson v St. Paul Fire and Marine Ins. Co.*, (1885) 99 NY 124, 1 NE 539; Staring (1993), § 11:1.

[6] *American Eagle Fire Ins. Co. v Eagle Star Ins. Co.* (1954, CA9 Cal) 216 F2dd 176; *Tokio Marine & Fire Ins. Co. v National Union Fire Ins. Co.* (1937, CA2 NY) 91 F2d; Staring (1993), § 11:1.

[7] *American Eagle Fire Ins. Co. v Eagle Star Ins. Co.* (1954, CA9 Cal) 216 F2dd 176; Staring (1993), § 11:1.

all terms other than the amount of risk and the premium thereon are considered binding upon the execution of the provisional binder.[8]

Because facultative reinsurance is deigned to cover a specific risk, such reinsurance often will incorporate standard terms from the underlying insurance policy. The parties to a facultative contract can incorporate underlying policy provisions by stating on a certificate that the reinsurance is subject to the "terms and conditions" of the underlying policy, that the reinsurance applies "as original", or simply that the contract contains a "full reinsurance clause".[9]

In *Progressive Casualty Ins. Co. v Reaseguradora Nacional de Venezuela*[10] a policy presented by the broker to the retrocessionaire contained, although the slip did not, a provision stating "subject to facultative reinsurance agreement" and referring to an agreement between the original insurer and certain London reinsurers and contained an arbitration clause. When the retrocedent tried to enforce it against retrocessionaires, the court held that New York, USA law recognises that not all terms need be in a binder and that certain stereotypical terms can be implied; in the particular case, a dispute of fact as to whether the arbitration clause was typical in such facultative agreement, made summary judgment on that point impossible.[11]

In contrast to facultative reinsurance, there can be great variation in the use of standard and manuscripted terms in treaty reinsurance. Where a treaty relationship is based on a slip only, the slip may refer to standard-form clauses available in the relevant market. If treaty reinsurance is based on formal wording, on the other hand, the parties may employ form language, manuscripted terms, or some combination of both as best suits their needs.[12]

2.1.3 Identification of the Contract

Good order requires reinsurance contracts to be in writing. In common usage they are, and so there will ordinarily be a signed memorandum sufficient to satisfy any real or assumed requirement for writing.

In *Exchange Mut. Fire Ins. Co. v Mutual Fire Ins. Co.*,[13] where there was an oral treaty the terms of which were in dispute, the court decided that if it was a contract

---

[8] *American Eagle Fire Ins. Co. v Eagle Star Ins. Co.* (1954, CA9 Cal) 216 F2dd 176, 178; Staring (1993), § 11:1.

[9] Thomas and Lyons (2012), pp. 72–79.

[10] *Progressive Casualty Ins. Co. v Reaseguradora Nacional de Venezuela* (1992, SD NY) 802 F Supp 1069; Staring (1993), § 11:1.

[11] *Progressive Casualty Ins. Co. v Reaseguradora Nacional de Venezuela* (1992, SD NY) 802 F Supp 1069; Staring (1993), § 11:1.

[12] Thomas and Lyons (2012), pp. 72–79.

[13] *Exchange Mut. Fire Ins. Co. v Mutual Fire Ins. Co.*, (1915) 59 Pa Super 240.

to begin with, the course of dealing thereafter showed disregard of every term and, as a consequence, each session was to be regarded as a separate contract.

An issue of the writing will probably not arise because the parties have not intended to reach a written agreement, but rather because it is claimed that, in the course of negotiations, an exchange of writings not clearly establishing mutual assent has been supplemented by an oral assent.[14]

In England, the Marine Insurance Act 1906 lays down some minimum requirements of writing, including the name of the reinsured, the identification of the subject-matter, the period, the amount reinsured and the signature of the reinsurer.[15] As with any other contract, the reinsurance contract must contain the particulars to make a complete bargain as to its essential features. Certainly, major material terms cannot be left out, without which the contract will not be performed, and some of these will vary with the circumstances of the contract.[16] Also, as in the case of other contracts, the standard rules may be supplemented by the usages of the market. The London practice is to circulate among the proposed reinsurers a slip with abbreviated particulars of the coverage desired, including usually references to a number of standard clauses. The reinsurers indicate and initial the percentage they will accept.

It is now settled law[17] that the initials of each reinsurer create a contract between him and the reinsured, binding on both for the percentage accepted by him, even though the full 100 % may not be attained on the slip.

Although in *Abrahams v Med. Re*[18] a lot of uncertainty surrounded the intention to enter into a contract and it was held that there was never a binding contract, nevertheless this case does not affect the general rule that an underwriter initialising a slip is also thereby bound.[19]

Also, it is theoretically possible for commercial men to enter, deliberately, into an agreement relating to liabilities arising under insurance contracts, which is binding in honour only.

In *Orion Insurance Co. Plc v Sphere Drake Insurance Plc*[20] it was held that the parties had entered into a "good will agreement" which they did not intend to be legally binding; however, for a court to reach such a conclusion is unusual, and the party asserting that there was no intention to create legal relations, bears a heavy burden of proof.

In *Home Insurance Co. v Administratia Asigurarilor De Stat*,[21] however, where the quota share treaty contained an arbitration clause providing that it shall be

---

[14] *Wetherell v Sentry Reinsurance, Inc*., (1990, ED Pa)743 F Supp 1157; Staring (1993), § 11:2.

[15] English Marine Insurance Act 1906, ss. 23, 24.

[16] Staring (1993), § 11:1.

[17] *General Reinsurance Corp. v Fennia Patria* (1983) 2 Lloyd's Rep 287 (CA).

[18] *Abrahams v Med. Re* [1991]1 Lloyd's Rep. 216.

[19] O'Niell and Woloniecki (1998), § 3–21.

[20] *Orion Insurance Co. Plc v Sphere Drake Insurance Plc* [1990]1 Lloyd's Rep. 465.

[21] *Home Insurance Co. v Administratia Asigurarilor De Stat* [1983]2 Lloyd's Rep. 674.

interpreted as an honourable engagement rather than as a legal obligation, it was held that this did not mean that the contract was binding in honour only.[22]

With regards to oral promises, in principle and subject to the proof of the intention of the parties, an unequivocal oral promise to sign a slip on particular terms would constitute a valid and legally enforceable contract. However, in *Sphere Drake Insurance Plc v Denby*[23] it was held—on the evidence—that a binding oral agreement for the provision of stop loss reinsurance had not been entered into.[24]

Both in London market slips and in requests and binders used in the USA and elsewhere, it is a practice not to set out the intended clauses in full but to refer to them by title or subject matter. If the clause, however, is not identified as one of a published set or one widely used and known by name to both parties, there may be difficulty in settling the ultimate wording. Thus, efforts have been made to produce standard or clearly identifiable clauses for reference.[25]

Whether in the slip or in a full contract subsequently issued, the contract will normally be treated as fully integrated and the parole evidence rule is illustrated in operation both in the USA and in England, both in favour of the slip and of the latter contract, depending on the circumstances.

In the USA, in *Wetherell v Sentry Reinsurance, Inc.*[26] the slip was taken to be the integrated contract and the subsequent certificate was of no effect.

In England, in *Youell v Bland Welch & Co.*,[27] the wording of the reinsurance contract was approved by the leading underwriter pursuant to authority in the slip. When a conflict appeared between the underlying policies and the reinsurance, so that the reinsurers were no longer on the risk when losses occurred, the reinsureds sought to introduce the slip as evidence to explain the contract in their favour but were barred by the parole evidence rule.[28]

Amendments to a reinsurance contract are governed by the same rules and usages as initial formation of the contract.

In the USA, in *Wetherell v Sentry Reinsurance, Inc.*[29] amendment was held to require mutual assent and thus, offer, acceptance and consideration. In *Hamilton Life Ins. Co v Republic Nat. Life Ins. Co.*[30] it was held that, where a contract had been fully integrated, oral amendment could be precluded by the parole evidence rule and that the same effect could be achieved by a contract provision that all amendments be written and signed.

---

[22] O'Niell and Woloniecki (1998), § 3–22.

[23] *Sphere Drake Insurance Plc v Denby* [2000]2 Lloyd's Rep. 550, QBD (Comm).

[24] O'Niell and Woloniecki (1998), § 3–23.

[25] Staring (1993), § 11:2.

[26] *Wetherell v Sentry Reinsurance, Inc.*, (1990, ED Pa)743 F Supp 1157.

[27] *Youell v Bland Welch & Co.* (1990)2 Lloyd's Rep 423 (QB).

[28] Staring (1993), § 11:3.

[29] *Wetherell v Sentry Reinsurance, Inc.*, (1990, ED Pa)743 F Supp 1157.

[30] *Hamilton Life Ins. Co v Republic Nat. Life Ins. Co.*, (1969, CA2 NY) 408 F2d 606.

In England, in *General Reinsurance Corp. v Fennia Patria*,[31] it was held that the effect of initialling a slip is the same, where the slip proposes an amendment as where it is the original proposal of a contract.[32]

2.1.4 The Contract Terms

The long and well established tradition that reinsurance transactions are a matter of "utmost good faith" between the parties has had a predictable effect on the preparation of reinsurance contracts. The typical reinsurance contract is a relatively short, concise document, noticeably lacking in the legalisms so characteristic of other types of contracts.

This underlying assumption of utmost good faith allows the companies to draft a document, that assumes that both parties are so knowledgeable on the subject matter to be dealt with and possess such a degree of sophistication as to preclude the necessity for long, expository declarations of intent and implementation.[33]

The apparent clarity of reinsurance contracts may be deceptive to the uninitiated because of words and short phrases that say a great deal more than they appear to, in the usages of insurance and reinsurance.

Of the expressions that make up the contract, cardinal to prove its existence are the clauses containing the names of the parties, the terms, the reinsurance clause, the amount expressed as proportion or excess point and limit and the premium or formula for calculating it. Of those, the reinsurance clause will probably draw the closest attention.[34]

Exclusions exist and are important in both proportional and excess loss treaties. Exclusions may refer to particular perils or certain difficult exposures, as well as whole classes of businesses. Among the common exclusions are, war, political risks, risks on property exceeding a certain value, nuclear risks and reinsurance written by the insurer. Some of the more sophisticated of those exclusions are the subject of standard clauses. Since excluded risks may be taken by inadvertence, a clause is sometimes included to provide temporary coverage of an excluded risk for a limited time, to permit the insurer to cancel it coverage or find protection. It is also

---

[31] *General Reinsurance Corp. v Fennia Patria* (1983) 2 Lloyd's Rep 287 (CA).

[32] In *General Reinsurance Corp. v Fennia Patria* (1983) 2 Lloyd's Rep 287 (CA) an amendment was proposed changing the excess point at which the reinsurance cover would attach. It has been initialled by only 2 of the 28 reinsurers on the contract when a major fire loss occurred, as to which it appeared that the amendment would affect the rights of all reinsurers. The circulation of the slip was halted and the reinsured sought to cancel it. The Court held on appeal that this was not feasible and that the amendment, if effective, was binding as to the two who signed it, and them only, since it was unacceptable to allow the reinsured an election to hold individual reinsurers to a contract or not, according to how he perceived his advantage after the loss; Staring (1993), § 11:3.

[33] Staring (1993), § 12:1.

[34] Staring (1993), § 12:1.

fair to assume that exclusions in reinsurance contracts contemplate parallel exclusions in the underlying policies. However, the reinsurance exclusion is valid regardless of the failure of the direct insurer, for whatever reason, to have excluded the risk in his policy.[35]

Warranties in reinsurance contract may reiterate warranties found, or supposed to be found in underlying policies and governing the subject of those policies. They are unlikely, however, to focus on the underlying policy itself. They are used principally to provide assurance of the underwriting information provided and of certain obligations undertaken by the reinsured. Thus, either the reinsured's retention or the maintenance of other insurance or reinsurance may be warranted. The warranted matters are, thus, likely to be the same as the representations of the reinsured relied on by the reinsurer. Restatements as warranties, in the contract, provide certainty and eliminate some disputes. Depending on the time to which the warranty refers, however, it may have the added effect of allowing the reinsurer to rescind the contract for breach of warranty with respect to facts that were true when the contract was made but later became untrue.[36]

Reinsurance may be subject to implied terms, but the implication of terms, with or without a following form clause, will depend upon their suitability to the contract. An implied term, in an underlying policy, however, may not be suitable to the reinsurance and may therefore not be implied in it or carried into it by a following form clause.[37] Reinsurance contracts are obviously related to the underlying contracts, but, in the absence of express reference, they are not related to the contracts that precede or follow them in time.[38] Where a reinsurance contract is based on a slip alone or on otherwise incomplete wording, courts may imply terms deemed necessary for the functioning of the parties' relationship. Both the parties' course of dealing and the custom and practice of the reinsurance industry can provide a basis for filling gaps in the writing to which a cedent and reinsurer have agreed.[39]

Reinsurance may also have terms supplied or interpreted by usage. Usages or customs, to be binding, must be well-settled, general in their applications and uniformly recognised as obligatory. There is, however, a limit to what usage or custom may dictate as it cannot restrict the power of the contracting parties to agree to terms.[40]

---

[35] *IPCI Ltd v Old Republic Ins. Co* (1991, ED Wis.), 758 F Supp 478; Staring (1993), § 12:1.

[36] English Marine Insurance Act 1906, s. 33; *Iron Trades Mut. Ins. Co. v Companhia de Seguros Imperia*, [1991] 1 Re LR 231, QB 1990; Staring (1993), § 12:3.

[37] Staring (1993), § 12:6.

[38] Staring (1993), § 12:7.

[39] *Reliastar Life Ins. Co. v IOA Re, Inc*, 303 F.3d 874, 881–882 (8th Cir. 2002); Thomas and Lyons (2012), pp. 72-10.

[40] *Chalaron v Insurance Co of North America* (1896) 48 La Ann 1582, 1585, 21 So 267, 269; Staring (1993), § 12:8.

In *General Reinsurance Corp. v Fennia Patria*,[41] the defendants contended that there remained an option to rescind all the contracts resulting from the lines written on a partially completed slip and that this result was said to flow either from the implication of a term, as and when each line is written, which is necessary to give business efficacy to the resulting contract or, alternatively, from a binding usage or practice in the reinsurance market.

The Court of Appeal held that no such option to rescind existed, and stated that every usage, custom or practice, which is imported into any transaction as a matter of binding obligation, whether in respect of a particular trade, branch of business or occupation, must be notorious, certain and reasonable,[42] and that there is a big difference between a course of conduct which is frequently or habitually followed in a particular commercial community as a matter of grace and a course which is habitually followed because it is considered that the parties have a legally binding right to demand it. For a practice to be a recognised usage, it need be established as a practice having a binding effect.[43]

In *Con-Stan Industries of Australia Pty Ltd v Norwich Winterthur Insurance (Australia) Ltd*[44] the High court of Australia stated that the existence of a custom or usage which will justify the implication of a term into a contract is a question of fact,[45] that there has to exist evidence that the custom relied on is so well known and acquiesced in that everyone making a contract in that situation is presumed to have imported it into the contract, and that a person may be bound by a custom notwithstanding that he had no knowledge of it.[46]

Moreover, usage cannot prevail if it contradicts the direct wording of the contract.[47] Finally, the force of usage or custom can only prevail and is limited to the community or market in which it is proved to obtain.[48]

[41] *General Reinsurance Corp. v Fennia Patria* (1983) 2 Lloyd's Rep 287 (CA).

[42] *Pacific & General Insurance Co. Ltd v Hazell* [1997] LRLR 65.

[43] *Cunliffe-Owen v Theather and Greenwood* [1967] 1 WLR 1421; O'Niell and Woloniecki (1998), pp. 3–20.

[44] *Con-Stan Industries of Australia Pty Ltd v Norwich Winterthur Insurance (Australia) Ltd* (1986) 64 ALR 481.

[45] *Nelson v Dahl* (1879) 12 Ch. D. 568.

[46] O'Niell and Woloniecki (1998), pp. 3–21.

[47] *Pink v American Surety Co.* (1940) 283 NY 290, 28 NE2d 842; Staring (1993), § 12:8.

[48] *Insurance Co. of North America v Hibernia Ins. Co.* (1891) 140 US 565, 570, 35 L Ed 517, 11 S Ct 909, where the USA Supreme court impliedly recognised the force of usage or custom but also held that a usage of New Orleans could not prevail in Philadelphia, where it was not followed or perhaps even known; Staring (1993), § 12:8.

2.2 Rules of Construction

Courts should recognise that reinsurance contracts are contracts negotiated at arms' length, between sophisticated parties rather than contracts of adhesion.[49] Indeed in the facultative reinsurance relationship, both the cedent and the reinsurer have the faculty or option to accept or reject every individual risk submitted.

Nevertheless, courts are split over whether reinsurance arrangements, which are negotiated by sophisticated business entities familiar with the business of reinsurance, should be governed by the same "contra preferentem" rules that often apply in the direct insurance context.

Some courts hold that the written terms embodied in reinsurance certificates and treaties should be enforced by courts without reference to contra-insurer rules of construction.[50] These courts hold that general contract law principles govern the interpretation of reinsurance contracts.[51]

Other courts hold that ambiguities in a reinsurance contract should be construed against the reinsurer.[52]

2.2.1 The Role of Industry Custom and Practice

The special and unique nature of reinsurance arrangements makes it imperative that arbitral tribunals consider industry custom and practice in interpreting reinsurance contracts.

Even outside the reinsurance context, basic principles of contract construction require that the terms of a contract are to be construed in light of the customs, practices, uses and terminology as generally understood in the particular trade or business.[53]

The reasons for considering industry custom and practice are even more compelling in the reinsurance context. The typical reinsurance agreement is relatively short and concise, using terms of art rather than lengthy, legalistic explications to

---

[49] *Unigard Sec. Ins. Co. v North River Ins. Co.*, 4 F.3d 1049, 1065/2d Cir. 1993); *International Surplus Lines Ins. Co v Fireman's Fund Ins. Co.*, No 88 C32 (N.D. Ill. Dec. 29,1989); Ostrager and Vyskocil (1996), p. 5-4.

[50] *Unigard Sec. Ins. Co. v North River Ins. Co.*, 4 F.3d 1049, 1065 /2d Cir. 1993); *In Re Pritchard & Baird Inc.*, 8 B.R. 265, 270–271 (D.N.J. 1980); *Arkwright-Boston Mfrs. Mut. Ins. Co. v Calvert Fire Ins. Co.*, 887 F.2d 437, 440 (2d. Cir. 1989); Ostrager and Vyskocil (1996), p. 5-5.

[51] Ostrager and Vyskocil (1996), p. 5-5.

[52] *Christiania Gen. Ins. Corp. v Great Am. Ins. Co.*, F.2d 268,278 (2d. Cir. 1992); *Westchester Resco Co v New England Reins. Corp.*, 818 f.2d 2, 3 (2d Cir. 1987); *Travellers Ins. Co. v Central Natal Ins. Co.*, 733 F. Supp. 522, 528 (D.Conn. 1990); *Justice v Stuyvesant Ins. Co.*, 265 F. Supp. 63, 65–66 (S.D.W.Va. 1967); Ostrager and Vyskocil (1996), p. 5-5.

[53] *Garza v Marine Transport Lines, Inc.*, 861 F.2d 23,27 (2d. Cir. 1988); *Walk-In Medical Centers, Inc. v Breuer Capital Corp.*, 861 F.2d 23,27 (2d. Cir. 1988); Ostrager and Vyskocil (1996), p. 5-6.

define the obligations of the parties.[54] The concise nature of the facultative certificate, which has developed in reliance upon the principle of utmost good faith, requires that the certificate be construed in light of industry custom and practice in order to effectuate the intent of the parties and too give proper meaning to the contract's technical terms.

Thus, in *Affiliated FM Ins. Co v Constitution Reins, Corp.*,[55] the Massachusetts Supreme Court reversed the trial court's finding that the parties' reinsurance contract was unambiguous and remanded for consideration of evidence of industry custom and practice.[56]

2.2.2 Interpretation and Construction

With respect to the interpretation and construction of reinsurance contracts, there is no reason for reinsurance contracts not to be interpreted and construed according to the rules for contracts generally.[57]

Reinsurance will usually be intended to be congruent, or nearly so, with the underlying policy. However, the wording of the reinsurance slip can be independently interpreted to terminate the period before the intended time and deny cover for serious losses.[58]

Reinsurance placed under treaty will absolutely follow the underlying policies, unless the treaty contains an exclusion that applies to the particular risk.[59] However independently the reinsurance may be viewed when its plain terms are different from those of the underlying policy, the later can greatly affect the interpretation and validity of reinsurance terms.

In *Forsokringsakteselskapet Vesta v Butcher*[60] where the proper law of the insurance contract was Norwegian law and that of the reinsurance was English law, it was vital to decide which law applied as the breaches of certain warranties, which arose, would render the insurance void under English law and not under Norwegian law. It was held, that a reinsurance contract, "back to back" with the original insurance and incorporating the same wording means that the wording in the reinsurance contract, must be governed by the same law as the original.[61]

---

[54] *Affiliated FM Ins. Co v Constitution Reins, Corp.*, 416 Mass. 839, 846, 626 N.E.2d 878, 882 (1994); Ostrager and Vyskocil (1996), p. 5-7.

[55] *Affiliated FM Ins. Co v Constitution Reins, Corp.*, 416 Mass. 839, 846, 626 N.E.2d 878, 882 (1994).

[56] *Travelers Ins. Co. v Central Natl Ins. Co.*, 733 F. Supp. 522, 528 (D.Conn. 1990); Ostrager and Vyskocil (1996), p. 5-9.

[57] Staring (1993), § 13:1.

[58] *Youell v Bland Welch & Co* (1990) 2 Lloyd's Rep. 423 QB; Staring (1993), § 13:3.

[59] *Glasgow Assurance Corp. v William Symondson & Co* 16 Com Cas 109, 110–111.

[60] *Forsokringsakteselskapet Vesta v Butcher* (1989)1 Lloyd's Rep 331.

[61] Staring (1993), § 13:3.

It is evident that the purported incorporation of all the terms of the original insurance policy in the reinsurance contract may not accord with the alleged "true" intention of the parties, if, i.e. they had clarified what their true intention was at the time the contract was made.

Thus, as observed by Lord Griffith in *Forsokringsakteselskapet Vesta v Butcher*,[62] "subject to the same terms and conditions" may make neither legal nor commercial sense, and this expression should not be taken literally. The approach of the courts to incompatible or inconsistent clauses in reinsurance contracts has been to make pragmatic sense of the muddle, by giving effect to what the courts regard as the commercial purpose of reinsurance.

Where the reinsurance contract is merely an endorsed version of the original insurance policy, the situation is equally problematic.

In *Home Insurance Co. of New York v Victoria-Montreal Fire Insurance Co.*,[63] where the contracts of insurance and reinsurance were identical and in format and a standard printed form of insurance policy, then in use in the USA, was amended by inserting "re-" before the word "insure" in the policy and attaching a typewritten slip so that the retrocession contract would appear to consist of the terms of the original policy of direct fire insurance, which appeared to have little relevance to reinsurance, it was held that according to the true construction of the instrument under dispute, so carelessly put together and so awkwardly patched, it was not to be regarded as applying to the reinsurance contract.

In *Municipal Mutual Insurance Ltd v Sea Insurance Co Ltd*[64] where excess of loss reinsurance slips provided "conditions as underlying", it was clear to the court that the phrase "conditions as underlying" had not necessarily meant that one must write into the terms of the reinsurance all the underlying terms adapting them to the reinsurance.

In *Australia Widows Fund Life Assurance Society Ltd v National Mutual Life Association of Australia Ltd*,[65] the Privy Council assumed that a statement contained in the proposal for a reinsurance contract that was on the same terms and conditions as the original policy, was effective to incorporate the clause on the proposal for reinsurance into the contract for reinsurance and, thus, to incorporate the terms of the original policy into the reinsurance contract.

In *Pine Top Insurance Co. Ltd v Unione Italiana Anglo Saxon Reinsurance Co. Ltd*,[66] where the slip provided, *inter alia*, "all terms, clause and conditions as original", where most of the terms, clause and conditions were inappropriate for a

---

[62] *Forsokringsakteselskapet Vesta v Butcher* (1989)1 Lloyd's Rep 331, at 337.

[63] *Home Insurance Co. of New York v Victoria-Montreal Fire Insurance Co.* [1907] AC 59.

[64] *Municipal Mutual Insurance Ltd v Sea Insurance Co Ltd* [1996] LRLR 265.

[65] *Australia Widows Fund Life Assurance Society Ltd v National Mutual Life Association of Australia Ltd* [1914] AC 634.

[66] *Australia Widows Fund Life Assurance Society Ltd v National Mutual Life Association of Australia Ltd* [1987]1 Lloyd's Rep. 476.

reinsurance contract, and where the original policies contained arbitration clauses and the reinsurance contract had its own arbitration clause, it was held that "as original" in the retrocession slip was a reference to those provisions in the original policies, which were intended by the parties to the retrocession to be identical to the risk assumed by the primary insurer. Thus, it was held that the arbitration clause was not incorporated in the retrocession contract, as there were none express wording of incorporation, which would have been required, to make the arbitration clause in the reinsurance contract a term of the retrocession contract.[67]

2.2.2.1 Presumptions in the Interpretation

The reinsurance relation often begins with the slip, which is the document containing the very basic terms of the agreement. The slip may be of high significance to interpret and define the parameters of the reinsurance relationship. If the slip is itself the reinsurance contract, then, the terms as identified on the slip will control the relationship between reinsurer and reinsured. If the terms of the final contract are clear, those terms will be enforced and any inconsistencies with the terms of the slip will usually have no impact. If the final contract contains terms that are ambiguous, the terms as identified on the slip can serve as a useful tool of interpretation and the tribunal might look back into the bargaining history, including the slip, in determining the intent of the parties to effect a proper interpretation of the reinsurance contract.[68]

2.2.2.2 The Function "As Original"

In the late nineteenth and twentieth centuries an underwriter who insured risks in which he was not an expert would refer to other policies that had already been taken out on the same subject matter and against the same risk and containing clauses worded as "warranted to be on the same rate, as original, terms and identical interest of ... Insurance Company". These clauses were interpreted by the courts as conditions precedent to the liability of the underwriters that the terms of the later insurance contract were identical to the earlier policy referred to.[69]

It is now settled that the incorporation wording does not encompass all of the provisions of the original insurance contracts: the phrase "all terms and conditions as original" is not to be read as comprising "all" terms of the original policy.[70]

---

[67] O'Niell and Woloniecki (1998), pp. 4–08.

[68] Thomas and Lyons (2012), p. 72-20.

[69] *Barnards* v *Faber* [1893] 1 QB 340; *Bancroft* v *Heath* (1901) 17 TLR 425; *Walker & Sons* v *Uzielli* (1896) Com Cas 452; *The Sulphite Pulp Co Ltd* v *Faber* (1895–1896) 1 Com Cas 146; *Beauchamp* v *Faber* (1898) 3 Com Cas 308; Gurses (2010), p. 51.

[70] *Pine Top Insurance Co Ltd v Unione Italiana Anglo Saxon Reinsurance Co Ltd* [1987] 1 Lloyd's Rep 476; *Municipal Mutual Insurance Ltd v Sea Insurance Co Ltd* [1996] CLC 1515, 1527; Gurses (2010), p. 51.

As a general rule, terms that are merely collateral will not be considered incorporated into the reinsurance contract. For example, a forum selection clause might be seen as a collateral term that should not be incorporated even if "as original" is included in the reinsurance contract.[71]

The terms germane to reinsurance, are confined to those provisions defining the period, the geographical limits and the nature of the risk undertaken by the reinsurer.[72]

Further, the incorporation clause is not to be interpreted as encompassing clauses which are inconsistent with the reinsurance agreement.[73] Even if a clause complies with other requirements, incorporation is not allowed to the extent that it contradicts the express provisions of the reinsurance.[74] It is also permissible to incorporate a term which refers to e.g. the "insurer" by manipulating it to read "reinsurer."[75]

2.2.2.3 Interpretation of the Original Policy Is Binding on the Reinsurer

In *North River Ins Co v CIGNA Reinsurance Co*,[76] the reinsurers were held to be liable for the defence costs that the assured had incurred and the reinsured had paid after an arbitration award which held the reinsured liable in this respect both under the Wellington Agreement and also under the interpretation of the original insurance independently of the Wellington Agreement.

It is noteworthy that the absence of an express exclusion of defence costs in the reinsurance contract, was one of the grounds for the holding that the reinsurers were liable for such costs.[77]

In this case, the arbitrator examined, *inter alia*, the original policy language; the policy wording did not expressly exclude payment of defence costs and the policy provided for payment of costs upon consent of the insurer, and, hence, held that North River was responsible for the incurred defence costs, because it had not met its burden of showing that those costs were excluded from the policy coverage.

---

[71] Thomas and Lyons (2012), p. 72-25.

[72] *Pine Top Insurance Co Ltd v Unione Italiana Anglo Saxon Reinsurance Co Ltd* [1987] 1 Lloyd's Rep 476; Gurses (2010), p. 51.

[73] *Municipal Mutual Insurance Ltd v Sea Insurance Co Ltd* [1996] CLC 1515; *Home Insurance Company of New York v Victoria—Montreal Fire Insurance Company* [1907] AC 59; Gurses (2010), p. 51.

[74] *Australian Widows' Fund Life Assurance Society, Ltd v National Mutual Life Association of Australasia* [1914] AC 634; Gurses (2010), p. 51.

[75] *CNA International Reinsurance Co Ltd* v *Companhia de Seguros Tranquilidade SA* [1999] Lloyd's Rep IR 289; Gurses (2010), p. 56.

[76] *North River Ins Co* v *CIGNA Reinsurance Co* 52 F.3d 1194 (3rd Cir. (NJ) Apr 13, 1995).

[77] Gurses (2010), p. 165.

North River initially appealed the arbitrator's ruling, but later dropped the appeal. CIGNA Re indemnified North River for liability under the policies but denied coverage for defence costs. The district court granted summary judgment to CIGNA. On appeal, the Third Circuit found the reinsurers liable for the defence costs, according to the original policy interpretation and the follow the fortunes doctrine. As to the function of the follow the fortunes clause, the Third Circuit noted that the follow the fortunes doctrine creates an exception to the general rule that contract interpretation is subject to *de novo* review.[78]

2.2.2.4 Commencement and Termination

Most contracts are specific about the contract period. The parties are free to fix by contract the time of commencement of risk and may also fix it before the date of the reinsurance contract and at the date of an underlying policy, subject to the principle of law that the loss must either not have occurred or be unknown to have occurred.[79] The expiration date of a facultative contract is the end of the reinsurer's risk. The expiration date of a reinsurance treaty is the end of the period when new cessions may be made, but not the reinsurer's risk on old cessions. Even though the time of the termination is stated in the contract, problems may arise from the wording or the circumstances.[80] Extended expiration clause may also be used, though they may raise questions regarding the terms and circumstances of the extension.[81] Cancellation of a reinsurance contract may also occur. In the case of treaty reinsurances, a special question will arise as to what and how much can be cancelled.

In *Manhattan Life Ins. Co v Prussian Life Ins. Co*[82] where the question that arose was whether the matters involved, and thus also cancellation, was severable, the court held that where a contract contains a plurality of promises, if the promises are agreed as a single whole, the contract is indivisible and a material breach goes to the whole contract and the attempt at selective cancellation of parts is therefore destructive of the whole contract.[83] Abandonment or termination by breach may also occur.

In *Fenton Insurance Co. Ltd v Gothaer Versicherungsbank VVaG*,[84] where the defendants reinsurers alleged that the plaintiff reinsured had never paid any

[78] Gurses (2010), p. 168.

[79] Staring (1993), § 14:1.

[80] *Milwaukee Mechanics' Ins. Co. v Palatine Ins. Co* (1900) 128 Cal 71, 75, 60 P 518; Staring (1993), § 14:2.

[81] *Globe & Rutgers Fire Ins. Co v Liberty Bell Ins. Co* (1936)16 Cal App 2d 76, 60 P2d 200; Staring (1993), § 14:2.

[82] *Manhattan Life Ins. Co v Prussian Life Ins. Co* (1924, CA2 NY) 296 F 39; Staring (1993), § 14:2.

[83] Staring (1993), § 14:3.

[84] *Fenton Insurance Co. Ltd v Gothaer Versicherungsbank VVaG* [1997]1 Lloyd's Rep. 172.

premium for the 3 years of the duration of a reinsurance treaty, it was held that the contract could have been accepted as having been terminated or abandoned by breach, when such a repudiatory breach was a thing writ in paper and accepted by the reinsurers as bringing the contract to an end.

In *Figre Ltd v Mander*[85] the reinsurance contract was also not held to have been repudiated as the non-payment of premium was due to an administrative error. However, in *Pacific & General Insurance Co. Ltd. v Hazell*[86] where the insurer expressly stated that he would pay no premium, this was held to be repudiatory as to the reinsurance contract.[87]

2.2.2.5 "Follow The Settlements"–"Follow The Fortunes"–"Follow The Forms"

"Follow The Settlements" is an expression used in reinsurance, denoting a contractual obligation that the reinsurer accept the settlements of the reinsured, or judgments against it, and pay accordingly.

Considered, *obiter*, by Branson J. in *Excess Insurance Co v Mathews*[88] the words "Follow The Settlements" were held to be obliging a reinsurer to pay when there had been a compromise of liability by the insurer or the reinsured, and were also held to be an advantage as to the way the law stood previously.

"Follow The Fortunes" is an expression used in reinsurance, denoting a fundamental legal relationship and sometimes, its implications. The distinctive feature of the relationship is that the reinsurer has placed its pen, as it were, in the hands of its cedents and its fortunes, to that extent, in their control. A "Follow The Fortunes" clause establishes the absolute congruence of the reinsurance with the underlying policies in period and risks.[89]

"Follow The Forms" is an expression used in reinsurance, carrying into the reinsurance contract all the relevant provisions of the underlying contract as a means of ensuring congruence. It is common in facultative reinsurances and unsuitable for treaty reinsurances because of the variety of underlying terms that it would purportedly incorporate in the reinsurance contract.[90]

---

[85] *Figre Ltd v Mander* Unreported, Jan. 27, 1998.

[86] *Pacific & General Insurance Co. Ltd. v Hazell* [1997] LRLR 65.

[87] O'Niell and Woloniecki (1998), § 3–25.

[88] *Excess Insurance Co v Mathews* (1925) 23 Ll.L.R. 71.

[89] In *River Thames Insurance Co Ltd v Al Ahleia Insurance Co. Ltd* [1973] 1 Lloyd's Rep. 2, Lord Denning M.R. described the contract as a "follow the fortunes" treaty; O'Niell and Woloniecki (1998), § 5–09.

[90] Staring (1993), § 18:1.

2.2.2.5.1 Construction of the "Follow the Settlements" Clause

It appears to be the case that between the 1920s and 1984 almost all reinsurance disputes were referred to arbitration. It was as late as 1985 that the follow the settlements clause first came to be analysed by the courts in *Insurance Co of Africa v SCOR (UK) Reinsurance Co Ltd.*[91] The comments of the Court of Appeal in construing the follow the settlements clause have been taken as definitive ever since. The court was of the view that the clause in *Insurance Co of Africa v SCOR (UK) Reinsurance Co Ltd*[92] was not to be construed in the same way as the "pay as may be paid" clause because of the absence of any reference to that clause. The Court of Appeal was of the view that where the reinsurer agreed to follow the settlement, it was not appropriate to impose any higher duty on the reinsured.[93]

2.2.2.5.2 The USA Approach

As a general principle, reinsurers are not obliged to make any payments to reinsured where the reinsured had no liability to the assured under the original policy, that is, where the reinsured has made a payment that was not legally bound to make. Thus, the English cases have established that the reinsured has to prove the loss in the same way as the assured has to do.

However, the parties may specify in the reinsurance contract that a settlement or other adjustment of loss between the assured and the reinsured is to be binding on the reinsurers. By so doing the reinsurer's obligation to indemnify the reinsured becomes dependent on the reinsurance policy terms, and not on the question of whether the insured suffered a loss as a matter of law under the original policy. It is seen that the same principles[94] apply in the United States.

In *Hastie* v *De Peyster*[95] and in *New York State Marine Ins Co* v *Protection Ins Co*[96] the courts pointed out the inconvenience caused by the rule regarding the reinsured has to prove the loss in the same way as the assured is required to do.[97] Today such clauses have two forms in the United States: "follow the settlements" or "follow the fortunes."

There appears however to be no standard form of settlement clauses in the US and, clauses are drafted individually in every case. The common feature of the settlements clauses is that they contain the expression "All claims involving this

[91] *Insurance Co of Africa* v *SCOR (UK) Reinsurance Co Ltd*, [1985] 1 Lloyd's Rep 312.

[92] *Insurance Co of Africa* v *SCOR (UK) Reinsurance Co Ltd*, [1985] 1 Lloyd's Rep 312.

[93] Gurses (2010), p. 113.

[94] *Michigan TP Participating Plan* v *Federal Ins Co*, 233 Mich App 422, (Mich. App. Jan 19, 1999).

[95] *Hastie* v *De Peyster* 3 Cai R. 190, NY Sup. 1805.

[96] *New York State Marine Ins Co* v *Protection Ins Co* 18 F. Cas 160 (CC Mass 1841).

[97] Gurses (2010), p. 132.

reinsurance, when settled by the company, shall be binding on the reinsurer . . . ." Provisions that contain such an expression is sometimes referred to as a follow the settlements clause, and sometimes as a follow the fortunes clause.

In England, a follow the fortunes clause came before the High Court in *Hayter* v *Nelson & Home Insurance Co.*[98] A follow the fortunes clause also came before Creswell J in *CGU International Insurance* v *AstraZeneca Insurance Co.*,[99] however, given that there was no decision what the wording meant and whether the parties had been right in their concession, the judge treated the policy as if there was no follow the settlements clause.[100]

2.2.2.5.2.1 "Back-to-Back" Cover

Under a facultative reinsurance contract, since the reinsurer takes a proportion or all of the risk that the direct insurer has insured, it is to be presumed that in the absence of clear words to the contrary the risks covered by the two contracts are consistent.[101]

This naturally leads to the result that if the reinsurance and original insurance contain identical terms, for instance where the reinsurance slip contains the clause of "as original" and there are no exclusion clauses which differ from the insurance contract, where the reinsured's liability is established under the original insurance, it follows naturally that reinsurer's liability is also established in that the construction of the terms of the original insurance is binding on the reinsurance.[102] The presumption may be inapposite, if the risk as presented to reinsurers differs materially from the risk as assumed by the reinsured.[103] Cover is not presumed to be back-to-back in non-proportional reinsurance contracts.[104] This may, nevertheless, be problematic where the original insurance and the reinsurance contracts are governed by different applicable laws. This is not uncommon in reinsurance contracts, where local insurers from various countries outside England take out

---

[98] *Hayter* v *Nelson & Home Insurance Co.* [1990] 2 Lloyd's Rep 265.

[99] *CGU International Insurance* v *AstraZeneca Insurance Co.*, [2006] Lloyd's Rep IR 409. Gurses (2010). Reinsuring Clauses, London. Lloyd's List, 134.

[100] Gurses (2010), p. 135.

[101] *American International Marine Agency of New York Inc* v *Dandridge* [2005] Lloyd's Rep IR 643; *Toomey* v *Banco Vitalicio De Espana SA de Seguros* [2004] Lloyd's Rep IR 354; *HIH Casualty and General Insurance Ltd* v *New Hampshire Insurance Co* [2001] 2 Lloyd's Rep 161; *Mann* v *Lexington Insurance Co* [2001] Lloyd's Rep IR 179; *Reliance Marine Insurance* v *Duder* [1913] 1 KB 265; *Citadel Insurance Co* v *Atlantic Union Insurance Co SA* [1982] 2 Lloyd's Rep 543.

[102] Gurses (2010), p. 33.

[103] *Gan Insurance* v *Tai Ping Insurance (No 1)* [1999] Lloyd's Rep IR 472.

[104] *AXA Reinsurance (U.K.) Plc. v Field* [1996] 2 Lloyd's Rep 233; *American Centennial Insurance Company v Insco Limited* [1996] LRLR 407; *Municipal Mutual Ins Ltd v Sea Ins Co Ltd* [1996] CLC 1515; *Goshawk Syndicate Management Ltd v XL Speciality Insurance Co* [2004] Lloyd's Rep IR 683.

reinsurance policies in the London Market, the policies of which usually are expressly governed by English law, whereas the relevant local law will be applicable to the original insurance contracts. Under English law, the construction of the wording of a contract is a matter for its applicable law. Difficulties arise where the two laws provide different meanings for the same words.[105]

2.2.2.5.2.2 Forms of Reinsurance Contracts

The clause whereby reinsurers agree to be bound by the same terms and conditions of the original insurance and to follow the settlements of their reinsureds is mostly used in proportional facultative reinsurance contracts. However, besides proportional facultative reinsurance, other types of reinsurance are available. Reinsurance contracts are classified based on the method by which the reinsured and reinsurer share the risk and the premium.[106]

This has led to their categorisation as proportional and non-proportional. Proportional reinsurance contracts may be either facultative or treaty, but non-proportional contracts are mainly written in the form of a treaty.

In proportional reinsurance the reinsurer and the reinsured share the risk and the premium on a proportional basis. The proportion that the reinsurer takes over depends on the agreement between the parties; it could be any figure between 1 and 100 %. It means that the reinsured transfers the premium according to the percentage of the risk that the reinsurer has agreed to take over. The reinsured, however, will generally be permitted a ceding commission consisting of an agreed proportion of the premium payable to the reinsurer. If a loss occurs, the reinsured pays for the loss and claims the amount from the reinsurer according to the reinsurer's proportion of the risk.

Proportional reinsurance operates on a horizontal basis, with the parties sharing the risk. Non-proportional reinsurance, by contrast, is vertical. The reinsured agrees to bear a part of the loss itself, and cedes the excess to the reinsurers. In other words the reinsurer's liability is triggered when the reinsured's liability has reached an agreed excess limit.

Facultative reinsurance contracts can be placed proportionally or, less commonly, non-proportionally. Under a proportional facultative reinsurance contract a single risk is reinsured on a proportional basis, so that the reinsured insures the risk and transfers it to the reinsurer according to the agreed proportions that the latter has agreed to reinsure. If the reinsurer[107] agrees to reinsure 100 % of the risk insured this type of contract is called "fronting." Parties sometimes enter into "fronting" agreements because local regulations only allow local insurers to insure the local risks and insurers may need reinsurance support to cover large risks.

[105] Gurses (2010), p. 34.

[106] *GE Reinsurance Corp (formerly Kemper Reinsurance Co) v New Hampshire Insurance Co* [2004] Lloyd's Rep IR 404.

[107] Gurses (2010), p. 2.

Fronting may also be necessary where the assured is not satisfied with the nominated insurer.

Facultative reinsurance contracts are generally in proportional form, so that the reinsured and the reinsurers share any loss in their agreed proportions. This structure makes it clear that the reinsurers and insurers are presumed to provide identical cover because they share the risk and the premium; in other words, it is normally expected that where the reinsured is liable, the reinsurer is liable. This is naturally subject to any specific exclusions of liability which the reinsurers have insisted upon and, as decided cases have shown, it may be affected by the application of different laws to the two contracts. In order to reflect the identical cover between the original insurance and reinsurance policy, the reinsurance slip (usually no formal policy wording is issued) contains the words "subject to the same terms and conditions as original" or only "as original" or "the full reinsurance clause."[108] The reinsurance policy wording in proportional facultative reinsurance contracts creates various controversial issues.[109]

A treaty is defined as a mechanism under which risks falling within its scope may be transferred to the reinsurer. A treaty is a method for reinsuring a large number of risks either by class or by way of whole account.

Proportional treaties are either surplus or quota share, where the reinsured transfers to the reinsurer an agreed proportion of all risks accepted. The most common type of non-proportional treaty is excess of loss reinsurance.[110] Proportional treaties are either quota share or surplus. In quota share reinsurance, the reinsurer agrees to automatically reinsure a fixed percentage of each risk subject to a maximum monetary amount per risk. Premium is shared pro rata but the reinsured is usually entitled to deduct ceding commission from the premium to be paid to the reinsurers for his efforts in issuing the original policy.

In surplus treaties, where the reinsured underwrites more than it is willing to bear from its own account, the surplus can be transferred to the reinsurer. The amount that the reinsured retains is called its "line" and the maximum value of the treaty will be expressed in terms of the number or lines that the reinsured finds satisfactory for his reinsurance requirements.

Excess of loss and stop loss treaties are non-proportional. The former are the most common. Stop loss reinsurance covers aggregate loss in respect of specified

[108] The full reinsurance clause is worded as follows: "Being a reinsurance of and warranted same gross rate, terms and conditions as and to follow the settlements of the company and that said company retains during the currency of this policy at least . . . on the identical subject matter and risk and in identically the same proportion on each separate part thereof, but in the event of the retained line being less than as above, underwriters' lines to be proportionately reduced."; Gurses (2010), p. 3.

[109] For example what is the purpose of inserting "as original" as a policy wording? Does the phrase "as original" incorporate the direct policy terms into reinsurance or does it simply confirm that original insurance and reinsurance are back-to-back and provide identical cover?; Gurses (2010), p. 3.

[110] Gurses (2010), p. 3.

class or classes of insurance. The stop loss reinsurers' liability is triggered where the reinsured's liability exceeds the premium income. Thus, it becomes clear that stop loss is a framework used to protect reinsureds' solvency rather than to expand reinsureds' capacity to insure. It is debatable if the most important other form of non-proportional treaty, stop loss reinsurance, should be regarded as reinsurance at all.

In *Toomey* v *Eagle Star Insurance Co Ltd (No 1)*[111] Hobhouse L.J. held that stop loss policies are not reinsurance and in *Wasa International Insurance Co Ltd* v *Lexington Insurance Co*[112] Lord Mance *obiter* confirmed this view. According to the judges in these cases a stop loss or similar policy taken out by an insurer is not reinsurance and operates as a whole account protection on a different basis. However, it should be remembered that the Financial Services and Markets Act 2000 treats stop loss policies as reinsurance for regulatory purposes.

A further classification of treaties is obligatory, non-obligatory and facultative obligatory. In obligatory treaties there is an obligation on both sides as regarded the ceding of risks: the reinsured is obliged to transfer all risks of a given description and the reinsurer is obliged to accept them. A non-obligatory treaty provides a framework under which individual risks accepted by the reinsured may be declared to the reinsurer and the reinsurer may choose to accept them on an individual basis. An intermediate possibility is the facultative obligatory treaty, under which the reinsured may choose whether or not transfer the risk but if he does so the reinsurer is obliged to accept it.[113]

2.2.2.5.2.3 Forms of Reinsurance in the United States

2.2.2.5.2.3.1 General In the USA most reinsurance disputes are resolved by arbitration[114] and there is typically no publicly available written decision explaining the reasons for the decision of the arbitrator panel.

There are relatively few judicial decisions involving reinsurance, and state courts, in the absence of a controlling authority by the state's higher court, often rely on decisions from other state's courts. Only a handful of those the state court decisions on reinsurance issues are decided by the highest state court. Unless the decisions are by the highest state or appellate courts, the court opinions on particular issues are not authoritative or binding, they are merely "persuasive authority" for other courts to consider on the strength of the reasoning.

Thus, there is little concerning reinsurance law that is firmly settled in the US by court decision, however, not all of the principles stated can be considered settled law.

---

[111] *Toomey* v *Eagle Star Insurance Co Ltd (No 1)* [1994] 1 Lloyd's Rep 516.

[112] *Wasa International Insurance Co Ltd v Lexington Insurance Co* [2009] 2 Lloyd's Rep 508, 518.

[113] Gurses (2010), p. 4.

[114] *Employer Reinsurance Corp* v *Laurier Indem Co* 2007 WL 1831775 (MD Fla); *Ott* v *AllStar Ins Corp* 99 Wis.2d 635, (Wis. Jan 06, 1981).

2.2.2.5.2.3.2 Types of Reinsurance A similar classification of reinsurance is seen in the USA reinsurance market, in that reinsurance is classified either as "pro rata" and "excess"—in other words, proportional and non-proportional or facultative and treaties. The contracts are the same as in English practice, just differently defined.

In *Ott* v *All-Star Ins Corp.*,[115] the Supreme Court of Wisconsin clarified that in pro rata types of reinsurance, the reinsurer and the reinsured share the risk and the premium in an agreed fixed proportion; in the excess reinsurance, however, the reinsurer becomes liable on a loss only when the loss exceeds an agreed policy amount.

Generally, the premiums for excess of loss reinsurance are lower than those for quota share reinsurance as the risks are not shared proportionately by the reinsured and reinsurer.[116] This amount, for which the insurer alone is responsible, is known as the insurer's "retention."

In *North River Ins Co* v *CIGNA Reinsurance Co*,[117] the United States Court of Appeals for the Third Circuit also touched upon the classification of reinsurance contracts. The Third Circuit defined facultative reinsurance as policy specific, all or a portion of a reinsured's risk under a specific contract of direct coverage will be indemnified by the reinsurer in the event of loss.[118]

Under "treaties" reinsurers agree to accept an entire block of business from the reinsured. An insurer who seeks to reduce potential financial losses from policies issued to a class of customers or an industry may purchase treaty reinsurance. As treaties cover an "entire block of business", they evaluate the overall risk pool, but not the individual risk being reinsured. This will include accepting all of the policies under the block of business, including those as yet unwritten. These last two statements are the key factors of treaties that differs them from facultative reinsurance which entails the ceding of a particular risk or policy.[119]

In facultative reinsurance, where the reinsurer and the reinsured share the risk and the premium, the reinsurer assesses the unique characteristics of each policy to determine whether to reinsure the risk and the amount of premium. Primary and excess insurers, unlike reinsurers, provide coverage directly to the assured. Primary and excess insurance policies both describe the kinds of liability that will be covered and specify dollar limits. Excess insurers generally replicate the coverage offered by the primary insurer; however, the excess insurer's liability is not triggered until the primary insurer's limit is exhausted.

---

[115] *Ott* v *All-Star Ins Corp* 99 Wis.2d 635, (Wis. Jan 06, 1981).

[116] *Travelers Cas and Sur Co* v *Certain Underwriters at Lloyd's of London* 96 NY.2d 583, (NY Oct 16, 2001).

[117] *North River Ins Co* v *CIGNA Reinsurance Co* 52 F.3d 1194 (3rd Cir. (NJ) April 13, 1995).

[118] *Travelers Cas and Sur Co* v *Certain Underwriters at Lloyd's of London* 96 NY.2d 583, (NY Oct 16, 2001).

[119] *Christiania General Ins Corp of New York v Great American Ins Co* 979 F.2d 268, CA 2 (NY), 1992; *Unigard Sec Ins Co, Inc v North River Ins Co* 79 NY.2d 576, (NY, May 05, 1992); *Progressive Cas Ins Co v CA Reaseguradora Nacional De Venezuela* 991 F.2d 42 (2nd Cir. (NY) April 06, 1993). Gurses (2010), p. 6.

Reinsurance, however, is a business between insurance companies in which an insurer, who has provided coverage to its assured, transfers all or part of that risk to other insurance companies (reinsurers) along with a portion of the premiums.

In *North River Ins Co* v *CIGNA Reinsurance Co*[120] the Third Circuit illustrated the relationship between excess insurers and reinsurers with an example of an excess insurer which issued a $100 million policy and retained a certain portion of the risk (e.g. the first $10 million of excess liability) and reinsure the balance with other insurance companies: reinsurance here is non-proportional excess of loss reinsurance. The excess insurer will pay the entire excess claim unless a claim exceeds the $10 million retained liability. If a claim exceeds $10 million, that portion of the claim exceeding $10 million will fall on the reinsurer who has accepted the next layer of liability up to the reinsurance policy limit.

2.2.2.6 Wording of Reinsurance Contracts

In both treaties and proportional facultative reinsurance, reinsuring clauses delimit the circumstances in which the reinsurer's liability will arise. In proportional facultative reinsurance the wording is not drafted in detailed terms; it is more usual in treaties for reinsuring clauses to be drafted in a more detailed fashion. The reason is that in proportional facultative reinsurance the purpose is to achieve a sharing of a single risk and the premium by providing closely matching or identical cover, so that there is no particular need to repeat what appears in the direct policy. However, treaties have the additional functions of expanding underwriting capacity and protecting the reinsured from insolvency.[121]

A treaty covers a series of underlying risks, and sometimes the reinsured's whole account is reinsured and the reinsurer undertakes to provide an indemnity for the excess losses above an agreed figure during the policy period. In facultative proportional reinsurance, when the assured suffers loss then, subject to any exceptions in the reinsurance contract, where the reinsured is liable, the reinsurer will be liable for the agreed proportion of the direct risk reinsured.

However, in treaties, the respective losses faced by reinsured and the reinsurer will deal with other matters, for instance, whether the reinsurer has agreed to cover losses which occurred within the policy period, or which were the subject of claims during the currency of the reinsurance. Furthermore, in the case of excess of loss treaties, the reinsurer will be liable only for losses in excess of the amount retained by the reinsured, so that it is important to define aggregating terms such as "occurrence" and "event," in order to determine the amount and number of the reinsured's retentions arising from a series of claims. Reinsurance treaties usually contain inspection clauses which entitle the reinsurer to examine the reinsured's

---

[120] *North River Ins Co* v *CIGNA Reinsurance Co* 52 F.3d 1194 (3rd Cir. (NJ) April 13, 1995).

[121] Gurses (2010), p. 7.

books and records relating to the business written by the reinsured and within the scope of the reinsurance.[122]

In proportional facultative reinsurance a single risk is reinsured by the reinsurer on a proportional basis: the parties share the risk and the premium: if the risk occurs, the reinsured becomes liable to pay the loss but becomes entitled to claim the relevant proportion of the reinsurer's contribution. The insurance and reinsurance policies are often drafted to provide identical (back-to-back) or at least closely matching cover. As it is usually the case that the reinsured's liability to the policyholder will trigger the reinsurer's liability, in entering into the reinsurance contract, a cover page (reinsurance slip) is appended to the original policy and the cover page usually contains the clause "subject to the same terms and conditions as original and follow the settlements of the reinsured" a clause sometimes expressed to be "the full reinsurance clause"[123] and sometimes only "as original and follow the settlements." These phrases are the most important wordings expressing the scope of the reinsurance.

Reinsurance slip policies also state the amount of premium to be paid and the reinsurer will in many cases add exclusion or limitation clauses which are not found in the underlying cover. It is worth noting that as administrative practice in the London Market, the slip may refer to a choice of forms: J1 or NMA 1779. J1 contains the clause "being a reinsurance of and warranted same gross rate, terms and conditions as and to follow the settlements of the [reassured]." NMA 1779 does not have a follow settlements clause. However it contains an obligation: "to pay or to make good to the Reinsured all such Loss as aforesaid as may happen to the subject matter of this Reinsurance, or any part thereof during the continuance of this Policy." It should be noted that a standard Full Reinsurance Clause is not seen in US reinsuring policies. The reinsuring clauses used in the United States reinsurance market are varied from one policy to another.[124]

2.2.2.7 Arbitration in Reinsurance Contracts

2.2.2.7.1 General

Reinsurance contracts have long typically attained arbitration clauses, the simple reasons for this choice being the speed, simplicity and privacy of arbitration.[125] As far as governing law is concerned, the Arbitration Act 1996, the FAA 1925 and the New York provide for the enforcement of arbitration agreements. Arbitration of reinsurance disputes can occur under the auspices of all the above mentioned legal instruments.[126]

---

[122] Gurses (2010), pp. 7–8.

[123] *Insurance Co of Africa* v *Scor (UK) Reinsurance Co Ltd* [1985] 1 Lloyd's Rep 312.

[124] Gurses (2010), p. 9.

[125] Staring (1993), § 21:1.

[126] Staring (1993), § 21: 2.

Although often reinsurance arbitrations are held *ad hoc*, nevertheless many organisations (LCIA, ICC, ARIAS) provide rules for the conduct and administration of such arbitrations.

The arbitration clause or special agreement is all important in reinsurance arbitrations, as it is the sole source of authority for which the law provides mechanisms of enforcement in an attempt also to fill gaps left by the parties. The arbitration clause may be as comprehensive or narrow as the parties agree.[127]

With regards to arbitrability, the latter depends on the scope of the arbitration clause and on the terms or policy of the governing law, as to whether the issue may be arbitrated or must be reserved to the courts. Although not infinitely broad, the policy of the law is so expansive that most questions of arbitrability must arise in relation to the clause, rather than the law.

Often, the questions arise as to when and how much of a dispute will be referred to arbitration by the court, and what issues, if any, will be determined by the court, either preliminary or on review of an arbitration award.[128]

With regards to discovery, statutes, such as the FAA 1925, make no direct provision for discovery in the sense of that process under the Federal Rules of Civil Procedure. Thus, in general, discovery in that sense is generally understood not to be available in arbitration, unless the parties have specially provided for it.[129]

It is extremely common to find arbitration clauses in various types of contracts, providing that any disputes arising from those contracts should be resolved by arbitrators. Unless the award is appealed, it is conclusive between the parties to the dispute, so that the award establishes the reinsured's liability to the assured.

The difficulty here is that there is much authority for the proposition that an arbitration award is binding only on the parties to it and indeed that its contents are confidential.[130]

However, it has been accepted that where the original insurance contract contains an arbitration clause, it is implicit in reinsurance contracts that the reinsurer agrees to be bound by the arbitration award even if the award is not fully consistent with strict law, subject to the reinsured having argued its case properly in the arbitration and exhausted all rights of appeal.[131]

In *North River Ins Co* v *CIGNA Reinsurance Co*[132] the USA Court of Appeals, Third Circuit noted that it found no difference in terms of a binding effect of a judgment or an arbitration award on reinsurers' liability.

---

[127] Staring (1993), § 21:4.

[128] Staring (1993), § 21:5.

[129] Staring (1993), § 22:2.

[130] *Associated Electric & Gas Insurance Services Ltd v European Reinsurance Co of Zurich* [2003] 1 All ER (Comm) 253; *Lincoln National Life Insurance Co v Sun Life Assurance Co of Canada* [2005] 1 Lloyd's Rep 606.

Gurses (2010), p. 107.

[131] Gurses (2010), p. 107.

[132] *North River Ins Co* v *CIGNA Reinsurance Co* 52 F.3d 1194, (3rd Cir. (NJ) Apr. 13, 1995); Gurses (2010), p. 107.

With regards to interim awards issued in order to grant relief or protection intended to be carried out by the parties before a final award, which therefore presents questions of authority and of finality for its limited purpose, provisions for such awards exist in many rules, such as the UNCITRAL Rules. In reinsurance case, where there was concern as to whether the managers of a reinsurance pool might be able to collect their damages from a member after a final award, the arbitrators established an escrow account and ordered funds paid into it by the member as security. This interim award was confirmed by the state courts which upheld the power of the arbitrators to grant interim relief and the jurisdiction of the district court to enforce it.[133]

2.2.2.7.2 Incorporation of Arbitration Clauses

An arbitration clause governs dispute resolution and as such it takes effect as a self-contained contract collateral to the substantive agreement.[134] As a result, because of the ancillary and separable nature of an arbitration clause, unless it is clearly and expressly provided, general words of incorporation do not operate on it.[135]

2.2.2.7.3 Incorporation from Direct Insurance into Reinsurance Contracts

In *Pine Top Insurance Co* v *Unione Italiana Anglo Saxon Reinsurance Co*[136] Home and Overseas Insurance issued insurance policies in respect of holiday travel, section 3 of which covered "Medical and other Expenses." They then reinsured their excess of loss under section 3. "General Conditions" of the reinsurance slip provided: "All terms, clauses and conditions as original. To pay as paid thereon, but subject nevertheless to the terms, clauses and conditions of this reinsurance." The original insurance issued by Home and Overseas contained an arbitration clause for

[133] *Pacific Reinsurance Management Corp. v Ohio Reinsurance Corp.* 935 F2d 1019, 1022–1023, 91 CDOS 4344, 91 Daily Journal DAR 6565 (9th Cir. Cal. 1991); *Insco Limited v Meadows Indemnity Co.*, 1993 WL 328376, Docket no CV 90 2935 SVW, 4 Mealey's Reins Rep, No. 5, C (CD Cal. 1993); *Yasuda Fire & Marine Ins. Co. of Europe v Continental Casualty Co.*, 37 F3dd 345 (7th Cir. Ill. 1994); *Meadows Indemnity Co. v Arkwright Mutual Ins. Co.*, 1996 WL 557513, Docket No. 88-0600, 7 Mealey's Reins. Rep. No 11, F (ED Pa 1996); See Ch. 22, § 22:7, G S Staring, *Law of Reinsurance*, CBC, NY, 1993.

[134] Gurses (2010), p. 64; *Bremer Vulkan Schiffbau und Maschinenfabrik v South India Shipping Corporation Ltd* [1981] AC 909; *Heyman v Darwins* [1942] AC 356; *Black Clawson International Ltd v Papierwerke Waldhof-Aschaffenburg AG* [1981] 2 Lloyd's Rep 446; *Harbour Assurance Co (UK) Ltd v Kansa General International Insurance Co Ltd* [1993] QB 701.

[135] Gurses (2010), pp. 64–65.

[136] *Pine Top Insurance Co* v *Unione Italiana Anglo Saxon Reinsurance Co.* [1978]1 Lloyd's Rep. 476.

the resolution of disputes between the assured and the insurer. The reinsurance contract between Home and Overseas and the reinsurer also contained an express arbitration clause for the disputes between "the reinsured" and "the reinsurer." The reinsurer transferred the risk to the retrocessionaire, but the retrocession contract did not contain an express reference to the arbitration clause as it only contained the "as original" wording. The retrocessionaire declined to pay under the retrocession agreement and reinsurers sought to refer the dispute to arbitration, and the issue which arose was whether the reinsurer could do so by relying on the incorporation of the arbitration clause into the retrocession agreement.

Gatehouse J held that the word "all" in the general conditions did not mean "all." Terms, which defined the risk, namely the period, the geographical limits and in this case section 3 could be incorporated but not the arbitration clause. Having clarified that "as original" in the retrocession referred to the original contract but not the reinsurance agreement, Gatehouse J. stated that the purpose of the as original clause was that the parties to this retrocession agreement were anxious to make sure that identical risks were covered. According to the learned judge, the "as original" wording was a convenient catch-all phrase which the parties to the retrocession contract used without considering whether it was repetitive and, therefore, strictly unnecessary.

Applying the settled principles of the bills of lading cases Gatehouse J. clarified that in order to incorporate the arbitration clause there should be an express reference to it in the retrocession slip. The judge also noted the wording of the arbitration clause, in that it referred to the disputes between the assured and the reinsured, and the judge did not manipulate the words to the "reinsurer" and "retrocessionaire" because such manipulation would not be appropriate.[137]

The main purpose for rendering the reinsurance on the same terms as original was explained as being the provision of matching cover. For that reason, only the terms defining the period, geographical limit and the nature of the risk were held to be carried across, and an arbitration clause was held not to have been incorporated. The arbitration clause was classified as ancillary or collateral to the contract of reinsurance. This proposition is now well established.[138]

In *Pine Top Insurance Co* v *Unione Italiana Anglo Saxon Reinsurance Co*,[139] Incorporation of terms from the direct policy should be distinguished from incorporation of terms from other sources, such as standard market wordings. In the latter case problems may arise from inconsistency between the standard terms and the express terms of incorporating contract which the court will be required to resolve.

---

[137] Gurses (2010), pp. 65–66.

[138] *Excess Insurance Co Ltd & Anor v Mander* [1995] CLC 838; *American International Speciality Lines Insurance Co v Abbott Laboratories* [2003] 1 Lloyd's Rep 267; *Cigna Life Insurance Co of Europe SA-NV & Ors v Intercaser SA de Seguros y Reaseguros* [2001] CLC 1356; *OK Petroleum AB v Vitol Energy SA* [1995] 2 Lloyd's Rep 160; Gurses (2010), p. 67.

[139] *Pine Top Insurance Co* v *Unione Italiana Anglo Saxon Reinsurance Co.* [1978]1 Lloyd's Rep. 476.

In *Axa* v *Ace Global Markets*,[140] the reinsurance was on "Full wording as EXEL 1.1.90." Gloster J found it possible to reconcile the arbitration clause in standard EXEL wording with the English choice of law and jurisdiction clause in the reinsurance slip by holding that the latter related to supervision of the arbitration and challenges to any award and, accordingly held that the arbitration clause was incorporated with other standard clauses in EXEL 1.1.90.

In *Axa* v *Ace Global Markets*,[141] the reinsurer applied for a declaration under section 72(1)(a) of the Arbitration Act 1996 that a reinsurance contract does not, on its true construction, include an arbitration agreement. The reinsurance contract is contained in a reinsurance slip which provided: "Full wording as EXEL 1.1.90 with additional clauses, deletions, endorsements, special condition and warranties (at no additional premium) as follows: ... This Contract shall be subject to English Law and Jurisdiction. Clause 15 of EXEL 1.1.90 is an arbitration clause in the following terms: 15.1 The parties agree that prior recourse to courts of law any dispute between them concerning the provisions of this contract shall first be the subject of arbitration. The issue on this application was whether or not, as a matter of construction, the reinsurance slip incorporated the arbitration clause contained in clause 15 of EXEL 1.1.90 into the reinsurance contract, notwithstanding the express incorporation of the English choice of law and jurisdiction clause in the slip."[142] Gloster J. noted that the reference to EXEL 1.1.90 is a reference to the "Joint Excess Loss Committee excess loss clauses" dated 1 January 1990. EXEL 1.1.90 were in fact a set of standard trade or market terms and conditions. They were, in reality, standard reinsurance contract wordings in common use, the wording was widely available to reinsurance professionals, and could be found on various London Market databases.

Referring to *AIG Europe SA* v *QBE International Insurance Ltd*[143] and *Excess Insurance Co Ltd v Mander*,[144] Gloster J. held that the correct approach to be adopted when considering whether or not a jurisdiction clause is incorporated into a contract, is for the court to "construe the language of the contract in the context of its commercial background and ask itself whether a consensus on the subject matter of the jurisdiction clause is clearly and precisely demonstrated." The EXEL 1.1.90 wording was not attached to the slip but the judge found that given the fact that the wording was widely used as standard terms, the drafters of the slip had its provisions well in mind.

The fact that the jurisdiction clause was specifically agreed, whereas the arbitration[145] clause was incorporated only by reference, led to the conclusion that, if, indeed, there was an irreconcilable conflict between the two provisions, the

[140] *Axa* v *Ace Global Markets* [2006] Lloyd's Rep IR 683.

[141] *Axa* v *Ace Global Markets* [2006] Lloyd's Rep IR 683.

[142] Gurses (2010), p. 66.

[143] *AIG Europe SA* v *QBE International Insurance Ltd* [2001]2 Lloyd's Rep. 268.

[144] *Excess Insurance Co Ltd v Mander* [1997]1 Lloyd's Rep. 119.

[145] Gurses (2010), p. 66.

specifically agreed jurisdiction clause would prevail, as was common ground between the parties.

Gloster J., nevertheless, concluded that the two clauses could be read together in such a way as to avoid both conflict and surplusage, to the effect that the parties envisaged the possibility that the proceedings might take place in court but only after arbitration.

Therefore, according to the learned Judge, the parties did not treat arbitration and judicial proceedings as mutually exclusive, but provided arbitration as a step which was to take place before any action in court.

As to the reference to English jurisdiction, Gloster J. construed it as referring to the supervision of the arbitration, to the law governing the arbitration in relation to matters arising in the course of the arbitration, and as fixing the appropriate court for any appeal proceedings in respect of the award.

Pine Top Insurance Co v *Unione Italiana Anglo Saxon Reinsurance Co*[146] and *Excess Insurance Co Ltd v Mander*[147] pre-dated the Arbitration Act 1996. Section 6 (2) of the Act provides that "the reference in an agreement to a written form of arbitration clause or to a document containing an arbitration clause constitutes an arbitration agreement if the reference is such as to make that clause part of the agreement." The wording of the section seems to allow the incorporation of an arbitration clause from one document into another via general words of incorporation.

The Departmental Advisory Committee on Arbitration Law (DAC) report paragraph 42 left the issue to the courts to decide and in *Trygg Hansa Insurance Co Ltd* v *Equitas Ltd*,[148] Raymond Jack QC ruled that this was a field in which the law should be clear, certain and well understood; therefore the Arbitration Act s. 6 (2) did not change the settled view.[149]

2.2.2.7.3.1 Incorporation of Terms

In the USA, it is accepted[150] that a follow the form clause in a policy of reinsurance incorporates by reference all the terms and conditions of the reinsured policy, except to the extent that the reinsurance contract by its own terms specifically defines the scope of coverage differently.[151]

---

[146] *Pine Top Insurance Co* v *Unione Italiana Anglo Saxon Reinsurance Co.* [1978]1 Lloyd's Rep. 476.

[147] *Excess Insurance Co Ltd v Mander* [1997]1 Lloyd's Rep. 119.

[148] *Trygg Hansa Insurance Co Ltd v Equitas Ltd* [1998]2 loyd's Rep. 439, applied in Cigna Life Insurance Co of Europe SA-NV & Ors v Intercaser SA de Seguros y Reaseguros [2001] CLC 1356; Gurses (2010), p. 67.

[149] Gurses (2010), p. 67.

[150] Under New York state law.

[151] *Aetna Cas and Sur Co* v *Home Ins Co* 882 F. Supp. 1328, (SDNY, March 27, 1995); *Travelers Cas and Sur Co* v *Ace American Reinsurance Co* 392 F. Supp.2d 659, SDNY, Oct 12, 2005.; *aff'd* by the Second Circuit: 201 Fed. Appx. 40, (2nd Cir. (NY) Oct 18, 2006); Gurses (2010), p. 92.

Unlike English law, however, incorporation of terms has not caused controversy, nor has there been much dispute regarding the terms that can be incorporated. There are, however, a few cases in which the courts have questioned the incorporation of dispute resolution provisions.[152]

2.2.2.7.3.2 Incorporation of Arbitration Clauses

In *Progressive Cas Ins Co* v *CA Reaseguradora Nacional De Venezuela*[153] (RNV) incorporation of an arbitration clause from the reinsurance into the retrocession agreement was at issue.

In this case, a group of Venezuelan insurance companies issued insurance to a subsidiary of Petroleos de Venezuela, SA, an oil and gas exploration and development company owned by the Venezuelan government. The Venezuelan insurers reinsured $10 million of the risk with RNV. RNV in turn retroceded this risk through Sedgwick Marine & Cargo Ltd, a London-based broker who placed 90 % of the retroceded risk with London-based reinsurers and placed the remaining 10 % with New York Marine Managers, Inc (NYMM), the underwriting agent for a group of reinsurers in the US. The policy that NYMM signed was stated to be "Subject to Facultative Reinsurance Agreement" and the Facultative Reinsurance Agreement (FRA) in question contained an arbitration clause in the following terms: "Any question or dispute arising between the contracting parties concerning the interpretation of this Reinsurance Agreement, which cannot be otherwise arranged, shall be settled by arbitration in London, England."

Two claims were brought by RNV which were rejected by the group of reinsurers in the US. The group of reinsurers in the US brought a declaratory judgment action seeking a declaration that RNV's claims were not covered by the policy. RNV argued that this action should be stayed on the ground that the parties agreed to bring any dispute to an arbitration proceeding.

The question therefore was whether the arbitration clause in the FRA was incorporated into the reinsurance agreement signed by NYMM, the underwriting agent of the group of reinsurers in the US.[154]

The USA Court of Appeals for the Second Circuit accepted RNV's position. The court noted that under New York law, in the absence of fraud or other wrongful conduct, a party who signed a written contract was bound by its terms as he was conclusively presumed to know the contents of the document and thus assented to them.[155] The court also found no sign that RNV or its broker misrepresented or concealed the terms of the policy; the term referring to the FRA plainly appeared in

---

[152] Gurses (2010), p. 92.

[153] *Progressive Cas Ins Co v CA Reaseguradora Nacional De Venezuela* 991 F.2d. 42, (2nd Cir. (NY) Apr 6, 1993).

[154] Gurses (2010), p. 92.

[155] Referring to *Level Export Corp* v *Wolz, Aiken & Co* , 305 NY 82, 87, (NY Feb 26, 1953); Gurses (2010), p. 93.

the document signed by NYMM. As a result, the group of reinsurers were bound by the all-policy terms, including the term referring to the FRA and its arbitration provision. The District Court had ruled that a trial was necessary to determine whether the policy identified the FRA with sufficient specificity to incorporate it by reference into the policy.

The Second Circuit disagreed: the FRA was directly and specifically identified by name and that any reasonable person would understand that the capitalised letters in the phrase "Subject to Facultative Reinsurance Agreement" indicated that a specific document was being referenced.

Furthermore, according to the Second Circuit, if the underwriting agent of the group of reinsurers was unfamiliar with the FRA, it should either have asked the London brokers, or objected to the provision before signing the policy. NYMM did not do either of these and therefore NYMM, which was described by the Second Circuit as a very sophisticated party, was assumed as a matter of law to have understood and agreed to all aspects of the policy.

Moreover, the Second Circuit referred to the position it had adopted in disputes, over incorporation of charterparty terms into bills of lading: "a broadly-worded arbitration clause which is not restricted to the immediate parties may be effectively incorporated by reference into another agreement."

Specifically, in the charterparty cases the court had ruled that a clause in a charterparty which provided for arbitration of "any and all differences and disputes of whatsoever nature arising out of this Charter" was binding on parties to a bill of lading which incorporated the charterparty by reference.[156]

Similarly, the Second Circuit found the FRA's arbitration clause was worded broadly enough to allow its effective incorporation by reference into other contracts. Moreover, the FRA's clause used the phrase "the contracting parties" and thus did not restrictively refer to the immediate parties to that contract by name. The group of reinsurers pointed out that the FRA's arbitration clause referred to disputes "concerning the interpretation of this Reinsurance Agreement" which applied only to disputes concerning the FRA even where the clause had been incorporated into another agreement.

The Second Circuit however rejected this challenge on the basis that it was inconsistent with prior case law in which the court had applied arbitration clauses using similar language to disputes arising out of other agreements into which they have been incorporated by reference.

Furthermore, according to the Second Circuit, adopting the American Reinsurers' position would make almost impossible to incorporate any arbitration clause into a second agreement.[157]

---

[156] Citing *Compania Espanola de Petroleos, SA* v *Nereus Shipping, SA*, 527 F.2d 966, 973 (2d Cir. Dec 12, 1975), cert. denied, 426 US 936, 96 S Ct 2650, 49 L.Ed.2d 387 (1976); Gurses (2010), p. 93.

[157] Gurses (2010), p. 93.

2.2.2.7.3.3 Incorporation of Arbitration Clauses: Lead Underwriter Clause

In *Cigna Life Insurance Company of Europe SA NV & Ors v Intercaser SA de Seguros y Reaseguros*,[158] the court considered whether the terms of an underlying policy and the reinsurance wording were incorporated into the reinsurance policy. The conditions per the reinsurance slip specified only that the reinsurance was to follow the terms of the original policy, and condition 7 referred to the inclusion of "all other terms and conditions as more properly defined by the Intercaser Reinsurance Contract".

When a dispute arose, Intercaser wished to arbitrate on grounds that the Intercaser Reinsurance Contract contained an arbitration clause which was incorporated into the reinsurance. Cigna Life contended that an arbitration clause could not be incorporated into a separate reinsurance contract by broad words of incorporation and that the slip made no express reference to the Intercaser Reinsurance Contract.

It was held that: (a) the arbitration clause had not been incorporated into the reinsurance slip; (b) that arbitration clauses are personal to the parties involved, and (c) that when the slip was scratched, terms of the Intercaser Reinsurance Contract had not even been agreed, so the clause in that contract could not have been incorporated into the slip.

It was found that certain of the claimants were not bound to arbitrate on the basis that they had never accepted the wording and as mentioned, because the wording was not incorporated into the contract. In any event, they were not bound to arbitrate merely because the lead underwriter had signed. Similarly, in the case of *Unum Life Insurance Co of America v The Israel Phoenix Assurance Co Ltd*,[159] the court had to consider whether a valid arbitration agreement existed between the parties, and this turned on whether the leading underwriter had authority to enter into an arbitration agreement on behalf of the claimant.

The court found that the agreement of Liberty Mutual, the lead underwriter, to arbitrate did not mean that the following market was also obliged to arbitrate. In this case, Mr Justice Smith found that absent special circumstances, general words of incorporation did not incorporate an arbitration agreement and did not bind the lead underwriter's following market to arbitration. Both of the above cases, serve to illustrate the fact that under English law it remains the general position that no person should be deprived of the right to access the English courts unless he has clearly chosen to follow a different route.[160]

---

[158] *Cigna Life Insurance Company of Europe SA NV & Ors v Intercaser SA de Seguros y Reaseguros* [2001] CLC 1356.

[159] *Unum Life Insurance Co of America v The Israel Phoenix Assurance Co Ltd* [2001] unreported.

[160] Leedham and Linker (2002).

2.2.2.7.3.4 Incorporation of Jurisdiction Clauses

In the *Anonymous Greek Co of General Insurances* ("*The Ethniki*") *v AIG Europe* (*UK*) & *Ors*,[161] the Court of Appeal considered whether a Greek jurisdiction clause contained in an underlying policy was incorporated into the reinsurance contract.

The Greek insurance company (Ethniki) insured a proportion of its business to AIG. AIG refused to pay a claim submitted under the reinsurance and Ethniki issued proceedings in Greece against AIG. AIG also commenced proceedings in England for negative declaratory relief for various breaches by Ethniki. Ethniki applied to have the English proceedings set aside, contending that the term "as original" was contained in the reinsurance contract and since the underlying policy contained a Greek jurisdiction clause, that jurisdiction clause was transported into the reinsurance.

It was held that the words "as original" do not serve to incorporate jurisdiction clauses from underlying policies into reinsurance contracts. References to "as original" relate only to the scope of the cover afforded by the particular policy. To bestow the Greek court with jurisdiction Ethniki would need to demonstrate clearly that was what the parties intended at the time of contracting.[162]

2.2.2.7.4 Utmost Good Faith in Reinsurance

Although both the general requirement of good faith in commercial transactions and the special requirement of utmost good faith in reinsurance are rules of implied obligations, there have always been important differences in their meanings.[163] Moreover, they were also created with different considerations in mind.

Utmost good faith in reinsurance evolved in a substantially different way and for substantially different reasons than ordinary commercial good faith. In effect, the concept of utmost good faith in reinsurance evolved mostly outside Courts, not so much as a legal rule but as the overarching embodiment of customs and practices.[164] Cedents and reinsurers of the past enjoyed longstanding, profitable relationships, and felt the need to draft contracts that covered every remote contingency. General conceptions such as utmost good faith were thought to be adequate to cover whatever occasional misunderstandings.

Nowadays, to assess the utmost good faith of a cedent a court may ask whether the cedent acted like a company that was wholly non-reinsured for the loss.

---

[161] *Anonymous Greek Co of General Insurances* ("*The Ethniki*") *v AIG Europe* (*UK*) & *Ors*, [2000] Lloyd's Rep. 34.

[162] Leedham and Linker (2002).

[163] Zeller (2000), p. 182.

[164] *Unigard Sec. Ins. Co. v North River Ins. Co.*, 4F 3d 1049, 1054 (2d Cir. 1993).

Although a number of courts have considered utmost good faith equivalent to a fiduciary duty, such a broad conception of utmost good faith is exaggerated.[165]

Not surprisingly, in view of the arms-length nature of reinsurance transactions, this view of utmost good faith generally has not held.[166] Thus, in *Zenith Insurance Co. v Employers Insurance of Wasau*,[167] the USA Court of Appeal for the Seventh Circuit became the first court to expressly disallow the reinsurance doctrine of utmost good faith in favour of the "general duty of good faith and fair dealing between the parties to a contract".[168] However, and despite the fact that the doctrine of utmost good faith has been considered by many courts since the proliferation of the reinsurance litigation in the late 1980s, the state of law in this area remains unsettled.[169]

2.2.2.7.5 Critique

The primary mistake of most courts considering reinsurance issues is blindly applying principles of original insurance. Before applying a rule of original insurance to reinsurance, an arbitrator must consider the circumstances of reinsurance that differentiate it from original insurance: two sophisticated business entities familiar with the customs and practices of insurance and reinsurance negotiate a contract of indemnity that necessarily places the information regarding the risks to be ceded in the hands of the ceding insured. Only after these circumstances are considered, can a coherent result be reached regarding the duties required by good faith under the contract. Although the parties can, and may, specifically contract in these areas for the expected conduct, historically, parties to a reinsurance contract have relied on an implied duty of "utmost good faith." The reinsurance market has changed due to the enormous environmental claims and the decline of profitability resulting in more contentious relationships.

These factors demonstrate that characterizing the reinsurance relationship as one of utmost good faith is no longer an accurate description. Formerly, differences had been settled by handshakes so as not to poison a profitable long-term business relationship.

Today, differences are more often resolved before courts and arbitrators. The sparseness of case law and precedent have placed courts in the unenviable position of developing a coherent jurisprudence. Arbitral courts should enforce the bargains

---

[165] *Mutuelle Generale Francaise Vie v Life Assurance Co of Pennsylvania*, 688 F. Supp. 386 (N.D. III, 1988); *American Reinsurance Co v MGIC Inv. Corp.* No 77 CH 1457 (Ill Cir. Ct. Ch. Cook County Oct. 20, 1987).

[166] *Christiania Gen. Ins. Corp v Great Am. Ins. Co.*, 979 F.2d 268, 280–281; Zeller (2000), pp. 185–186.

[167] *Zenith Insurance Co. v Employers Insurance of Wasau*, 141 F3d 300 (7th Cir. 1998).

[168] *Zenith Insurance Co. v Employers Insurance of Wasau*, 141 F3d 300 (7th Cir. 1998) at 308.

[169] Zeller (2000), p. 190.

of these sophisticated and experienced parties. Absent express terms, however, courts should adopt information-forcing default rules: the mere nondisclosure rule for initial disclosure of the risk and the good faith/prejudice rule for notice of a claim.[170]

References

Gurses O (2010) Reinsuring clauses. Lloyd's List, London

Leedham R, Linker S (2002) Reinsurance disputes: how, where and who to sue. Bus Law Rev 23:86

Staring GS (1993) Law of reinsurance. CBC, New York

O'Niell PJ, Woloniecki J (1998) The law of reinsurance. Sweet and Maxwell, London

Ostrager BR, Vyskocil MK (1996) Modern reinsurance law and practice. Glasser Legal Works, Little Falls

Thomas JE, Lyons S (eds) (2012) New Appleman on insurance law – library edition, vol 7, Property insurance (chapters 71–79 §§ 71.01–79.06). Lexis Nexis, Los Angeles

Thomas SW (1992) Utmost good faith in reinsurance: a tradition in need of adjustment. Duke Law J 41:1548

Zeller MC (2000) Divergent conceptions of the reinsurance doctrine of utmost good faith. In: Diaconis J, Gurevitz M (eds) Reinsurance law and practice. New legal & business developments in a changing global environment. Practising Law Institute, New York, pp 182–195

[170] Thomas (1992), p. 1597.

The Need for Reinsurance Arbitration: The Legal Framework

Arbitration is a commonly favoured alternative dispute resolution (ADR) method in reinsurance, hence reinsurance agreements, most often, contain arbitration clauses. In the most representative jurisdictions favouring arbitration as an ADR method, the corresponding legal framework also adheres to this favourism over arbitration. In England, the Arbitration Act 1996 redefines the relationship between arbitrators and the courts and clearly favours arbitration by stating that the object of arbitration is to obtain the fair resolution of disputes by an impartial tribunal without unnecessary delay or expense. This, *inter alia*, justifies the wide use of arbitration also in reinsurance. In the USA, the Federal Arbitration Act (FAA), acts as the primary source of arbitration law and enunciates a liberal policy in favour of arbitration. In Germany, arbitration is also more and more widely used and favoured, especially for reinsurance disputes. The German Arbitration Act forms the Tenth Book of the Code of Civil Procedure (*Zivilprozessordnung*) (ZPO) and establishes the principles and rules for the conduct of arbitration proceedings. All of the jurisdictions favour arbitration and practically transmit the continuous market need for arbitration in reinsurance.

3.1 General Introductory Remarks on Arbitration in Reinsurance

Arbitration clauses in reinsurance contracts are commonly included and favoured by parties. Courts require most reinsurance claim disputes to be arbitrated if the parties had agreed in writing to arbitrate the dispute, but much depends on the scope of the arbitration clause.

Arbitration enables parties to a reinsurance contract to have disputes determined by a tribunal knowledgeable about the subject. There is no law requiring reinsurance disputes to be arbitrated, and certain reinsurers, particularly facultative reinsurers, prefer to litigate. Parties to arbitration agreements can also waive the right to

K. Noussia, *Reinsurance Arbitrations*, DOI 10.1007/978-3-642-45146-1_3,

arbitrate.[1] If a reinsurance contract contains an arbitration clause, however, the clause is likely to be found valid and enforceable if it was consented to by the cedent and the reinsurer.[2]

Many reinsurance agreements contain arbitration clauses with the hope that disputes can be resolved quickly and efficiently by persons knowledgeable about the reinsurance industry.

In practice, the process has been less streamlined than originally envisioned, because cedents and reinsurers have turned to the courts to litigate about whether they have to arbitrate, how the arbitration should be conducted and whether they have to live with the resolution of the arbitrators. The result has been the development of a significant body of decisional law that should be valuable to help counsel form strategic judgments for arbitration proceedings.[3]

Cedent companies and reinsurers may draft arbitration clauses as they desire. Although there is no standard or typical arbitration clause, the content of a basic reinsurance arbitration clause is being provided, for reference, herein below:

> Any dispute or other matter in question between the Company and the Reinsurer, arising out of or relating to the formation, interpretation, performance or breach of this Contract, whether such dispute arises before or after the termination of this Contract, shall be settled by arbitration.
>
> Arbitration shall be initiated by the delivery of a written notice of demand for arbitration by one party to the other within a reasonable time after the dispute has arisen.
>
> If more than one reinsurer is involved in the same dispute, all such reinsurers shall constitute and act as one party for the purposes of this Article, provided, however, that nothing herein shall impair the rights of such reinsurers to assert several, rather than joint, defenses or claims, not be construed as changing the liability of the Reinsurer under the terms of this Contract from several to joint.
>
> Each party shall appoint an individual as arbitrator and the two so appointed shall then appoint a third arbitrator. If either party refuses or neglects to appoint an arbitrator within sixty (60) days, the other party may appoint the second arbitrator. If the two arbitrators do not agree on a third arbitrator within sixty (60) days of their appointment, each of the arbitrators shall nominate three individuals. Each arbitrator shall then decline two of the nominations presented by the other arbitrator.
>
> The third arbitrator shall then be chosen from the remaining two nominations by drawing lots. The arbitrators shall be active or retired officers of insurance or reinsurance companies or Lloyd's London Underwriters; the arbitrators shall not have a personal or financial interest in the result of the arbitration.
>
> The arbitration hearings shall be held in (City, State, Country), or such other place as may be mutually agreed.
>
> The language to be used in the arbitral proceedings will be . . ..
>
> Each party shall submit its points of claims to the arbitral tribunal, within the time designated by it.
>
> The arbitral tribunal will guide the parties as to discovery and will issue an award within reasonable time after the conclusion of the arbitral proceedings.[4]

[1] Hammesfahr and Wright (1994), p. 266.

[2] Hammesfahr and Wright (1994), p. 266.

[3] Hummer (1996), p. 228.

[4] Hammesfahr and Wright (1994), pp. 266–268.

The traditional purpose of arbitration is to enable the parties in a reinsurance contract to have disputes resolved and settled by a tribunal experienced in reinsurance transactions by avoiding the formal and public proceedings in civil court justice.

Arbitration has a long tradition in the field of reinsurance. One and very important reason why parties to a reinsurance contract resort to arbitration is the fact that awards commonly remain unpublished and are consequently only known and accessible to the parties involved. Arbitration awards are therefore not available as a source of reinsurance law, and since they become public in very few cases, their limited value as such source must be taken into consideration.[5]

3.2 The Legal Framework in England

Prior to 1997, the English law on arbitration had to be sought in at least three statutes (the Arbitration Acts 1950, 1975 and 1979, in addition to which the Limitation Act 1980 governed the issue of when arbitration proceedings were commenced so as to terminate the running of any relevant limitation periods, and sections of other statutes applied to specific forms of arbitration) as well as numerous judicial decisions.

The need for a unified body of arbitration law has, however, long been felt by the commercial community. In 1985 the United Nations Commission on International Trade Law (UNCITRAL) produced a Model Law on International Commercial Arbitration. Although the government decided, on the advice of the Department of Trade and Industry's Departmental Advisory Committee on Arbitration Law (DAC), that the UNCITRAL Model Law was not suitable for adoption in England (the Scottish Arbitration Act was nevertheless based on it), the DAC recommended a new Arbitration Act, one of the requirements of which would be: "...that it should, so far as possible, have the same structure and language as the Model Law, so as to ensure its accessibility to those who are familiar with the Model Law."

The efforts of the DAC culminated in the production of the Arbitration Act 1996, which received Royal Assent on 17 June 1996. The Act consolidates and amends the previous Arbitration Acts.[6] The Act itself provides that it will apply to arbitral proceedings commenced on or after the date on which it is brought into force, irrespective of when the relevant arbitration agreement was made (section 84). The Secretary of State is given power to include, m an order bringing the Act into force, any transitional provisions which appear to be appropriate. The substantive provisions of the Act came into force on 31 January 1997, save that its implementation with respect to the statutory recognition of honourable engagement arbitration provisions is confined to arbitration agreements made on or after 31 January

[5] Geiger (2000), pp. 135–136.

[6] Barlow Lyde and Gilbert LLP (2009), § 26-1.

1997. The authorities on the meaning and effect of honourable engagement clauses will, therefore, continue to be relevant to reinsurance arbitrations in the future, provided that the parties agreement to arbitrate was concluded before 31 January 1997.

The usual procedure followed in the course of a reinsurance arbitration entails the following stages: (a) service of the reinsurance arbitration notice, (b) appointment of the reinsurance arbitration panel, (c) exchange of pleadings, statements' of parties' cases, or other written submissions, (d) filing of any interlocutory applications to arbitrators or to the court (such as e.g. amendment of pleadings, applications for further disclosure or inspection, applications for security for costs etc.), (e) disclosure and inspection of documents, (f) instruction of the experts, (g) pre-hearing review, (h) conduct of the hearing, (i) issue of award whether final or interim, (j) hearing as to the costs, (k) award re costs, (l) appeal, (m) payment or enforcement of the award.[7]

In England, the Arbitration Act 1996 redefines the relationship between arbitrators and the courts. The arbitrators are the prime movers for the purpose of ensuring procedural justice and enjoy extended powers. As a corollary, the court's powers have been restricted to a subsidiary, supporting role. The procedure for making applications to the court in circumstances where the court is empowered to intervene in the arbitral process (e.g. to appoint an arbitrator where the appointment procedure laid down by the arbitration agreement has failed, to secure compliance with a peremptory order made by an arbitral tribunal, to compel the attendance of witnesses at a hearing, or to determine a preliminary point of law is governed by Part 62 of the Civil Procedure Rules (read with its accompanying practice direction which sets out a comprehensive code in this respect).[8]

3.2.1 Scope of the Arbitration Act 1996

Unusually for a piece of English legislation, the Arbitration Act 1996 contains a number of statements of general principle.

Section l recites that: "... the object of arbitration is to obtain the fair resolution of disputes by an impartial tribunal without unnecessary delay or expense; ... the parties should be free to agree how their disputes are resolved, subject only to such safeguards as are necessary in the public interest...[and] the court should not intervene except as provided by [the Act]."

Section 1 reflects an explanatory memorandum which accompanied the Bill (which subsequently became the Arbitration Act 1996) when it was introduced in December 1995.

---

[7] Barlow Lyde and Gilbert LLP (2009), § 26-2.

[8] A detailed discussion of the procedural rules would, however, go beyond the scope of this book.

The memorandum stressed the importance of the concept of party autonomy and stated that the provisions of the Bill come into play to support the arbitration only when the parties have not decided what should happen. The Bill reflects the view that the decision of the parties to choose a private tribunal rather than the courts to resolve their dispute must be respected.

The powers of the arbitrators have therefore been strengthened and the role of the courts is limited to those occasions when it is obvious that either the arbitral process needs assistance or that there has been or is likely to be a clear denial of justice.

The majority of the provisions of the Act apply where the "seat of the arbitration" is in England and Wales, or in Northern Ireland: section 2(1); a number of its provisions, however, apply even if the seat is outside England, Wales or Northern Ireland, or if the seat of the arbitration has yet to be designated or determined, e.g. section 7 (separability of arbitration agreement), sections 9–11 (stay of legal proceedings) and section 66 (enforcement of arbitral awards). Similarly, the powers of the court under section 43 (securing the attendance of witnesses) and section 44 (general powers exercisable in support of arbitral proceedings) apply if the seat is outside England, Wales or Northern Ireland, or if the seat of the arbitration has yet to be designated or determined, although the court has, in such circumstances, a discretion to refuse to exercise any such powers.

The seat of the arbitration is defined is the juridical rather than the geographical location of the proceedings, although the two may be the same.[9] The seat may be designated by the parties to the agreement, or by any arbitral institution invested with appropriate power, or by the arbitrators if so authorised. If the seat is not chosen in this manner, it will be determined by having regard to the parties' agreement and all other relevant circumstances.

An agreement to refer to arbitration any disputes arising out of a reinsurance contract may be included in a clause in the contract, or it may be contained in a separate agreement. Such agreement may be oral or in writing, but the English Arbitration Act 1996 only applies where the arbitration agreement is in writing (section 5).

This expression is widely defined so as to include an agreement which is evidenced in writing, or an oral agreement which refers to written terms (section 6). Moreover, references to anything being written include its being recorded by any means: this is an apparent reference to paperless Communications, including electronic placements of reinsurance.

The majority of reinsurance treaty wordings contain detailed arbitration clauses. Such clauses would clearly qualify as agreements in writing for the purposes of section 5 of the Act. It is not uncommon, however, for reinsurance disputes to arise at a stage before a wording has been produced and when the contract is still in the form of a slip. Provided that there is a clear indication in the slip that the parties

[9] Barlow Lyde and Gilbert LLP (2009), §§ 26-2, 26-3, 26-4.

intended to refer any disputes to arbitration, the Act will apply. For this purpose, the mere words "Arbitration Clause" are probably sufficient.[10]

On the other hand, if the substance of an agreement relating to disputes is that they should be referred to a procedure, outside the normal court system but in the nature of a judicial enquiry, intended to provide for a final and binding determination, then the agreement is an arbitral agreement within the meaning of the Act, notwithstanding that the words "arbitrator" or "arbitration" are conspicuous by their absence.[11]

In *David Wilson Homes* v *Survey Services and Another*,[12] a "QC clause" in the following terms in an insurance contract was held to constitute an arbitration agreement: "This contract is governed by the laws of England and any dispute arising hereunder between the assured and the insurers shall be referred to a Queen's Counsel of the English Bar to be mutually agreed between the insurers and the assured or, in the event of disagreement, by the chairman of the Bar Counsel."

In *Trygg Hansa Insurance Co. Ltd* v. *Equitas Ltd*,[13] it was held that section 6 of the Act did not supersede the existing body of authority relating to incorporation by reference of arbitration clauses from other documents. In the circumstances, the words "as original" or ". . . to follow the same terms . . . as the policy of the primary insurers" in a reinsurance contract were not sufficient to transpose into the latter contract an arbitration clause in the primary policy. What was required was a clear and specific reference to the arbitration clause, and not merely general words of incorporation.[14]

3.2.1.1 Equity Clauses

Although several market associations have suggested model arbitration clauses, there is no standard or uniform arbitration clause used by all market participants. Among other things though, it is particularly common in reinsurance contracts to expressly stipulate that market practices and principles shall be considered in addition to the strict rules of law.

The underlying rationale of such "equity" and "honourable engagement" clauses is to underpin the importance of the utmost good faith principle also with respect to the determination of reinsurance disputes. In other words, where the entire

[10] *Hobbs Padgett & Co. (Reinsurance) Ltd v J CKirkland Ltd* [1969] 2 Lloyd's Rep 547 (CA); Barlow Lyde and Gilbert LLP (2009), §§ 26-2, 26-3, 26-4.

[11] Barlow Lyde and Gilbert LLP (2009), §§ 26-2, 26-3, 26-4.

[12] *David Wilson Homes* v *Survey Services and Another* [2001] 1 All ER (Comm) 449 (CA).

[13] *Trygg Hansa Insurance Co. Ltd v Equitas Ltd* [1998] 2 Lloyd's Rep 439 (QB Com Ct).

[14] *Cigna Life Insurance Company of Europe SA-NV v Intercaser SA de Seguros y Reaseguros* [2001] Lloyd's Rep IR 821 (QB Com Ct).

transaction is based on utmost good faith, then the same spirit should apply to the resolution of related disputes.[15]

English courts have considered equity clauses in reinsurance contracts as the argument was raised that such clause was binding in honour only and not in law, and that such clause would deny any contractual obligation. The courts, however, were generally disinclined to follow such argument and concluded that equity clauses do not oust the jurisdiction of the courts but only oust the rules and technicalities of interpretation. According to the courts, such clauses indeed create a legally binding agreement to arbitrate and to abide by an award.[16]

Reinsurance transactions cannot be outside the scope of the law and public policy. Despite such business orientated approach, reinsurance contracts must likewise comply with the established general rules and standards of insurance contract law.[17] Hence the remaining effort of equity clauses to grant arbitrators some flexibility in construing contracts of reinsurance.[18]

English, as well as German, law do not impose restrictions insofar as the use of arbitration clauses in reinsurance contracts is concerned.[19] There are situations, particularly in slip reinsurance, where the legally valid incorporation of an arbitration clause can be doubtful. A slip, for instance, may attempt too incorporate by reference in the reinsurance contract an arbitration clause contained in the underlying policy. English courts have held that general words of incorporation were not sufficient to incorporate an arbitration clause into the reinsurance in the absence of an express intention.[20] *Equitas & Ors v Trygg Hansa*[21] is a case which addresses the question whether a "written agreement" requirement pursuant to s. 6(2) of the Arbitration Act 1996 has changed the law on the incorporation of reinsurance arbitration clauses.[22] In that case the judge indicated that s. 6(2) of the Arbitration Act 1996 did not stipulate how it was to be determined whether the reference in an agreement to a written form of arbitration clause or to a document containing an arbitration clause is such as to make that clause part of the Agreement. It was also stated that existing authorities on that issue should basically continue to apply but at the same time it was questioned whether the fact that the relevant authorities

---

[15] Geiger (2000), p. 136.

[16] *Eagle Star Insurance Company Ltd. v Yuval insurance Company Ltd.*, [1978]1 Lloyd's Rep. 357; Geiger (2000), p. 136.

[17] *Home and Overseas Insurance Company Ltd v Unione Italiana Anglo Saxon Reinsurance Company* [1978]1 Lloyd's Rep. 476; Geiger (2000), p. 137.

[18] Geiger (2000), p. 137.

[19] Geiger (2000), p. 137.

[20] Geiger (2000), p. 137.

[21] *Equitas & Ors v Trygg Hansa* Dec. 1997 (unreported).

[22] The English Arbitration Act 1996 in s. 6 (2) provides: "The reference in an agreement to a written form of arbitration clause or to a document containing an arbitration clause constitutes an arbitration agreement if the reference is such to make the clause part of that agreement". In Germany s. 11031(3) of the ZPO stipulates the same; Geiger (2000), p. 138.

required express reference whereas s. 6(2) of the Arbitration Act 1996 did not seem to contain such prerequisite.

In the light of this, the court reviewed the DAC report on the Arbitration Act 1996[23] and decided that whether general reference is sufficient to incorporate also an arbitration clause in a reinsurance contract is a matter for courts to decide. Hence, following the above, the court was not convinced that s. 6(2) of the Arbitration Act 1996 sought to impose any change in the law and was satisfied that this view was also reflected in the Arbitration Act 1996. For all of the above reasons, the Court followed *Excess Insurance Company v Mander*[24] and came to the conclusion that the arbitration clauses had not been incorporated in to the reinsurance contract by means of mere reference. This view appears to be supported as consistency and certainty are of particular importance as concerns the issue of whether disputes are to be arbitrated or litigated.[25]

Reinsurance is many centuries old. Reinsurance underwriters early learned the wisdom of tempering their operation with prudence, and used the security of their colleagues and competitors to balance and protest their accounts.

During the last century the scope of reinsurance has gradually widened while latterly a great range of technical developments has been evolved and many sophisticated practices have been introduced. There has also been a considerable shift if emphasis and today many of the reinsurances are designed to produce a profit for the reassured as well as the reinsurer.[26]

Despite the care given by brokers and others to the preparation of a reinsurance contract, there will always be the occasion when a dispute arises that defies agreement between the parties to the contract. At one time there seemed to be no option but to resort to litigation, and, in direct insurance, this procedure is still adopted in many cases.

In the case of reinsurance contracts, the parties are both practitioners in the insurance industry and prefer to avoid the unwelcome publicity of the courts. Accordingly, it is preferable that disputes be settled outside the courts by independent arbitration.[27]

3.2.1.2 Honourable Agreement Clauses

Parties are free to establish procedures in the arbitration agreement, and the parties or arbitration panels are free to require any procedures deemed necessary to resolve the dispute in as fair and expeditious a manner as possible.

[23] No 42 of the DAC Report on the English Arbitration Act 1996.
[24] *Excess Insurance Company v Mander* [1995] L.R.L.R. 385.
[25] Geiger (2000), p. 138.
[26] Brown and Reed (1981), p. 1.
[27] Brown and Reed (1981), pp. 166–167.

The cedent and reinsurer typically each provide the arbitration panel with their own submission of the case, describing the nature of the dispute, the amount in dispute and their respective positions.

At an evidentiary hearing, arbitration panels generally are free to reject evidence without regards to the legal rules of evidence.[28]

Most reinsurance agreements include an honourable agreement clause which typically instructs arbitrators to interpret the contract as an "honourable engagement" and not merely as a legal obligation and relieves arbitrators from following the strict rule of law. This language reflects the overriding practicality inherent in reinsurance relationships and embodies the mutual duty of good faith.[29]

The relationship between a ceding insurer and its reinsurers has often been described as an "honourable undertaking". Reinsurance is considered an honourable engagement because the nature of the reinsurance relationship requires a high degree of trust and confidence between the reinsured and the reinsurer.

Often, this concept is expressed by an "honourable agreement" clause found in the arbitration provision of a reinsurance contract.[30] An honourable engagement clause generally provides that an arbitration panel may determine any dispute which is subject to arbitration in accordance with good faith and equity.

3.3 Reinsurance in the USA

3.3.1 General

The law governing rights and obligations under contracts of reinsurance is well developed in the USA as one might expect for a commercial field as standing and widespread as the reinsurance industry.

Indeed, New York is probably the only state whose case law can be said to have addressed most of the major issues in the context of reinsurance disputes.

That being said, it is also certainly true that reinsurance contracts are a sub-category of commercial contracts, and hence the well developed body of general contract law principles may be drawn upon to fill in the gaps. Moreover, courts often borrow principles from the somewhat analogous direct insurance context.

There are several reasons for the relative paucity of controlling reinsurance specific case law in most USA jurisdictions.

---

[28] Hammesfahr and Wright (1994), pp. 308–309.

[29] *Pacific Reinsurance Mgmt. Corp. v Ohio Reinsurance Corp.*, 935 F2d 1019, 1022–1023; Thomas et al. (2011), § 40-23.

[30] Ostrager and Vyskocil (1996), §§ 5-01, 5-03, 5-04.

One leading reason is that most reinsurance contracts contain arbitration clauses, so most reinsurance disputes are resolved outside the traditional state court system.

In addition, and due to the fact that treaties have been more likely than facultative covers to contain an arbitration clause, a disproportionate number of USA reinsurance court decisions involve facultative covers rather than treaties.

Further skewing of the law may be caused by the fact that many of the USA reinsurance court decisions are rendered in the context of long-tail losses (e.g. asbestos, environmental pollution etc.). These court decisions may involve the interpretation of clauses that are not of widespread use.

A further challenge in the USA is of course the federalist nature of its legislation, i.e. the existence of 50 separate bodies of substantive law as well as a dozen federal circuits interpreting federal substantive law, which in theory ought to be uniform. This creates choice-of-law challenges, particularly since many reinsurance contracts do not specify which state's or nation's substantive law is to be applied in the dispute.[31]

The upshot is that in most USA jurisdictions there is oftentimes no other legal precedent to give definite guidance to the reinsurance professional, where the substantive issue may be late notice, accumulation or allocation of losses, non-disclosure etc.

American reinsurance lawyers therefore must often resort to the reinsurance case law of other states—as persuasive but not binding authority—or to insurance law or general contract law principles, or to evidence of reinsurance custom and practice, when advising their clients and advancing arguments to the USA courts.[32]

Most reinsurance treaties include a clause providing for resolution of disputes through arbitration and USA courts strongly favour the enforcement of arbitration provisions.

Historically reinsurance disputes were the exception rather than the rule, as a result of the in part, practice of utmost good faith. The parties to reinsurance agreements were usually well known to each other viewed their relationship as an honourable undertaking and sought to avoid serious disputes.

However, with the influx of new reinsurers in the 1980s, the capacity of the reinsurance market swelled, competitive pressures intensified and prices were cut. Investment income increased but so did loss ratios and hence many of the newcomers did not survive. As the complexion of the reinsurance market changed, disputes increased. The volume of litigation however, remains relatively low, due in part to the inclusion of arbitration clauses in most reinsurance treaties and many facultative agreements.[33]

---

[31] *Unigard Security Ins. Co. v North River Ins. Co.*, 79 N.Y.2d 576 (1992) (New York law); *Keehn v Excess Ins. Co. of America*, 129 F2d 503 (7th Cir. 1942) (Illinois law); Barlow Lyde and Gilbert LLP (2009), pp. 935–936.

[32] Barlow Lyde and Gilbert LLP (2009), pp. 935–936.

[33] Bank and Winters (1989), p. 323.

Even in the absence of an arbitration provision, the parties to a reinsurance contract may agree after the fact to arbitrate a particular dispute, not least due to the fact that arbitration enables parties to a reinsurance agreement to have their disputes adjudicated by a tribunal that is knowledgable about the reinsurance industry. Also, arbitrators may be able to eschew fidelity to strict rules of law pursuant to "honourable engagement" clauses.

The arbitration clause in a reinsurance contract typically sets forth the type of dispute subjected to arbitration, the initiation of the arbitration process, the process of selecting the arbitration panel and the qualifications of the arbitrators, the place and time of the arbitration hearing, the governing law, the procedures and time frames to be followed and the enforcement of the arbitral award.

The presumption favouring arbitrability of a particular dispute is strengthened when the language in the arbitration clause defining arbitrable disputes is "broad".[34] An example of a "broad" language is provided in the BRMA Arbitration Clause[35]: "...this clause defines arbitrable matters as "any dispute or other matter in question between the Company and the Reinsurer arising out of, or relating to, the formation, interpretation, performance or breach of this Contract." Such a language is intended to grant arbitrators broad authority to hear disputes that could arise under or with respect to the contract.

Parties are free to limit by agreement the claims they wish to arbitrate.[36] In determining whether a particular dispute is arbitrable, Courts typically engage in a two-part enquiry: whether there is an agreement to arbitrate and whether the scope of the agreement encompasses the asserted claims.[37] Courts can also sever arbitrable claims for non arbitrable claims.

The arbitration clause is also a starting point for the determination of the remedies that can be imposed by an arbitral panel, including equitable remedies such as pre-judgment attachment, prejudgment-interest[38] or security.[39]

Consistent with the federal policy favouring arbitration, Courts have been reluctant to find that an arbitrator exceeded his authority in ordering relief, where the arbitration agreement does not specifically restrict the arbitrator's authority.[40]

---

[34] *Leadertex Inc. v Morganton Dyeing & Finishing Corp.*, 67 F.3d 20,27 (2d Cir. 1005); Thomas et al. (2011), § 40-22.

[35] Thomas et al. (2011), § 40–45.

[36] *Hartford Accident and Ind. Co. v. Swiss Reinsurance Am. Corp.*, 246 F.3d 219,223 (2dCir. 2001); Thomas et al. (2011), § 40-22.

[37] *Hartford Accident and Ind. Co. v. Swiss Reinsurance Am. Corp.*, 246 F.3d 219,223 (2dCir. 2001); Thomas et al. (2011), § 40-22.

[38] *Rhone-Poulenc Inc. v Gould Elecs. Inc.*, 1998 US Dist. LEXIS 15848, at 7–8 (N.D. Cal. 1998); Thomas et al. (2011), § 40-22.

[39] *Advest Inc. v Mccarthy*, 914 F2d, 6, 10–11; Thomas et al. (2011), § 40-22.

[40] *Mich. Mut. Ins. Co. v Unigard Sec. Ins. Co.*, 44F3d 826; *Mutual Fire Marine and Inland Ins. Co. v Norad Reinsurance Co*, 868 F2d 52,56 (3d Cir. 1989); *Rhone-Poulenc Inc. v Gould Elecs. Inc.*, 1998 US Dist. LEXIS 15848, at 7; *Ace Capital Re: Overseas Ltd v Central United Life Ins. Co.* 398 F.3d 24, 29 (2d. Circuit 2002); Thomas et al. (2011), § 40-22.

Arbitrators may award temporary equitable relief where necessary so as to ensure that the final award is meaningful.[41]

Courts may also look to the parties submissions of the issues to the arbitrators to determine the scope of the arbitrator's power to grant relief.[42] Non-signatories to an arbitration agreement may be included in an arbitration with signatories, under the justification of principles of contract, agency and estoppel.[43]

Finally, the right to arbitrate a dispute may be waived if a party fails to comply with the terms of the arbitration agreement, excessively delays commencing arbitration or takes action that is inconsistent with the arbitration process.[44]

3.3.2 The Legal Framework in the USA

3.3.2.1 The Federal Arbitration Act (FAA)

The FAA,[45] which applies to arbitrations arising from transactions that affect interstate or international commerce, is the primary source of arbitration law in the US and enunciates a liberal policy in favour of arbitration.[46]

Another body of law governing and favouring commercial arbitration in the USA is the New York Convention which applies to arbitrations arising from commercial transactions where at least one party is not a USA citizen or where the arbitration has some reasonable relation with one or more foreign states even if all parties are USA citizens.[47]

Whether a claim is arbitrable is a legal question for a court to decide, unless there is clear and unmistakable evidence that the parties have agreed to arbitrate arbitrability.[48]

[41] *Pacific Reinsurance Mgmt. Corp. v Ohio Reinsurance Corp.*, 935 F2d 1019, 1022–1023; Thomas et al. (2011), § 40-22.

[42] *Mutual Fire Marine and Inland Ins. Co. v Norad Reinsurance Co*, 868 F2d 52,56 (3d Cir. 1989); Thomas et al. (2011), § 40-22.

[43] *Gulf Guarr. Life Ins. Co v Conn. Gen. Life Ins. Co.*, 975 F. Supp 839, 841–842; Thomas et al. (2011), § 40-22.

[44] *Menorah Ins. Co. v INX Re. Corp.*, 72 F.3d 218, 221–222 (1st Cir. 1995); Thomas et al. (2011), § 40-22.

[45] FAA, 9 USC §§1 et seq.

[46] *Argonaut Ins. Co. v Travelers Ins. Co.* 744 N.Y.S. 2d. 24, 25 (NY App. Div. 2002); *Progressive Cas. Ins. Co. v C.A. Reaseguradora Nacional de Venez*, 991 F2d, 42,45 (2d Cir. 1993); Thomas et al. (2011), § 40-22.

[47] 1958 NY Convention on the Recognition and Enforcement of Arbitral Awards, 9 USC § 202; Thomas et al. (2011), § 40-22.

[48] *First Option of Chi. Ins. v Kaplan*, 514 US 938, 944 (1995); Thomas et al. (2011), § 40-22.

Although arbitration is favoured by Courts, it will not be ordered unless the parties have agreed to arbitrate their dispute.[49]

As stated above there must be clear and unmistakable evidence that the parties have agreed to arbitrate,[50] although most Courts seem as a practical matter to rule in favour of arbitrability or to remand the question of arbitrability to arbitrators. In addition, the duty to arbitrate is limited by scope of the particular arbitration clause to which the parties have agreed, so certain types of disputes, such as tortuous interference or bad faith, might be found to be outside the scope of an arbitration clause governing contractual performance.[51]

If an arbitration provision is ambiguous as to how the arbitration should be structured, the ambiguity should be decided by the arbitrators.[52]

In the past, courts were averse to the enforcement of private arbitration agreements.[53] In enacting the FAA in 1925, the Congress intended to overrule all common law hostility toward arbitration and wanted to enlist the courts in assisting in the maintenance and enforcement of the arbitration system and arbitration agreements.

The Supreme Court has interpreted the FAA as evidencing a strong federal policy favoring arbitration. Today, courts recognize that the court system benefits from the resulting conservation of judicial resources, and alternatives to litigation for dispute resolution are favored by all federal circuits.

Because the purpose of the FAA is to ensure judicial enforcement of private arbitration agreements, its substantive rules apply to both state and federal courts with respect to arbitrations within the scope of the Act.

The FAA governs proceedings on agreements to arbitrate when the agreement is in writing and the contract involves interstate commerce.[54] It requires courts to enforce all arbitration agreements when one party either sues in court on an arbitrable dispute or otherwise does not cooperate with the arbitration proceedings.[55]

When considering whether to enforce an arbitration agreement, a court must determine: (1) whether there is a valid written agreement to arbitrate and (2) whether the dispute falls within the scope of the arbitration agreement. Any doubts about the scope of an arbitration clause must be resolved in favor of arbitrability, given the strong federal policy favoring arbitration.[56]

[49] *Ace Capital Re*: *Overseas Ltd v Central United Life Ins. Co.* 398 F.3d 24, 29 (2d. Circuit 2002); Thomas et al. (2011), § 40-22.

[50] *First Option of Chi. Ins. v Kaplan*, 514 US 938, 944 (1995); Thomas et al. (2011), § 40-22.

[51] *Argonaut Ins. Co. v Travelers Ins. Co.* 744 N.Y.S. 2d. 24, 25 (NY App. Div. 2002); Thomas et al. (2011), § 40-22.

[52] *Dorinco Reinsurance Co. v Ace American Insurance Co*, 2008 US Dist. LEXIS 4593 (ED. Mich. Mar. 5, 2008); Thomas et al. (2011), § 40-22.

[53] *Kulukundis Shipping Co. v Amtorg Trading Corp.*, 126 F.2d 978 (2d Cir. 1942) (discussing the history of the hostility of courts to arbitration).

[54] 9 U.S.C. §§ 1–2 (2005).

[55] 9 U.S.C. §§ 1–2 (2005).

[56] Tagvoryan (2005), p. 155.

If the court determines that a dispute is subject to arbitration as agreed in the contract, it has two principal ways of enforcing the arbitration clause. It can either stay the court proceedings pending arbitration under section 3, or issue an order compelling arbitration under section 4.

In other words, if a party to a contract containing an arbitration clause brings an action in court, the other party may petition the court to either "stay the trial of the action" pending arbitration of the dispute or petition the court for an order directing the arbitration to proceed in the manner agreed.

Thus, it is clear that the FAA reserves certain powers to the courts when the dispute is arbitrable. The question then becomes whether courts can exercise other powers not exclusively reserved to them by the Act, specifically their equitable power of granting provisional remedies over arbitrable disputes. Under California state law, parties can seek a preliminary injunction to maintain the status quo pending arbitration. Federal law is less clear.[57]

3.3.2.2 The Interplay Between the FAA, the McCarran-Ferguson Act and the New York Convention

The McCarran-Ferguson Act was enacted to preserve the longstanding prerogative of the States to regulate the insurance industry. States have acted in accordance with this statute to declare arbitration agreements in insurance contracts invalid. However, the Senate has since ratified the New York Convention and appended implementing legislation to the FAA that obligates domestic courts to recognize arbitration agreements in all international contracts.

In an odd convergence of authority, a functional conflict arises between these three bodies of law: the federal law says that state law controls in this area, even over other federal law that might incidentally cover the subject of insurance; the reverse-preemptive state law instructs that arbitration agreements are void in all circumstances; and a later-in-date treaty and corresponding implementing legislation purportedly compel enforcement of the agreement. A resolution of this conflict is required.[58]

In the case of *Goshawk Dedicated Lmtd. v Portsmouth Settlement Co. I.*[59] in the district court for the Northern District of Georgia, a British insurer attempted to enforce an arbitration agreement contained within a reinsurance agreement with a Georgia-based investment company. The reinsurer resisted, invoking the McCarran-Ferguson Act and arguing that Georgia law quite clearly states that arbitration agreements in insurance contracts are void as a matter of public policy.

[57] Tagvoryan (2005), p. 155.

[58] Murphy (2008), p. 1535.

[59] *Goshawk Dedicated Lmtd. v Portsmouth Settlement Co. I.* 466 F. Supp. 2d 1293, 1297 (N.D. Ga. 2006).

The court held that even though the arbitration agreement would be invalid in a domestic setting, special considerations pertaining to international commercial arrangements counseled that this arbitration agreement should be enforced. It also ruled that the New York Convention controlled pursuant to the policies recognized in the context of international commerce that strongly favor enforcement of arbitration clauses.

In so concluding, the court specifically rejected a prior decision of the Second Circuit, which held that the New York Convention was not self-executing, and, therefore, did not preempt a similar anti-arbitration statute in Kentucky.[60] Thus, reasoned the Second Circuit, the implementing legislation of the Convention—as a part of the FAA—was reverse-preempted pursuant to the McCarran-Ferguson Act.[61] The Northern District of Georgia reached these results even though it was clear at the time that, despite the FAA's strong policy favouring the enforcement of arbitration agreements, arbitration clauses in insurance contracts-at least in the domestic context-are generally unenforceable in Georgia.[62]

Although it is argued that the outcome in *Goshawk Dedicated Lmtd. v Portsmouth Settlement Co. I.*[63] was the correct one, it is also argued that the doctrinal basis on which courts should rely when faced with this conflict need be expanded.

Courts should invoke any of four doctrines to enforce arbitration agreements in international reinsurance contracts: (1) *pacta sunt servanda* and the corresponding obligation to abide by the text of a ratified treaty; (2) the "Charming Betsy canon's" teaching that domestic law should not be interpreted in a manner that conflicts with international law and obligations; (3) the "last-in-time rule", which gives the force of law to the latest expression of the state's will in a certain area; and (4) the Supreme Court's jurisprudence enforcing international arbitration agreements in a host of situations based on notions of international commercial comity, cooperation, and efficiency.[64]

Despite the generally preemptive effect given to section 9-9-2 by the McCarran-Ferguson Act and the decisions of the 11th Circuit and Supreme Court of Georgia, the *Goshawk Dedicated Lmtd. v Portsmouth Settlement Co. I.*[65] opinion focused on two reasons why the New York Convention should nonetheless control. As a

---

[60] *Stephens v Am. Int'l Ins. Co.*, 66 F.3d 41, 45 (2d Cir. 1995).

[61] *Stephens v Am. Int'l Ins. Co.*, 66 F.3d 41, 45 (2d Cir. 1995).

[62] *Goshawk Dedicated Lmtd. v Portsmouth Settlement Co. I.* 466 F. Supp. 2d 1293, 1302 (N.D. Ga. 2006). *McKnight v Chicago Title Ins. Co., Inc.*, 358 F.3d 854, 858–859 (11th Cir. 2004) (concluding that the FAA does not preempt Georgia's anti-arbitration statute due to the McCarran-Ferguson Act); *Love v Money Tree, Inc.*, 614 S.E.2d 47, 49 (Ga. 2005) (holding that the McCarran-Ferguson Act "prohibits the [FAA] from preempting" Georgia's anti-arbitration statute); Murphy (2008), p. 1537.

[63] *Goshawk Dedicated Lmtd. v Portsmouth Settlement Co. I.* 466 F. Supp. 2d 1293, 1297 (N.D. Ga. 2006).

[64] Murphy (2008), p. 1542.

[65] *Goshawk Dedicated Lmtd. v Portsmouth Settlement Co. I.* 466 F. Supp. 2d 1293, 1297 (N.D. Ga. 2006).

precursor, the court rejected the postulate that the New York Convention should apply because the McCarran-Ferguson Act was not intended to apply to international arbitration agreements. The court then held, first, that the New York Convention supersedes the McCarran-Ferguson Act and, second, that the New York Convention applies to the agreement because Portsmouth's state law defense of the anti-arbitration clause falls outside the scope of the affirmative defenses allowed under the Convention.[66]

When analysing the friction between a unique federal statute, a widely accepted international treaty, and aggressive state legislation it needs be determined whether the outcome in *Goshawk Dedicated Lmtd. v Portsmouth Settlement Co. I.*[67] was the correct one; namely, whether the New York Convention should be given deference over state anti-arbitration statutes notwithstanding the federalist mandate of the McCarran-Ferguson Act.

It should also be noted that the arbitration of a reinsurance contract of the sort addressed in *Goshawk Dedicated Lmtd. v Portsmouth Settlement Co. I.*[68] constitutes the business of insurance as envisioned in the McCarran-Ferguson Act.

However, if we also consider the issue in the context of three traditional doctrines concerned with international law, i.e. the *pacta sunt servanda* doctrine, the Charming Betsy canon, and the last-in-time rule, their basic application in federal courts and the manner in which they should be applied, in the context of a conflict between purportedly reverse-preemptive state statutes and the New York Convention, it will be noted that none of these traditional doctrines are available for use and constructs a rubric, by which courts can enforce agreements to arbitrate in international reinsurance contracts based solely upon the jurisprudence of the U.S.A. Supreme Court, concerning international commercial arbitration and the Court's use of international policy and comity, to justify the enforcement of these agreements, notwithstanding the general proscription against their enforcement in a domestic context.[69]

3.3.2.3 Doctrines Regarding the Use and Implementation of International Law

Once it has been determined that the state anti-arbitration statutes regulate the business of insurance, the operative conflict with which courts struggle arises.

---

[66] *In re Arbitration Between West of Eng. Ship Owners Mut. Ins. Ass'n (Luxembourg) & Am. Marine Corp.*, Nos. 91-3645, 91-3798, 1992 WL 37700, at *4–5 (E.D. La. Feb. 18, 1992) ("The McCarran-Ferguson Act does not apply to contracts made under the Convention, as it was intended to apply only to interstate commerce, not to foreign commerce."); Murphy (2008), p. 1543.

[67] *Goshawk Dedicated Lmtd. v Portsmouth Settlement Co. I.* 466 F. Supp. 2d 1293, 1297 (N.D. Ga. 2006).

[68] *Goshawk Dedicated Lmtd. v Portsmouth Settlement Co. I.* 466 F. Supp. 2d 1293, 1297 (N.D. Ga. 2006).

[69] Murphy (2008), p. 1544.

Under the standard operation of the McCarran-Ferguson Act, the state anti-arbitration laws would reverse-preempt any federal regulation incidental to the realm of insurance regulation.

Theoretically, this would include the New York Convention's implementing legislation. However, the New York Convention provides an impediment to the normal operation of the preemption mechanism. A treaty on a specific topic occupies a peculiarly supreme position within the hierarchy of controlling law.[70]

Courts must then decide between enforcing the New York Convention, which makes no specific reference to insurance regulation or deferring to the state anti-arbitration statute.

Additionally, even if the court decides that the McCarran-Ferguson Act supersedes any state regulation due to its status as the supreme law of the land, the plain language of the implementing legislation still does not mandate the enforcement of arbitration agreements.

Recall that section 206 states that courts "may" order arbitration to be held upon finding a valid arbitration agreement.[71] Because the implementing legislation controls where a treaty is not self-executing, it seems that judges have only the option of enforcing the agreement-an outcome that raises doubt and uncertainty, neither of which benefits international commerce.[72]

If the goal is to ensure the enforcement of the arbitration agreement, two solutions may be found to the problem that this conflict presents. First, under two canons of statutory construction and a basic doctrine of international obligation, courts should interpret the implementing legislation consistently with the New York Convention in order to implement its object and purpose. The result would be mandatory arbitration when the parties are bound by another wise valid arbitration agreement.

Under the *pacta sunt servanda* doctrine, the Charming Betsy canon, and the last-in-time rule, courts are bound to enforce the implementing legislation of the New York Convention over any contrary state law that might be preemptive under the McCarran-Ferguson Act.

Moreover, they must enforce the implementing legislation in a manner that is consistent with the original language of the Convention.

Second, the U.S.A. Supreme Court has developed jurisprudence over the last 50 years that speaks specifically to this issue.

The Court has manifested its intent to raze any barriers to international commerce, including courts' reluctance to implement valid arbitration agreements. Resting on principles of international economic efficiency and comity, the Court

---

[70] U.S. CONST. art. VI, 2 "[All Treaties made, or which shall be made, under the Authority of the United States, shall be the supreme Law of the Land]" 133. 9 U.S.C. 206 (2006); Murphy (2008), p. 1556.

[71] 9 U.S.C. 206 (2006).

[72] Posner (1999), pp. 647–648 ("[W]hen public policy demands that certain kinds of contracts not be enforced, it is important that parties know what these restrictions are in advance."); Murphy (2008), p. 1557.

has forcefully stated that relying solely on domestic law for disputes in international commerce is insufficient and impracticable.

Based on these precedents, the Court has expressed a clear preference for interpreting the implementing legislation and state laws in a manner that advances international commercial cooperation. Each solution is examined in turn.[73]

3.3.2.3.1 The "Pacta Sunt Servanda" Doctrine

One of the most basic principles of international law is embodied in the doctrine of *pacta sunt servanda*. The doctrine is based on the ancient ideal of the sanctity of contract. The generally accepted terms of this doctrine are codified in Article 26 of the Vienna New York Convention on the Law of Treaties (VCLT) stating "...every treaty in force is binding upon the parties to it and must be performed by them in good faith".

Moreover, a state "may not invoke the provisions of its internal law as justification for its failure to perform a treaty." As a corollary to that directive, states are generally bound to interpret treaties "in good faith in accordance with the ordinary meaning to be given to the terms of the treaty in their context and in the light of its object and purpose."

Pacta sunt servanda, and the corresponding respect accorded to obligations arising under international conventions, is perhaps the most important principle of international law.

The United States signed but has not ratified the VCLT; nevertheless, the positive obligation of *pacta sunt servanda* binds the United States as customary international law and a general principle of international law recognized by nations throughout the world. Though its application in domestic courts sparks consternation in commentators, customary international law remains a rule of decision for contests of an international nature.[74]

Customary international principles have "the force of law ... from acceptance by common consent of civilized communities of rules designed to foster amicable and workable commercial relations."[75] Even critics recognize that courts have almost unanimously endorsed the idea of customary international law as binding and substantive. Therefore, as perhaps the most basic tenet of customary international law, the "pacta sunt servanda" doctrine deserves a corresponding degree of deference.

---

[73] Murphy (2008), p. 1557.

[74] Bradley and Goldsrmith (1999), pp. 815, 817; ("This critique reveals that the modern position [that customary international law is binding, substantive law] is founded on a variety of questionable assumptions and that it is in tension with fundamental constitutional principles. We conclude that, contrary to conventional wisdom, [customary international law] should not have [supreme status]."); Murphy (2008), p. 1557.

[75] *Lauritzen v Larsen*, 345 U.S. 571, 581–582 (1953).

Moreover, the U.S.A. Executive Branch has already recognized the customary international law implications of the doctrine of "pacta sunt servanda". Thus, even though the United States has not yet ratified the VCLT, the doctrines of "pacta sunt servanda" and faithful observation of treaties represent customary international law binding upon the United States.

Accordingly, under the "pacta sunt servanda" doctrine U.S.A. courts must directly enforce the provisions of the Convention, including those mandating the enforcement of arbitration agreements that fall within the auspices of the New York Convention. This includes those agreements contained in contracts between citizens of states who are party to the New York Convention—the United States and Great Britain among them.

Domestic courts may refuse to enforce arbitration agreements only upon a showing that the agreement would be "null and void" or contrary to the public policy of the state of one of the parties to the agreement. This public policy exception has been interpreted narrowly, usually requiring the dissolution of an arbitration agreement only where the agreement violates basic notions of "morality and justice."[76]

In *Goshawk Dedicated Lmtd. v Portsmouth Settlement Co. I.*[77] the arbitration agreement did not fall under either of the exceptions, and the court was, therefore, bound to enforce the arbitration agreement faithfully and in accordance with the terms of the New York Convention.

Moreover, recall that states cannot invoke provisions of internal law as justification for failure to perform a treaty. Therefore, domestic courts may not invoke state law provisions that hinder the performance of the New York Convention. State anti-arbitration statutes fall squarely into this category.

Under a strict interpretation of the "pacta sunt servanda" doctrine courts may not ignore the obligations conferred by the New York Convention by relying on conflicting state anti-arbitration laws.[78] Some may, however, see this conclusion as inconsistent with the basic principle that implementing legislation controls over the express language of a treaty.

This is particularly evident in this case, where adherence to the "pacta sunt servanda" doctrine would require enforcement of all valid arbitration agreements, but the implementing legislation allows courts discretion in making that judgment. In a case such as this, courts must, at the least, interpret the implementing legislation and domestic law consistently with the intended object and purpose of the New York Convention.

---

[76] *Parsons & Whittemore Overseas Co., Inc. v Societe Generale de L'Industrie du Papier (RAKTA)*, 508 F.2d 969, 973 (2d Cir. 1974) (noting that the purposes of the Convention permitted only a "narrow reading of the public policy defense"); *Fotochrome Inc. v Copal Co. Ltd*, 517 F.2d 512, 513 (2d Cir. 1975).

[77] *Goshawk Dedicated Lmtd. v Portsmouth Settlement Co. I.* 466 F. Supp. 2d 1293, 1297 (N.D. Ga. 2006).

[78] Murphy (2008), p. 1561.

The "travaux preparatoires" reveal that the drafters of the New York Convention believed that a provision requiring the enforcement of arbitration agreements was of the utmost importance to the successful operation of the treaty. They understood that the original object and purpose of the treaty—the recognition and enforcement of arbitral awards—could be effectuated only if courts enforced the agreements under which the awards would be promulgated. The New York Convention was thus concluded with a dual purpose—to enforce both awards and agreements. Domestic court judgments must reflect this intent, and, therefore, must enforce valid arbitration agreements that they are presented with. Indeed, the FAA to which the legislation implementing the New York Convention was appended, states that courts must stay any judicial proceeding "referable to arbitration" when presented with a valid arbitration agreement in writing.[79]

Despite the preeminence of the "pacta sunt servanda" doctrine some courts are hesitant to rely squarely on the doctrine due to its sparse treatment in the context of domestic law by the Supreme Court.

As an alternative, courts may base their obligation to enforce arbitral agreements upon two rules of statutory construction devised by the Court: the Charming Betsy canon and the last-in-time rule.[80]

3.3.2.3.2 The Charming Betsy Canon

The Supreme Court has always interpreted domestic statutes in a manner such that they do not conflict with international law. This canon of statutory construction has been memorialised as the Charming Betsy canon.

It is so named from the first invocation of the canon by Chief Justice Marshall in *Murray v Schooner Charming Betsy*.[81] There, the Court held that "an act of Congress ought never to be construed to violate the law of nations if any other possible construction remains."

---

[79] 9 U.S.C. para. 3 (2006).

[80] Murphy (2008), p. 1562.

[81] *Murray v Schooner Charming Betsy*, 6 U.S. (2 Cranch) 64 (1804). The case arose out of the conflict with France at the turn of the nineteenth century. Congress had passed the Non-Intercourse Act of 1800, which prohibited commerce between U.S. and French citizens. Act of Feb. 27, 1800, 2 Stat. 7. Enforcement of the statute was vested in the U.S. Navy, which was under orders to capture any ship suspected of trading with France. The Charming Betsy had sailed from Baltimore under a U.S. flag and U.S. captain to St. Thomas, where it was purchased by Mr. Shattuck. Shattuck was born in the U.S., but had moved to St. Thomas, a Danish territory, when he was very young and had thence become a Danish citizen. While captained by Shattuck, the Charming Betsy was captured by the U.S. Navy under suspicion of trading with Guadaloupe, a French dependency, in violation of the Non-Intercourse Act. Shattuck argued that the seizure violated international law because he was a citizen of a neutral country. The Court agreed, and construed the Act as not applying to Shattuck because he was not a U.S. citizen—the result of a contrary construction being that the application of the Act would have violated international laws of neutrality; Murphy (2008), p. 1562.

Since its inception, the Charming Betsy canon has been reaffirmed consistently, often without reconsideration. Along with the interpretation ascribed to the Charming Betsy case, courts have typically extended the canon by applying the general presumption that statutes do not apply extraterritorially, particularly where doing so might conflict with international law.[82]

The canon has been recognized as a method of interpretation of substantive law, not just a jurisdictional limit on federal courts.

Moreover, courts have reinterpreted the canon over time to incorporate both customary international law and U.S.A. treaties within the collection of substantive international law with which federal statutes should not be construed to conflict.

Thus, federal law may not be construed incongruously with both the New York Convention and the customary law obligation to effectuate its object and purpose.

The Charming Betsy canon encourages the enforcement of international arbitration agreements in cases such as *Goshawk Dedicated Lmtd. v Portsmouth Settlement Co. I.*[83] for the following reasons: first, the canon instructs courts to interpret the McCarran-Ferguson Act in such a manner that it does not violate international law. Because treaties are binding codifications of international law as conceived by the canon, the McCarran-Ferguson Act must be interpreted in a manner that does not contravene the New York Convention. The simplest method of construction to achieve consistency would be for courts to hold that international arbitration agreements in insurance contracts do not constitute the business of insurance; state statutes applied to these agreements would lack preemptive effect under the McCarran-Ferguson Act. The agreements would then be governed by federal law—namely, the implementing legislation of the New York Convention—which would encourage their enforcement. However, because the court in the 11th Circuit, and the Supreme Court of Georgia have all previously recognized that arbitration agreements are indeed included within the business of insurance, an alternative solution is required.

Urging courts to hold that the New York Convention and its implementing legislation constitute federal legislation with a direct aim of regulating the business of insurance, not ancillary legislation with an incidental impact on the field of insurance regulation, provides this alternate solution.

Under section 1012(b) of the McCarran-Ferguson Act, no federal legislation may supersede any state law concerning insurance unless such legislation specifically relates to the business of insurance.

Construing the New York Convention and its implementing legislation to fall within this exculpatory clause would avoid conflict and thrust the implementing legislation to the top of the hierarchy of governing law concerning agreements to arbitrate in international reinsurance contracts.

[82] Murphy (2008), p. 1563.

[83] *Goshawk Dedicated Lmtd. v Portsmouth Settlement Co. I.* 466 F. Supp. 2d 1293, 1297 (N.D. Ga. 2006).

Once it is established that the New York Convention and its implementing legislation directly regulate the business of insurance, the courts must interpret the Federal Arbitration Act, including the implementing legislation, in a manner consistent with the obligations set forth in the New York Convention. This requires courts to interpret the rather ambiguous permissive language in section 206 in accordance with the affirmative obligation of the New York Convention to enforce arbitral agreements in international commercial transactions. Though section 206 states that courts may enforce arbitration agreements, courts are bound by the Charming Betsy canon to interpret this provision as requiring the enforcement of arbitration agreements unless they run afoul of the affirmative defenses prescribed by the New York Convention. While judicial sleight of pen transmuting permissive language into mandatory language may seem counterintuitive, it is a fairly standard practice.

Courts regularly interpret the term "may" as a mandatory instruction to bring legislation within constitutional bounds or effectuate the overarching object and purpose of the act. The final instruction of the Charming Betsy canon is that courts may not interpret the state anti-arbitration statutes and the McCarran-Ferguson Act to apply extraterritorially where such application would violate principles of international law embodied in the New York Convention. As mentioned earlier, this canon is most often invoked to limit the potential jurisdiction of the courts in applying U.S.A. federal law extraterritorially. This concept might be applied to prevent American judicial interference with a privately conducted and agreed-upon method of resolution in an international commercial venture.

Thus, this application of the canon would require courts to enforce the arbitration agreement according to the intent of the private contracting parties, and not to apply conflicting federal or state legislation extraterritorially to a contract of a truly international nature. Proper application of the Charming Betsy canon leads to the conclusion that the McCarran-Ferguson Act cannot preclude the enforcement of valid arbitration agreements which fall within the framework of the New York Convention.[84]

3.3.2.3.3 Last-in-Time Rule

The Supreme Court has always recognized a distinction between self-executing and non-self-executing treaties, holding that only the former are judicially enforceable absent implementing legislation. Congress eliminated a potentially troubling analytical hurdle in this case when it enacted legislation to implement the New York Convention in 1970.

Therefore, the New York Convention has the status accorded to treaties under the Constitution as the "supreme law of the land," subject only to any restrictions

---

[84] Murphy (2008), p. 1568.

imposed by the implementing legislation. Congress has the inherent ability to override treaties by enacting domestic laws.

This proposition is in accord with the treatment of federal law as compared to treaties ratified with the advice and consent of the Senate; each is treated on par with the other. Such equality introduces the question of which body of law should apply if a federal statute and a ratified treaty concerning the same subject are in conflict with each other. It is well settled that, where conflict arises, courts are bound to construe and give effect to the latest expression of the sovereign will.

Therefore, when a statute and treaty conflict, the legal principle that is "last in date" will control and serve as the applicable substantive law. This rule of decision is commonly known as the "last-in-time" rule and has been upheld and reaffirmed in many contexts.

Most commonly, the principle is invoked to support the proposition that Congress has the ability to override treaties through federal law. This congressional prerogative is not subject to doubt. However, only once has the Supreme Court applied the last-in-time rule to hold that a treaty can override an earlier federal statute, and despite its apparent viability, the application of the rule in such a manner has been exceedingly rare in the lower courts.

In the context of international reinsurance contracts, the difficult question is whether the New York Convention conflicts with either the McCarran-Ferguson Act or the state anti-arbitration statute that provides the actual substantive rule of decision.

If the controlling law is actually state law, then there would be little doubt as to the superiority of the New York Convention and its implementing legislation, and the last-in-time rule would not be necessary.

But, if the McCarran-Ferguson Act is controlling and determinative, then the important issue is whether the New York Convention and the Act truly conflict. There can be no preemption of the McCarran-Ferguson Act by the New York Convention under the last-in-time rule unless the statute cannot be enforced without antagonizing the treaty. Under this formulation, the New York Convention is predominant. The enforcement of the reverse-preemption mechanism of McCarran-Ferguson antagonises the Convention. The application of the Act creates a functional conflict whereby the McCarran-Ferguson Act and the New York Convention are irreconcilable. The McCarran-Ferguson Act serves as a vehicle through which state substantive law voiding arbitration agreements emerges as a federal rule of decision when that law regulates the business of insurance.

The New York Convention is quite clear that arbitration agreements must be enforced unless the agreement falls under one of the affirmative defenses provided by the Convention. Because the business of insurance does not fall within those defenses, enforcement of the McCarran-Ferguson Act frustrates the operation of the New York Convention. The anti-arbitration statute, by way of the McCarran-Ferguson Act, seeks to preclude arbitration, whilst the New York Convention seeks to facilitate it. Therefore, the last-in-time rule would be applied to resolve the conflict between the McCarran-Ferguson Act (not the state statute) as the vehicle for substantive law and the Convention.

The New York Convention was ratified in 1970 whereas the McCarran-Ferguson Act in 1945 and thus the New York Convention is the expression of congressional will last in date and as such it should serve as the rule of decision for courts where a conflict presents itself. Even if the express language of New York Convention does not control because it is not self-executing, the same interpretation results from the conflict between the implementing legislation and the McCarran-Ferguson Act.

When section 206 is read in a mandatory manner consistent with the Charming Betsy canon, the same conflict arises between the mandatory instruction of the implementing legislation. The Court has minced no words in making it clear that for a treaty to preempt a federal statute, or vice-versa, there must be a clear conflict between the two provisions and the preemptive mechanism of the Act. Because the implementing legislation is the last in date of all of the documents considered it controls vis-a-vis the McCarran-Ferguson Act.

Thus, under the last-in-time rule and the practice of treaty preemption, the New York Convention (or its implementing legislation interpreted consistently with the Convention) should control over the McCarran-Ferguson Act. This conclusion is consistent with the application of *pacta sunt servanda* and the Charming Betsy canon.[85]

3.3.2.4 Enforcement of Arbitration Agreements for the Purpose of International Commercial Comity and Cooperation

In addition to the support various canons of interpretation provide for the enforcement of international arbitration agreements, the jurisprudence of the U.S. Supreme Court also supports enforcement of an agreement like that in *Goshawk Dedicated Lmtd. v Portsmouth Settlement Co. I.*[86]

Because of the above-described difficulties with invoking international doctrines or applying various canons of statutory interpretation, it may be easier to rely upon the language and precedent of the Court to reach the same conclusion. Both federal and state court precedent support the application of, and adherence to, functional decisional principles that reinforce overarching commercial public policy goals in the face of contrary state law.

Milliken v Pratt,[87] a Massachusetts state court decision from 1878, was the first to recognize the importance of facilitating multi-state and interstate transactions.

In *Milliken v Pratt*,[88] the Supreme Judicial Court of Massachusetts applied the substantive law of Maine to "validate a contract which would be otherwise invalid under the personal Massachusetts law of one of the parties".[89]

---

[85] Murphy (2008), p. 1568.

[86] *Goshawk Dedicated Lmtd. v Portsmouth Settlement Co. I.* 466 F. Supp. 2d 1293, 1297 (N.D. Ga. 2006).

[87] *Milliken v Pratt*, 125 Mass. 374 (1878).

[88] *Milliken v Pratt*, 125 Mass. 374 (1878).

[89] Murphy (2008), p. 1569.

It has been argued that this decision can be interpreted as the functional subordination of a state rule for the purpose of facilitating certainty and predictability in multi-State transactions.[90] This conclusion is important because the Supreme Court has similarly gone to great lengths to subordinate American rules to facilitate certainty and predictability in multi-national transactions.

Further on, the U.S.A. Supreme Court indicated a similar willingness to acquiesce to general notions of commercial policy in *The Bremen v Zapata Off-Shore Co.*[91] There, the Court vacated a Fifth Circuit decision that all forum-selection clauses were unenforceable as contrary to public policy.

In a decision inspired by the need of furthering a general policy facilitating international economic relations, the Court held that despite the general unenforceability of the forum-selection clause, lower courts should adopt a doctrine whereby such clauses are prima facie valid and should be enforced unless enforcement is show by the resisting party to be unreasonable under the circumstances.

The Court went on to explain the basis for its decision: the expansion of American business and industry will hardly be encouraged if, notwithstanding solemn contracts, we insist on a parochial concept that all disputes must be resolved under our laws and in our courts.

The case of *The Bremen v Zapata Off-Shore Co.*[92] evinced a judicial predilection for rules of decision that further international commercial comity and cooperation. Thus, the decision helped to develop international law and comity as cognizable reasons to uphold and enforce clauses in purely international agreements.[93]

Milliken v Pratt,[94] and *The Bremen v Zapata Off-Shore Co.*[95] alone provide a sufficient basis on which courts may decide that notions of commercial comity trump domestic laws to the contrary. The U.S.A. Supreme Court, however, has been much more specific in its acceptance of general principles of international law and comity in the enforcement of international arbitration agreements. On at least three occasions, the Court has relied on principles of international commercial comity and predictability to enforce an international arbitration agreement, even though a similar agreement would have been unenforceable in the domestic context.[96]

---

[90] *Bernkrant v Fowler*, 360 P.2d 906 (Cal. 1961) (applying Nevada law over California law to further a multi-State policy common to both California and Nevada to protect the expectations of the parties to a multi-State transaction).

[91] *The Bremen v Zapata Off-Shore Co*, 407 U.S. 1 (1972).

[92] *The Bremen v Zapata Off-Shore Co*, 407 U.S. 1 (1972).

[93] Murphy (2008), pp. 1569–1570.

[94] *Milliken v Pratt*, 125 Mass. 374 (1878).

[95] *The Bremen v Zapata Off-Shore Co*, 407 U.S. 1 (1972).

[96] *Vimar Seguaros y Reaseguros, S.A. v M/V Sky Reefer*, 515 U.S. 528,537–538 (1995); *Mitsubishi Motors Corp. v Soler Chrysler-Plymouth, Inc.*, 473 U.S. 614, 629 (1985); *Scherk v Alberto Culver Co.*, 417 U.S. 506, 517–519 (1974).cf. *Missouri v Holland*, 252 U.S. 416, 435 (1920) ("Where a national interest of very nearly the first magnitude is involved. It can be protected only be national action in concert with that of another power . . .. We are of the opinion that the treaty and statute must be upheld [over a conflicting state statute]."); Murphy (2008), pp. 1569–1570.

These cases illustrate that international agreements to arbitrate are enforceable despite public policy concerns that might warrant a contrary decision if the agreement were purely domestic.

This conclusion offers great prospective benefit to courts faced with conflicting precedent with regard to public policy concerns and arbitration agreements. Those courts may undertake an analysis of the persuasive Supreme Court precedent in favor of the enforcement of agreements to arbitrate, notwithstanding any proposed domestic obstacles. The subsequent outcome, preferably enforcing the agreement to arbitrate, will be based not only upon general ideals of international comity and international commercial policy, but also on the specific recognition by the Supreme Court of the importance of equilibrium and consistency within the international commercial realm.

A national policy favoring the arbitration of international commercial agreements will become increasingly important in the coming years. Many federal courts have recognized that the enforcement of international arbitration agreements follows necessarily from the Supreme Court's jurisprudence, and that pattern should not change.

Under the doctrine of *pacta sunt servanda*, the Charming Betsy canon, and the last-in-time rule, the New York Convention and its implementing legislation should be enforceable over a state anti-arbitration statute empowered as reverse-preemptive by the McCarran-Ferguson Act.

Moreover, proper construction of both the New York Convention and implementing legislation, leads to the conclusion that valid international arbitration agreements—falling under the New York Convention—should be enforced.

However, even if none of those canons are applied, the purpose underlying the New York Convention still applies to purely international disputes. This is true even in the face of considerable and significant domestic policy concerns such as antitrust rights.

The Supreme Court has held that international comity and policy dictate that private international arbitration agreements must be enforced in order to secure the international commercial order and to encourage international discourse and trade. This analysis may be unique, but its outcome is not. It has not been rare for lower courts to enforce international arbitration agreements under the New York Convention notwithstanding an anti-arbitration statute falling under the auspices of the McCarran-Ferguson Act.[97]

---

[97] *Antillean Marine Shipping Corp. v. Through Transp. Mut. Ins., Ltd.*, No. 02-22196-Civ., 2002 WL 32075793 (S.D. Fla. Oct. 31, 2002); *Jantran, Inc. v Sphere Drake Ins., P.L.C.*, No. Civ. A.2:96CV085-D-B, 1997 WL 88259 (N.D. Miss. Feb. 18, 1997); *Continental Ins. Co. v Jantran, Inc.*, 906 F. Supp. 362 (E.D. La. 1995); *McDermott Int'l, Inc. v Underwriters at Lloyd's of London*, Civ. A. No. 91-841, 1992 WL 37695 (E.D. La. Feb. 14, 1992); *Assuranceforeningen Skuld (Gjensidig) v Apollo Ship Chandlers, Inc.*, 847 So. 2d 991 (Fla. Ct. App. 2003). However, in the domestic context, the results of the lower courts are more varied in deciding whether the McCarran-Ferguson Act enables state anti-arbitration statutes to reverse preempt federal law in the insurance context. Compare *Hamilton Life Ins. Co. v Republic Nat'l Life Ins. Co.*, 408 F.2d

In *Goshawk Dedicated Lmtd. v Portsmouth Settlement Co. I.*,[98] the Northern District of Georgia followed the path trodden by previous pioneers to conclude that the international instrument controls in a conflict between a New York Convention vital to the successes of international commerce and a federal statute committed to retaining the long-preserved sovereignty of the Several States in an area of regulation that is unmistakably committed to them. The conclusion was the correct one, and future courts faced with the same conflict should take heed of *Goshawk Dedicated Lmtd. v Portsmouth Settlement Co. I.*[99] and of the ruling in *Mitsubishi Motors Corp. v Soler Chrysler-Plymouth, Inc.*,[100] in the enforcement of international arbitration agreements under the New York Convention.[101]

3.3.2.5 Reinsurance Policies Under the Bermuda Form

The Bermuda in its standard form is a type of direct excess liability insurance. It was specifically designed to respond to the need for such direct liability insurance in the wake of the catastrophes that plagued policyholders in the 1980s that revealed structural weaknesses in traditional CGL policies, not least the long-tail liabilities that came back to haunt insurers.[102]

606 (2d Cir. 1969) (holding that the McCarran-Ferguson Act does not preclude the application of the FAA because the state arbitration statute was not one regulating the business of insurance, but a method of handling contract disputes generally), *Triton Lines, Inc. v S.S. Mut. Underwriting Assoc.*, 707 F. Supp. 277 (S.D. Tex. 1989) (holding that the FAA preempted a state anti-arbitration provision in the insurance code because a disputed claim, and its subsequent resolution, is not the business of insurance), and *Bernstein v Centaur Ins. Co.*, 606 F. Supp. 98 (S.D.N.Y. 1984) (holding that the FAA preempted a state policy against arbitrating insurance claims because the state did not have a statute that specifically prohibited arbitration in the insurance industry), with *McKnight v Chicago Title Ins. Co., Inc.*, 358 F.3d 854 (11th Cir. 2004) (holding that a portion of the Georgia Arbitration code was "law regulating the business of insurance" and thus reverse-preempted the FAA by way of the McCarran-Ferguson Act), *Mut. Reinsurance Bureau v Great Plains Mut. Ins. Co., Inc.*, 969 F.2d 931 (10th Cir. 1992), cert denied 506 U.S. 1001 (1992) (holding that an arbitration clause in a Kansas reinsurance agreement was unenforceable under a Kansas statute excluding insurance contracts as valid arbitration agreements because the McCarran-Ferguson Act precluded application of the FAA), and *Eden Financial Group, Inc. v Fidelity Bankers Life Ins. Co.*, 778 F. Supp. 278 (E.D. Va. 1991) (holding that the FAA does not preempt a state receivership statute concerned with the arbitration of insurance company disputes because the McCarran-Ferguson Act provides that it is the province of the states to regulated the business of insurance).

[98] *Goshawk Dedicated Lmtd. v Portsmouth Settlement Co. I.* 466 F. Supp. 2d 1293, 1297 (N.D. Ga. 2006).

[99] *Goshawk Dedicated Lmtd. v Portsmouth Settlement Co. I.* 466 F. Supp. 2d 1293, 1297 (N.D. Ga. 2006).

[100] *Mitsubishi Motors Corp. v Soler Chrysler-Plymouth, Inc.*, 473 U.S. 614, 629 (1985).

[101] Murphy (2008), pp. 1569–1575.

[102] Scorey et al. (2011), p. 15.

Reinsurance policies based upon the Bermuda Form usually *adopt* the Law of Construction and Interpretation Clause found in Article VI.O of Form XLGO4 and the arbitration agreement in Article VI.N of Form XL004.

Thus, disputes arising from the reinsurance policy are resolved by way of arbitration, with the contract usually governed by New York law, as amended. The reinsurance structure gives rise to three particular issues in terms of dispute resolution.

First, it is necessary to be certain as to the identities of the parties to the arbitration agreement. If there are separate contractual arrangements between the captive and the reinsurer and between the captive and the policyholder, there will similarly be separate arbitration agreements.

As a matter of English law, it is difficult to see how the reinsurer can arbitrate against the policyholder, who is a stranger to the contract, unless there is a separate ad hoc agreement to permit this. However, it can be pointed out that the arbitration condition says any 'party' may initiate arbitration by notifying the other party *or parties of* its intent to do so.

It has been suggested that, by implication, this clause recognizes, that there may be more than two parties, to an arbitration. If this were thought desirable, a reinsurer initiating an arbitration on an issue affecting the policyholder would be well advised to send the notice of arbitration to both the named entity and the named insured. If the named insured, as policyholder, objects or ignores the notice of arbitration, there is little mileage in pursuing the point.

Secondly, assuming that the policyholder is a stranger to the arbitration agreement, the party holding all the relevant documents regarding the underlying claims, litigation and resulting liability is a third party to the reinsurance and a non-party to the arbitration.

As a result, the reinsurer is unable to seek orders for disclosure of documents from the tribunal against such third parties, which may give rise to procedural and evidential difficulties.

Under section 43 of the Arbitration Act 1996, the reinsurer is able to invoke the assistance of the court in order to secure the attendance of third parties as witnesses or to compel them to disclose documents. Given that the underlying policyholder is usually a corporation outside the jurisdiction of the English courts, this offers little practical assistance. Technically, the captive insurer faces the same predicament; however, the alignment of interests between the underlying policyholder and the captive means that the underlying policyholder will quite often volunteer to provide relevant documents, either directly or via the captive. If there is a refusal to provide such relevant material, adverse inferences may be drawn by an arbitral tribunal in certain situations.

Thirdly, for whatever reason,[103] the underlying policyholder may seek to involve itself as a party to any arbitration, either as co-claimant with the captive

[103] An underlying policyholder may wish to participate because it feels that it is the ultimate beneficiary of any award against the reinsurer in favour of the captive insurer. Also, it may be that a

insurer or alone.[104] It will be necessary to ensure that such an arrangement is documented by agreement at an early stage so as to be certain that the arbitral tribunal has jurisdiction over the policyholder.

If the policyholder is willing to become a party in this way, the reinsurer is presented with an immediate solution to the issue of disclosure and evidence because the underlying policyholder is no longer a stranger to the proceedings. However, one must let overcome the difficulty that the underlying policyholder is *prima facie* a third party to the reinsurance and, importantly, the separate arbitration agreement.[32]

3.4 Reinsurance in Germany and Arbitration Within It

Germany is one of the world's largest and most influential reinsurance markets. The global reinsurance market uses arbitration as its traditional method of dispute resolution. As a result, reinsurance arbitration is a frequent phenomenon in Germany.

Reinsurance arbitration is growing in Germany, and can be expected to continue to grow, as the insurance and reinsurance markets soften since 2008, and disputes again become more commonplace amongst the large players.

Most reinsurance arbitrations are held pursuant to ad hoc agreements rather than conducted, pursuant to institutional rules. The form and content of ad hoc arbitration clauses frequently leave much to be desired. They tend towards the lengthy and complex, regardless of the practicalities of the process, and the need for flexibility.

One common feature is the tendency of such clauses to invoke market practice; the desirability of such a solution is not always evident, as what is truly representative of market practice is frequently more likely to turn out to be a matter of personal prejudice, historical obscurity and local mannerism, rather than a truly ascertainable practice.

Another feature of reinsurance arbitration clauses is the requirement for the arbitrators to be qualified in certain respects, notably as regards their experience and longevity within the insurance or reinsurance market. Often, such clauses can limit unnecessarily the number of people capable of conducting an efficient and competent arbitration process, by reference to qualifications that have little to do with either the relevant contract, branch of reinsurance, or the method of dispute resolution selected.

---

claimant in an arbitration has a residual concern about the tribunal's perception of the interposition of a captive insurer and therefore, for presentational reasons, wishes to ensure that the underlying policyholder retains a presence before the tribunal; Scorey et al. (2011), p. 28.

[104] For a case where the reinsurer sought to join the underlying policyholder as a party to an arbitration, see *Ace American Insurance Co. v Huntsman Corp.*, 2008 WL 44)3101 (SDIcx, Slip Copy 2008) which applied Second and Fifth Circuit jurisprudence, including New York law; Scorey et al. (2011), p. 28.

The reinsurance market is, although financially large, very small in terms of the number of players operating within it. Clauses which seek to prescribe the qualifications of the arbitrators by reference to their experience within this small market are liable to limit the growth of a suitably experienced and competent pool of reinsurance arbitrators, as the requirements of independence and impartiality can be strained by the imposition of such qualifications.

Nevertheless, there is no real call in Germany for a specialist set of institutionalised arbitration procedural rules and regulations specifically tailored for the reinsurance market; such regulations can lead both to uncertainties as to their meaning and effect, as a result of their novelty on the one hand, and a lack of flexibility in their application on the other. Neither would be of benefit to the parties.

The notion that Germany has been of scarcely any importance as a seat for international arbitration has been a commonplace amongst lawyers and legal scholars for many years, but that perception is now changing.

Germany's adoption of the UNCITRAL Model Law on International Commercial Arbitration together with a case-law strongly in favour of arbitration, a growing body of expertise and Germany's geo-political situation in Europe are all strong objective reasons which speak for a choice of German seat.

3.4.1 Statistical and Anecdotal Evidence

The most readily available statistics are those of the ICC. In 2001, there were 566 new references to arbitration. Within those arbitrations, 118 German parties were involved. By way of comparison, there were 195 USA parties and 89 English parties. In terms of parties Germany is important in international arbitration.

This is not a new development: over a period of at least 25 years, Germany has consistently provided the third largest number of parties to ICC arbitration, following only the United States and France.[105]

The number of German arbitrators, too, although proportionally smaller, is also significant. In 2001, 92 German arbitrators were appointed, 45 nominated by the parties and 47 appointed by the ICC. By way of comparison, 117 English arbitrators were appointed, of which two-thirds (76) were nominated by the parties.

This, too, is no new trend. Over the 11 year period 1989–1999, the number of German arbitrators (580) was exceeded only by Switzerland (1,113), the United Kingdom (718) and the United States (592).[106] Again, Germany's importance in this respect can hardly be said to be of little importance.

The picture is different when one looks at the occurrence of a German seat. The number of ICC arbitrations in 2001 with a German seat (24) was disproportionately

[105] 933, 1202 and 1387 parties respectively; Craig et al. (2000), p. 155.

[106] Craig et al. (2000), p. 155.

low to the number of German parties. By way of comparison, the United Kingdom's figure of 61 arbitrations was nearly three times as great as Germany's but with only three-quarters of the number of parties. Over the period 1989–1999, of the total 3,393 seats of ICC arbitration, only 138 (or 4.5 %) were in Germany. This contrasts with 1,056 (33 %) in France, 773 (25 %) in Switzerland and 318 (8.5 %) in the United Kingdom.[107]

To call Germany's significance of scarcely any importance in this respect is perhaps an exaggeration, but there appears to be at least a disproportionately low occurrence of seat. On the evidence of the 1989–1999 figures, this is not due to any preference of the ICC: the ratio of seats fixed by the ICC to seats agreed by the parties was broadly the same for both France and Germany (at 1:4) and considerably higher than the ratio for the other principal seats (the United States and the United Kingdom at about 1:6 and Switzerland at about 1:8).

These figures suggest on the contrary that the relative incidence of seat between different countries has much more to do with the choice of the parties. It would be wrong to assess "importance" solely by reference to statistics.

In addition to the relatively high incidence of German arbitrators and parties, Germany's procedural law has had a profound influence on the development of international practice as a whole, and German jurisprudence is likely to play an increasingly important role in the sphere of international arbitral law as a result of Germany's adoption of the Model Law. This is particularly the case given that, until now, none of the most popular arbitral seats in Europe has done so.[108]

Moreover, Germany's adoption of the Model Law has itself catalysed the adoption of the Model Law in turn by a number of East European nations. Also, within Germany there is a strong and unmistakable sense that international arbitration has come of age.

In daily practice, arbitration clauses with a German seat in English-language, international contracts are now commonplace and it has been estimated that four-fifths of German companies' export contracts for plant and engineering equipment contain arbitration clauses. The most recent figures of the German Institution of Arbitration (DIS) also paint a healthy picture, with 77 new proceedings in 2002, up from 30 in 1999, a significant number for a national arbitral institution.

There has also been a sustained growth of interest in international arbitration within the legal community. Membership of DIS is growing and attendance at arbitration conferences has noticeably increased in the last few years. Such conferences have begun regularly to be conducted wholly or partly in English, taking on an increasingly comparative content. There are now a number of centres of expertise in international arbitration within or allied to universities (for instance, the Heidelberg Centre for International Dispute Resolution, and the Center for Transnational Law and the Rechtsinstitut für Europäische und Internationale Zusammenarbeit ("RIZ"), both in Cologne).

---

[107] Craig et al. (2000) and Hunter (2003), p. 155.

[108] Hunter (2003), pp. 155–156.

In conclusion, while the instance of a German seat in international arbitrations remains statistically low, the interest of the German legal community in international arbitration has certainly grown. It is valid to ask whether this is likely to become reflected in an increase of importance of Germany as a place of international arbitration.[109]

3.4.2 An Empirical Evaluation

Which factors might have caused Germany's poor statistical representation as a seat and whether these are historical or intrinsic: in other words, how they are likely to affect Germany's position in the coming years?

Many reasons and factors have been put forward for the relative paucity of arbitrations with a German seat, such as the argument of an outdated arbitration law. Despite its strong support of party autonomy and flexibility, there were a number of aspects of the old law which militated against Germany as an arbitral seat. These have been swept away by the new statute. A variety of political-historical grounds in a broader sense have contributed to the pre-eminence of capitals such as London, Paris, Zurich and Vienna as arbitral centres. Such historical factors are important to the extent not only that bodies of expertise and experience have built up in those cities, but also that they have no doubt created something of an "IBM factor": London or Paris are safe choices for an arbitral seat, whereas Frankfurt might still be regarded by many as maverick.

However, this is no solid basis in the long term for a self-perpetuating hierarchy if it is not directly linked to concrete comparative benefits, and important new centres can develop rapidly with a conjunction of favourable circumstances, as the example of Stockholm has shown.

Another factor is the existence of minimum scale fees for lawyers. These can appear disproportionately large in high-end cases. It is fair to say that this is true only in the largest cases, although even in more modest cases the stages of accrual are front-loaded and not well matched to the usual course of an international arbitration.

In fact, the applicability of such scale fees is determined not by the choice of seat but by the seat of the lawyer's practice, and there is a good basis to exclude them in an international arbitration in any event. However, the perception alone is reason enough for the applicability of such scales to be expressly excluded from international arbitration. The crucial question is to ask how Germany now measures up as a neutral seat on objective criteria today.[110] The following is a selection of such criteria and a summary assessment of Germany's fulfilment of them.

[109] Hunter (2003), pp. 155–156.

[110] Hunter (2003), pp. 155–156.

3.4.3 Party Neutrality

Here one is confronted immediately by the conundrum that the single and most obvious cause of Germany's relatively low incidence of seat is precisely because there are so many German parties.

It is significant in this respect that the United States, which has consistently provided the highest number of parties to ICC arbitration (1,202 in 1989–1999), also has a relatively low incidence as a seat (247 in the same period); conversely, Switzerland, which has a relatively low number of parties (398 in the period 1989–1999) has a relatively high number of seats (773).

This factor is unavoidable. It is not undesirable. Indeed, the more German parties adopt arbitration as a means of dispute resolution in their international affairs, the greater the pool of experience and expertise within Germany becomes. Provided it has objective advantages, Germany will still be a possible forum even for those disputes involving a German party, particularly where German law applies, and there remains of course a vast number of other contracts where it could be a neutral forum if regarded as objectively suitable.

3.4.4 Arbitral Law and Environment

Apart from neutrality, the most relevant criterion in any choice of seat is the existence of an efficient, culturally sensitive and supportive environment in which to conduct international proceedings. Crucial in this respect is a modern and suitable arbitral law and its consistent and pro-arbitral application by the state judiciary.

Germany's adoption of the UNCITRAL Model Law (with some desirable changes) is both a concrete measure of the fulfilment of this criterion and also a sign of Germany's appreciation of, and desire to meet, the needs of the international arbitral community.

That alone is not enough. Such a political will must also be reflected in the application of the arbitral law by the courts in arbitral proceedings and the acceptance of international norms by arbitral tribunals in practice. Germany can fairly be said to provide an environment which is able to satisfy the expectations of international commercial parties in their choice of arbitration environment and which compares favourably with the more established seats.

3.4.5 Substantive Law

Germany has one of the most developed civil and commercial laws in Europe and is supported by a vast body of learning in jurisprudence and legal literature. This has both had a profound influence on the substantive (and procedural) law of many other countries and is also frequently cited to fill legislative or jurisprudential voids in other civil law legal systems (particularly in the former Eastern Bloc countries which have only fairly recently adopted or reinstituted new civil and commercial codes).

While it is not necessary that the seat of arbitration be linked to the choice of substantive law of the contract, there is a great deal of sense in doing so and it is very commonly done. German law is a good choice of governing law for an international contract and, whether German law or a system with a substantive relationship to it is chosen to govern a contract, arbitration in Germany also makes considerable sense.

3.4.6 Expertise and Infrastructure

Germany is one of the largest industrial economies in the world and it is also thought to be the world's second largest legal market.[111] There is a thriving international arbitration community as well as a strong tradition of comparative law. In particular, a large number of German lawyers in commercial practices have either studied or worked abroad, very often in the United States. This leads to a large choice of both arbitrators and counsel.

Germany's national arbitration institution, the Deutsche Institution für Schiedsgerichtsbarkeit, or "DIS", is also well-established. Its origins lie in the Deutscher Ausschuss für Schiedsgerichtswesen (DAS), which was founded in 1920. Today, DIS is an active organisation, administering its own arbitration rules as well as representing ICC Germany in ICC arbitration matters and promoting arbitration generally through committees, publications, know-how and seminars. On the technical side, the importance and size of German industry and commerce provides a large platform for the supply of expert services.

3.4.7 Convenience

Germany is located centrally within Europe and has excellent accessibility. Frankfurt is particularly favoured in this respect, not least with the best-served airport in Continental Europe lying 15 min from the city centre.

---

[111] Total expenditure on legal fees in 2000 was estimated to about US$7.5 billion.

3.4.8 Language

Most international arbitration is now conducted in English, even between non-English parties. The standard and occurrence of proficiency in English in Germany, certainly among international commercial lawyers, is extremely high. Of the ICC arbitrations in Germany in 2002, only a quarter were conducted in German. One in seven DIS arbitrations in the same year was conducted in English.

3.4.9 Confidentiality

Germany provides a particular degree of confidentiality in the context of applications to the court. In common with German civil practice as a whole, court judgments are as a matter of practice published without disclosing the identity of the parties to the underlying dispute. Law reports therefore do not disclose the names and addresses of the parties or other material which would tend to enable them to be identified.[112]

During the course of the arbitration, the tribunal and party attorneys are bound by the strict rules of confidence governing judicial deliberations and lawyers as a whole. Subject to any express agreement, the parties' position is governed by the general law of confidence.[113]

3.4.10 The Practice of Arbitration in Germany

3.4.10.1 Brief History

Germany has a long tradition of arbitration, and of respecting party autonomy in particular. As far back as the thirteenth and fourteenth centuries, arbitration flourished and awards were enforceable just like state court judgments, with no right of appeal.

Following a decline in status in the eighteenth century, arbitration enjoyed a revival in the nineteenth century when, together with the rise of the idea of self-determination in contractual dealings (party autonomy), new commercial arbitration tribunals were instituted together with the ability of parties to exclude access to state justice by mutual agreement[10]. Arbitral law was codified in 1877, and this remained in force (with revisions in 1930 and 1986) until the present revision of the law in 1998. Although criticised in certain respects, this law too supported the

[112] Hunter (2003), pp. 155, 157.

[113] Hunter (2003), pp. 155, 158.

principle of party autonomy, the concept of which has therefore been embedded in German procedure for a considerable time.

3.4.10.2 The Procedural Framework

The German Arbitration Act forms the Tenth Book of the Code of Civil Procedure (*Zivilprozessordnung*). The Act came into force on 1 January 1998. The Code of Civil Procedure (ZPO, §§1025 et seq) establishes general principles for arbitration proceedings. §§ 1051 ZPO et seq. state that the arbitral tribunal must apply the law designated by the parties.

If the parties have failed to specify which national law will apply as the substantive law of the contract, then the arbitral tribunal should apply the law of the country to which the subject of the proceedings is most closely linked (ZPO § 1051 para.2). The Code of Civil Procedure (ZPO, §§ 1025 *et seq.*) applies to all arbitral proceedings where the place of arbitration is situated in Germany.

Certain sections—the dismissal of a court action where there is valid arbitration agreement, court provision of interim measures, court assistance in taking evidence and other judicial acts, and enforcement of foreign awards—apply irrespective of seat. The concept of place, in common with most other modern arbitral laws, is a juridical (or normative) rather than an empirical one. The determination of place in the award itself is decisive (§ 1054 III of the Code of Civil Procedure/ Zivilprozessordnung).

The German Arbitration Act incorporates the complete UNCITRAL Model Law with very few exceptions. It was decided as a matter of policy to subordinate the national law to the Model Law's aim of harmonisation, with a view to the fact that the latter was built on worldwide consensus and provided what was regarded internationally as a trusted and accessible system of rules. It was felt moreover that the Model Law could be adopted without fundamental changes to the existing law (subject to curing a number of perceived previous deficiencies). Therefore to a substantial extent the former case law remains effective.

Article 186 of the VVG prohibits direct application of the VVG provisions to reinsurance. Reinsurance contracts in Germany are governed by the Civil Code (BGB) to the extent that such general statutory provisions are compatible with the contractual relationship as it exists and do not conflict any other provisions.

As the direct insurer and reinsurer are carrying on a commercial trade in Germany they are subject to the Lawson trading established in the Commercial Code (HGB, §§ 48–58, 341e–341h, 343–372, 84-92c, 346, 778–900). Codified statutes apart reinsurance law is also determined by reinsurance practice and market usage.

3.4.10.3 Applicability

Contrary to the UNCITRAL Model Law, the Act is applicable to all arbitrations with a German seat, whether national or international. Similarly, the commercial requirement of Article 1 (1) has been expanded by reference to a broad concept of arbitrability, consistent with—and indeed, in some respects even broader than—the general freedom of parties to determine their rights with regard to one another.

Essentially, all claims are arbitrable to the extent they are assessable in financial terms ("vermögensrechtlich") or, where not, they fall within the scope of such rights as the parties are able to determine themselves as a matter of law (§ 1030 of the Code of Civil Procedure/Zivilprozessordnung).

3.4.10.4 Formal Requirements

The formal requirements for the validity of an arbitration agreement are relaxed as against the Model Law, allowing in particular for deemed assent by silence (§ 1031 II of the Code of Civil Procedure/Zivilprozessordung).

3.4.10.5 Constitution of Tribunal

A party may apply to the court (within a very short timeframe) if disadvantaged by the preponderant rights of another party in constituting the tribunal (§ 1034 II of the Code of Civil Procedure/Zivilprozessordnung).

3.4.10.6 Judicial Support and Control

One very important aspect of the German Arbitration Act is the extent and nature of judicial support and control of the arbitral process. In common with the UNCITRAL Model Law, the court may not intervene save where provided by the Act (§ 1026 of the Code of Civil Procedure/Zivilprozessordnung).

As a rule, this function has been given to the regional Courts of Appeal (*Oberlandesgerichte*). In normal civil procedure, these would be the courts of second instance, only one step below the Federal Supreme Court (*Bundesgerichtshof*). The allocation of most of the court functions under the Arbitration Act to this small number of higher level courts was expressly with the objects of concentrating competence in a small number of tribunals and of shortening the available appeal process.

From the perspective of a Common Law lawyer, used to concentration of arbitration applications in the Commercial (and in certain cases in the Technology & Construction) Courts in London, and in practice even on a very few individual judges, the allocation of arbitration business on a regional rather than a centralised basis even to this high level of court is an apparent disadvantage.[114]

By German standards, however, the concentration of arbitration business on what is a very high level of court was a significant concession in itself. In Bavaria and Rheinland-Pfalz, this concentration has gone further, with all arbitration business allocated in the former case to the Bavarian Supreme Court of Justice (*Bayerisches Oberstes Landesgericht*) and in the latter to a single "senate" of the Court of Appeal in Koblenz.

The German Arbitration Act in fact allows for an even further concentration by agreement between different states, but while this would be desirable from the point of view of promoting Germany internationally, it is difficult to imagine it happening in practice.

In any event, there has largely been a consistent and favourable application of arbitral law between the various regional Courts of Appeal. In a provision aimed at speeded up applications to the court, the procedure allows for a decision to be made without an oral hearing.

One sensible and helpful exception to the concentration of business in the regional Courts of Appeal is that applications for judicial assistance to the arbitral process (by or with the consent of the tribunal) are to be made to the lowest suitable level of court, equivalent to the English County Courts (*Amtsgerichte*). This has benefits to a party to international arbitration. First, appearance before such courts requires no German qualification, so it is available to foreign counsel.

Secondly, it is informal and quick. In a further departure from the Model Law, court assistance is not restricted to the taking of evidence but extends to other judicial acts such as service of process (§ 1050 of the Code of Civil Procedure/ Zivilprozessordnung).[115]

Finally, the German Arbitration Act contains some additional provisions in relation to interim measures (§ 1041 II of the Code of Civil Procedure/Zivilprozessordnung). In particular, the court may "recast" an interim measure of a tribunal if necessary for the purposes of enforcement. There is also express provision for mandatory compensation to an injured party who has been subjected to a wrongfully obtained interim measure.

3.4.10.7 Choice of Law

In another departure from the UNCITRAL Model Law, the German Arbitration Act provides that, where the parties have not chosen an applicable substantive law, the tribunal shall apply the law of the state with which the subject-matter of the proceedings is most closely connected (a rather simplified version of the Rome Convention, § 1051 II of the Code of Civil Procedure/Zivilprozessordnung).

---

[114] Hunter (2003), pp. 155, 158.

[115] Hunter (2003), pp. 155, 159.

3.4.10.8 Majority Decision

The German Arbitration Act provides a sensible amendment to the effect that, where an arbitrator refuses to take part in a decision, the other arbitrators may make the decision without him unless the parties have agreed otherwise (§ 1052 II of the Code of Civil Procedure/Zivilprozessordnung).

3.4.10.9 Saving of Arbitration Agreement

In a further departure from the UNCITRAL Model Law designed to deal directly with what was previously regarded as a serious defect of German law, the German Arbitration Act provides that, in the case of a successful challenge to an arbitral award, the arbitration agreement becomes again operative unless the parties have agreed otherwise (§ 1059 V of the Code of Civil Procedure/Zivilprozessordnung).

3.4.10.10 Costs

There is a new provision expressly conferring jurisdiction on the tribunal to allocate costs between the parties taking into consideration all the circumstances, in particular the outcome. The section also allows the tribunal to make a separate award on costs after the termination of the arbitral proceedings (§ 1057 of the Civil Procedure/Zivilprozessordnung).

3.4.10.11 Finality

In common with the UNCITRAL Model Law, there is no provision for an appeal on the merits. Also in common with the UNCITRAL Model Law, the time for setting aside an award is limited to 3 months from receipt of the award. However, the German Arbitration Act contains stricter provisions than the UNCITRAL Model Law in this context where a request has been made to the tribunal for correction or interpretation of the award (§ 1059 III of the Civil Procedure/Zivilprozessordnung). In what must be regarded as a particularly "pro-arbitration" departure from the Model Law "domestic" awards (i.e. awards made in a German seat arbitration) have the same effect between the parties as a final judgment of the court (§ 1060, 1055 of the Code of Civil Procedure/Zivilprozessordnung). "Foreign" awards are enforceable much as one would expect, consistent with the New York Convention. Additionally, the German Arbitration Act provides for a provisional, *ex parte* procedure.

3.4.10.12 Application of the New Law in Practice

The application of the German Arbitration Act by the German courts has on the whole been supportive of arbitration.

3.4.10.13 Validity of Arbitration Clause

In a dispute concerning a poorly drafted clause, evidence was given that whereas one party had intended to introduce a phrase so as to *retain* the jurisdiction of the state courts, the other party had interpreted the same words as excluding such jurisdiction. The court held that this latter was the only interpretation which made sense and that the court proceedings should accordingly be dismissed in favour of arbitration.[116] In another decision, the Bundesgerichtshof rejected a challenge to the validity of an arbitration agreement which provided for a choice between two alternative tribunals.[117] There is, however, one decision which appears out-of-line with international practice. The Bundesgerichtshof decided that aclaimant's impecuniosity was a ground of "impossibility of performance" of the arbitration agreement and refused to dismiss court proceedings.[118] However, this decision was in a small domestic dispute and it is to be hoped that the decision would be different in a case involving international parties.[119]

3.4.10.14 Public Policy

German courts interpret the public policy ground of challenge restrictively (§ 1059 II No. 2(b) of the Code of Civil Procedure/Zivilprozessordnung). In a decision concerning the enforcement of an English Award,[120] the Bundesgerichtshof rejected a challenge to recognition and enforcement on two grounds. First, since the applicant had had the opportunity to invoke bias before the English state courts, there was no need for this issue to be raised before the German court. Secondly, an alternative ground of challenge (based upon § 826 of the Civil Code/Bürgerliches Gesetzbuch, and therefore a substantive rather than a procedural right to challenge the enforceability of a judgment under German law), was held to be inapplicable as the merits of the case were governed by material law of England and a notion similar to the substantive right under the Civil Code did not exist in English law.[121]

---

[116] *OLG Stuttgart*, judgment of 27.7.2001, 4 U 251/00.

[117] *BGH*, decision of 30.1.2003, III ZB 6/02.

[118] *BGH*, NJW 2000, 3720 et seq.

[119] Hunter (2003), pp. 155, 159.

[120] *BGH*, decision of 1.2.2001. III ZR 332/99.

[121] Hunter (2003), p. 160.

3.4.10.15 Enforcement

In a decision on Article IV of the New York Convention, the Federal Supreme Court held that where the existence and the authenticity of the arbitral award were undisputed, it would be a mere technicality ("leere Förmelei") to insist on the original award being produced, reducing this requirement of Article IV to an evidential rather than a substantive rule.[122]

Similarly, the Bayerische Oberstes Landesgericht held that the requirement of Article IV § 2 of the New York Convention that a translation of the award into German must be submitted was not a requirement for the admissibility of the application for enforcement in Germany, since the Arbitration Act contained a more favourable provision than the New York Convention (§ 1064 III of the Code of Civil Procedure/Zivilprozessordnung).[123]

3.4.10.16 Judicial Appointment

In reaching a decision in 2001 concerning the release of a state judge to act as arbitrator in a private dispute, the Administrative Court in Frankfurt recognised the legislative aim of encouraging arbitration as an alternative means of dispute resolution, and thereby increasing the attractiveness of Germany as a place of international trade and relieving the burden on the state courts, as being in the public interest.[124]

3.4.11 Arbitrating in Germany in Practice

German law, both in legislation and in jurisprudence, provides a satisfactory procedural environment for the conduct of an international arbitration. One may wonder if this equally applies to arbitration procedure in practice.

As would be expected, and in conformity with the UNCITRAL Model Law, the parties are in general free to determine the procedure themselves and, failing such agreement, the arbitral tribunal may conduct the arbitration in such manner as it considers appropriate (§ 1042 III, IV of the Code of Civil Procedure/Zivilprozessordnung).

The question arises whether, within such freedom and perhaps even as a result of it, the choice of a German seat will in practice determine a particular type of procedure which might be unfamiliar to an Anglo-Saxon party. It is impossible to lay down any hard and fast rules in this respect: the procedure in any particular

[122] *BGH*, decision of 17.8.2000, III ZB 43/99, and *OLG Köln*, decision of 27.3.2001, 9 Sch 06/01.

[123] *BayObLG*, decision of 11.8.2000, 4 Z Sch 05/00.

[124] *VG Frankfurt*, decision of 12.11.2001, 9 E 5148/00(1).

arbitration depends very heavily upon the particular parties and the particular tribunal, and having a seat in Germany does not prescribe any particular combination of parties or tribunal. An interesting starting-point is to ask whether the determination of a German seat brings with it the legitimate expectation or presumption of a particular procedure which the tribunal (whether German or not) is bound to follow. For instance: "Given the fact that parties must deliberately opt into German law, it would be odd not to include the basic principles underlying German civil practice. Thereby, the parties by choosing Germany as a seat should be considered to have chosen continental-style procedure, but this is refutable."[125] The question whether and, if so, by reference to what criteria, such a presumption should be taken to have been made in relation to any seat is beyond the scope of this article. Irrespective of this question in theory, however, the choice of a German seat (as with any seat) is likely in practice to be reflected to some extent in certain procedural tendencies, manifesting the underlying culture. The following is a summary of the kind of points which might be encountered.[126]

3.4.11.1 "Inquisitorial" Versus "Adversarial"

The traditional contrast between what are often called the "adversarial" aspects of Anglo-Saxon proceedings and the "inquisitorial" style of civil proceedings is exaggerated.

It is certainly the case that the respective roles of the judge and the advocate vary between the two generic legal cultures. For instance, a witness before a German court would generally be called and questioned directly by the judge and there would be little (although often some) cross-examination.

Similarly, there will tend to be a lesser degree of preparation of evidence for trial in Germany in terms of factual witnesses, expert reports or disclosure and a greater emphasis on and judicial control over what evidence is relevant and therefore admissible.[127]

However, contrary to a common misconception among Common law lawyers, the burden of introducing the facts and circumstances of a case in Germany is on the parties and not the court, just as in Anglo-Saxon procedure. To this extent, both procedures are at their heart adversarial.

Moreover, in international arbitration, the presentation of factual evidence is in practice—in Germany as in England—now very commonly made in the form of the delivery of witness statements by the parties in advance of the hearing and by direct examination, cross-examination and re-examination by the parties' counsel.

Where it may differ from traditional common law procedure in practice, is[128]: (a) in that the tribunal will have limited patience with protracted or aggressive

---

125 Hunter (2003), p. 160.

126 Hunter (2003), p. 160.

127 Hunter (2003), p. 160.

128 Hunter (2003), p. 161.

cross-examination, (b) the tribunal will generally allow considerable freedom with the scope of re-examination and re-re-examination, (c) in that in German civil procedure a party may not be a witness. Experienced arbitral tribunals in Germany, as elsewhere, will ignore this distinction. A trace of it may sometimes be detected in the background in the form of an apparently greater distrust of party witnesses. For instance, it is not uncommon for factual witnesses to be excluded from the hearing room until they have delivered their evidence: to an English lawyer, this would usually only be directed where dishonesty has been alleged, (d) in that while verbatim transcripts are now fairly common, the German judicial practice of recording the gist of factual evidence in the form of a summary dictated by the tribunal is also sometimes followed.

A distinction can also appear in the field of expert evidence. In German civil procedure, expert evidence is given by tribunal-appointed experts. Party-appointed experts will often be allowed in arbitration but their reports will generally be treated as party submissions and not as evidence. However, in reality, there is little if any real difference in the weight attached to it. Provided an Anglo-Saxon lawyer is aware of the possible existence of such differences when approaching the directions hearing, none of them will prove to be an obstacle in practice and one can confidently expect a procedure that accords with the expectations of efficient international practice.

3.4.11.2 Discovery

In German civil practice, there is no procedural duty for a party to participate in investigating the facts of the case and there is in general terms no such thing as discovery.

Since 1 January 2002 the revised § 142 of the ZPO enables a court to order disclosure from a party or a third party. There has been much discussion about the implications of this section and whether, as against parties, it even extends at all the rules from those limited provisions which existed before.

Certainly, it would be wrong to compare this in any way to US-style pre-trial disclosure, but the provision at least demonstrates some willingness to proceed along a road previously treated as an abomination of common law procedure.

Discovery must in any event be seen in the context of the fact that a German court has no power to sanction a party for non-compliance, except in the limited and formal sense that the non-compliance itself can be regarded as circumstantial evidence and that the party can be precluded from submitting the same document later.

No additional power is given to a Court by the German Arbitration Act to exercise any greater authority in the context of arbitral proceedings. Moreover, the Act contains a qualification to the corresponding provision in the UNCITRAL

Model Law, expressly allowing the court to decline a request for court assistance as "inadmissible", a modification made intentionally to exclude USA-style applications for disclosure.

In practice, the tribunal may very well allow an application for disclosure of a particular document or class of document and certainly has power to do so (§ 1042 IV).

However, it can be assumed that there will be a strong prejudice against extensive or "train of enquiry" discovery exercises and applications for such may well be considered inadmissible in the absence of the agreement of both parties.

Contrary to the perception of many German lawyers, this differs little from the USA courts' attitude to pre-trial discovery in arbitration[25], although it is fair to say that this view is not always shared by Anglo-Saxon counsel.

In any event, an acceptable compromise has been found in the form of the IBA Rules on the Taking of Evidence in International Commercial Arbitration and these Rules are very often referred to as a guide to accepted international practice.

The general principle of the Rules is that, consistent with efficiency and economy in the taking of evidence in general, the burden is on each party to produce in advance the evidence on which it intends to rely and there will be only limited and specific disclosure in addition. This creates an efficient dynamic and also reflects the more informal and consensual context of international arbitration and the practical limitations of the tribunal's powers.

In this context, and in the context of admissibility of evidence generally, English practitioners should be conscious of the fact that, under German law (in common with most other civil laws), there is no holistic concept as such of either privilege or without prejudice save in the rather limited sphere of an attorneys (and some other professionals) duty of confidentiality to his client and his corresponding right not to give evidence of such matters in court.

Given the general absence of a broad discovery procedure and of any power of enforcement, this is rarely likely to arise as an issue save in relation to the specific but nonetheless important areas of undesired disclosure in relation to settlement offers, mediators, and illegally obtained evidence.[129]

Here again a working compromise is likely to be found, not least by reference to the IBA Rules. Nevertheless, it is a field where a broader jurisprudence in international disputes is desirable.

3.4.11.3 Costs

Differences in relation to costs may arise in one of three ways.

First, while there is a similar presumption, although less strong than in England, that costs (both those of the tribunal and of legal representation) will be awarded to the winner, the means of assessment may well be different.

[129] Hunter (2003), p. 161.

An arbitration tribunal has flexibility to award costs as it deems fit. However, whereas an English practitioner would expect costs to be awarded by reference to success or failure on issues and limited by some concept of reasonableness, the expectation of a German lawyer will be for costs to be awarded by reference to the proportion the damages and other remedies actually awarded holds to the original claims.

It should therefore obviously not be assumed that the English practice will prevail. This should be borne in mind particularly when issuing a claim or counterclaim, as exaggeration of the amount when formulating the claim may well have an adverse costs impact later irrespective of the amount of costs objectively tied to the time spent arguing the particular issue.

Secondly, before state courts, German lawyers are bound by a statutory regulation to charge a minimum fee, and this is still quite often applied to fix the actual remuneration in litigation save in larger commercial cases, not least as it also fixes the maximum fees recoverable by one party from another in litigation.

As mentioned above, as a matter of law the application of scale fees to counsel's representation in international arbitration is determined not by the seat of the arbitration but by reference to where the relevant counsel has his seat of practice and it should therefore not be a factor in a choice of seat. Moreover, it is generally thought that it can be avoided in the case of an international arbitration by means of an express choice of foreign law governing the lawyer's retainer. However, it would be better if this were expressly regulated.

Thirdly, there is no formal equivalent in German procedure of a sealed offer common under English law. The nearest equivalent is a formal acknowledgement of a claim or a part of it but, since this acts both as a conclusive determination of that element of liability and is therefore also directly admissible in evidence, it lacks the tactical element of the English offer, the more so where costs are assessed by relation to sums awarded and not time spent.

Combined with the lack of rules concerning "without prejudice" correspondence, this can complicate seeking protection for a respondent's position. The lack of such protection is substantially offset if costs are awarded in the German manner by reference to sums awarded as a proportion of claims asserted.[130]

3.4.11.4 Res Judicata/Jura Novit Curia

A technical but nonetheless potentially important distinction between Anglo-Saxon and German procedure relates to the parallel concepts of *res judicata* and *jura novit curia*.

In normal procedure, since there is a presumption that the judge knows the law, the definition of a claim and the relief sought (i.e. the financial or other remedy) is sufficient.

[130] Hunter (2003), p. 162.

Hence, the burden on a party to plead its case is limited to the requirement to bring all the facts upon which the claim is brought before the tribunal and it is not necessary to plead the particular causes of action as an English lawyer would understand the expression.

Consistent with that, too, the theory of *res judicata* and issue estoppel is narrower than would be the case in common law. The *res judicata* is strictly limited to the operative part of the court judgment (i.e. the particular order for relief) and does not extend to its reasoning.

Therefore, if a party claims a debt due or other performance due under a contract, the parties in a subsequent action are not estopped from arguing the existence or validity of the contract, but only from denying the finding in relation to the particular claim.

Since § 1055 of the Code of Civil procedure/Zivilprozessordnung stipulates that an arbitral award has the same effect between the parties as a judgment, it follows that the effect of an award in *res judicata* is also the same as that of a court judgment.

The potential significance of this may arise in two respects: (a) provided the facts have been stated sufficiently, there can be what seems to an English lawyer to be a lack of specificity with regard to the formulation of a cause of action in the early stages, and there is equally little scope for raising issues of costs or jurisdiction in relation to amendments or the manner of pleading. This might be said to correspond in any event to the generally more informal and procedurally less technical nature of arbitration proceedings internationally, and (b) in that adverse findings of fact in the body of an award are normally not binding as *res judicata* in future proceedings, although they can certainly be expected to be prejudicial[28].

In practice, as with so many theoretical distinctions of this nature, this is rarely likely to be of any relevance and in the context of the lack of any form of revision au fond it may in any event be considered preferable on the rare occasions when it is.[131]

3.4.11.5 Settlement

One area where litigation practice is significantly different between Germany and England is the role of the judge in the context of settlement. Under the civil procedure rules, a judge has a duty to endeavour to achieve settlement between the parties. This commonly takes the form of the judge addressing both parties at the first procedural hearing, warning them of the risks and costs of litigation and indicating particular weaknesses in their cases. This duty has not been carried forward into the German Arbitration Act, although it does feature in § 32.1 of the DIS Arbitration Rules.

[131] Hunter (2003), p. 162.

It will be evident perhaps in a greater willingness on the part of a German tribunal to become involved in settlement, and in particular to indicate an initial view of the strengths and weaknesses of the parties' positions. This will only ever be done with the express consent of the parties but, contrary to English experience, a tribunal's offer to do this would be regarded as a normal and acceptable part of its function and there may therefore be a greater cultural pressure to accept it. Again, this may be said to conform to a general tendency of judicial encouragement to settlement even in common law jurisdictions.

3.4.11.6 Critique

Germany is very well placed to become an important place of international arbitration, in terms both of seat and more generally of a concentration of expertise. The principal obstacle to this process is subjective (perception) rather than objective. The adoption of the UNCITRAL Model Law is an important step in effecting the necessary transition and the impact of this over the long term could be considerable. Provided Germany now applies—and is seen to apply—the UNCITRAL Model Law in a coherent and sensible way, Germany will almost inevitably become one of the leading sources of jurisprudence in international commercial arbitration. This will in turn breed familiarity, transparency and reassurance to international users and a greater willingness to accept it as a neutral seat.

Leaving aside the question of disqualification as a neutral forum arising from the fact of the high number of German parties, there are also other strong objective criteria by reference to which it can confidently be predicted that Germany will become a leading international seat and centre of international arbitration expertise. The eastward expansion of the European Union will favour Germany in this, as also Germany's position, both geographically and culturally, in the centre of Europe.[132] It would be foolish to pretend that arbitration under a German (or, indeed, any "civil law" seat) does not sometimes present unfamiliarities and challenges to a common law lawyer. However, it would certainly be wrong to conclude from this that the differences result in an inferior form of process.

For one thing, none of the cultural differences summarised above, would be regarded as surprising elements of an arbitration by a "civil law" lawyer, and they will be largely familiar to most "common law" lawyers experienced in international proceedings. Indeed, apart from the possible application of the fixed costs provisions, all these different aspects, are likely to be encountered to at least some extent in any international arbitration with a significant civil law content.

It is certainly not the case that they are any more likely to occur, or likely to be any more strongly applied, in a German seat, than an arbitration in any of the main "civil law" seats. Secondly, suitably adjusted to an international environment, many of these differences, particularly those regarding evidence and disclosure, should

[132] Hunter (2003), p. 163.

properly be regarded as consistent with the trend of the norms of best practice in international arbitration.

There are nonetheless areas where improvements could be made, not least to assist in changing historic perceptions and to provide an impetus to change. Among these are a greater concentration of arbitration business in single senates of the Regional Courts of Appeal, ideally even across State boundaries, and a dialogue between the judiciary and practitioners to ensure transparency and responsiveness to the needs of international arbitration practitioners; the development of an holistic theory of admissibility to protect privilege and without prejudice to match the gradual acceptance of targeted disclosure; and the amendment of the regulations regarding the fixed scales of remuneration to allow complete and unequivocal freedom in the sphere of international arbitration. None of these should be seen as determinative factors in the choice of seat, but they are nonetheless important in terms of external perception. In the meantime, there are strong objective reasons why Germany will continue to increase in importance both as a seat and as a centre for international arbitration practice.[133]

3.5 Overall Conclusions

Arbitration clauses are commonly used in reinsurance contracts as well as frequently opted for by parties. Courts will require that reinsurance claim disputes be arbitrated if the parties had agreed in writing to arbitrate the dispute; however, a lot will also depend on the scope of the arbitration clause. Arbitration also enables parties to a reinsurance contract to have disputes determined by a tribunal expert in that business sector. Having said all of the above, it should be noted that no law detects reinsurance disputes to be arbitrated, and certain reinsurers, particularly facultative reinsurers, will prefer to litigate. In addition, parties to arbitration agreements may waive the right to arbitrate. However, in most cases where a reinsurance contract contains an arbitration clause, the clause is likely to be found valid and enforceable if it was consented to by the cedent and the reinsurer. One pertinent need for inserting arbitration clauses into reinsurance agreements is the hope that disputes will be resolved quickly and efficiently. However, practically speaking, at times the process has been less streamlined than originally envisioned, because cedents and reinsurers have turned to the courts to litigate about certain issues pertinent to the reinsurance arbitration proceedings. This, nevertheless, does not underestimate the value of arbitration in reinsurance. Cedent companies and reinsurers may draft arbitration clauses as they desire and there is no standard or typical arbitration clause. Another very important reason why parties to a reinsurance contract resort to arbitration is the fact that awards commonly remain

[133] Hunter (2003). Arbitration in Germany—A Common Law Perspective, SchiedsVZ Heft 4, 155. 162.

unpublished and are consequently only known and accessible to the parties involved.

An agreement to refer to arbitration any disputes arising out of a reinsurance contract may be included in the contract, or in a separate agreement. The English Arbitration Act 1996 only applies where the arbitration agreement is in writing. In the USA, the FAA enables and favours arbitration. The FAA applies to arbitrations arising from transactions that affect interstate or international commerce, and encapsulates a policy in favour of arbitration. The German Arbitration Act regulates arbitration and is contained in the Tenth Book of the ZPO. Consistent with the federal policy favouring arbitration, reinsurance disputes will be primarily arbitrated where parties have agreed so. In Germany reinsurance arbitration is also widely used. Not least, Germany's adoption of the UNCITRAL Model Law on International Commercial Arbitration together with a body of case-law strongly favouring arbitration and a growing body of expertise constitute objective reasons which promote the choice of a German seat in arbitrations.

References

Barlow Lyde and Gilbert LLP (2009) Reinsurance practice and the law. Informa, London
Bank JF, Winters P (1989) Reinsurance arbitration: a U.S. perspective. J Ins Reg 7:323
Bradley CAJ, Goldsmith JL (1999) Customary international law as federal common law: a critique of the modern position. Harv Law Rev 110:815
Brown RH, Reed PB (1981) Marine reinsurance. Witherby & Co, London
Craig WL, Park WW, Paulsson J (2000) International chamber of commerce arbitration, 3rd edn. Oceana Pubn Incorporated, Dobbs Ferry
Geiger H (2000) The comparative law and economics of reinsurance. Nomos Verlagsgesellschaft, Baden-Baden
Hammesfahr RW, Wright SW (1994) The law of reinsurance claims. Andrews Professional Books, Westtown
Hummer P (1996) Reinsurance arbitrations from start to finish: a practitioner's guide. Def Couns 63:228–236
Hunter R (2003) Arbitration in Germany – a common law perspective. SchiedsVZ Heft 4:155
Murphy JL (2008) Law triangle: arbitrating international reinsurance disputes under the New York convention, the McCarran-Ferguson Act, and Antagonistic State Law. Vand J Transnatl Law 41:1542
Ostrager BR, Vyskocil MC (1996) Modern reinsurance law and practice. Glasser Legal Works, Little Falls
Posner EA (1999) Arbitration and the harmonization of international commercial law: a defense of Mitsubishi. Va J Int Law 39:647
Scorey D, Geddes R, Harris C (2011) The Bermuda form. OUP, Oxford
Tagvoryan A (2005) A secret in one district is no secret in another: the cases of Merril Lynch and preliminary injunctions under the FAA. Pepp Disp Resolut Law J 6:147
Thomas JE et al (eds) (2011) New Appleman insurance law practice guide, vol 4, Separate lines of insurance. Lexis Nexis, Los Angeles

The Reinsurance Arbitration Clause

Arbitration clauses are widely used in reinsurance contracts. Such clauses are drawn by parties as they desire, i.e. either narrowly or broadly. A narrowly drawn arbitration clause will render only the specific issues within its scope arbitrable. Broadly-worded arbitration clauses will also normally be construed to encompass extra-contractual claims. Arbitration clauses contained in reinsurance agreements, entail that any arising dispute will be sought to be resolved by arbitration. Although it could be argued that there is no difference between litigation and arbitration—in the sense that in each proceeding a neutral third party decides the dispute between the parties and issues a binding decision—procedurally there are dramatic differences. However, any doubt concerning the scope of arbitrable issues should be resolved in favour of arbitration. Case law demonstrates the tendency to support the conclusion of the existence of the intent to arbitrate, in simple phrases purporting so. The importance of the arbitration panel's qualifications and the process of selecting an arbitrator and umpire are matters of great concern in any arbitration. Parties choose to arbitrate reinsurance disputes for reasons such as—*inter alia*—to avail themselves of the arbitrators' knowledge of industry custom and practice because, often, judges are unlikely to possess more than a cursory understanding of the customs and practices of the insurance/reinsurance industry.

4.1 Introductory Remarks

Many reinsurance contracts, particularly reinsurance treaties, contain arbitration clauses.

Arbitration provides parties with an opportunity to submit disputes to a panel of industry experts under a process which is, at least in theory, less time-consuming, less expensive and less disruptive than traditional litigation.

K. Noussia, *Reinsurance Arbitrations*, DOI 10.1007/978-3-642-45146-1_4,

Arbitration can be the means by which cedents and reinsurers obtain a fair and expeditious resolution of disputes based on the arbitrators' knowledge of industry custom and practice without the restrictions imposed by the judicial system.[1]

Reinsurance arbitrations are generally commenced when one party demands arbitration in writing, identifying the parties, the contracts at issue, the nature of the claims and issues involved and sometimes specifying the petitioning party's arbitrator and enclosing his or her curriculum vitae. An arbitration agreement may specify the information that must be included in the arbitration demands. In response the opposing party should identify the contact person for all communications, its appointed arbitrator, enclosing his or her curriculum vitae and any claims by the opposing party.[2]

4.1.1 The Arbitration Clause

A threshold determination for any dispute that arises between a cedent and reinsurer is whether the dispute falls within the scope of an arbitration clause contained in the applicable reinsurance contract.

The Supreme Court has held that the business of insurance is commerce and, therefore, that interstate insurance transactions (including, by implication, interstate reinsurance transactions) constitute interstate commerce subject to federal Substantive law.[3]

Accordingly, the enforceability of arbitration clauses contained in reinsurance contracts arising from interstate transactions is governed by the FAA,[4]

The FAA pre-empts state law, and the state courts may not apply state statutes that invalidate arbitration.[5]

The FAA empowers district courts to order parties to an arbitration agreement to submit to arbitration.[6] The FAA reflects "an emphatic federal policy in favor of arbitral dispute resolution."[7] It requires that district courts shall order that parties

[1] Ostrager and Vyskocil (1996), pp. 14-01, 14-03.

[2] Thomas and Lyons (2012), pp. 77-43, 77-44.

[3] *United States v South-Eastern Underwriters Ass'n*, 322 U.S. 533 (1944). *Hart v Orion Ins. Co.*, 453 F.2d 1358 (10th Cir. 1971); Ostrager and Vyskocil (1996), §§ 14-01, 14-04.

[4] 9 U.S.C. § 1, *et seq*; *Vimar Seguros Y Reaseguros, S.A. v M/V Sky Reefer*, 115 S. Ct. 2322, 2329 (1995) (*citing Allied Bruce Termine* v Dobson*, 115 S. Ct. 834 (1995)); Ostrager and Vyskocil (1996), §§ 14-01, 14-04.

[5] Ostrager and Vyskocil (1996), pp. 14-01, 14-04.

[6] US—9 U.S.C. § 4; *Volt Information Sciences v Board of Trustees*, 489 U.S. 468, 478 (1989) (the FAA "requires courts to enforce privately negotiated agreements to arbitrate, like other contracts, in accordance with their terms"); Thomas and Lyons (2012), pp. 77-43, 77-44, 77-46.

[7] *Mitsubishi Motors Corp. v Soler Chrysler-Plymouth, Inc.*, 473 U.S. 614, 631 (1985); Thomas and Lyons (2012), pp. 77-43, 77-44, 77-46.

arbitrate issues within the scope of an arbitration agreement.[8] The FAA does not create an independent basis for federal subject matter jurisdiction. Therefore, an independent basis for subject matter jurisdiction must exist in order for a federal court to entertain a petition to compel arbitration.[9] In a domestic arbitration, a federal court has the power to compel arbitration only within the district in which it is located.[10] By contrast, in an arbitration proceeding subject to the New York Convention,[11] a federal court has the power to compel arbitration outside of the district in which it is located. Parties are also deemed to consent to personal jurisdiction when they agree to arbitrate a dispute in a particular jurisdiction.[12]

Relying upon the congressional mandate contained in the FAA, in *Moses H. Cone Memorial Hosp. v. Mercury Constr. Corp.*,[13] the Supreme Court clarified that any doubts concerning the scope of arbitrable issues should be resolved in favour of arbitration, whether the problem at hand is the construction of the contract language itself or an allegation of waiver, delay, or a like defence to arbitrability.[14]

[8] *KPMG LLP v Cocchi*, No. 10-1521, 2011 U.S. LEXIS 7924, at *6 (U.S. Nov. 7, 2011); *AT&T Technologies, Inc. v Communications Workers of America*, 475 U.S. 643, 650 (1986) (there is a presumption of arbitrability "unless it may be said with positive assurance that the arbitration clause is not susceptible of an interpretation that covers the asserted dispute"); Under the FAA, courts may only decide "certain gateway matters, such as whether the parties have a valid arbitration agreement at all or whether a concededly binding arbitration clause applies to a certain type of controversy."; *Howsam v Dean Witter Reynolds, Inc.*, 537 U.S. 79 (2002); Thomas and Lyons (2012), pp. 77-43, 77-44, 77-46.

[9] *Serv. Partners, LLC v Am. Home Assur. Co.*, No. CV-11-01858-CAS(Ex), 2011 U.S. Dist. LEXIS 67207, at *5 n.2 (CD. Cal. June 20, 2011) (federal subject matter jurisdiction existed because of diversity of citizenship under 28 U.S.C. § 1332); Thomas and Lyons (2012), pp. 77-43, 77-44, 77-46.

[10] *Federated Rural Elec. Ins. Co. v Nationwide Mut. Ins. Co.*, 874 F. Supp. 1204, 1210 (D. Kan. 1995).

[11] Convention on the Recognition and Enforcement of Foreign Arbitral Awards (New York, 1958).

[12] *Unionmutual Stock Life Ins. Co. of Am. v Beneficial Life Ins. Co.*, 774 F.2d 524, 527 (1st Cir. 1985) ("When Beneficial agreed to arbitrate in Portland, Maine, and agreed that Maine law would govern the contract, it impliedly consented to the personal jurisdiction of Maine courts."); *Hamilton Life Ins. Co. v Republic Nat'l Ins. Co.*, 408 F.2d 606 (2d Cir. 1969). Similar to courts' analyses of parties' selection of choice of law, *see* Section 77.03[4] above, courts may refuse to enforce parties' choice of forum if found to be unfair or unreasonable; *Unionmutual Stock Life Ins. Co. of Am. v Beneficial Life Ins. Co.*, 774 F.2d 524, 527 (1st Cir. 1985) (choice of forum not unreasonable because "the agreement to arbitrate in Portland, Maine was made between two commercially sophisticated insurance companies of equal bargaining power."); Thomas and Lyons (2012), pp. 77-43, 77-44, 77-46.

[13] *Moses H. Cone Memorial Hosp. v Mercury Constr. Corp.*, 460 U.S.1, 24–25 (1983).

[14] *Shearson/American Express v McMahon*, 482 U.S. 220 (1987); *Mitsubishi Motors Corp. v Soler Chrysler-Plymoutb, Inc.*, 473 U.S. 614, 626 (1985); *Southland Corp. v Keating*, 465 U.S. 1 (1984); *First Options of Chicago, Inc. v Kaplan*, 115 S. Ct. 1920, 1924 (1995) (courts should apply ordinary state-law contract principles when determining whether the parties agreed to arbitrate a certain matter); Ostrager and Vyskocil (1996), pp. 14-04, 14-05.

Thus, broadly-worded clauses that seemingly encompass all disputes relating to the contract will be given that effect.[15]

However, the policy favouring arbitration does not supplant the intent of the parties as the primary factor in determining the scope of an arbitration clause.[16]

A narrowly drawn arbitration clause will render only the specific issues within its scope arbitrable.[17] Thus, in *Associated Indemnity Corp. v Home Insurance Co.*,[18] where the arbitration clause stated that "[s]hould an irreconcilable difference of opinion arise as to the *Interpretation* of this contract, it is hereby mutually agreed that, as a condition precedent to any right of action hereunder, such difference shall be submitted to arbitration",[19] the Sixth Circuit upheld the district court's denial of a motion to compel arbitration because there was no dispute over interpretation of the contract language.[20]

An arbitration clause may be incorporated by reference into other agreements, binding non-parties to the original agreement, provided that the clause is not restrictively worded.[21]

Typically, arbitration clauses in reinsurance contracts are phrased broadly enough to encompass any disputes involving the interpretation of the contract and the parties' rights thereunder.

In *Selcke v New England Insurance Co.*,[22] the Seventh Circuit held that the interpretation and enforcement of implied contract terms were arbitrable. *Selcke v New England Insurance Co.*[23] involved a setoff claim premised on a provision of the Illinois insolvency statute. The court applied the rule of Illinois law that statutory provisions in existence at the time of contracting formed a part of the contract in holding that the set-off claim was arbitrable.[24]

---

[15] *AT&T Technologies, Inc. v Communications Workers of America*, 475 U.S.643, 650 (1986).

[16] *S.A. Mineracao da Trindade Samitri v Utab, Int'l, Inc.*, 745 F.2d 190, 193 (2d Cir. 1984). Futter v Guthrie, 565 F.2d 259, 261 (2d Cir. 1977); *Lukens Steel Co. v United Steelworkers of Am. (AFL-CIO)*, 989 F.2d 668, 672 (3d Cir. 1993) [quoting *F. Harkins Co. v Waldinger Corp.*, 796 F.2d 657, 660 (3d Cir. 1986), cert. denied, 479 U.S. 1059 (1987)]. *Shearson Lehman Hutton, Inc. v Wagoner*, 944 E2d 114, 121 (2d Cir. 1991); *Seaboard Coast Line RR. Co. v Trailer Train Co.*, 690 F.2d 1343, 1352 (11th Cir. 1982). *Syufy Enterprises v North Cal State Ass'n ofl.AT.S.E Locals*, 631 E2d 124, 126 (9th Cir. 1980), cert. denied, 451 U.S. 983 (1981); *AfecdW S.PA. v Necchi Sewing Machine Sales Corp.*, 348 F.2d 693, 696 (2d Cir. 1965), cert. denied, 383 U.S. 909 (1966); Ostrager and Vyskocil (1996), pp. 14-01, 14-04, 14-05.

[17] *McDonnell Douglas Finance Corp. v Pennsylvania Power & Light Co.*, 858 E2d 825, 832 (2d Cir. 1988). *Associated Brich Mason Contractors of Greater N.Y, Inc. v Harrington*, 820 F.2d 31, 35 (2d Cir. 1987). *Prudential Lines, Inc. v Exxon Corp.*, 704 F.2d 59, 64 (2d Cir. 1983); Ostrager and Vyskocil (1996), pp. 14-01, 14-06, 14-07.

[18] *Associated Indemnity Corp. v Home Insurance Co.*, 19 F.3d 1432 (6th Cir. 1994).

[19] 19 F.3d at 1432 (emphasis added).

[20] Ostrager and Vyskocil (1996), pp. 14-01, 14-06, 14-07.

[21] *Progressive Casualty Ins. Co. v CA. Reaseguradora National de Venezuela*, 991 E2d 42 (2d Cir. 1993).

[22] *Selcke v New England Insurance Co.*, 995 F.2d 688 (7th Cir. 1993).

[23] *Selcke v New England Insurance Co.*, 995 F.2d 688 (7th Cir. 1993).

[24] 995 E2d at 689.

Broadly-worded arbitration clauses will also normally be construed to encompass extra-contractual Claims, such as fraud in the inducement.[25]

4.1.1.1 Can the Arbitration Clause Cover All Disputes?

The arbitrators' powers derive from the contract under which they are appointed.

In the past, the inclusion of an arbitration agreement within the written contract has given rise to the possibility that certain disputes apparently fall outside the ambit of the arbitrators' jurisdiction, irrespective of the width of the language of the arbitration agreement.

The logical proposition, simply stated, is that if there is something wrong with the contract whereby it can be rescinded or avoided, then as the arbitration clause forms part of the contract, it also must fall away.

Such restrictions obviously limit the effectiveness of arbitration agreements and, commencing with the landmark decision of *Heyman* v *Darwins Limited*,[26] the courts have attempted to overcome this logical difficulty by establishing the principle of separability.

The principle is based on the artifice that the arbitration agreement, even if incorporated with the main written contract, effectively constitutes a separate agreement and, in most circumstances, will stand independently of the main contract. It is as if the parties had entered into a separate arbitration agreement. The concept of separability only comes into consideration where the arbitration agreement forms part of an integrated written contract. If the arbitration agreement forms a separate written contract executed at the same time as the main contract or, as in the case of *ad hoc* arbitration agreements, it is entered into separately, either after the contract was concluded but before any dispute has arisen or after a dispute has arisen, there is very little which the arbitrator cannot decide.[27]

In *Heyman* v *Darwins Limited*,[28] the issue was whether the arbitrator had jurisdiction to decide whether the contract was brought to an end by an accepted repudiation. The House of Lords was unanimous in deciding this in the affirmative and, in doing so, initiated the principle of separability in English law.

Subsequent developments in the law have led to the scope of this principle being explored further and appreciated more clearly. Once the doctrine of separability is adopted, there is little logical reason to limit the type of dispute which can be

---

[25] *Prima Paint Corp.* v *Flood & Conklin Manufacturing Co.*, 388 U.S. 395.

[26] *Heyman* v *Darwins Limited* (1942) 72 Ll L Rep 65; Barlow Lyde and Gilbert LLP (2009), §§ 25.4.2, 25-8/2.

[27] Barlow Lyde and Gilbert LLP (2009), §§ 25.4.2, 25-8/2.

[28] *Heyman* v *Darwins Limited* (1942) 72 Ll L Rep 65; Barlow Lyde and Gilbert LLP (2009), §§ 25.4.2, 25-8/2.

determined by the arbitrators, provided that the arbitration clause itself is not directly impeached.[29]

Since *Heyman* v *Darwins Limited*,[30] the courts have gradually extended the ambit of the arbitrators' jurisdiction. Disputes as to the avoidance of contracts for innocent or negligent misrepresentation, undue influence, or duress might be referred to arbitration.

In *Mackenderv Feidia AG*,[31] the Court of Appeal had to decide the position in relation to a case where the contract was voidable. Specifically, the Court of Appeal considered whether an exclusive jurisdiction clause could be relied upon in the context of a contract of insurance which was alleged to have been avoided on the ground of material non-disclosure.

Lord Diplock stated that it is sometimes sought to assimilate the concept of the avoidance of a voidable contract with the concept of "non est factum" which prevents a contract ever coming into existence at all. He went on to state that it is often argued that innocent misrepresentation or, in the case of contracts of insurance, non-disclosure of material facts vitiates consent and makes the apparent consent of the party misled, no consent at all and that this is specious as what is really meant is that the party did in fact consent but would not have done so if he had known then what he knows now and that fraud may raise other considerations into which it is not necessary to go.[32]

In *Craig v National Indemnity Company*,[33] Lloyd J held the same reasoning applied to an arbitration clause.

The doctrine of separability was reviewed in its entirety by Steyn J and the Court of Appeal in *Harbour Assurance Company (UK) Limited* v *Kansa General International Insurance Company Limited & Others*.[34] The central issue in dispute concerned the alleged illegality of certain reinsurance contracts, and whether any such illegality had the effect of rendering the contracts in question void *ab initio*.

In this context, the court was required to consider whether the arbitration clause in each contract survived the allegation of initial illegality so that the Substantive dispute, i.e., whether the contracts actually were illegal, could be determined in arbitration.

It can be discerned from his judgment that Steyn J.'s sympathies lay with the defendants, who argued that the arbitration clauses survived the allegation. In considering this question, Steyn J. considered the objective of separability as a

---

[29] For example, if it were argued by one of the parties that he was induced by fraud to sign an agreement containing an arbitration clause believing it to be a different agreement.; Barlow Lyde and Gilbert LLP (2009), §§ 25.4.2, 25-9.

[30] *Heyman* v *Darwins Limited* (1942) 72 Ll L Rep 65; Barlow Lyde and Gilbert LLP (2009), §§ 25.4.2, 25-9.

[31] *Mackenderv. Feidia AG* [1967] 2 QB 590.

[32] Barlow Lyde and Gilbert LLP (2009), §§ 25.4.2, 25-9.

[33] *Craig v National Indemnity Company* (25 July 1980, unreported).

[34] *Harbour Assurance Company (UK) Limited* v *Kansa General International Insurance Company Limited & Others* [1992] 1 Lloyd's Rep 81 and [1993] 1 Lloyd's Rep 455.

whole and noted the increasing trend to develop the principle in different jurisdictions. He concluded that logically there is no obstacle to an arbitration agreement surviving the initial invalidity of a contract. He also concluded that disputes concerning fraud are capable of falling within the scope of an arbitration agreement and went on to further comment that, logically, now that the principle of separability is established, there should be nothing to prevent disputes as to initial illegality also being decided by the arbitrators. Further, he held that he was bound, however, by previous authority in the Court of Appeal, to hold that the separability principle does not extend to *ab initio* illegality of a contract.[35]

In the USA courts routinely exercise their power to compel arbitration in reinsurance disputes and have held that the words "arbitration" or "arbitration clause" in a reinsurance agreement suffice for an enforceable arbitration agreement when supplemented by reinsurance industry custom and practice.[36]

4.1.1.2 A Suggested Arbitration Clause

A typical reinsurance provision in reinsurance agreements provides for arbitration as an ADR method for any dispute or claim arising out of the said reinsurance agreement and stipulates the details of the arbitral proceedings, i.e. the way of initiating the arbitration, the place where arbitration shall be held, the consistency of the arbitral panel and the way of the appointment for the arbitral panel, the

[35] Barlow Lyde and Gilbert LLP (2009), §§ 25.4.2, 25-9, 25-10.

[36] *Guarantee Trust Life Ins. Co. v American United Life Ins. Co.*, No. 03 C 4250, 2003 U.S. Dist. LEXIS 22777, at *7 (N.D. 111. Dec. 18, 2003) (compelling arbitration where slip provided merely "arbitration clause"); *Zurich Am. Ins. Co. v Cebcor Serv. Corp.*, No. 02 C 2283, 2003 U.S. Dist. LEXIS 10346, at *6–7 (N.D. 111. June 16, 2003) (compelling arbitration where Reinsurance Cover Note provided for "arbitration"); *CNA Reinsurance Co. v Trustmark Ins. Co.*, No. 01 C 1652, 2001 U.S. Dist. LEXIS 7523 (N.D. 111. June 5, 2001); *Allianz Life Ins. Co. of N. Am. v American Phoenix Life & Reinsurance Co.*, No. 99–802, 2000 U.S. Dist. LEXIS 7216, at *12 (D. Minn. Mar. 28, 2000) (compelling arbitration, concluding that phrase "arbitration clause" in reinsurance placement slip constituted valid arbitration agreement where retrocedents provided substantial evidence that "'arbitration clause' is, standing alone, common language in reinsurance placement slips; that such slips are often the only formal manifestation of agreement between the parties to ongoing transactions; and that these words have a distinct meaning in the industry"); *Tulsa Gen. Ins. Agency, Inc. v CIGNA Reinsurance Co.*, No. 92-457-NJ (E.D. Okla. Feb. 12, 1993), 3 Mealey's Reins. Rpt. No 23 a B-2 (parties concluded valid arbitration agreement where signed placement slip provided "arbitration clause" even though reinsurer did not sign treaty that contained complete arbitration clause); See however, *Frank B. Hall Co. of Colo. v Colorado Sch. Dists. Self-Ins. Pool*, No. 92 CV 225 (Colo. Dist. Ct. Mar. 30, 1993), 3 Mealey's Reins. Rpt. No. 24 at D-1 (refusing to compel arbitration, concluding that the phrase "arbitration clause" in reinsurance placement slip, where formal agreement was never concluded, did not constitute a valid arbitration agreement, notwithstanding reinsurers' argument that slips could be supplemented by industry custom and practice); Thomas and Lyons (2012), §§ 77.04[2], 77-43, 77-44, 77-47, 77-48.

requirements to be borne by the arbitrators so as to qualify to be members of the said panel, as well as details for the arbitral decisions to be issued.

ARIAS, the reinsurance and Insurance arbitration society of the International Association for Insurance Law (or AIDA, from the initials of its French title namely "Association Internationale de Droit des Assurances"), has produced its own recommended arbitration clause. It is suggested that the stipulated requirements of the arbitrators should be widened to reflect the current reality; namely that professionals—both accountants and lawyers—are more frequency used as arbitrators.

Indeed, it is often helpful to the tribunal to be able to call upon legal expertise because the final decision must be based on Substantive law. It is not uncommon to find a tribunal of arbitrators, drawn solely from the marketplace, calling upon the services of a lawyer to draft the final award.

Also, issues of procedure and law will inevitably occur throughout the arbitration and, provided the market is adequately represented by two arbitrators, it seems sensible to ensure that the award is technically sound by incorporating legal expertise into the tribunal.

The ARIAS arbitration clause recommends that in order to qualify as members of the tribunal, the arbitrators shall (unless the parties otherwise agree) be persons (including those who have retired) with not less than 10 years' experience of insurance or reinsurance within the industry or as lawyers or other professional advisers serving the industry.[37]

4.2 The Everlasting Struggle: Arbitration or Litigation?

Many people ask, what is the difference between litigation and arbitration today anyway? Commercial arbitration, especially reinsurance arbitration, has become complex, costly, and time consuming.

Fundamentally, there is no difference between litigation and arbitration because in each proceeding, a neutral third party decides the dispute between the parties and issues a binding decision.

Procedurally, however, there are dramatic differences.

The underlying basis of dispute resolution in the courts differs greatly from that of arbitration. It is concerned, primarily, with precedent, which is intended to create some certainty in respect of dispute resolution.

In other words, if a particular legal issue has been resolved at an earlier date and, in particular, in a higher court, later parties to a dispute are bound by that decision.

Thus a body of case law is created and published, allowing lawyers to provide their clients with clear advice as to whether a particular case is meritorious or otherwise.

[37] Barlow Lyde and Gilbert LLP (2009), §§ 25.4.2, 25.4.5, 25-12, 25-13.

Arbitrators, on the other hand, while being bound by the published decisions of the courts, cannot add their own decisions to this body of precedent, and therefore such rulings exist in isolation.

Until some time ago, the reinsurance dispute which could not be negotiated to a satisfactory conclusion was the exception rather than the rule. In those circumstances arbitration, and even the honourable engagement clause, provided the flexibility to deal with these one-off disputes.

However, attitudes have now changed, and more and more reinsurance disputes are finding their way not only to arbitration but also into the court System.

It is certainly arguable that in those circumstances it may well be in the interests of the reinsurance market that a body of published reinsurance law should be established as soon as possible, so that the market can be advised on the merits of particular disputes.

Indeed, a considerable body of reinsurance law has developed over the last 20 years in the Commercial Court, and this has provided some assistance to the reinsurance market and to its legal advisers.[38]

In addition, arbitration is a consensual dispute resolution mechanism generally founded on a contract provision that requires all disputes be resolved by arbitration instead of litigation. Because it is generally a contract right, courts enforce arbitration clauses.

In the USA, the federal policy in favour of arbitration developed many years ago and was made part of the law by Congress when the FAA was enacted. Most states also favour arbitration and have similar laws and court decisions enforcing arbitration clauses.

The biggest difference between litigation and arbitration is the decider of the dispute.

In court, of course, it is a judge, either elected or appointed, but who is an employee of the government (or a judge and a jury if you really want to have fun with a reinsurance dispute).

In arbitration, the decider is an arbitrator or a panel of arbitrators, who are private citizens being paid by the parties to resolve the dispute.

In reinsurance, the practice has been to have a panel of three arbitrators chosen from either active or former executive officers of insurance or reinsurance companies. In other words, industry "experts" act as the arbitrators in reinsurance disputes.

Another big difference is the rules. In court, litigation is governed by either state or federal procedural rules. These rules cover all aspects of the litigation, from commencement through appeals.

In commercial arbitration there may or may not be rules. The rules in commercial arbitration may come from arbitral bodies like the American Arbitration Association, or the International Chamber of Commerce, or in international arbitration the UNCITRAL Arbitration Rules.

[38] Barlow Lyde and Gilbert LLP (2009), §§ 25.5.1, 25-12, 25-13.

In reinsurance disputes, the parties may agree to use the Procedures for the Resolution of U.S.A. Insurance and Reinsurance Disputes, which were promulgated by a task force of insurance and reinsurance industry professionals, or may agree to procedures before the arbitration panel that suit both the parties and the arbitrators. Unlike other forms of commercial arbitration, it is rare that a reinsurance arbitration will take place under the auspices of an arbitral organization or tribunal with rules and procedures that must be followed.

Flexibility of the process is another significant difference between litigation and arbitration. In court, there is very little flexibility. The case will be tried in the courthouse, and the rules make clear how the process will unfold. In arbitration, the parties and the arbitrator may find that the arbitration hearing should be held in more than one location or that only briefs and oral argument are necessary to decide the case. Because commercial arbitration is a private, confidential, and consensual procedure, the parties and the arbitrator may adopt unique methods for resolving the dispute.

Of course, a huge difference between litigation and arbitration is confidentiality. In court, your dispute is on public display and anyone can sit and watch the trial. In arbitration, the process is private and confidential. Reinsurance arbitrations are private, confidential proceedings that are not open to public or competitor scrutiny. This is another reason why many insurers and reinsurers would rather arbitrate than litigate. While the industry rumour mill may leak some information, the fact is that in most commercial arbitration disputes, only the parties and the arbitrator see the evidence and hear the testimony. Information about arbitrations often does find its way into the industry press, especially if a party goes to court to seek to confirm or vacate an arbitration award, for the most part, the details of the award and the dispute are kept confidential.[39]

Finally, another major difference is the ability to appeal. In court, the right of appeal exists by statute. In commercial arbitration, generally there is no right of appeal. While there are some ways to challenge an arbitration award, courts construe these grounds narrowly, and it is rare to see an arbitration award vacated.[40]

Why do reinsurance contracts have arbitration clauses? In general, most reinsurance contracts, especially reinsurance treaties, contain an arbitration clause.

Arbitration clauses in reinsurance contracts tend to be very broad. This means that virtually any dispute or disagreement concerning the interpretation or application of any part of the reinsurance contract, including its formation, must be decided by arbitration.

But why choose arbitration? Arbitration has been the traditional method of dispute resolution for reinsurance disputes for many decades.

Insurance and reinsurance companies would rather have their disputes resolved by a panel of industry experts who will decide disputes based on industry custom and practice.

---

[39] Schiffer (2006).

[40] Schiffer (2006).

Traditional reinsurance arbitration clauses relieve the arbitrators from following the strict rules of law and specifically require the arbitrators to consider the reinsurance contract as an honourable engagement rather than a strict legal obligation. This way, instead of a judge that knows nothing about the industry and who will construe the reinsurance agreement like any commercial contract, reinsurance disputes are determined based on industry business practices by industry experts.[41]

4.2.1 Procedural Difficulties in Arbitration

There are other procedural limitations facing parties to an arbitration agreement. Many of these difficulties, result from the fact that, primarily, the arbitrators' powers rest on contract rather than on the statutory or inherent jurisdiction of the courts.

Arbitrators' powers may be limited when they are obliged to resolve a dispute as to the validity of the contract and procedural problems may also arise when joining third parties to an arbitration.

Despite the enhanced powers provided by the Arbitration Act 1996, it may still be necessary for arbitrators to resort to the courts in order to force parties into action. This is only possible once all other remedies provided for by the arbitral process itself have been exhausted. The necessity to proceed in this way may deprive the arbitration of what should be one of its main advantages, namely speed.[42]

4.2.2 Arbitration: The Quick Result

One of the main arguments put forward in support of arbitration is the fact that, generally, the reinsurance dispute can be resolved a good deal more quickly than if it were to go through the courts.

It is certainly true that if both parties to the arbitration are acting in good faith and attempt to co-operate with the arbitration panel, it is possible to resolve disputes relatively speedily by agreeing, for example, to isolate the key issues in dispute and limit the disclosure of documentary evidence.

Unfortunately, it is often the case that one party, or perhaps both, does not wish to co-operate, and in those circumstances, arbitration can be delayed. It should be remembered, however, that one of the purposes of the CPR is to ensure that court proceedings are not delayed; the extensive case management powers now available to the judiciary mean that judges can and do intervene to monitor the parties'

[41] Schiffer (2006).

[42] Barlow Lyde and Gilbert LLP (2009), §§ 25.5.2, 25-14.

adherence to the timetable which is set at the time of the "case Management conference".

Since the implementation of the CPR, therefore, litigation may be a speedier means by which to resolve disputes than arbitration, which continues to be reliant upon the parties working together to resolve their differences.[43]

4.2.3 The Advantages of Expert Knowledge

It has been suggested that arbitrations not only allow flexibility, but also that they enable the panel to include members with commercial expertise and market knowledge.

Arbitral tribunals are often made up of three members, with two of the arbitrators being market men such as underwriters, and a third arbitrator, who acts as chairman, being a lawyer.

The advantage of having members of the panel who are market men with extensive reinsurance experience is that the parties are given the option to dispense with any need to call expert evidence if, for example, the issue in dispute is an underwriting matter and the two lay arbitrators are underwriters with knowledge of the class of business which is the subject matter of the arbitration.

In this way, both time and costs are likely to be saved. It must be remembered, however, that the final decision of the arbitral panel has to be made in accordance with substantive law. Consequently, a lawyer is often better equipped to make such a decision than an underwriter or a broker. It is for this reason that lawyers are frequently appointed to arbitral panels as the umpire or third arbitrator.

There is a further advantage to having a legally qualified umpire or third arbitrator: the Arbitration Act 1996 requires the panel to give reasons for its decision unless the parties agree to dispense with reasons, and lawyers—particularly barristers or retired judges—are of course accustomed to expressing their opinions in writing.

Also, nearly all reinsurance disputes which are litigated find their way to the Commercial Court, which has the task of dealing specifically with commercial disputes. Thus, judges concerned in resolving such disputes have themselves developed an in-depth knowledge of the reinsurance market. The judges will also be drawn from the Commercial Bar and they are likely to have gained knowledge of reinsurance law and the market during the course of their practice. When this is added to considerable legal expertise, it does make the Commercial Court an attractive way of resolving disputes, if it seems unlikely that they can be concluded in a less formal manner.[44]

---

[43] Barlow Lyde and Gilbert LLP (2009), §§ 25.5.3, 25-15.

[44] Barlow Lyde and Gilbert LLP (2009), §§ 25.5.4, 25-15.

4.2.4 Where Avoidance of Precedent Is Preferred

Certainly, arbitrations can be useful if the parties to the contract wish to resolve their dispute without setting a precedent for the future. In the past, there has been a certain reluctance by the reinsurance market to publicise its differences. The entire arbitration process, from service of a notice requesting arbitration to the making of an award, is (in theory at any rate) private and confidential. Generally, no-one other than the parties to the reference (and, if employed, their legal advisers) is entitled to have access to the pleadings, the evidence, the award or the arbitrators' reasons, subject to qualifications which emerge from *Hassneh Insurance Company of Israel v* Mew[45]and subsequent cases.[46]

4.2.5 The Relative Costs of Litigation and Arbitration

It is sometimes suggested that arbitration proceedings are a good deal cheaper than litigation. It is certainly the case that, if the parties are sensible and use the flexibility of arbitration to restrict the issues, the size of the panel and the evidence called, arbitration can prove to be a less expensive method of resolving disputes.

However, experience suggests that such good sense is often absent, and in those circumstances there is little difference between the cost of arbitration and that of litigation.

Almost inevitably, in reinsurance disputes the parties will be represented by both solicitors and barristers, and the form of the disclosure process and hearing would be much the same as in a court of law.

In addition, it is often forgotten that, in litigation, the judge and the court facilities are paid for by the taxpayer. This is not the case in arbitration, where the parties may be required to fund not only the arbitrators' fees and umpire's fees, but also the arbitration rooms, transcript facilities, and any other associated costs. This can substantially add to the overall expense of resolving a dispute.

4.2.6 Joining Third Parties to the Proceedings

One of the advantages of litigation over arbitration is that under Part 20 of the CPR, third parties may be joined to proceedings commenced by the original claimant (s) against the original defendant(s).

[45] *Hassneh Insurance Company of Israel vMew* [1993] 2 Lloyd's Rep 243 (QB Com Ct).
[46] Barlow Lyde and Gilbert LLP (2009), §§ 25.5.5, 25-15, 25-16.

Arbitration, by contrast, is confined to those parties who are bound by an arbitration clause or a separate arbitration agreement. In the context of reinsurance, this issue is of particular relevance where brokers are concerned.

For example, in proceedings in which a reinsured is suing a reinsurer for non-payment of Claims, the reinsurer may wish to assert a defence of misrepresentation or non-disclosure based on the broker's presentation at the time of placement. The reinsured may, if the reinsurer's defence is upheld, have a claim for damages against the broker.

In arbitration proceedings, it is improbable that any claim by the reinsured against the broker could be determined at the same time as the principal dispute, as the broker would not be party to any reinsurance contract containing an arbitration clause and would be most unlikely to agree subsequently to be a party to the arbitration.

The reinsured in such a situation would need to wait for an arbitration award to be made against it, and then bring a separate claim against the broker to indemnify it for amounts which it had been unable to recover from the reinsurer.

In litigation, both claims could be heard together. A further advantage of litigation over arbitration in relation to third parties is that, under Rule 31.17 of the CPR, an application may be made to the court to order disclosure from third parties. Again this might be of particular relevance in seeking documents from a broker who is not party to proceedings between a reinsured and a reinsurer.

By contrast, in the case of *BNP Paribas* v *Deloitte & Touche LLP*,[47] Morison J. held that there was no power under section 43 of the Arbitration Act 1996 by which a court could order a third party to an arbitration to make disclosure of documents.

Therefore, especially in a situation where a broker may have made a misrepresentation or non-disclosure, or have useful and relevant documents, the parties to a potential reinsurance dispute might prefer to waive the provisions of any arbitration clause and pursue their dispute through the courts, so as to make use of the wider rights against third parties which that system affords.[48]

4.2.7 The Flexibility of Arbitration

While it is sometimes commented that there is no real difference between formal arbitration and court proceedings, there is certainly no obligation upon the parties (unless the arbitration agreement provides otherwise, and the parties can vary this by consent in any event) for the arbitration process always to mirror the procedures of a court.

---

[47] *BNP Paribas* v *Deloitte & Touche LLP* [2003] EWHC 2874 (Comm).

[48] Barlow Lyde and Gilbert LLP (2009), §§ 25.5.6, 25-16, 25-17.

The Arbitration Act 1996 gives the arbitrators wide powers to decide procedural and evidential issues where the parties have been unable to agree upon these themselves. Consequently, one of the principal advantages of arbitration is that the parties can decide the procedures and adopt a timetable which best suits the issues in dispute.

There is no obligation, for example, to produce formal pleadings if the parties can agree instead to set out their case in written submissions, to which the documents upon which they rely as evidence to support their respective cases may be attached.

Even if the parties wished to have formal pleadings, there is no reason why the documents which they intend to produce in evidence cannot be exchanged at the same time as the pleadings are served, in order to circumvent the need for formal lists of documents (or a separate disclosure stage generally).

Witnesses do not necessarily have to be called to give oral evidence; it may be quicker and simpler to rely purely on written statements. The crucial point is that arbitrations allow the parties the flexibility to create their own procedures to suit the dispute in question. Of course, this only works if the parties are co-operating with one another.

The advantage of referring a dispute to the Commercial Court, on the other hand, is that a formal structure is already in place for the resolution of that dispute. The court can impose sanctions upon parties who do not comply with its directions and has wide case management powers which allow judges to take an active role in ensuring that the parties do not delay unduly in reaching a conclusion to their dispute. Sometimes, therefore, a court can be a better forum in which to resolve a reinsurance dispute than an arbitral tribunal.[49]

4.3 The Arbitration Procedure

The FAA does not prescribe a particular form or method that must be utilized by a party invoking its right to arbitration to commence arbitration proceedings. A demand for arbitration can be in the form of a pleading or letter.[50]

Section 4 of the FAA allows a party aggrieved by the alleged "failure, neglect or refusal of another" to abide by a written arbitration agreement to petition a federal district court for an order compelling arbitration.[51] Section 4, however, does not provide an independent basis for federal subject matter; accordingly, an independent basis for federal jurisdiction, such as diversity of citizenship, must exist.[52]

[49] Barlow Lyde and Gilbert LLP (2009), §§ 25.5.6B, 25-17.

[50] Ostrager and Vyskocil (1996), §§14-03, 14-15–14-16.

[51] 9 U.S.C. § 4.

[52] *Moses H. Cone Memorial Hosp. v Mercury Constr. Corp.*, 460 U.S. at 26 n. 32; Ostrager and Vyskocil (1996), §§ 14-17–14-18.

Where an independent basis for federal jurisdiction does exist, a federal court has the power to compel arbitration only within the district in which it is located.[53] A common circumstance which gives rise to federal question jurisdiction in a proceeding to compel arbitration is where the reinsurance contract involves foreign entities and thus falls within the New York Convention.[54]

Section 203 of the FAA expressly provides that an action or proceeding falling under the New York Convention shall be deemed to arise under the laws and treaties of the United States and that the district courts of the United States shall have original jurisdiction over such an action or proceeding, regardless of the amount in controversy.[55]

Where the New York Convention does not apply and diversity does not exist, a party wishing to compel arbitration must do so in state court.[56]

4.3.1 Does the Arbitration Agreement Cover the Dispute?

Where the parties have incorporated an agreement to arbitrate into their contract the next issue is to determine whether that clause covers the dispute that has arisen.

In the common law system, prior to the decision of the House of Lords in *Fiona Trust v Privalov*[57] two lines of argument had been developed by parties who wished to assert that an agreement to arbitrate did not apply in the particular circumstances of the dispute that had arisen: (1) that the agreement did not apply because the contract had been avoided or (2) that the agreement was not broad enough to cover the dispute.

In relation to the argument that the agreement did not apply because the contract had been avoided, even before the passage of the Arbitration Act 1996, English courts had refused to allow arbitration agreements to be frustrated by the allegation that the contract in which they were found was voidable. A line of authority held that the arbitration agreement was a separate and distinct agreement from the contract agreement. As such, even if the main agreement fell away, the arbitration agreement would remain valid as per the doctrine of separability which was also given effect in section 7 of the Arbitration Act 1996.

The second argument that the agreement is not wide enough to cover the dispute has also attracted a considerable amount of judicial analysis. The focus of the

---

[53] *Federated Rural Elec. Ins. Co. v Nationwide Mut. Ins.* Co., 874 F. Supp. 1204, 1210 (D. Kan. 1995).

[54] 9 U.S.C. § 201, *et seq.*

[55] *Injones v Sea Tow Services Freeport N.Y, Inc.*, 30 F.3d 360 (2d Cir. 1993.9 U.S.C. § 203; Ostrager and Vyskocil (1996), §§ 14-17–14-18.

[56] Ostrager and Vyskocil (1996), §§ 14-17–14-18.

[57] *Fiona Trust v Privalov* (2008)1 Lloyd's Rep. 254.

analysis was on construing the precise terms used in a number of arbitration agreements.

The high water mark of this approach was the decision of Hirst J. in *Ethiopian Oil Sea Pulses Export Corporation v Rio del Mar Foods Incorporated*[58] where Hirst J. considered the words used in arbitration clauses to circumscribe the arbitrator's powers "arising out of" and "arising in connection with" and sought to assess their breadth.

The House of Lords dealt with both of those issues in *Fiona Trust v Privalov*[59] which certified the function of the principle of separability and in the light of which (judgment) it seems now that almost any dispute arising under a reinsurance contract with a standard arbitration clause will now be dealt with by way of arbitration even if the dispute goes to the illegality or validity of the actual contract itself.[60]

4.3.2 Provisions with Ambiguous Scope

Because arbitration is a creature of contract, parties to a reinsurance agreement are free to contract for the scope of issues that they will submit to arbitration should there be a dispute in the future.

Difficulties arise, however, when the parties' intentions regarding the scope of arbitration are not clearly expressed in the reinsurance agreement. Lack of clarity over the scope of arbitration may lead to a dispute that has to be settled in court. Even worse, litigation over a poorly drafted arbitration clause may result in a judicial interpretation that is contrary to the parties' intentions.

One of the more significant examples of litigation over reinsurance arbitration provisions involves an arbitration clause that does not clearly set out the scope of what conflicts are arbitrable. Many arbitration clauses provide that only matters affecting the interpretation of a reinsurance agreement are to be arbitrated. When this language is used, disputes can arise over whether certain disputed issues address the interpretation of the agreement as opposed to the formation of the agreement.

Courts consistently review the breadth of the arbitration clause and, if it is narrow, do not compel arbitration of claims outside the scope of the clause. Narrow arbitration clauses, however, may be appropriate where the parties want certain disputes to be litigated in court and not subject to arbitration (e.g., fraud in the inducement). If that is the case, parties should make this clear in the drafting of their dispute resolution clause.

---

[58] *Ethiopian Oil Sea Pulses Export Corporation v Rio del Mar Foods Incorporated* (1990)1 Lloyd's Rep. 86.

[59] *Fiona Trust v Privalov* (2008)1 Lloyd's Rep. 254.

[60] Barlow Lyde and Gilbert LLP (2009), pp. 782–783.

If, however, parties want all disputes concerning the contract subject to arbitration—whether the dispute is about the formation, interpretation, or application of the contract—then the dispute resolution clause should be written broadly and clearly to ensure that there is no ambiguity about the broad scope of the clause.

Lastly, if the parties want all disputes concerning the contract subject to arbitration but wish to limit arbitral authority in specific ways—such as by excluding attorney and arbitrator fees from the range of sanctions open to arbitrators—the parties must clearly and expressly state the intent to limit arbitral authority as part of their arbitration agreement.

4.4 Considering the Obligation to Arbitrate

The reinsurance relationship is considered one of good faith, and is historically viewed as long-term and the reinsurance agreement is traditionally considered to be an "honourable engagement".

As a result, parties have historically sought means other than litigation to resolve their disputes and have felt a strong incentive to preserve their relationship and settle disputes through negotiation.

Where the parties cannot reach a negotiated settlement, arbitration is the traditional method of dispute resolution. In fact, the reinsurance industry has utilized the arbitration process since at least the early 1800s, when arbitration clauses were commonly used in English marine reinsurance contracts.[61]

4.4.1 The Agreement to Arbitrate

The parties must agree to arbitrate, and a party may not be forced to arbitrate a dispute unless that party has agreed that arbitration will be the method by which that dispute is to be resolved.[62] Reinsurance contracts, therefore, almost always include an arbitration clause.

In *CNA Reins. of London Ltd. v Home Ins. Co.*,[63] where the summary slip did not indicate arbitration and the contract wording that would have included provision for arbitration was never signed, a federal district court stated that an evidentiary

[61] Holmes and Sutin (1996), p. 544.

[62] *Merit Ins. Co. v Leatherby Ins. Co.*, 714 F.2d 673 (7th Cir.); Holmes and Sutin (1996), p. 545.

[63] *CNA Reins. of London Ltd. v Home Ins. Co.*, 85 Ciiv. 5681–5801, 1985 U.S. Dist. LEXIS 13296 (S.D.N.Y. Dec. 2, 1985).

hearing could be required to determine whether and exactly what issues the parties may have intended to arbitrate.[64]

In *North Carolina League of Municipalities v Clarendon Nat'l Ins. Co.*,[65] an arbitration clause was enforced in a reinsurance binder, even when the plaintiffs were seeking cancellation of the binder. Plaintiffs sued for a refund of premiums paid to a reinsurance company under a binder pending negotiation of a reinsurance agreement. The binder provided for arbitration of any dispute between the parties. On a motion by the reinsurer to compel arbitration, the court held that the arbitration clause applied to the dispute in question, including the issue as to whether a binding contract of coverage was formed.[66]

4.4.2 Scope of the Agreement to Arbitrate

Because reinsurance contracts typically contain an agreement to submit disputes to arbitration, the usual issue thus becomes whether the dispute in question falls within the scope of the agreement to arbitrate.

As an overarching and overly general principle, efforts to establish that a given issue is beyond the scope of the arbitration agreement generally fall. Federal policy strongly favours arbitration, and any doubts concerning the scope of arbitrable issues should be resolved in favour of arbitration.[67]

Nevertheless, courts do examine the particular language of the arbitration agreement and compare that language to the particular issue in dispute. Courts have developed general, yet sometimes inconsistent, guidelines for determining whether the parties intended a particular dispute to be arbitrated, attempting to classify arbitration clauses as "broad" or "narrow."

The law is clear in its position that a party "cannot be required to submit to arbitration any dispute which he has not agreed to so submit."[68] The question whether the parties have submitted a particular issue to arbitration, *i.e.*, the question of arbitrability, is "an issue for judicial determination unless the parties clearly and

---

[64] *CNA Reins. of London Ltd. v Home Ins. Co.*, 85 Ciiv. 5681–5801, 1985 U.S. Dist. LEXIS 13296 (S.D.N.Y. Dec. 2, 1985); *Frank B. Hall Co. of Colo. v Colo. School Dist. Self-Insurance Pool*, No 92 CV 225 (Colo. Dist. Ct. 1993; Holmes and Sutin (1996), p. 545.

[65] *North Carolina League of Municipalities v Clarendon Nat'l Ins. Co.*, 733 F. Supp. 1009/E.D.N. C. 1990).

[66] Holmes and Sutin (1996), pp. 546–547.

[67] *Moses H. Cone Memorial Hosp. v Mercury Constr. Corp.*, 460 U.S. 1, 24–25 (1983). While the FAA is not an independent source of federal jurisdiction (*Mesa Operating Ltd. Partnership v Louisiana Interstate Gas*, 797 F.2d 238, 240 (5th Cir. 1986), it is a substantive rule applying in the state as well as federal courts (*Southland Corp. v Keating*, 465 U.S. 1 (1984); Holmes and Sutin (1996), p. 547.

[68] Reliastar Life Ins. Co. v EMC Nat'l Life Co., 564 F.3d 81, 85 (2d Cir. 2009).

unmistakably provide otherwise."[69] U.S.A. courts presume that parties intended to resolve all disputes by arbitration where the parties' agreement contains an arbitration clause.[70] In deciding, whether the parties agreed to arbitrate a certain matter, courts apply state contract law governing the formation of contracts.[71] Non-signatories can consent to arbitration by participating in the arbitration without objection.[72]

Courts will generally compel arbitration of claims that a party breached the reinsurance contract where the agreement contains an arbitration provision.[73] Courts will enforce party agreements limiting the scope of arbitrable issues.[74] Courts frequently distinguish between "broad" and "narrow" arbitration clauses in determining the scope of arbitrable claims. Arbitration provisions that specify that "any disputes" "relating to" the parties' transactions or agreement shall be determined by arbitration, or words to that effect, are typically deemed to be "broad" arbitration provisions.[75] An arbitration clause that provides for arbitration of disputes "arising out of or relating to" the contract, would in most cases be

---

[69] *Howsam v Dean Witter Reynolds, Inc.*, 537 U.S. 79, 83 (2002).

[70] *First Options of Chicago, Inc. v Kaplan*, 514 U.S. 938, 945 (1995) (the FAA "insists upon clarity before concluding that the parties did not want to arbitrate a related matter"); *AT&T Tech., Inc. v Communications Workers*, 475 U.S. 643, 650 (1986) ("In the absence of any express provision excluding a particular grievance from arbitration, we think only the most forceful evidence of a purpose to exclude the claim from arbitration can prevail."); *Moses H. Cone Mem'l Hosp. v Mercury Constr. Corp.*, 460 U.S. 1, 24–25 (1983) ("the FAA establishes that, as a matter of federal law, any doubts concerning the scope of arbitrable issues should be resolved in favor of arbitration, whether the problem at hand is the construction of the contract language itself or an allegation of waiver, delay or a like defense to arbitrability").

[71] *Progressive Cas. Ins. Co. v CA. Reaseguradora National de Venezuela*, 991 F.2d 42, 45–46 (2d Cir. 1993); *Trustmark Ins. Co. v Transamerica Occidental Life Ins. Co.*, 484 F. Supp. 2d 850, 853 (N.D. 111. 2007).

[72] *Am. Ins. Managers, Inc. v Guar. Ins. Co.*, No. 1:07-CV-1615-MBS, 2011 U.S. Dist. LEXIS 34029 (D.S.C. Mar. 29, 2011) (arbitrator had authority over corporate officers' liability, although they did not sign the agreement, because they "vigorously participated" in the arbitration and did not object to the arbitrability of the issue).

[73] *Southern Underwriters, Inc. v Hansa Reinsurance Co. of Am.*, No. 93-0498-CIV-MORENO (S.D. Fla. June 21, 1993), 4 *Mealey's Reinsurance Rpt. No.* 5 at B-l ("Southern brought this action seeking enforcement of payment under the contract. As such, it is covered by the expansive language of the arbitration clause."); *Nissan Fire & Marine Ins. Co., Ltd. v Fortress Re, Inc.*, No. 1:02CV00054, 2002 U.S. Dist. LEXIS 19542 (M.D. N.C. Feb. 25, 2002); *Nationwide Gen. Ins. Co. v Investors Ins. Co. of Am.*, 332 N.E.2d 333, 336 (N.Y. 1975) (compelling arbitration where "the parties entered into a reinsurance agreement and ... the appellant relying on the agreement has submitted a claim for reimbursement.. . . This is a dispute 'touching the construction meaning or effect of the agreement'" and thus arbitrable).

[74] *Harleysville Mut. Ins. Co. v GE Reinsurance Corp.*, No. 02–171, 2002 U.S. Dist. LEXIS 8064, at *10–11 (E.D. Pa. May 6, 2002) (refusing to compel arbitration because arbitration clause allowed either party to elect litigation over arbitration when the amount in controversy exceeded $2 million, and the claims at issue exceeded that amount).

[75] Thomas and Lyons (2012), pp. 77-53, 77-54.

classified as a "broad" arbitration clause.[76] In contrast, a "narrow" arbitration clause would often provide for arbitration of only those disputes "arising under" the contract.[77] Narrow clauses therefore limit arbitrable issues only to those issues relating directly to interpretation and performance of the contract containing the clause.[78] Arbitrators, rather than courts, are presumptively empowered to decide procedural issues.[79]

Else put, an arbitration clause phrased in language that could be narrowly construed would permit arbitration of reinsurance disputes concerning performance or breach of the provisions of the contract.[80]

Where the parties agreed to arbitrate any dispute "in connection with" the reinsurance agreement, questions pertaining to the interpretation and effect of a subsequent modification of the terms of the contract, and to a party's right to reformation may be arbitrable.

---

[76] *Prima Paint Corp. v Flood & Conklin Mfg. Co.*, 388 U.S. 395 (1967); Holmes and Sutin (1996), p. 547.

[77] *S.A. Mineracao Da Trindade-Samitri v Utah Int'l, Inc.*, 745 F.2d 190, 194 (2d Cir. 1984) (applying federal law); Holmes and Sutin (1996), p. 547.

[78] *Associated Indem. Corp. v Home Ins. Co.*, 994 U.S. App. LEXIS 3742 (6th Cir. Feb. 24, 1994) ("The language of the arbitration clause at issue is narrow and expressly applies solely to issues involving irreconcilable differences of opinion as to the interpretation of the language of the contract between the parties. Home has failed to identify any provision of the contract requiring interpretation, let alone arbitration. There is no duty to arbitrate in the absence of a bona fide issue of contract interpretation."); *N.H. Ins. Co. v Canali Reinsurance Co.*, No. 03 Civ. 8889 (LTS) (DCF), 2004 U.S. Dist. LEXIS 6180, at *3, *6 (S.D.N.Y. Apr. 12, 2004) (refusing to compel arbitration where narrow arbitration clause submitted to arbitration "all disputes or differences arising out of the interpretation of this agreement," and the dispute concerned whether the reinsurer failed to deposit funds into a trust account pursuant to the reinsurance agreement: "Because there is no indication that there is any dispute over the calculation of the amounts due, there is nothing in the Petition that even remotely implicates a need for interpretation of the Reinsurance Agreement."); *Gerling Global Reinsurance Corp. v Home Ins. Co.*, 752 N.Y.S.2d 611, 613, 618 (N.Y. App. Div. 2002) (reinsurer's restitution claims were not arbitrable, where reinsurer alleged that it mistakenly paid billings based on cedent's incorrect allocation of losses, where narrow arbitration clause provided for arbitration "should an irreconcilable difference of opinion arise as to the interpretation of this contract;" concluding that the dispute did not turn on the interpretation of the contract, but instead on the cedent's erroneous loss allocation); *Argonaut Ins. Co. v Travelers Ins. Co.*, 744 N.Y.S.2d 24, 25 (N.Y. App. Div. 2001) (dispute was not arbitrable where the certificates required arbitration where "an irreconcilable difference arises as to the interpretation of this contract" and "defendant failed to specify any provision of the certificates requiring interpretation"); Thomas and Lyons (2012), pp. 77-53, 77-54.

[79] *Howsam v Dean Witter Reynolds, Inc.*, 537 U.S. 79, 83–84 (2002) ("procedural questions which grow out of the dispute and bear on its final disposition are presumptively not for the judge, but for an arbitrator, to decide."); *Dockser v Schwartzberg*, 433 F.3d 421, 426 (4th Cir. 2006) ("only when there is a question regarding whether the parties should be arbitrating at all" is a question of arbitrability raised for the court to decide); *Certain Underwriters at Lloyd's, London v Westchester Fire Ins. Co.*, 489 F.3d 580, 585 (3d Cir. 2007); Thomas and Lyons (2012), pp. 77-53, 77-54.

[80] *NECA Ins. Ltd. v National Union Fire Ins. Co.*, 595 F. Supp. 955, 958 (S.D.N.Y. 1984). *Schacht v Beacon Ins. Co.*, 742 F.2d 386 (7th Cir. 1984) (applying federal and Illinois law) (arbitration held proper means to enforce contract).

In *American Home Assur. Co. v American Fidelity & Cas. Co.*,[81] a letter accompanying an addendum reducing a reinsurance rate was clearly intended to be read with the addendum and hence constituted a modification of the original reinsurance contract and, therefore, any dispute with respect to and meaning and effect of the reinsurance contract addendum reducing the premium and the accompanying letter providing for "adequate amendment" in case of a loss ratio exceeding 65 % of gross premiums on a basis to be mutually arranged were arbitrable under a provision for arbitration of controversies "in connection with" the agreement.

The court held that a reformation of a contract involves a claim falling within a provision to arbitrate disputes "arising out of" or "in connection with" a contract so that reformation of the addendum reducing the reinsurance rate would be arbitrable.[82]

Some feel that arbitrators are ill-equipped to decide such issues as fraud in the inducement, reformation for mutual mistake or the issue of arbitrability itself and that the arbitration process does not permit sufficient discovery to arrive at the truth of such allegations.

At the other end of the spectrum, the arbitration process is thought by some needlessly to prolong collection of balances in cases where litigation could more quickly dispose of weak or fanciful defences.

Such concerns are increasingly addressed by including in an otherwise traditional arbitration clause language to the effect that "disputes concerning the validity of this Agreement or any part thereof and actions for payment of admitted balances shall be submitted to a court of competent jurisdiction." And obviously under a very broad agreement that all disputes and differences are to be submitted to arbitration, practically any issue that could be raised must be arbitrated.

In *Hamilton Life Ins. Co. of New York v Republic Nat. Life Ins. Co.*[83] the New York federal court determined that such a provision embraces defenses of fraud in inducement of contract generally, lack of consideration, failure to comply with conditions precedent, illegality of subject matter of contract, and breach of contract, as well as question of the reinsurer's liability to the insurer.

In *Nationwide Gen. Ins. Co. v Investors Ins. Co. of America*,[84] where the language of an arbitration clause covered all disputes relating to the meaning and interpretation of the agreement or any article contained in the agreement, or the rights or liabilities of either party, a dispute concerning interpretation of whether the insurer was entitled to reimbursement for a judgment rendered against it for failure

---

[81] *American Home Assur. Co. v American Fidelity & Cas. Co.*, 356 F.2d 690 (2nd Cir. 1966) (applying New York law).

[82] Holmes and Sutin (1996), p. 549.

[83] *Hamilton Life Ins. Co. of New York v Republic Nat. Life Ins. Co.*, 291 F. Supp. 225 (S.D.N.Y. 1968).

[84] *Nationwide Gen. Ins. Co. v Investors Ins. Co. of America*, 37 N.Y.2d 91, 332 N.E.2d 333, 371 N.Y.S.2d 463 (1975).

to settle or whether the agreement applied only to judgments rendered against the insurer within policy limits was arbitrable.[85]

However, if the arbitration clause were broadly construed, arbitrable issues need not be limited to the terms of the contract,[86] but may also include related tortious conduct.[87] Precise language is often less important in a given factual situation than is the court's view of its mandate to resolve doubts in favour of arbitrability. On the other hand, neither party to the contract can be required to submit to arbitration any issue that it clearly had not agreed should be arbitrated.[88]

In *Medical Insurance Exchange of California v Certain Underwriters at Lloyds, London*,[89] the court analysed the question of whether a reinsurer and its cedent should be compelled to arbitrate a dispute where the insurer alleged misrepresentation, concealment, nondisclosure, and fraud. The plaintiff was a physician-owned insurance company providing medical malpractice insurance to health care providers. After hundreds of claims were asserted, against a group of cardiologists insured by the plaintiff, the latter agreed to defend those insureds against the claims, and provided notice of same to the reinsurers. When a tentative global settlement of the lawsuits was reached, the plaintiff agreed to contribute to the settlement and notified the reinsurers regarding the details of the arrangement. The plaintiff alleged that the reinsurers led the plaintiff to believe that the settlement would be covered under the reinsurance policies in question.[90] After the insurer made the settlement payment, it requested reimbursement from the reinsurers. The reinsurers rejected that request, asserting that because the plaintiffs had allocated the settlement amount among all the individual claimants such that the individual allocations did not exceed $75,000 per claimant, no reinsurance coverage had been triggered under the policies. The insurer responded that it could have structured the settlement in a different manner had the reinsurers taken that position before the settlement had been finalized.[91] The plaintiff filed suit, alleging breach of contract and breach of the implied covenant of good faith and fair dealing. The reinsurers demanded arbitration pursuant to the agreements between the parties. The plaintiff rejected that demand, claiming that because the action against the reinsurers involved allegations of misrepresentation, concealment, nondisclosure, and fraud,

---

[85] Holmes and Sutin (1996), p. 550.

[86] *Meadows Indem. Co. v Baccala & Shoop Ins. Servs., Inc.*, 760 F. Supp. 1936 (E.D.N.Y. 1991). *Morgan v Smith Barney, Harris Upham & Co.*, 729 F.2d 1163 (8th Cir. 1984); Holmes and Sutin (1996), p. 550.

[87] *Pierson v Dean, Witter, Reynolds, Inc.*, 742 F.2d 334 (7th Cir. 1984) (applying federal law).

[88] *Morgan v Smith Barney, Harris Upham & Co.*, 729 F.2d 1163 (8th Cir. 1984); Holmes and Sutin (1996), p. 550.

[89] *Medical Insurance Exchange of California v Certain Underwriters at Lloyds, London*, No. C 05-2609 PJH, 2006 WL 463531 (N.D. Cal. Feb. 24, 2006); Chiafullo et al. (2007), p. 459.

[90] *Medical Insurance Exchange of California v Certain Underwriters at Lloyds, London*, No. C 05-2609 PJH, 2006 WL 463531 (N.D. Cal. Feb. 24, 2006) at *2; Chiafullo et al. (2007), p. 460.

[91] *Medical Insurance Exchange of California v Certain Underwriters at Lloyds, London*, No. C 05-2609 PJH, 2006 WL 463531 (N.D. Cal. Feb. 24, 2006) at *2; Chiafullo et al. (2007), p. 460.

the dispute fell outside the parties' arbitration agreement.[92] Moving to compel arbitration, the reinsurers claimed the exception for misrepresentation claims was intended to cover contract formation issues leading to rescission claims.[93]

After a detailed analysis of the intent of the parties in inserting into the arbitration provision the exception for allegations of misrepresentation, the court determined that the arbitration provision was not ambiguous on its face but that under California law a provision is ambiguous if it is capable of two or more reasonable constructions.[94]

Finding that the language satisfied that test for ambiguity, the court rejected the insurer's argument that there was no need to look to the extrinsic evidence.

In proceeding to grant the motion to compel arbitration, the court found that the lead underwriter intended, and Carvill [the intermediary] and the reinsurers understood that the lead underwriter intended, that the exception to the arbitration requirement be applied only where the validity or formation of the contract was being challenged. As Carvill was acting as the insurer's intermediary, the court charged the insurer with Carvill's knowledge of the lead underwriter's intent, regardless of whether Carvill had actually communicated that intent to the insurer.[95]

4.4.3 Arbitrability

Courts generally decide issues of arbitrability—that is, whether parties have agreed to submit a dispute to arbitration—while arbitrators decide issues of procedure.[96] "Questions of arbitrability" include "the kind of narrow circumstance where contracting parties would likely have expected a court to have decided the gateway matter, where they are not likely to have thought that they had agreed that an

---

[92] *Medical Insurance Exchange of California v Certain Underwriters at Lloyds, London*, No. C 05-2609 PJH, 2006 WL 463531 (N.D. Cal. Feb. 24, 2006) at *2; Chiafullo et al. (2007), p. 460.

[93] *Medical Insurance Exchange of California v Certain Underwriters at Lloyds, London*, No. C 05-2609 PJH, 2006 WL 463531 (N.D. Cal. Feb. 24, 2006) at *13; Chiafullo et al. (2007), p. 460.

[94] *Medical Insurance Exchange of California v Certain Underwriters at Lloyds, London*, No. C 05-2609 PJH, 2006 WL 463531 (N.D. Cal. Feb. 24, 2006) at *15; Chiafullo et al. (2007), p. 460.

[95] *Medical Insurance Exchange of California v Certain Underwriters at Lloyds, London*, No. C 05-2609 PJH, 2006 WL 463531 (N.D. Cal. Feb. 24, 2006) at *17; Chiafullo et al. (2007), pp. 460–461.

[96] *Stolt-Nielsen S.A. v AnimalFeeds Int'l. Corp.*, 130 S. Ct. 1758, 1775 (2010) ("In certain contexts, it is appropriate to presume that parties that enter into an arbitration agreement implicitly authorize the arbitrator to adopt such procedures as are necessary to give effect to the parties' agreement.. . . Procedural questions which grow out of the dispute and bear on its final disposition are presumptively not for the judge, but for an arbitrator, to decide."); *Howsam v Dean Witter Reynolds, Inc.*, 537 U.S. 79, 84 (2002) ("[Procedural questions that grow out of the dispute and bear on its final disposition are presumptively not for the judge, but for an arbitrator, to decide."); *First Options of Chicago, Inc. v Kaplan*, 514 U.S. 938, 944 (1995); Thomas and Lyons (2012), pp. 77-51, 77-52.

arbitrator would do so, and consequently, where reference to the gateway dispute to the court avoids the risk of forcing parties to arbitrate a matter that they may well not have agreed to arbitrate."[97] Examples of "gateway disputes" that should be decided by courts—not arbitrators—include: (1) disputes regarding "whether the parties are bound by a given arbitration clause"; and (2) "a disagreement about whether an arbitration clause in a concededly binding contract applies to a particular type of controversy."[98]

In *Employers Insurance Co. of Wausau v Century Indemnity Co.*,[99] the insurer had entered into a number of reinsurance agreements, including two with Wausau. When Century's reinsurers refused to reimburse Century for certain claims, Century demanded that they participate in a consolidated arbitration to determine liability. Wausau acknowledged that it was required to arbitrate but claimed that it could not be required to participate in a consolidated arbitration. Wausau filed suit in federal district court seeking a declaratory judgment to that effect.[100] Wausau argued that the issue of whether consolidation was allowed, was, in the absence of clear evidence that the parties had intended the arbitrator to decide a question of arbitrability to be determined by the court.

Century took the opposite position, arguing that the question was a procedural one that needed to be resolved by the arbitrator unless the arbitration agreement reserved it for the court.

The trial court determined that the question of whether a consolidated arbitration could be compelled was itself a question for the arbitrator rather than the court. Citing *First Options of Chicago, Inc. v Kaplan*,[101] the Seventh Circuit affirmed. The court distinguished between questions of arbitrability and issues that are merely procedural in nature but that do not impact on arbitrability. Finding that the

[97] *Howsam v Dean Witter Reynolds, Inc.*, 537 U.S. 79, 83–84 (2002); Thomas and Lyons (2012), pp. 77-51, 77-52.

[98] *Howsam v Dean Witter Reynolds, Inc.*, 537 U.S. 79, 84 (2002). Parties can agree to arbitrate; *First Options of Chicago, Inc. v Kaplan*, 514 U.S. 938, 943 (1995) ("parties may agree to arbitrate arbitrability."); *Anderson v Pitney Bowes, Inc.*, No. C 04-4808SBA, 2005 U.S. Dist. LEXIS 37662, at *2 (N.D. Cal. May 4, 2005) (parties can "contract around this default rule by assigning the determination of arbitrability to an arbitrator"); If "the parties clearly and unmistakably empowered an arbitrator to determine arbitrability, the Court must compel arbitration of the gateway issues as well." *Anderson v Pitney Bowes, Inc.*, No. C 04-4808SBA, 2005 U.S. Dist. LEXIS 37662, at *7 (N.D. Cal. May 4, 2005); *Air Line Pilots Ass'n, Int'l v Midwest Express Airlines, Inc.*, 279 F.3d 553, 555 (7th Cir. 2002) ("when an arbitration clause is so broadly worded that it encompasses disputes over the scope or validity of the contract in which it is embedded, issues of the contract's scope or validity are for the arbitrators."). Parties clearly and unmistakably empower arbitrators to determine arbitrability where they expressly adopt institutional arbitration rules that empower arbitrators to decide issues of arbitrability. *Contec Corp. v Remote Solution Co.*, 398 F.3d 205, 208 (2d Cir. 2005); Thomas and Lyons (2012), pp. 77-51, 77-52.

[99] *Employers Insurance Co. of Wausau v Century Indemnity Co.*, 443 E3d 573 (7th Cir. 2006); Chiafullo et al. (2007), p. 459.

[100] *Employers Insurance Co. of Wausau v Century Indemnity Co.*, 443 E3d 573 (7th Cir. 2006) at 574; Chiafullo et al. (2007), p. 459.

[101] *First Options of Chicago, Inc. v Kaplan* 514 U.S. 938 (1995); Chiafullo et al. (2007), p. 459.

question of whether an arbitration agreement forbids consolidated arbitration is a procedural one, the Seventh Circuit held that the question is to be resolved by the arbitration panel.[102]

4.4.4 Intent to Arbitrate

The reinsurance industry has undergone material changes, including deterioration of the industry's preference to abide by the customs and practices of the industry and to arbitrate disputes.[103]

For a dispute to be arbitrated there must be a written agreement to arbitrate and the dispute must be arbitrable, i.e. fall within the scope of the arbitration agreement.

In the U.S.A., the Supreme court has held, in *Moses H. Cone Memorial Hospital v Mercury Constr. Corp.*[104] that any doubt concerning the scope of arbitrable issues should be resolved in favour of arbitration.[105]

When a party seeks to avoid arbitration, a court may be faced with a motion to compel it. The issue of whether the dispute is subject to arbitration, under the arbitration clause, may arise. If a court determines that the dispute falls within the arbitration agreement, the court must refer the dispute to arbitration under the merits.[106]

The issue of whether a reference to arbitration on a reinsurance slip is sufficient to compel arbitration has been adjudicated. In *P.B. Hall Company of Colorado v Colorado School Districts Self Insurance Pool*,[107] it was held that reference to a placement slip and memorandum of reinsurance is insufficient to find that the parties agreed to arbitration.

However, this court's decision may be considered exceptional as in the London and other markets, the placement slip evidences the intention of the parties. Moreover, although courts may be reluctant to find a written agreement to arbitrate where none can be proved, they generally view arbitration clauses broadly.[108]

---

[102] *Employers Insurance Co. of Wausau v Century Indemnity Co.*, 443 E3d at 577; Chiafullo et al. (2007), p. 459.

[103] McDonald (2001), p. 338.

[104] *Moses H Cone Memorial Hospital v Mercury Constr. Corp.* 460 US 1 (1983).

[105] Hammesfahr and Wright (1994), p. 279.

[106] *Moses H Cone Memorial Hospital v Mercury Constr. Corp.* 460 US 1 (1983); Hammesfahr and Wright (1994), p. 279.

[107] *P.B. Hall Company of Colorado v Colorado School Districts Self Insurance Pool*, No 92 CV 225 (Col Dist. Ct. March 21, 1993), 3 Mealey's Reins. Rep. No 24.

[108] *Meadows Indemnity Co. v Arkwright Mutual Ins. Co.*, 1996 WL 557513, Docket No. 88-0600, 7 Mealey's Reins. Rep. No 11, F (ED Pa 1996); *Usher Syndicate Ltd Inc v Figgie International Inc.* 1987 US Dist. LEXIS 13,340 (S.D. Fla. 1987); *Southern Underwriters Inc v Hansa Reinsurance Company of America*, No 39-0498-CIV Moreno (S.D. Fla., June 21, 1993), 4 Mealey's Reins. Rep. No 5; Hammesfahr and Wright (1994), pp. 278–279.

Many times parties to a reinsurance treaty have attempted to avoid arbitration when there was, at a minimum, an implied intent to arbitrate disputes. Assuming a dispute and one of the parties commencing suit in a state court, what options are available for the party seeking to enforce the arbitration provision?[109] What can a party wishing to protect its agreement to arbitrate do to guarantee that if and when arbitration is needed, the arbitration agreement can be enforced?[110]

Both the FAA 1925 and the New York Convention require a court to enforce the parties' agreement to arbitrate. A dispute over arbitration is subject to the New York Convention when one of the parties to the agreement is a foreign company, and the country of the foreign company is a signatory to the convention. The FAA 1925 may also apply to an action brought under the convention.

In *North Carolina League of Municipalities v Clarendon National Insurance Co.*,[111] a federal district court addressed the issue whether the phrase "arbitration clause" in the placement slips was sufficient to show an intent to arbitrate. Both parties had accepted the placement slips without reservation, and a treaty containing the full language of the terms of any arbitration also had been circulated between the parties. However, the treaty was never signed.

Placing great emphasis and weight on the custom of the reinsurance industry, the court concluded it was the industry custom to use abbreviated terms in placement slips. It held that the phrase arbitration clause in the placement slips dispositive on the issue of arbitration and thus enough to compel arbitration, concluding that industry custom conclusively established an intent to arbitrate. In support of its decision, the court noted extrinsic evidence, including the failure by either party to modify the arbitration agreement. The court's decision was both proper and logical because it was based on the nature of the reinsurance industry. Its reliance on the custom of the industry is also consistent with the approach taken by arbitrators.

In *Allianz Life Insurance Co. of North America v American Phoenix Life and Reassurance Co.*[112] the plaintiff, Allianz, was the retrocessionaire of American Phoenix, Phoenix Home Life Mutual Insurance Co. and Sun Life Assurance Co. of Canada. The parties entered into three separate contracts for retrocessional coverage and the relevant slips were silent on the issue of arbitrating disputes except they contained the single phrase arbitration clause. When a dispute arose, Allianz sued the retrocedents in Minnesota state court, seeking rescission of the contract and damages. The case was removed to the USA District court for Minnesota, and the retrocedents sought to compel arbitration based on the inclusion of "arbitration clause" in the placement slips. The Allianz court stated that the phrase "arbitration clause," while sparce, had significant meaning in the reinsurance industry. The

[109] McDonald (2001), p. 334.

[110] McDonald (2001), p. 338.

[111] *North Carolina League of Municipalities v Clarendon National Insurance Co.* 733 F. Supp. 1009 (E.D.N.C. 1990).

[112] *Allianz Life Insurance Co. of North America v American Phoenix Life and Reassurance Co.* 2000 US Dist. Lexis 7216 (D. Minn).

court concluded that based on the customs and practices of the industry, the phrase "arbitration clause" had considerable meaning and was enough o compel arbitration.

However, in *Frank B. Hall Inc. v Colorado School Districts Self-Insurance Pool*,[113] the court did not compel arbitration based on the phrase "arbitration clause." The decision in *Frank B. Hall Inc. v Colorado School Districts Self-Insurance Pool*[114] illustrates the potential danger reinsurers and reinsureds face when confronted with litigation over issues steeped in the customs and practices of the reinsurance industry.[115]

More recent decisions, illustrate the trend to support the conclusion of the existence of the intent to arbitrate, in simple phrases purporting so.

In *Hartford Accident and Indemnity Co. v Swiss Reinsurance Co. of America*[116] the court applied a broad standard for arbitration and held that claims yet to be submitted by the insurer to the reinsurer may be joined in the arbitration of pending disputes. Since each claim made to the reinsurer involved a similar calculation, the court stated, common arbitration potentially could resolve each dispute.

In *Security Life Insurance Co. of America v Hannover Life Reinsurance Co. of America*[117] the court considered contradictory language in the reinsurance contract. On the one hand, the contract stated that "arbitration is the sole remedy for disputes arising under this agreement." On the other hand, the contract noted that either party may request arbitration, and a service of suit clause provided that the parties must submit to the jurisdiction of any court of competent jurisdiction.

Sorting it out, the court stayed the proceeding and ordered the parties to submit to arbitration. The court noted that the reinsurance contracts fell within the protection of the FAA and stated that it was its practice to stay litigation when the parties have agreed to arbitrate.[118]

As per the FAA and cases interpreting it, it is noted that the enforcement of arbitration agreements is favoured. In other words, when a contract contains an arbitration provision, there is a presumption of arbitrability that is overcome only it can be shown and proven that the dispute in question is outside the coverage of the arbitration clause.[119]

---

[113] *Frank B. Hall Inc. v Colorado School Districts Self-Insurance Pool* No. 92-CV-225 (Colo. Dist. Ct. March 26, 1993).

[114] *Frank B. Hall Inc. v Colorado School Districts Self-Insurance Pool* No. 92-CV-225 (Colo. Dist. Ct. March 26, 1993).

[115] McDonald (2001), p. 338.

[116] *Hartford Accident and Indemnity Co. v Swiss Reinsurance Co. of America*, 246 F.3d 219 (2d Cir. 2001).

[117] *Security Life Insurance Co. of America v Hannover Life Reinsurance Co. of America*, 2001 WL 392412 (D. Minn.).

[118] McDonald (2001), p. 337.

[119] *Moses H. Cone Memorial Hosp. v Mercury Constr. Co.*, 460 U.S. 1, 24 (1983); *Associated Brick Mason Contractors v Harrington*, 820 F.2d 31, 35 (2d Cir. 1987). *Continental Casualty Co. v Certain Underwriters at Lloyd's*, No. C-92-4094-DLJ (N.D. Cal. April 19, 1993), reprinted in

As we have seen above, Courts have consistently applied this broad federal mandate to order reinsurance disputes to arbitration.[120]

However, Courts have been less than consistent, in their approach to whether commercial tort claims, such as fraud in the inducement, misrepresentation, conspiracy, etc., which often are raised in the course of reinsurance disputes, must be arbitrated. Of course, the parties always have the option of agreeing to arbitrate all their claims, including those that would not be arbitrable but for that agreement. When they cannot agree, however, a court has the power to decide whether to stay the litigation over those claims that are not arbitrable pending a resolution of those claims that can be arbitrated.[121] Decisions of the arbitrators may have *res judicata* or collateral estoppel effects on any claims that are not arbitrated.[122]

It follows from the above that parties who wish to eliminate arbitration from reinsurance treaties should be prepared to amend the treaties so that they will more closely resemble other complex commercial contracts outside of the reinsurance industry.

The problem with this proposition however is that even relatively simple reinsurance treaties are usually signed after the coverage period expires, with the parties relying on the placement slip in the interim.

Simply put, the reinsurance industry does not facilitate the drafting of complex contracts before performance. This is readily evident by examining how business has always been done. Treaties were never that important historically because they were never relied on or used. The parties knew what was expected of each other and they held to those expectations.

The problem today is that parties may no longer bind themselves to the custom and practice of the industry as stringently as they once did. However, the reinsurance transaction of today still leaves little room for the drafting and negotiation of complex contracts prior to performance. This puts the parties in a difficult position. To suggest further drafting and negotiation may risk the entire deal, but not to suggest clarifying certain terms may risk having the agreement enforced according to the intent of the parties.

The resulting problem is that a party to a reinsurance deal now has a window of opportunity, depending on the circumstances of how the business transaction was consummated, i.e. if and when a formal treaty is signed, to avoid arbitration.

Mealey's Litig. Rep.: Reins., Vol. 4, No. 3, at B-1 (June 9, 1993), recons. denied, 1993 WL 299232 (N.D. Cal. July 21, 1993). In *McCreary Tire & Rubber Co. v CEAT, S.p.A., 501 F.2d 1032, 1037 (3d Cir. 1974)* it was stated: "*. . .there is nothing discreti*onary about [Section 3 of the FAA]. It states that district courts shall at the request of a party to an arbitration agreement refer the parties to arbitration." And in *United Steelworkers of Am. v Warrior and Gulf Navigation Co.*, 80 S.Ct. 1347, 1353 (1960) it was stated: ". . .the court can refuse to compel arbitration only when there is "positive assurance that the arbitration clause is not susceptible of an interpretation that covers the asserted dispute". . ."; Hummer (1996), p. 229.

[120] *Clarendon Nat'l Ins. Co. v Transam. Ins. Co.*, No. 92 CIV 1483 (LMM), 1992 WL 122781 (S.D. N.Y. May 22, 1992).

[121] Hummer (1996), p. 230.

[122] Hummer (1996), p. 230.

The representative case law selected and discussed above shows that this situation has the potential to render well-intended and bargained-for arbitration clauses hanging in the wind.

Perhaps a solution would be to include a slightly more detailed arbitration clause in the placement slips, perhaps largely boilerplate, familiar to the parties, which leaves room for amendments to be made when the actual treaty is finalised.

If a dispute arises before consummation of the treaty, or if the treaty is never drafted and signed, the boilerplate provisions in the placement slip will control. Such a contract should be no less enforceable than the "arbitration clause" language used to compel arbitration,[123] and perhaps such language would have been enough to have justified compelling arbitration in *Frank B. Hall Inc. v Colorado School Districts Self-Insurance Pool.*[124]

Regardless of what safeguard is ultimately used, the point remains that not all participants in the reinsurance industry are playing by the rules established long ago, and in order to see that the intent of any reinsurance transaction is realized, the parties should be careful to take small steps, which will not upset the nature of the transaction, aimed at ensuring the rules are followed.[125]

4.4.5 The Arbitration Notice

Under section 14 of the Arbitration Act 1996, the parties are free to agree when arbitral proceedings are to be regarded as commenced for purposes of the Limitation Act or of any relevant contractual limitation period.

In the absence of any such agreement, the time of commencement of arbitral proceedings depends upon the relevant provisions of the arbitration agreement: if the arbitrator is named or designated in that agreement, the proceedings are commenced when one party serves on the other a written notice requiring submission of the matter in dispute to the person so named or designated; where the arbitrators are to be appointed by the parties, proceedings are commenced by service of a written notice in which one party requires the other to appoint an arbitrator or to agree to the appointment of an arbitrator; and where the arbitrators are to be appointed by a person other than the parties, arbitral proceedings are commenced when one party gives written notice to the designated appointor requesting him to make an appointment in respect of the dispute. Service of the arbitration notice is dealt with by section 76 of the Act.

Service may take place in any manner agreed by the parties. In the absence of such agreement, a notice may be served by any means shown to be effective. In

---

[123] In the case law discussed above.

[124] *Frank B. Hall Inc. v Colorado School Districts Self-Insurance Pool* No. 92-CV-225 (Colo. Dist. Ct. March 26, 1993).

[125] McDonald (2001), p. 338.

particular, a notice may be sent by ordinary pre-paid post to the addressee's last known principal residence or place of business or, in the case of a body corporate, its registered or principal office.

Notwithstanding that the Arbitration Act 1996 provides for a significant relaxation as compared with the previous rules on Service of arbitration notices, it will nevertheless remain prudent to provide for a means of proving that delivery of the notice has actually taken place. In case of difficulty, an application can be made to the court to direct service in a particular manner or to dispense with Service altogether, provided that any powers which the arbitrators may have in this respect have first been exhausted (section 77).[126]

4.4.6 Response to the Arbitration Notice

Once the notice has been served, the respondent should respond to it in the terms provided by the arbitration notice, if it in turn is in accordance with the terms of the arbitration agreement. For example, if the respondent is invited to appoint an arbitrator within a specified time or to agree to the appointment of an arbitrator, he should do so within the specified time, otherwise he will suffer the consequences of his default. If the respondent intends to make a counterclaim, then he should specify this in his notice so as to ensure that the reference will also be in respect of his counterclaim, otherwise the arbitration panel will have no jurisdiction over the counterclaim.[127]

4.4.7 Demanding Arbitration

Either party to the reinsurance agreement max commence an arbitration by making a demand on the other to arbitrate. Although most arbitration clauses require that the demand be in writing, the demand is generally no more than a simple, single-page document requesting arbitration. Once a demand for arbitration is made, the responding party usually has 30–60 days in which to appoint its arbitrator.

The procedures necessary to initiate arbitration are, of course, controlled by the language of the arbitration clause. When the arbitration clause fails to specify a time limit in which to respond, the demanding party should set a reasonable time limit. If the opposite party fails to respond to the demand or refuses to arbitrate, the demanding party may petition the court to compel arbitration under section 4 of the FAA. The arbitration must proceed in the district in which the petition is filed. Thus, the filing party may obtain the strategic advantage of determining the situs of

[126] Barlow Lyde and Gilbert LLP (2009), §§ 26.3.1.1, 26-5.

[127] Barlow Lyde and Gilbert LLP (2009), §§ 26-3, 26-4, 26-4/1.

the arbitration. In order for an arbitration agreement to be subject to the mandatory provisions of the Act, it must meet five criteria:

- It must be in writing
- It must involve interstate or foreign commerce
- The arbitration clause itself must not have been induced by fraud or be otherwise voidable
- The party seeking enforcement must not have waived its right to insist on arbitration and
- The other party to the contract must have failed to arbitrate pursuant to the contract terms.[128]

Courts also compel arbitration against non-signatories to reinsurance agreements under the following theories:

- *Agency*. Courts have compelled arbitration under agency theories.[129]
- *Estoppel*. Courts have held non-signatories bound by an arbitration clause when the non-signatory takes advantage of certain provisions of the agreement containing the arbitration provision.[130]
- *Incorporation*. Reinsurance contracts contain valid arbitration clauses when they incorporate all terms of an underlying reinsurance contract and the underlying contract contains an arbitration clause.[131] Similarly, courts have compelled

[128] Bank and Winters (1989), pp. 323–324.

[129] *Fencourt Reinsurance Co. Ltd. v ITT Indus., Inc.*, No. 06-4786, 2008 U.S. Dist. LEXIS 47724, at *20–27 (E.D. Pa. June 20, 2008) (compelling arbitration on agency grounds); *North River Ins. Co. v Transamerica Occidental Life Ins. Co.*, No. 3:99-CV-0682-L, 2002 U.S. Dist. LEXIS 10637, at *20 (N.D. Tex. June 12, 2002) (compelling reinsurer to arbitrate under agency theory, because its managing agent entered into reinsurance contracts on its behalf); Thomas and Lyons (2012), §§ 77.04[3][b], 77-48, 77-49.

[130] *International Ins. Agency Servs., LLC v Revios Reinsurance U.S., Inc.*, No. 04 C 1190, 2007 U.S. Dist. LEXIS 22229, at *14–19 (N.D. ***111***. Mar. 27, 2007) (compelling reinsurance intermediary to arbitrate under estoppel theory); *Fencourt Reinsurance Co. Ltd. v ITT Indus., Inc.*, No. 06-4786, 2008 U.S. Dist. LEXIS 47724, at *27–31 (E.D. Pa. June 20, 2008) (compelling arbitration on estoppel grounds, concluding that non-signatory reinsurer was bound by arbitration clause because it took advantage of other provisions of the agreement); Thomas and Lyons (2012), §§ 77.04[3][b], 77-48, 77-49.

[131] *Clarendon Nat'l Ins. Co. v Lan*, 152 F. Supp. 2d 506, 519–521 (S.D.N.Y. 2001) (compelling non-signatory to arbitrate where it signed guaranty that incorporated an agreement which contained a broad arbitration clause); *Burlington Ins. Co. v Trygg-Hansa Ins. Co. AB*, 9 F. App'x 196, 202 (4th Cir. 2001) (reinsurer's claim for declaratory relief relating to "Reconfirmation of Agreement" was arbitrable where it contained no arbitration clause but "include[d] all provisions of the Reinsurance Agreements, including the arbitration clauses.... Thus, it is clear that the ROA includes and is subject to the arbitration clauses included in the Reinsurance Agreements."); *Century Indem. Co. v Certain Underwriters at Lloyd's, London*, 584 F.3d 513, 555 (3d Cir. 2009) (affirming order compelling arbitration, concluding that retrocessional agreements incorporated arbitration clauses in reinsurance treaties where they provided that all terms of the reinsurance treaties applied to the retrocessional agreements); But see *Union Ins. Co. v Hull & Co.*, No. 4:10-cv-0337-JEG, 2011 U.S. Dist. LEXIS 147014 (S.D. Iowa Dec. 19, 2011)

arbitration of disputes arising from separate, related agreements where the parties' reinsurance contract contained a broad arbitration provision.[132]

- *Third-Party Beneficiary*. "Where a party's claims arise out of the underlying contract to which he was an intended third-party beneficiary, he is bound by the contract's terms, including an arbitration provision."[133]
- *Veil-Piercing*. Courts have compelled arbitration under veil-piercing theories.[134]

Arbitration agreements can survive a release of a reinsurance agreement that does not expressly abrogate the arbitration provision.[135]

4.4.8 Avoiding Arbitration

Responding parties may defend against a petition to compel arbitration on various grounds, including lack of jurisdictions.[136] They may additionally contend that there is no agreement between the parties, that the dispute is not arbitrable, that the agreement was induced by fraud, that the demanding party waived its right to arbitrate, or that multiple parties and multiple actions bar resort to arbitration.[137]

(refusing to compel arbitration of claim that cedent's insurance agent breached underwriting guidelines in placing direct-side policy, where guidelines contained no arbitration clause, were not incorporated into agreement between the parties, and the agreement's arbitration clause was narrow); Thomas and Lyons (2012), §§ 77.04[3][b], 77-48, 77-49.

[132] *Northbrook Indem. Co. v First Automotive Servs. Group*, No. 3:07-cv-61424, 2008 U.S. Dist. LEXIS 61424 (M.D. Fla. Aug. 1, 2008); *Gulf Guar. Life Ins. Co. v Connecticut Gen. Life Ins. Co.*, 957 F. Supp. 839, 841–842 (S.D. Miss. 1997); *National Am. Ins. Co. v Scor Reinsurance Co.*, 362 F.3d 1288, 1291–1292 (10th Cir. 2004) (compelling arbitration under hold harmless agreement relating to bonds as to which reinsurer served as co-surety with cedent, and which did not contain arbitration clause, where the parties' reinsurance treaty contained broad arbitration clause and reinsured the bonds at issue, concluding that the hold harmless agreement and the treaty were "closely related"); Thomas and Lyons (2012), §§ 77.04[3][b], 77-48, 77-49.

[133] *Doeff v Transatlantic Reinsurance Co.*, No. 07-2110, 2007 U.S. Dist. LEXIS 91879, at *(E.D. Pa. Dec. 13, 2007); See also: *Continental Cas. Co. v Certain Underwriters at Lloyd's London*, No. 02 Civ. 960 (TPG), 2004 U.S. Dist. LEXIS 4060, at *13–14 (S.D.N.Y. Mar. 15, 2004) (compelling reinsured to arbitrate as a third-party beneficiary of agreement containing arbitration clause); *Fencourt Reinsurance Co. Ltd. v ΓΓT Indus., Inc.*, No. 06-4786, 2008 U.S. Dist. LEXIS 47724, at *31–33 (E.D. Pa. June 20, 2008) (compelling arbitration where reinsurer was listed as third-party beneficiary of agreement containing arbitration clause); Thomas and Lyons (2012), §§ 77.04[3][b], 77-48, 77-49.

[134] *ProNational Ins. Co. v Axa Liabs. Mgrs, Inc.*, No. 2008-PEG-2022-S (N.D. Ala. Jan. 11, 2010); *Monumental Life Ins. Co. v R.A.J. Holdings, Inc.*, No. 99-1224, 1999 U.S. Dist. LEXIS 13035 (E.D. La. Aug. 18, 1999); Thomas and Lyons (2012), §§ 77.04[3][b], 77-48, 77-49.

[135] *Continental Ins. Co. v Allianz Ins. Co.*, No. 00 Civ. 4548 (JSM), 2001 U.S. Dist. LEXIS 3191, at *11–12 (S.D.N.Y. Mar. 23, 2001); Thomas and Lyons (2012), §§ 77.04[3][b], 77-48, 77-49.

[136] *Freemeont Indemnity Co. v Pt. Reasuransi Umum Indonesia*, No C.87-1209 (N.D. Caal. Filed March 23, 1987); Bank and Winters (1989), p. 324.

[137] Bank and Winters (1989), p. 324.

4.4.9 Lack of a Written Agreement to Arbitrate

The FAA requires that there be a written agreement among the parties to arbitrate.[138] Even this seemingly simple requirement has led to litigation.[139]

In *Atlantica Ins. Co., Ltd v Pan Atlantic Group, Inc.*[140] the 11 plaintiffs were foreign insurance and reinsurance companies belonging to the Pan-Atlantic Group ("PAG") reinsurance underwriting syndicate. A company became a member of the syndicate by subscribing to the Memorandum of Agreement ("MoA") with Pan-Atlantic underwriters Limited, Pan-Atlantic group, Inc., its subsidiaries and affiliates ("The Underwriting Manager"). PAG and the plaintiffs begun arbitration under the MoA. PAG then sought to include another corporation, "Pan-Atlantic Reinsurance Company Ltd" ("PARCO") as a claimant in the arbitration, contending that PARCO, an affiliate, was a proper party to the arbitration because of the contract language and its role as an underwriting manager.

The court found that it was not essential for PARCO to be specifically mentioned in the MoA. The references to subsidiaries and affiliates, plus PARCO's activities as an underwriting manager were held to be sufficient to establish an agreement to include PARCO in the arbitration proceedings.[141]

4.4.10 The Dispute Is Not Arbitrable

The most popular defence to arbitration is the allegation that the arbitration clause is not broad enough to encompass the dispute at issue. Arbitration clauses use various phrases to define the scope of arbitrable issues. However, the clauses usually refer to disputes arising under this agreement or arising out of or relating to the agreement.

Courts may construe differently these very similar phrases. Some courts restrict the "arising under" language to controversies capable of complete resolution by a procedure specified in the agreement, such as a contractual formula for equitable adjustments in costs and price or a contractual provision extending time under appropriate circumstances. Under this view, even claims for breach of contract are excluded, since such disputes cannot be resolved by the terms of the contract.[142] The phrase "arising out of" has generally been held to permit arbitration of a

---

[138] 9 U.S.C.§ 2.

[139] *C.V. Starr & Co. v Boston Reinsurance Corp.*, 190 Cal. App. 3d 1637, 236 cal. Rptr 167 (1987) interpreting the California Arbitration Act.; Bank and Winters (1989), p. 324.

[140] *Atlantica Ins. Co., Ltd v Pan Atlantic Group, Inc.* No 86-6363 (S.D.N.Y. June 24, 1987); Bank and Winters (1989), p. 325.

[141] Bank and Winters (1989), p. 325.

[142] *Bethlehem Steel Corp. v Grace Line Inc.*, 416 F.2d. 1096 (D.C. Cir. 1969); Bank and Winters (1989), p. 325.

broader range of disputes, including claims for breach of contract, recision and damages.[143] The language "arising under, out of, or in connection with, or in any manner relating to" has been given the broader scope.[144]

4.4.11 Fraud

Another tactic used to avoid arbitration is that of alleging that the reinsurance agreement was induced by fraud and hence is unenforceable. Most courts however, have adopted the theory of separability holding that only fraud in the inducement of the arbitration clause itself is grounds for avoiding arbitration. The issue of fraudulent inducement of the underlying contract must be determined by the arbitration panel, rather than by the court.[145]

4.4.12 Waiver of the Right to Arbitrate

A party's own conduct may preclude it from exercising its right to pursue arbitration. For example, a party may waive its right to arbitration if it fails to comply with the excess terms of the arbitration agreement, or if it excessively delays commencing arbitration or if it takes stapes inconsistent with the arbitration process.

Failure to comply with contractual time limitations for initiating arbitration may result in a waiver of the right to arbitrate. A party's excessive delay in initiating arbitration may violate the doctrine of laches and waive the right to arbitrate.[146] Also, a cedent or reinsurer is presumed to waive the right to arbitrate, when he takes actions inconsistent with the arbitration process, such as litigation actions.

However, a party to a reinsurance contract containing an arbitration clause does not waive the right to arbitrate merely by filing suit against a non-party, even if that action is related to the dispute being arbitrated.[147] But, a party's failure to raise

[143] *Sherk v Alberto-Culver Co.*, 417 U.S. 506 (1974); Bank and Winters (1989), p. 325.

[144] *Mediterranean Enterprises Inc. v Ssanvong Corp.*, 708 F. 2d 1458 (9th Cir. 1983), *American Home Assur. Co. v American Fidelity & Casualty Co.*, 356 F.2d 690 (2d Cir.1966), *Makress Lingerie Inc. v international Ladies Garment Workers Union*, 395 F. Supp. 110 (S.D.N.Y. 1975); Bank and Winters (1989), p. 325.

[145] *Prima Paint Corp. v Flood & Conklin Mfg. Co.* 288 U.S. 395 (1967); *Robert Lawrence Co. v Devonshire fabrics, Inc.*, 271 F.2d 402 (2d Cir. 1959); Bank and Winters (1989), p. 328.

[146] *Home Assurance Company v Belvedere Insurance Company*, 1992 U.S. Dist. LEXIS 33, 214 (2d Cir. 1992); Hammesfahr and Wright (1994), p. 285.

[147] *Usher Syndicate Ltd Inc v Figgie International Inc.* 1987 US Dist. LEXIS 13,340 (S.D. Fla. 1987); Hammesfahr and Wright (1994), pp. 284–285.

arbitration as a defence to litigation has been held to act as a waiver,[148] and participating in the litigation discovery process may constitute a waiver.[149] Consequently, cedents and reinsurers must exercise arbitration rights carefully.[150]

Arbitration demands must, also, be typically served and failure to do so may have significant consequences. If the arbitration is improperly served, a party may argue that the time period has commenced. The arbitration demand may also be held insufficient, thus rendering the demand null and void.[151]

Consistent with the strong federal policy favouring arbitration, most courts are reluctant to find that a waiver of a right to arbitration has occurred.[152] The party asserting waiver bears the burden of demonstrating that it has suffered prejudice as a result of the opposing party's failure to seek arbitration sooner.[153] Mere participation in a lawsuit will not result in a waiver.[154] Even if a party propounds substantial discovery demands, prejudice will not necessarily be established.[155]

The responding party may also seek to avoid arbitration by contending that the demanding party waived its right to arbitrate. Waiver is not easily established, and inconsistent behaviour alone is insufficient as proof. The mere filing of a complaint does not constitute a waiver. The essential test is whether the pursuit of a remedy other than arbitration has worked substantial prejudice to the other party.[156]

Waiver was also raised as a defence to arbitration in *Usher Syndicate Ltd. Inc. v Figgie International Inc.*,[157] whereby Figgie, a party to a reinsurance contract sought arbitration of a dispute with plaintiffs. Concurrently, Figgie instituted a related action in federal court against various defendants who were not parties to the reinsurance agreement. Plaintiffs argued that Figgie, by filing the collateral action, waived its right to arbitrate.

The court found no waiver, noting that the only method by which Figgie could effectively enforce its rights against those persons and entities who were not parties to the reinsurance agreement was to institute the collateral suit. In these

[148] *Ohio-Sealey Mattress Mfg. Co. v Kaplan*, 545 F. Supp. 765 (ND Ill. 1982) aff'd 712 F2d 270 (7th Cir. 1983); Hammesfahr and Wright (1994), p. 286.

[149] *Krammer v Hammond*, 943 F.2d 176 (2d Cir. 1991); Hammesfahr and Wright (1994), p. 286.

[150] Hammesfahr and Wright (1994), p. 286.

[151] *England Reinsurance Corp. v Tennessee Ins. Comp.*, 780 F. Supp 73 (D. Mass. 1991); Hammesfahr and Wright (1994), pp. 286, 287.

[152] *Sevinor v Merrill Lynch, Pierce, Fenner & Smith, Inc.*, 807 F.2d 16 (1st Cir. 1986).

[153] *Menorah Ins. Co., Ltd. v INX Reins. Corp.*, 72 F.3d 218 (1st Cir. 1995).

[154] *Sevinor v Merrill Lynch, Pierce, Fenner & Smith, Inc.*, 807 F.2d 16 (1st Cir. 1986).

[155] *Sevinor v Merrill Lynch, Pierce, Fenner & Smith, Inc.*, 807 F.2d 16 (1st Cir. 1986); Ostrager and Vyskocil (1996), pp. 14-10–14-14.

[156] *Commercial Metals Co. v International Union Marine Corp.*, 294 F. Supp. 570, 573 (S.D.N.Y. 1968), *ATSA of California Inc., v Continental Ins. Co.*, 702 F.2d 172, 175 (9th Cir. 1983), amended 754 F.2d 1394 (9th Cir. 1985), *Martin Marietta Aluminum Inc. v General Electric Co.*, 586 F.2d 143, 146 (9th Cir. 1978); Bank and Winters (1989), p. 328.

[157] *Usher Syndicate Ltd. Inc. v Figgie International Inc.*, No 87-1079 (S.D. Fla. Oct. 22, 1978); Bank and Winters (1989), p. 328.

circumstances the court held that filing the suit was not inconsistent with Figgie's right to require arbitration of its dispute with plaintiffs.[158]

4.4.13 Multiple Parties and Multiple Actions

Parties also sometime argue that the existence of multiple parties and multiple actions bar resort to arbitration. Attempts have been made to avoid arbitration by filing class actions, or by initiating suits against not only the party with whom the arbitration agreement exists but also against third parties such as agents or brokers. The courts have held that the addition of third parties will not bar arbitration.[159] However, the effect of class action procedures on the right to arbitrate claims remains unresolved.[160]

4.4.13.1 Class Action in Reinsurance Arbitration

Litigation has also resulted from ambiguity over whether arbitration agreements under separate contracts underlying larger reinsurance programs call for consolidated or class arbitration as opposed to separate arbitrations. The clear trend among courts is to defer to arbitrators the question of consolidation, finding that the question is procedural.

In *Certain Underwriters at Lloyd's London v Westciester Fire Insurance Co.*,[161] a dispute arose as to whether separate contracts underlying a reinsurance program must have separate arbitrations or whether they must be consolidated for purposes of arbitration. The court cited extensive precedent for the proposition that where a reinsurance agreement is silent, the issue of whether parties are entitled to individualized arbitration or to consolidated arbitration is a procedural question for arbitrators to decide.

In *Dorinco Reinsurance Co. v ACE American Insurance Co.*[162] the cedent entered into a common reinsurance agreement (as well as individual slip agreements) with 16 separate reinsurers. A dispute arose as to whether each one of the 16 reinsurers was entitled to its own arbitration panel or whether all of the reinsurers had to arbitrate as a group.

[158] *Usher Syndicate Ltd. Inc. v Figgie International Inc.*, No 87-1079 (S.D. Fla. Oct. 22, 1978) at *2; Bank and Winters (1989), p. 328.

[159] *Lawson Fabrics Inc. v Akzona Inc.* 355 F. Supp. 1146, 1151 (S.D.N.Y: 1973), *Hilti Inc. v Oldach*, 392 F.2d 368, 369 n.2 (1st Cir. 1968); Bank and Winters (1989), p. 328.

[160] *Southland Corp. v Keating*, 465 U.S. 1 (1984); Bank and Winters (1989), p. 328.

[161] *Certain Underwriters at Lloyd's London v Westciester Fire Insurance Co.*, 752 N.Y.S.2d 611 (N.Y. App. Div. 2002).

[162] *Dorinco Reinsurance Co. v ACE American Insurance Co.* No. 07-12622, 2008 WL 192270 (E. D Mich. Jan. 23, 2008).

The court concluded that the arbitration provision was ambiguous in addressing each reinsurer's right to separate arbitration proceedings. The court held that the arbitrators should determine the structure of the parties' arbitration absent an express provision in the arbitration agreement.

Yet, in a recent non-reinsurance case, *Stolt-Nielsen S.A. v Animalfeeds International Corp.*[163] the U.S.A. Supreme Court held that class arbitration cannot be imposed upon the parties unless there is a contractual basis for concluding that the parties agreed to it. While *Stolt-Nielsen S.A. v Animalfeeds International Corp.*[164]provided that silence on the issue of class arbitration is not commensurate with consent, it would nevertheless be prudent for parties to expressly state in their arbitration agreements that they do not consent to class arbitration.

Hence, it is concluded that many arbitration clauses need clarity. Of course, no contract provision will be immune from a party's challenge to its meaning, but these cases help reveal areas of ambiguity that can be addressed by providing clear language reflecting the parties' intent. Very often, parties to a reinsurance contract give short shrift in the negotiating process to the dispute resolution clause, often accepting boilerplate language from the reinsurance intermediary or from the cedent. And while marketing and underwriting personnel would rather assume that disputes will never happen, care in drafting the dispute resolution clause will inure to the benefit of both parties when the inevitable disputes do arise.

In *Pedcor Management Co. Inc. v Nations Personnel of Texas*[165] North American Indemnity (NAI), a Belgian company, entered into reinsurance contracts with 408 ERISA Plans throughout the US, all of which provided for arbitration of any dispute between the parties in connection with the contract. The ERISA Plans intervened in a suit originally brought by NAI against the third party administrator for negligent intervention, claiming that NAI defaulted on the payment of claims under the reinsurance contracts. The District Court entered a "take nothing" judgment against NAI and then held a hearing to discuss the possibility of certifying a class for purposes of an arbitration against NAI. The Court certified a class for all ERISA plans that bought reinsurance from NAI whose claims had not been paid. Pedcor appealed. The Fourth Circuit affirmed.

The Court noted the US Supreme Court's holding in *Green Tree Financial Corp. v Bazzle*[166] that when an arbitration clause does not expressly forbid a class action and the arbitration clause language is broad enough to embrace the class certification issue, that issue is one for the arbitrator to decide. The Fourth Circuit determined that since NAI's reinsurance agreements stated that "arbitrations shall be governed by the laws of the state of Texas" it was broad enough to encompass the FAA which was incorporated into state law. The Court stated that the simultaneous

[163] *Stolt-Nielsen S.A. v Animalfeeds International Corp.* 130 S. Ct. 1758 (2010).

[164] *Stolt-Nielsen S.A. v Animalfeeds International Corp.* 130 S. Ct. 1758 (2010).

[165] *Pedcor Management Co. Inc. v Nations Personnel of Texas*, 343 F.3d 355 (4th Cir. 2003).

[166] *Green Tree Financial Corp. v Bazzle* 123 S.Ct. 2402 (2003).

applicability of the FAA into state law would preempt a Texas court from making a class-certification decision because the FAA preempts inconsistent state law.

4.4.14 *Service of a Demand for Arbitration*

This must comply with the arbitration clause in the treaty, and generally the demand will set forth the relief sought. A letter usually is sent demanding arbitration and granting the other party 30 days to respond. Timely demand for arbitration is also important under Section 4 of the FAA.[167] After making a demand for arbitration, if necessary, applications to judicial courts should be made (for example, to compel arbitration, stay proceedings, or consolidate arbitration proceedings).

4.4.15 *Selection of Arbitrator*

The initial step is contacting and interviewing possible candidates to learn about their previous positions and/or possible conflicts that may exist.[168]

4.4.15.1 Selection of the Umpire

Usually the two parties choosing arbitrators select an umpire from a list submitted by the parties. If a decision cannot be reached, it is common for the parties to strike two of the other's names (if three had originally been submitted) and then "draw lots," which essentially means flipping a coin or using some other equivalent to choose between the remaining two.

4.4.15.2 Statement of Position

As with any arbitration, once the panel is selected, the parties are directed to prepare and submit a written statement outlining the issues to the panel of arbitrators and possibly to exchange the statements.

[167] (FAA), 9 U.S.C. Section 1 et seq.

[168] A directory of arbitrators is maintained on the website of the Reinsurance Association of America, available at www.reinsurancearbitrators.com; McDonald (2001), p. 330.

4.4.15.3 The Arbitration Panel

The importance of the arbitration panel's qualifications and the process of selecting an arbitrator and umpire are matters of great concern in any arbitration. The number of arbitrators is a matter to be decided by the parties. The method of appointing arbitrators may be provided for in the arbitration agreement, depending on how detailed the latter is.

A reinsurance contract may provide that a panel of three arbitrators is to decide for the dispute concerned or that one sole arbitrator may be appointed. In selecting a party arbitrator, a party should consider that the arbitrator understands the issues involved, is not necessarily predisposed towards the opposite party's opinion and can forcefully articulate his view.

Also, reinsurance contracts will often have strict deadlines for selecting arbitrators, with a penalty of allowing the opposing party to select both party arbitrators.[169]

In *New England Reinsurance Corporation v Tennessee Ins. Comp.*,[170] the U.S.A. district court for the district of Massachusetts held that an 8 day delay, absent bad faith, in advising the reinsurer of the selection of its party arbitrator did not cause the cedent to forfeit its right to select its party arbitrator.

But in *Evanston Ins. Comp. v Gerling Global Reins. Corp.*[171] it was held that failure to advise the opposing party of the arbitrator selection within the contractually agreed upon time was improper.

Arbitrators should be qualified enough to deal with the issues of the dispute involved. Thus, they are often current or retired officers or directors of an insurance or reinsurance company. They also need to be impartial and unbiased so as to make their own determination fee from the influence of the other parties.

In addition, arbitrators and umpires should disclose any possible bias to the parties as soon as they become aware of the possibility of an impartiality or bias issue, because it may result in the arbitrator's disqualification.[172]

Courts have strictly enforced time limits for the appointment of arbitrators. Arbitration provisions typically identify certain minimal criteria the arbitrators

[169] *Re Arbitration between Employers Insurance of Wasau and Certain Underwriters at Lloyd's*, No 91-CIV-529 (1992, Wis. Cir. Ct Marathon Cty), 3 Mealey's Reins. Rep. No. 13; Hammesfahr and Wright (1994), p. 296.

[170] *New England Reinsurance Corporation v Tennessee Ins. Comp.*, 780 F. Supp. 73 (D. Mass 1991).

[171] *Evanston Ins. Comp. v Gerling Global Reins. Corp.*, 1990 WL 141, 442 (ND Ill 1990) 1 Mealey's Reins. Rep. No 11; Hammesfahr and Wright (1994), p. 297.

[172] *Employers Ins. of Wasau v National Fire Ins. Company*, 933 F.2d 1481 (9th Cir. 1991). *Metropolitan Property and Casualty Ins. Company v J C Penney Casualty Ins. Company*, 780 F. Supp. 885 (D. Conn. 1991). *Merit Ins. Company v Leatherby Ins. Company*, 714 F.2d 673 (7th Cir.), 464 US (1009) 1983. *International Insurance Company v Certain Underwriters at Lloyd's London*, No 88 C 9838 (N.D: Ill, Sept. 8, 1992) 3 Mealey's Reins. Rep. No 10; *Northwestern National Ins. Comp. v Allstate Ins. Company*, No 88-C-480 (ED Wisc. Sept. 13, 1993), 4 Mealey'S Reins. Rep. No 10, B-1; Hammesfahr and Wright (1994), pp. 298–302.

must meet, such as being disinterested current or former officers of an insurance or reinsurance company.

Courts have, at times, refused to hear prehearing challenges, leaving the litigant with little choice but to proceed to arbitration and raise a challenge to any subsequent award, or have entertained prehearing challenges.[173]

Arbitration agreements typically include provisions stipulating the number of arbitrators and their qualifications, the timing and method by which the panel is to be selected and whether one arbitrator is to act as an umpire or chairman of the panel. In the U.S.A. if the agreement is silent on the method for selecting arbitrators or if the parties "fail to avail themselves" of the procedures agreed upon for selecting arbitrators, a Court is authorised under the FAA[174] to appoint one or more arbitrators upon application by a party.[175]

4.4.15.3.1 Qualifications of Reinsurance Arbitrators

Most reinsurance disputes are resolved through arbitration as opposed to litigation. Indeed, it is the rare reinsurance treaty or facultative certificate that does not contain an arbitration clause. Equally rare is a reinsurance contract arbitration clause that does not provide for a tripartite arbitration panel. In other words, each party selects an arbitrator and the arbitrators then select an umpire.

The reinsurance industry elects to submit its disputes to arbitration so that a panel of industry experts can resolve the issues involved through a process that is generally less time consuming, expensive and formal than traditional court proceedings. In fact, most judges are unlikely to possess more than a cursory understanding of the customs and practices of the insurance/reinsurance industry.[176] By utilising arbitrators, the parties to a reinsurance dispute avail themselves of the arbitrators' knowledge of industry custom and practice.

Due to the purposeful informality of the arbitration process, a degree of uncertainty is present in arbitration that is not prevalent in litigation. Judicial precedent or the application of evidentiary rules does not strictly bid arbitrators, unlike judges. Rather, arbitrators are expected to apply their experience, personal knowledge of the industry and their individual sense of fairness. While benefits unquestionably inure to the reinsurance industry from its reliance on arbitration as a means of dispute resolution, the process, by its very nature, raises issues not generally contested in the context of litigation.

---

[173] Hummer (1996), p. 231.

[174] FAA, 9 USC §5.

[175] *Pacific Reinsurance Mgmt. Corp. v Ohio Reinsurance Corp.*, 935 F2d 1019, 1022–1023; *AIG Global Trade and Political Risk Ins. Co. v Odyssey Am. Reinsurance Corp.*, 2006 US Dist. LEXIS 73258 at 15–17 Thomas et al. (2011), § 40-23.

[176] Given the prevalence of arbitration provisions in reinsurance treaties and certificates, courts are infrequently called upon to resolve reinsurance disputes, thereby lessening the opportunities for the judiciary to gain an understanding of the industry; Kareken et al. (2000), p. 141.

One fundamental issue that parties to an arbitration procedure must consider is whether to challenge the qualifications of the selected arbitrators. Because of the significant authority vested in the arbitrators, the right of a party to seek to disqualify an arbitrator who does not meet the requirements contained in the arbitration agreement becomes a powerful tool in shaping the arbitration.

If a party believes challenging the arbitrator's qualifications is appropriate, it must concomitantly also determine when, and in what forum, it should raise such a challenge. While many arbitration agreements contain requirements that the arbitrators be "disinterested" or "impartial," the fact that an arbitration agreement does not contain such a requirement should not prevent a party from challenging an arbitrator's qualifications to serve on a particular panel. Arbitrators should be financially disinterested and not under any party's control. Otherwise, arbitration becomes a far less reliable method of dispute resolution.[177]

Arbitrators should be willing to make a full disclosure of ail potential conflicts of interest. Thus, nominated arbitrators should disclose their contacts with the parties and any prior arbitration proceedings involving the same or similar issues.

If the potential arbitrator has been involved with a particular issue in the past, the arbitrator's decision concerning that issue should be disclosed so that any predilection in favour of one side or the other might be determined. Also, if the arbitrator is to be professionally involved with the issue to be arbitrated in the foreseeable future, this should be disclosed.

The arbitration process must remain an economically viable alternative to formal litigation. If an unqualified arbitrator is allowed to hear the matter and a party cannot challenge the arbitrator's qualifications until after a decision is rendered, considerable time, effort and money are likely to be wasted.

Accordingly, challenges to a particular arbitrator's qualifications should be undertaken as early in the process as possible. Such a challenge should begin with the arbitrators themselves.

If a truly unqualified arbitrator remains after the matter is raised with the panel, courts should be willing to hear such challenges. Unless a court is ultimately receptive, one of the major purposes of the parties' agreement to arbitrate, an economic resolution of the dispute, will be frustrated. To protect the integrity of the process, any potential bias of an arbitrator needs to be disclosed early and any challenge to such an arbitrator should be resolved before the arbitration proceeds.

4.4.15.3.2 Appointment of the Panel

Most commonly in English reinsurance arbitrations, the arbitration panel will consist of either a sole arbitrator or two arbitrators sitting with or without an umpire. This contrasts with the Continental and American approach in which the panel often consists of three arbitrators.

---

[177] Kareken et al. (2000), p. 141.

The arbitration agreement may make specific provisions for the appointment of one or more arbitrators and an umpire, and the parties should have regard to these provisions when seeking to appoint an arbitrator.

If the arbitration agreement provides that each of two parties is to appoint one arbitrator, there is a presumption that a third arbitrator is to be appointed, who will act as chairman of the tribunal rather than as umpire [section 15(2)]. Unless the parties agree to the contrary, the chairman has a casting vote: section 20(4). If the arbitration agreement is silent with regard to the number of arbitrators to be appointed, there is a presumption that the tribunal should consist of a sole arbitrator: [section 15(3)]. The parties are free to agree on the procedure for appointing the arbitrator or arbitrators and any chairman or umpire [section 16(1)]. If there is no agreement, section 16 further provides a detailed timetable for appointments to be effected. Subject to the parties not agreeing otherwise, a sole arbitrator must be appointed within 28 days after service of a request for such appointment. In the case of a panel consisting of two or three arbitrators, each party must make its appointment within 14 days of being requested to do so, and the two arbitrators so appointed must appoint the third member of the panel forthwith (if he is to be a third arbitrator) or at any time prior to a substantive or interlocutory hearing (if he is to be an umpire).

Where the arbitration agreement contemplates a panel of two or more arbitrators, and one party refuses to make an appointment, the other may appoint his nominee as sole arbitrator, which appointment will become effective if the defaulting party does not make an appointment within 7 days of receiving an appropriate notice (section 17). If the arbitration agreement expressly or impliedly provides for a reference to a sole arbitrator, but the parties cannot agree upon a choice and no provision has been made for a third party to make the appointment, an application may be made to the court for the necessary appointment (section 18).

Section 27 sets out the procedure where an arbitrator ceases to hold office and the parties have not reached agreement as to how the vacancy should be filled. Section 27 (3) provides that section 16 (Procedure for appointment of arbitrators) shall apply in relation to the filling of any vacancy as in relation to an original appointment.

The relationship between sections 16 and 27 was considered in *Federal Insurance Co.* v *Transamerica Occidental Life Insurance Co.*[178] On 14 June 1999, the arbitrator appointed by Transamerica resigned his appointment through ill health. A question arose as to whether Transamerica had 30 days to nominate a new arbitrator (which was the period provided for the initial appointment in the arbitration clause in the relevant reinsurance contract), or only 14 days pursuant to section 16(5) of the Arbitration Act, which provides that, where the tribunal consists of three arbitrators, each party shall appoint one arbitrator not later than 14 days after service of a request by the other party to do so.

---

[178] *Federal Insurance Co. v Transamerica Occidental Life Insurance Co.* [1999] 2 Lloyd's Rep 286 (QB Com Ct).

The parties had not agreed a procedure for the appointment of a substitute arbitrator, so there were rival contentions as to whether the correct time period was 14 or 30 days. Federal was concerned that the hearing, which was set for 5 July, would be lost if Transamerica did not appoint a substitute arbitrator within 14 days. Rix J. pointed out that section l(b) of the Act provides that the parties are free to agree how to resolve their disputes. Against this background, he decided in favour of a 30-day period, construing section 16(1) when read together with section 27 (3) as if it provided that the parties are free to agree on the procedure for appointing the arbitrator or arbitrators, and any such agreement shall apply in relation to the filling of any vacancy as in relation to an original appointment.

In the absence of any specific provisions in the arbitration agreement, the parties are free to choose an arbitrator with either a legal or market background. Arbitration clauses may however restrict the parties' choice of arbitrator. If the court is called upon to assist in the process of appointment, it must have due regard to the agreement of the parties in this respect (section 19).

One often encounters, in London market reinsurance contracts, the following provision in an arbitration clause: "The arbitrators and umpire shall be disinterested executive officials of insurance or reinsurance companies or current or retired underwriting members of Lloyd's." It is difficult and time-consuming enough to find an arbitrator suitably qualified to hear a reinsurance dispute even without such limitations being placed on the potential nominees to the arbitration panel.

Had an argument presented in *Pan Atlantic Group Incorporated* v *Hassneh Insurance Company of Israel Ltd*[179] been successful, this task would have been made even more difficult. The case concerned a challenge to the qualifications of an arbitrator. Hassneh had appointed John Butler—at that time the legal officer of the Mercantile & General Reinsurance Company Plc—as its arbitrator in a dispute arising out of a quota share reinsurance agreement. The agreement included an arbitration clause containing the provision that the arbitrators and umpire shall be disinterested executive officials of insurance or reinsurance companies. After his appointment, but prior to the hearing of the arbitration, Mr. Butler retired from the Mercantile & General Re to take up an appointment as a consultant to Barlow Lyde and Gilbert. Pan Atlantic thereupon applied to the court for a declaration that Mr Butler was not qualified to continue to act as Hassneh's arbitrator. The basis of Pan Atlantic's argument was that, although Mr Butler was indubitably qualified in terms of the relevant words of the arbitration clause at the date of his appointment, he was now no longer an official of a reinsurance Company and was therefore disqualified. Both Hirst J. and the Court of Appeal rejected Pan Altantic's application. In its judgment, the Court of Appeal set out Mr Butler's impressive qualifications and expertise: he had worked for the Mercantile & General Re for 29 years, the latter 25 as its legal officer; he was a non-practising barrister as well as the then President of the Association Internationale de Droit des Assurances (the International

[179] *Pan Atlantic Group Incorporated v Hassneh Insurance Company of Israel Ltd* [1992] 2 Lloyd's Rep 120 (CA).

Association for Insurance Law, known as AIDA—the acronym coming from the initials of its French title) and of the British Insurance Law Association (BILA, which is the national chapter of AIDA established in the UK); he was the initiator of AIDA's Reinsurance and Insurance Arbitration Society (ARIAS); and over the past 10 years he had frequently been appointed as an arbitrator in insurance and reinsurance disputes. He was also one of the co-authors of "Butler & Merkin on Reinsurance Law". In the light of this evidence, it was not surprising that the Court of Appeal considered Mr Butler "as well-qualified as anyone to sit as an arbitrator, his experience enhanced by his new-found association with leading insurance solicitors".

The Court of Appeal held that the purpose of the qualification in the arbitration clause was to ensure that the right sort of individuals sat as arbitrators, rather than to ensure that those appointed as arbitrators kept their expertise up-to-date.

The court rejected an argument that there was a risk that an arbitrator's knowledge might become obsolete. It was more important that arbitrators should be familiar with market practice at the time when the dispute arose, and that was ensured by the requirement that they should be serving employees at the time of their appointment.

The court pointed out that the pool of arbitrators capable of being called upon to sit in reinsurance disputes in London is a relatively small one, at any rate in relation to the volume of work available. In addition, those who might be expected to be allowed to take time to sit as arbitrators would normally be senior employees.

It would be ridiculous if, on accepting appointment, an arbitrator were impliedly expected to undertake to remain employed (assuming this was a matter within his own choice) until the final determination of the arbitration. If that were indeed the true construction of the clause, the court pointed out, the number of those willing to accept appointment as arbitrators might be even more diminished.

It is, generally speaking, probably preferable not to limit the parties' choice of potential arbitrators too rigorously, and to leave it to their good sense to nominate someone who holds the requisite qualifications. A strict construction of a qualification provision can lead to results which the parties probably did not envisage.

For example, in *Employers Insurance of Wausau* v *Certain Underwriters at Lloyd's*[180] the arbitration clause required the arbitrators to be "executive officers of insurance companies". The nomination of a director of an Insurance Company as an arbitrator was held to be invalid because the terms "executive officer" and "director" had distinct and mutually exclusive meanings under Wisconsin law.

ARIAS, the AIDA Reinsurance and Insurance Arbitration Society mentioned above, has issued a recommended arbitration clause for use in reinsurance disputes which, while seeking to ensure that those nominated as arbitrators have the relevant expertise, aims at the same time at giving the parties a considerable measure of flexibility in their choice of nominees. The provision which ARIAS recommends

---

[180] *Employers Insurance of Wausau* v *Certain Underwriters at Llayd's*, No. 91-CV-529, slip op. at 6–8 (Wis. Cir. Ct., Marathon County, October 14, 1992).

reads as follows: "The arbitrators shall be persons (including those who have retired) with not less than 10 years' experience of insurance or reinsurance within the industry or as lawyers or other professional advisers serving the industry." The rules of natural justice provide that the arbitrator should be a disinterested and unbiased person. Such a person can, on occasion, prove difficult to find even in a retired member of the reinsurance market.

In the USA the party-appointed arbitrator usually becomes an advocate for the party appointing him.

Two notable decisions in 2009 concerned the appointment of replacement arbitrators during the course of a hearing.

First, in *WellPoint, Inc. v John Hancock Life Ins. Co.*[181] the Seventh Circuit ruled that a party seeking to challenge the appointment of a replacement arbitrator must do so at the time of the appointment, or else lose its ability to make such a challenge. During the course of the arbitration, plaintiff obtained new counsel and requested that its party-appointed arbitrator resign. After plaintiff proposed two separate replacement arbitrators, who were rejected by defendant, defendant's party-appointed arbitrator suggested that the remaining panel members propose three replacement arbitrators from which plaintiff could choose. Plaintiff agreed to this procedure and chose one of those replacements. Defendant agreed that the arbitrator chosen by plaintiff satisfied the prerequisites for service on the panel.

Plaintiff ultimately prevailed in an arbitration against defendant and later petitioned the District Court for confirmation of the award. Defendant cross-moved to vacate the arbitration award, on the grounds that the arbitration panel exceeded its authority by accepting the resignation of plaintiff's initial arbitrator and subsequently filling the vacancy in a manner not specified in the arbitration agreement. The District Court confirmed the panel's award, and denied defendant's cross-motion to vacate. Defendant then appealed.

The arguments raised by defendant to the Seventh Circuit in support of its motion to vacate were identical to those addressed by the District Court. The Seventh Circuit rejected this argument, relying upon Section 5 of the FAA, which sets forth a rule that applies to the "mid-stream" loss of an arbitrator. That section provides that, in "filling a vacancy," as well as in other circumstances, the court can appoint an arbitrator upon the application of either party to do so. Thus, having failed to object to the replacement arbitrator at the time of appointment, defendant had effectively waived its right to do so, and the arbitrators acted within their authority by filling the vacancy.

The Seventh Circuit further rejected defendant's argument that a party may also challenge an arbitrator's "mid-stream" appointment under Section 10(a)(4) of the FAA after the conclusion of an arbitration, noting that this would improperly permit an objecting party to wait until after the proceeding to make such a challenge, resulting in delay and inefficiency.

---

[181] *WellPoint, Inc. v John Hancock Life Ins. Co.* 576 F.3d 643 (7th Cir. 2009).

Rather, defendant's own participation in the substitution process estopped it from later challenging the replacement arbitrator's appointment, despite the fact that defendant specifically reserved its right to do so.

The second noteworthy decision, namely that in the case of *In the Matter of the Petition of Ins. Co. of North America against Public Service Mut. Ins. Co.*,[182] involved an arbitrator who resigned from a panel for health reasons prior to the rendering of an award. Because the arbitration agreement did not specify how to deal with appointing a replacement, the U.S. District Court for the Southern District of New York held that the arbitration had to start over from the beginning, with each party having the opportunity to select its own party-appointed arbitrator.[183]

Thereafter, upon learning from one of the parties that the previously ill arbitrator's health had improved such that he was actively seeking employment, the court granted the plaintiff's motion for relief pursuant to Fed. R. Civ. P. 60(b)(2) and (6), and vacated its prior ruling.

The court noted that had it been aware of this fact at the time of its previous order, it could have reappointed the arbitrator under Section 5 of the FAA, because the arbitration clauses in the reinsurance contracts at issue were silent with respect to the procedure to be followed to fill a vacancy created by the death or resignation of an arbitrator.

Accordingly, pursuant to that statute, the court reappointed the "resigned" arbitrator to the panel and ordered the parties to continue the arbitration proceedings as they were before the arbitrator's initial withdrawal.[184]

Unlike the U.S.A. position, where the party-appointed arbitrator usually becomes an advocate for the party appointing him, the party-appointed arbitrator in an English reinsurance arbitration is expected to adopt a neutral approach and come to an independent decision on the facts before him.

English arbitrators acting as advocates have been appointed in the past, in the context of shipping or commodity disputes, and may be appointed in the future, but this concept is considered to be on the wane, and generally speaking it is not common or appropriate in the reinsurance context.

Section 24(l) (a) of the Arbitration Act 1996 provides that an arbitrator may be subject to removal by the court if "circumstances exist that give rise to justifiable doubts as to his impartiality". A natural extension of this neutral role is that the party appointing an arbitrator should not attempt to ascertain from him, in advance of his appointment, whether he would be sympathetic to that party's arguments. Further, once appointed, the arbitrator may not in any circumstances communicate privately, with either party, without the knowledge and consent of his co-arbitrator and of the other party. All documents and evidence which the party-appointed arbitrator might receive must be disclosed and copied to the other members of the

[182] *In the Matter of the Petition of Ins. Co. of North America against Public Service Mut. Ins. Co.* No. 08-cv-7003 (S.D.N.Y.).

[183] Kanefsky and Diubaldo (2009), p. 9.

[184] Kanefsky and Diubaldo (2009), p. 9.

tribunal. In practice, upon appointment an arbitrator will generally request a copy of the arbitration agreement and any other documents which evidence the parties' agreement to arbitrate. He should ensure that any contractual limitation provisions within the arbitration agreement have been complied with and he should ensure that he has jurisdiction to arbitrate in the dispute.[185]

4.4.15.3.3 Critique

A critical area of change between the approach of the previous arbitration regime and that of the Arbitration Act 1996 is the framework within which arbitrations are meant to be conducted. The key elements are party autonomy, arbitrator empowerment and court support rather than court intervention.

The Arbitration Act 1996 provides a coherent framework against which the parties should be able to devise an appropriate procedure. The parties are at liberty to agree—either in the arbitration agreement or at any time thereafter—how the arbitration is to proceed and what evidence is to be taken.

Section 34 sets out a non-exhaustive check-list of points to be addressed including the venue and timetable for the proceedings; the language in which the proceedings are to be conducted and whether any documents need to be translated; whether pleadings are to be used; whether—and if so which—documents should be disclosed; whether and to what extent there should be oral or written submissions or evidence; whether strict rules of evidence as to admissibility or weight of any material should be applied; and whether and to what extent the tribunal should itself take the initiative in ascertaining the facts and the law.

In the absence of such agreement, the tribunal itself is able to determine all procedural and evidential matters, in addition to which it has other powers to enable it to maintain the impetus of the proceedings. The powers of the parties and of the arbitrators are limited only in so far as there are matters in relation to the conduct of legal proceedings which are more properly within the province of the courts, such as the preservation of evidence, the compulsion of witnesses to attend a hearing, and the enforcement of peremptory orders.

Even powers such as these are, however, for the most part available to the arbitrators, subject to any contrary agreement by the parties. In such circumstances, the court may act only after all available arbitral remedies have been exhausted. The powers exercisable by arbitrators are subject to the safeguard that, as a matter of overriding principle, the tribunal is bound to act fairly and impartially between the parties, avoiding unnecessary delay and expense and giving each party a reasonable opportunity of putting its case and dealing with the case of its opponent (section 33). If the arbitrators fail to observe such principles, they are susceptible to being removed from their positions, having their remuneration reviewed, or having their award set aside.

[185] Barlow Lyde and Gilbert LLP (2009), §§ 26.3.2, 26-5–26-8.

The spirit of the Arbitration Act 1996, however, is that such sanctions should be exercised only in respect of acts or omissions of the arbitrators which the court regards as indefensible. A party aggrieved by any aspect of arbitral proceedings must act promptly to preserve its rights in this regard.

Parties will lose any right to object to the jurisdiction of the tribunal, the conduct of the arbitration, non-compliance with the provisions of the Act or the arbitration agreement, or any other irregularity affecting the tribunal or the proceedings, if objection is not taken either immediately or within any period prescribed by the Act, the arbitral agreement, or the tribunal.

It is therefore incumbent upon a party with knowledge of grounds for an objection to raise the matter promptly or else lose its rights to object. A party will not, however, lose the right to object if it can show that "... at the time [it] took part or continued to take part in the proceedings, [it] did not know and could not with reasonable diligence have discovered the grounds for the objection" [section 73 (1)].[186]

4.4.15.3.4 Arbitrator Partiality

In *Nationwide Mutual Insurance Co. v Home Insurance Co.*,[187] the Sixth Circuit analyzed claims of bias regarding a party-appointed arbitrator. Nationwide sought vacatur of an arbitration award issued in a reinsurance dispute with Home Insurance Company, claiming that Home's party-appointed arbitrator evidenced partiality because of his "alleged nondisclosure of certain business and social relationships with Home." The trial court had rejected Nationwide's argument, relying on *Apperson v Fleet Carrier Corp.*,[188] which held that evident partiality may be found "only where a reasonable person would have to conclude that an arbitrator was partial to one party to the arbitration."[189]

In considering the claim, the Sixth Circuit noted that the FAA presumes that arbitration awards will be confirmed[190] and that a court may vacate an arbitration award only in limited circumstances, including "where there was evident partiality or corruption in the arbitrators, or either of them.'"[191]

Nationwide argued that the court should only apply *Apperson v Fleet Carrier Corp.*,[192] in "actual bias" cases "where the evident partiality claim is based on facts

[186] Barlow Lyde and Gilbert LLP (2009), §§ 26.4, 26-9, 26-10.

[187] *Nationwide Mutual Insurance Co. v Home Insurance Co.* 429 F.3d 640 (6th Cir. 2005); Chiafullo et al. (2007), p. 461.

[188] *Apperson v Fleet Carrier Corp.* 879 F.2d 1344 (6th Cir. 1989); Chiafullo et al. (2007), p. 461.

[189] *Nationwide Mutual Insurance Co. v Home Insurance Co.* 429 F.3d 640 (6th Cir. 2005) at *644; Chiafullo et al. (2007), p. 461.

[190] 9 U.S.C. § 9 (1999); Chiafullo et al. (2007), p. 461.

[191] 9 U.S.C. §10(a)(2) (2006); Chiafullo et al. (2007), p. 461.

[192] *Apperson v Fleet Carrier Corp.* 879 F.2d 1344 (6th Cir. 1989); Chiafullo et al. (2007), p. 461.

known or disclosed and objected to by the challenging party prior to or during the arbitration.'"[193] In a case where there is an alleged non-disclosure, Nationwide argued, such nondisclosure alone "mandates vacatur under either a 'reasonable impression of bias' or 'appearance of bias' standard.'"[194]

The court disagreed, holding that *Apperson v Fleet Carrier Corp.*,[195] supplied the correct standard even in nondisclosure cases and that the party alleging bias must show "more than an amorphous institutional predisposition toward the other side.'"[196] The court wrote, "[T]he alleged partiality must be direct, definite, and capable of demonstration, and 'the party asserting it . . . must establish specific facts that indicate improper motives on the part of the arbitrator.'"[197]

Applying *Apperson v Fleet Carrier Corp.*,[198] the Sixth Circuit found that the arbitrator had made full and timely disclosures regarding his business relationship with Home and that Nationwide had failed to make any showing as to how those disclosures manifested evident partiality.

The court further found that the arbitrator's "social engagements" upon which Nationwide relied to show partiality "did not constitute improper or prohibited *ex parte* contacts."[199]

The court rejected Nationwide's argument "that it had a contractual right to withdraw its consent to the second panel's authority because [the allegedly inadequate] disclosures rendered [the arbitrator] unacceptable to Nationwide."[200]

4.4.16 Challenging an Arbitrator: The Position Under the FAA

In making a decision to challenge an arbitrator, including when and where to assert such a challenge, an appreciation of how the courts view their role in the arbitration

[193] *Nationwide Mutual Insurance Co. v Home Insurance Co.* 429 E3d 640 (6th Cir. 2005) at *644; Chiafullo et al. (2007), p. 461.

[194] *Nationwide Mutual Insurance Co. v Home Insurance Co.* 429 E3d 640 (6th Cir. 2005) at *644; Chiafullo et al. (2007), p. 461.

[195] *Apperson v Fleet Carrier Corp.* 879 E2d 1344 (6th Cir. 1989); Chiafullo et al. (2007), p. 461.

[196] *Nationwide Mutual Insurance Co. v Home Insurance Co.* 429 E3d 640 (6th Cir. 2005) at *644 [quoting *Andersons, Inc. v Horton Farms, Inc.*, 166 E3d 308, 329 (6th Cir. 1998)]; Chiafullo et al. (2007), pp. 462–463.

[197] *Nationwide Mutual Insurance Co. v Home Insurance Co.* 429 E3d 640 (6th Cir. 2005) at *644 [quoting *Consol. Coal Co. v. Local 1643, United Mine Workers of Am.*, 48 E3d125, 129 (4th Cir. 1995)]; Chiafullo et al. (2007), p. 462.

[198] *Apperson v Fleet Carrier Corp.* 879 E2d 1344 (6th Cir. 1989); Chiafullo et al. (2007), p. 462.

[199] *Nationwide Mutual Insurance Co. v Home Insurance Co.* 429 E3d 640 (6th Cir. 2005) at *648–649 [quoting *Consol. Coal Co. v. Local 1643, United Mine Workers of Am.*, 48 E3d125, 129 (4th Cir. 1995)]; Chiafullo et al. (2007), p. 462.

[200] *Nationwide Mutual Insurance Co. v Home Insurance Co.* 429 E3d 640 (6th Cir. 2005) at *649 [quoting *Consol. Coal Co. v. Local 1643, United Mine Workers of Am.*, 48 E3d125, 129 (4th Cir. 1995)]; Chiafullo et al. (2007), p. 462.

process is critical. The legal foundation of the arbitration process is simply the law of contracts, and therefore an arbitration clause is generally viewed by courts as nothing more nor less than an agreement within a contract. As such, under the law, an arbitration clause should be treated the same as any other contractual provision. This precept is the basic tenet behind the FAA[201] and the New York Convention.[202]

In *United States v South-Eastern Underwriters Ass'n*[203] the Supreme Court held that the business of insurance is commerce, and accordingly interstate insurance transactions which implicitly includes reinsurance transactions, constitute interstate commerce subject to federal substantive law. Therefore, the FAA governs the enforceability of arbitration clauses contained in reinsurance treaties or certificates resulting from interstate transactions.[204]

The Supreme Court has interpreted the definition of "commerce" in the FAA[205] to be an expression of Congressional intent that the FAA's reach be as broad as is permitted by the Commerce Clause of the United States Constitution.

The decision further held that the FAA preempts state law, and state courts may not apply state statutes to invalidate arbitration agreements. The Court has vigorously enforced the legislative mandate set forth in the FAA favouring arbitration as a means of resolving commercial disputes.

It is important to note here that parties to an arbitration agreement can circumvent application of the FAA or the New York Convention. For example, the parties may agree that the arbitration procedures of a particular State will apply and even though such an agreement may frustrate some element of the FAA or the New York Convention, the parties' choice, that is freedom of contract, will generally be honoured.[206] While the parties may choose state law, most states have adopted the Uniform Arbitration Act, which is patterned after the FAA.

4.4.17 Removal or Resignation of Arbitrators

The court may, on the application of any party to arbitral proceedings, remove an arbitrator on any of the following grounds (section 24(1) of the Arbitration Act):

(a) That circumstances exist, which give rise to justifiable doubts as to the arbitrator's impartiality;

[201] 9 U.S.C.A. Sub section i-16 (1970 & Supp. 1998); Kareken et al. (2000), p. 142.

[202] 9 U.S.C.A. Sub section 201–208 (Supp. 1998); Kareken et al. (2000), p. 142.

[203] *United States v South-Eastern Underwriters Ass'n* 322 U.S. 533 (1944).

[204] Kareken et al. (2000), pp. 142–143.

[205] *Allied-Bruce Terminix Cos. v Dobson*, 513 U.S. 265 (1995); Kareken et al. (2000), pp. 142–143.

[206] *Volt Info. Sciences, Inc. v Bored of Trustees of Leland Stanford Junior Univ.*, 489 U.S. 468 (1989).

(b) That the arbitrator does not possess the qualifications required by the arbitration agreement[207];
(c) That the arbitrator is physically or mentally incapable of conducting the proceedings or that there are justifiable doubts as to his capacity to do so; or
(d) That he has refused or failed to conduct the proceedings properly or to use all reasonable despatch in conducting the proceedings or in making an award.

In relation to the ground specified in (a) above, the courts have clarified the standard to be applied when deciding whether to remove an arbitrator for possible bias.

In *AT & T Corp* v. *Saudi Gable Co*,[208] the Court of Appeal confirmed that, notwithstanding the precise words ("justifiable doubts") which appear in section 24 (1) (a) of the Arbitration Act, the test for removing an arbitrator is the same as that to be applied to any other person acting in a judicial capacity: an arbitrator will accordingly be removed if it can be shown that there is a "real danger" that he is biased. If an application is made under the ground specified in (d) above, the applicant must also show that he has suffered, or would otherwise suffer, substantial injustice.[209]

4.4.17.1 The Power of Arbitrators in Reinsurance Arbitrations

Arbitration is a creature of a contract, and the powers that arbitrators possess originate from the parties, who agree to confer specific powers on the arbitrators, either through an arbitration clause in the contract or through a separate agreement.[210] Typically, arbitration clauses found in reinsurance agreements confer broad power on arbitrators with respect to certain procedural or substantive issues. Where an arbitration clause enumerates specific powers to arbitrators, it is rare that parties challenge an exercise of those powers. Parties often challenge an arbitrator's actions, however, where the arbitrator acts in a manner not expressly provided for in the contract. In such instances, courts will look to the language of the parties' contract, as well as the statute regulating arbitration, i.e. the Arbitration Act 1996 in England, or in the U.S.A. the FAA, to determine whether an arbitrator has exceeded his powers.[211]

[207] Barlow Lyde and Gilbert LLP (2009), §§ 26.10.2, 26-24/1.

[208] *AT & T Corp* v *Saudi Gable Co* [2000] 2 Lloyd's Rep 127 (CA).

[209] Barlow Lyde and Gilbert LLP (2009), §§ 26.10.2, 26-24/2.

[210] For example, reinsurance contracts often contain "honourable engagement" clauses and similar language which courts have interpreted as providing arbitrators with wide discretion to interpret procedural and substantive issues and interpret an agreement with regard to the intent of the parties. A sample honourable engagement clause is as follows: "*The Panel shall interpret this Agreement as an honourable engagement rather than as merely a legal obligation and shall make its decision considering the custom and practice of the applicable insurance and reinsurance business.*"; DiUbaldo (2008), p. 83.

[211] *Banco de Seguros del Estado v Mut. Marine Office, Inc.*, 344 F.3d 255, (2d Cir. 2003).

Case law, especially in the USA, suggests that courts often struggle to grasp the extent of arbitral powers pursuant to the interplay between arbitration agreements contained in reinsurance contracts, industry custom and practice, and the FAA. In effect, the result has, often, been contradictory and resulted in inconsistent decisions in this area of law.

With regards to the emerging areas of the law governing certain procedural powers of arbitrators which have impacted and will continue to impact reinsurance arbitrations, we will further on examine the powers of arbitrators with respect to consolidation, non-party discovery, confidentiality, summary adjudication and the enforceability of a hold harmless agreement.[212]

Because the duty to arbitrate is contractual, courts are generally supportive of whatever contractual limitations the parties place on the process. When a contract is silent on a procedural matter related to the arbitration, courts usually will leave such matters to the arbitrators to decide. Thus, courts have left it to the arbitrators to determine such matters as venue, whether to require prehearing security, and choice of law.[213]

4.4.17.2 Disqualifying an Arbitrator

A party seeking to challenge the qualifications of an arbitrator is faced with the procedural question of when to bring such a challenge. Some courts hold that a challenge can be made only after the arbitration is concluded in the context of a motion to vacate the award.[214] Other courts hold that a challenge can be made during the course of the arbitration proceeding, before an award is issued.[215]

Even the judiciary's stated preference to have disputes resolved via arbitration, and its reticence to involve itself in arbitrations, a party seeking to challenge an arbitrator's qualifications faces a difficult decision: when and in what forum to raise a challenge to an arbitrator. Yet, disqualification of a party's arbitrator is a matter that courts will not treat lightly.

A party contemplating to seek disqualification of its opponent's arbitrator or the umpire should exercise a high degree of cautious professionalism before proceeding. Such action should be undertaken only when the challenging party has sufficient proof to substantiate its claim that the person in question does not meet the

---

[212] DiUbaldo (2008), p. 84.

[213] Hummer (1996), p. 233.

[214] *Florasynth, Inc. v Pickholz*, 750 F.2d. 171 (2d Cir. 1984). *Michaels v Mariforum Sbipping, S.A.*, 624 F.2d 411 (2d Cir. 1980). *Old Republic Ins. Co. v Meadows Indem. Co. Ltd.*, 870 F. Supp. 210 (N.D.I11.1994). *Corporate Printing Co. v New York Typographical Union No. 6*, 601 F. Supp. 323 (S.D.N.Y. 1984). *Marc Rieh & Co., A. G. v Transmarine Seaways Corp, of Monrovia*, 443 E Supp. 386 (S.D.N.Y. 1978). *Andarko Petroleum Corp. v Panhandle Eastern Corp.*, Del. Ch. Ct. Sept. 21, 1987; Ostrager and Vyskocil (1996), §§ 14.03b, 14-34.

[215] *Astoria Medical Group v Health Ins. Plan of Greater New York*, 11 N.Y.2d at 132, 182 N.E.2d at 86, 227 N.Y.S.2d at 403.

prerequisites for service or cannot be impartial. Failure to take this care will result in frivolous motions that will only serve to increase judicial reluctance to become involved in these challenges.

The courts appear to be split on the issue of when a party seeking to challenge the qualifications of an arbitrator should bring such a challenge. A significant number have held that a challenge to an arbitrator's qualifications can only be made after the arbitration is concluded and must be brought in the context of a motion to vacate the arbitration award.[216]

In these cases the party seeking to disqualify an arbitrator relies on the FAA in support of its disqualification argument. However, the FAA does not deal directly with the issue of arbitrator disqualification. Instead, section 10(a)(2) of the FAA provides that courts may vacate an award where there is evident partiality or corruption of an arbitrator and does not speak to the disqualification of arbitrators.

These courts concluded that the relief requested pursuant to the FAA could not be granted, regardless of merit, because the, FAA does not give the judiciary authority to disqualify an arbitrator. In other words, without an award these courts viewed themselves as powerless to consider the presence or absence of arbitrator partiality under the FAA.

Other courts have recognized that if a provision of the contract dealing with arbitration qualification has not been met, a condition precedent to the commencement of the arbitration may be lacking and the arbitrator's qualifications and appointment may be challenged.[217]

Effective challenges to an arbitrator's qualifications prior to the issuance of an award have not been statutorily based. Rather, two arguments have received some recognition.

First, parties have argued that the conditions of the contract or agreement addressing arbitration cannot be satisfied using a biased or unfit arbitrator.

---

[216] *Aviall, Inc. v Ryder Sys., Inc.*, 110 F.3d 892 (2d Cir. 1997). *Florasynth, Inc. v Pickholz*, 750 F.2d 171 (2d Cir. 1984). In *Re Michaels v Mariforum Shipping, S.A.*, 624 F.2d 411 (2d Cir. 1980); *Sanko S.S. Co. Ltd. v Cook Indus. Inc.*, 495 F.2d 1260 (2d Cir. 1973). *Old Republic Ins. Co. v Meadows Indem. Co.*, 870 F. Supp. 210 (N.D Ill. 1994). *Corporate Printing Co. Inc. v New York Typographical Union No. 6*, 601 F. Supp 323 (S.D.N.Y. 1984). *Marc Rich & Co., A.G. v Transmarine Seaways Corp. of Monrovia*, 443 F. Supp. 386 (S.D.N.Y. 1978). *Andarko Petroleum Corp. v Panhandle Eastern Corp.*, (No.87381 Del. Ch. Sept. 21, 1987), aff'd, 545 A.2d 1171 (Del. 1988).

[217] *Argonaut Midwest Ins. Co. v General Reinsurance Corp.*, 1998 U.S. Dist. LEXIS 12497, 1998 WL4142 (N.D. Ill. Aug. 6, 1998). In *Re Certain Underwriters at Lloyd's, London v Continental Cas. Co.*, 1997 U.S. Dist. LEXIS 11934, 1997 WL 461035 (N.D. Ill. Aug. 11, 1997) (mem. and order). *Fremont Indemn. Co. v Assicurazoni Generali SpA*, No. CV94-7908 (C.D. Cal., Mar. 7, 1995) (order). *Fireman's Fund Ins. Co. v Sorema North American Reinsurance Co.*, No. C94-3617SC (N.D. Cal., Feb. 8, 1995) (order). *Evanston Ins. Co. v Kansa Gen. Int'l Ins. Co.*, No. 94C4957 (N.D. Ill. Oct. 17, 1994 and Jan. 13, 1995) (mems. and orders). *Int'l Ins. Co. v Certain Underwriters at Lloyd's*, London, No. 1:88-CV-09838 (N.D. Ill. Dec. 30, 1992) (order). *Metropolitan Property & Cas. Ins. Co. v J.C. Penny Cas. Ins. Co.*, 780 F. Supp. 885 (D. Conn. 1991); *Third Nat'l Bank In Nashville v Wedge Group, Inc.*, 749 F, Supp. 851 (M.D. Tenn. 1990).

Second, parties have contended that failing to disqualify an unqualified arbitrator would permit the arbitration to proceed in a fashion that is invalid under general contract principles or in contravention of equitable principles.

While there are no specific requirements for arbitrator qualifications in any statute in the United States,[218] many reinsurance contracts typically contain some fairly generic arbitrator prerequisites. For example, common qualification requirements include that the arbitrators be "active or former officers or executives of insurance or reinsurance companies" or that the arbitrators; be "neutral," "disinterested" or "impartial."[219]

In *Evanston Insurance Co. v Kansa General International Insurance Co.*,[220] the arbitration provision required that the arbitrators be "disinterested." Evanston, the cedent, had entered into reinsurance contracts with both Kansa and another reinsurer, Gerling Global. Prior to the dispute between Evanston and Kansa, a non-payment issue arose between Evanston and Gerling Global. The reasons for non-payment by Gerling were made known to Evanston and were, in part, based on a review of a confidential report prepared by a Gerling consultant who had reviewed Evanston's books and records.

Thereafter, when a dispute over the same claims arose between Evanston and Kansa and Kansa appointed Gerling's officer as its arbitrator, Evanston objected on the grounds that Kansa's nominated arbitrator was not "disinterested" as required by the parties' written agreement to arbitrate. When presented with the issue, the District Court concluded it had the authority under Sections 4 and 5 of the FAA, as part of its ability to enforce arbitration agreements, to disqualify. The issue of whether Gerling's officer was "disinterested" was never reached, however, as he withdrew from the proceeding.

Recently, in the same district, another judge exercised jurisdiction over a controversy similar to the one in the *Evanston Insurance Co. v Kansa General International Insurance Co.*[221] case. The case of *Matter of the Arbitration between Argonaut Midwest Insurance Co. v General Reinsurance Corp.*,[222] involved an arbitration agreement requiring that the arbitrators be "officials of insurance or

[218] A California court has noted that "we have no statutory provisions fixing the qualification of arbitrators." *Cecil v Bank of America Nat'l Trust and Sav. Ass'n*, 236 P.2d 4-08, 410 (Cal. Ct. App. 1951).

[219] Some arbitration provisions may call for application of the Rules of the American Arbitration Association. Under Section 18 of these rules a party may have an arbitrator replaced if any circumstances are disclosed by the arbitrator prior to the hearing which tend to suggest bias.

[220] *Evanston Insurance Co. v Kansa General International Insurance Co.* 1994 U.S. Dist. LEXIS 19219, 1995 WL 23063 (N.D. Ill. 1994).

[221] *Evanston Insurance Co. v Kansa General International Insurance Co.* 1994 U.S. Dist. LEXIS 19219, 1995 WL 23063 (N.D. Ill. 1994).

[222] *Matter of the Arbitration between Argonaut Midwest Insurance Co. v General Reinsurance Corp.* 1998 U.S. Dist. LEXIS 12497 (N.D. Ill. 1998).

reinsurance companies authorized to transact business in. . .the United States. . .and writing the kind of business about which differences have arisen."[223]

When a dispute between the insurer and the reinsurer arose and the arbitration agreement was invoked, the reinsurer designated an arbitrator who met the qualifications. However, before the arbitration panel was fully empaneled, the arbitrator retired. Argonaut contended that his retirement disqualified the arbitrator and demanded that the reinsurer appoint a replacement arbitrator. When the reinsurer failed to do so, Argonaut sought relief in federal court. In exercising its jurisdiction over the dispute, the *Matter of the Arbitration between Argonaut Midwest Insurance Co. v General Reinsurance Corp.* court[224] relied on the *Evanston Insurance Co. v Kansa General International Insurance Co.*[225] case. It emphasized that "[w] here the parties to the arbitration agreement did not expressly provide for [a] contingency, it is appropriate for the court to consider evidence of the parties' general intent to engage in arbitration of their underlying dispute to interpret the [arbitration agreement].'"[226]

The *Matter of the Arbitration between Argonaut Midwest Insurance Co. v General Reinsurance Corp.* court[227] acknowledged that several courts have held that federal district courts do not have the power under the FAA to rule on pre-award challenges to nominate arbitrators, but distinguished the controversy before it from the factual situations in those cases. The court in *Matter of the Arbitration between Argonaut Midwest Insurance Co. v General Reinsurance Corp.*[228] reasoned that because the issue before it was the interpretation of the arbitration agreement, not a challenge to an arbitrator based on possible bias or prejudice, it had jurisdiction. It ruled in favour of the reinsurer, holding that retirement did not disqualify the arbitrator. It denied Argonaut's motions to grant it authority to appoint a replacement arbitrator and to compel arbitration before a panel of arbitrators that did not include the reinsurer's appointed arbitrator.

Such challenges to arbitrators are necessarily only as good as the contracts upon which they are based.

---

[223] *Matter of the Arbitration between Argonaut Midwest Insurance Co. v General Reinsurance Corp.* 1998 U.S. Dist. LEXIS 12497 (N.D. Ill. 1998) at 3–4.

[224] *Matter of the Arbitration between Argonaut Midwest Insurance Co. v General Reinsurance Corp.* 1998 U.S. Dist. LEXIS 12497 (N.D. Ill. 1998).

[225] *Evanston Insurance Co. v Kansa General International Insurance Co.* 1994 U.S. Dist. LEXIS 19219, 1995 WL 23063 (N.D. Ill. 1994).

[226] *Matter of the Arbitration between Argonaut Midwest Insurance Co. v General Reinsurance Corp.* 1998 U.S. Dist. LEXIS 12497 (N.D. Ill. 1998) at 2.

[227] *Matter of the Arbitration between Argonaut Midwest Insurance Co. v General Reinsurance Corp.* 1998 U.S. Dist. LEXIS 12497 (N.D. Ill. 1998).

[228] *Matter of the Arbitration between Argonaut Midwest Insurance Co. v General Reinsurance Corp.* 1998 U.S. Dist. LEXIS 12497 (N.D. Ill. 1998).

In *Certain Underwriters at Lloyds, London v Continental Casualty Co.*[229] three separate disputes had arisen between Underwriters and Continental Casualty under two separate reinsurance contracts with two different arbitration clauses. Continental Casualty named two senior claim officials with Travelers Insurance as arbitrators. Underwriters objected to the nominations and sought disqualification of both candidates on the grounds that: (1) Underwriters and Travelers were then arbitrating essentially the same issues; (2) the appointees were personally involved in Travelers' dispute with Underwriters; and (3) the law firm representing Continental Casualty in the arbitration had an attorney–client relationship with Travelers.

The court noted the distinction between a vacation of an award based on arbitrator bias pursuant to the FAA and a disqualification based on the parties' written agreement to arbitrate. The court acknowledged that it could disqualify an arbitrator if that person failed to meet the requirements contained in the parties' written agreement to arbitrate, but could not disqualify an arbitrator solely under the FAA.

The arbitration clauses in the two contracts between Underwriters and Continental Casualty, however, contained no arbitrator qualification requirements other than that they be officials of insurance companies. Without a contractual basis upon which to consider disqualifying the Continental Casualty arbitrators, the court believed it was left with no alternative but to conclude that Underwriters' motion amounted to nothing more than an impermissible FAA challenge. Therefore, the court denied Underwriters' motion to disqualify.[230]

While the failure of a proposed arbitrator to meet a qualification explicitly set forth in the arbitration provision is certainly a strong basis on which to obtain pre-award relief, some courts have nevertheless persisted in refusing to hear a pre-award challenge to an arbitrator's qualifications. For example, in *Employers Insurance of Wausau v Jackson*,[231] the Wisconsin Court of Appeals determined that Underwriters' failure to name a qualified arbitrator within 30 days of the request for arbitration constituted a failure to avail themselves of the method for selecting an arbitrator set forth in the arbitration agreement. The trial court had further concluded that the arbitrator selected by Underwriters was not qualified as he was not an "executive office[r] of an insurance compan[y] domiciled in the U.S.A."[232] as specified in the arbitration clause of the reinsurance contract.

Although the Wisconsin Court of Appeals upheld the trial court's adverse selection ruling on the basis of Underwriters' untimely identification of its proposed arbitrator, as to the qualification issue it found that "the circuit court should not review an arbitrator's qualifications at this stage of the arbitration process."[233]

---

[229] *Certain Underwriters at Lloyds, London v Continental Casualty Co.* 1997 U.S. Dist. LEXIS 11934, 1997 WL 461035 (N.D. Ill 1997).

[230] *Roth v Carvel Corp.*, 905 F. Supp. 196 (S.D.N.Y. 1995).

[231] *Employers Insurance of Wausau v Jackson* 505 N.W.2d 147 (Wis. Ct. App. 1993).

[232] *Employers Insurance of Wausau v Jackson* 505 N.W.2d 147 (Wis. Ct. App. 1993) at 149.

[233] *Employers Insurance of Wausau v Jackson* 505 N.W.2d 147 (Wis. Ct. App. 1993) at 153.

The Wisconsin Supreme Court affirmed the Court of Appeals ruling,[234] but did not address the issue of whether the arbitrator chosen by Underwriters was an "executive," since the Court of Appeals had not affirmed the trial court's decision on that basis.

In light of the foregoing case law, certain initial action is called for. If an appointed arbitrator fails to meet the qualifications explicitly set forth in the arbitration provision, opposing counsel must be advised of the arbitrator's lack of qualification and requested to identify an alternate candidate. As noted, the allegedly unqualified arbitrator, or the party proposing the arbitrator may withdraw the nomination once the qualification issue is raised. Should the allegedly unqualified arbitrator not withdraw, then seeking the pre-arbitration award intervention of the court can and should be a viable alternative.

A compelling argument can be made that an arbitrator's failure to meet an explicitly stated qualification is a prerequisite to entering into the arbitration process that warrants the court's pre-award involvement.

The second method of challenging an arbitrator is less definitive than relying upon a specific contractual provision. This method relies upon equitable principles. If there is not a specific qualification requirement calling for the arbitrators to be neutral, disinterested or impartial, courts may read such a requirement into the arbitration clause, since it is an implicit fundamental requirement of an arbitrator.

However, the level of impartiality a court requires of an arbitrator will likely differ depending upon whether the arbitrator whose partiality is at issue is a party appointed arbitrator or an umpire in a tripartite arbitration.

The standard of impartiality/disinterest is, of course, heightened if the challenged arbitrator is the umpire and one would expect the court to be more likely to entertain a pre-award motion to disqualify if the challenged arbitrator is the umpire.[235]

While the majority of courts have not held arbitrators, including the third "neutral" arbitrator or umpire, to the same standard as judges in determining whether an arbitration award should be vacated based on bias,[236] this does not

---

[234] *Employers Insurance of Wausau v Jackson* 527 N.W.2d 681 (Wis. 1995).

[235] A detailed discussion of the distinction courts have drawn between party appointed arbitrators and a third "neutral" arbitrator or umpire is beyond the scope of this article. For cases discussing the distinction, however, see: *Astoria Med. Group v Health Ins. Plan of Greater N.Y.*, 182 N.E.2d 85, 87 (N.Y. 1962) stating that "there has grown a common acceptance of the fact that the party-designated arbitrators are not and cannot be 'neutral.' at least in the sense that the third arbitrator or a judge is" and *Instituto Resseguros do Brasil v First State Ins. Co.*, 577 N.Y.S.2d 287, 288 (App. Div. 1991) explaining that a party designated member of a tripartite arbitration tribunal "is not expected to be neutral in the same sense as a judge or arbitral umpire".

[236] *Apperson v Fleet Carrier Corp.*, 879 F.2d 1344, 1353 (6th Cir. 1989), cert. denied, 495 U.S. 947 (1990). *Toyota of Berkeley v Automobile Salesmen's Union Local 1095*, 834 F.2d 751, 755 (9th Cir. 1987), cert. denied, 486 U.S. 1043 (1988). *Sheet Metal Workers Int'l Ass'n Local Union #420 v Kinney Air Conditioning Co.*, 756 F.2d 742, 745–746 (9th Cir. 1985). *Morelite Const. Corp. v New York City Dist. Council Carpenters Benefit Funds*, 748 F.2d 79, 83–84 (2d Cir. 1984). *Merit Ins. Co. v Leatherby Ins. Co.*, 714 F.2d 673, 678–679 (7th Cir. 1983).

mean that the courts should lessen disclosure requirements imposed on the arbitrators.

In order to fully gain the benefits of arbitration as a primary method of dispute resolution, namely minimization of time and expense, at the outset of the arbitration the parties should investigate the proposed arbitrators and require them to disclose any facts that might give rise to suspected bias.

By undertaking the investigation prior to or (luring the organizational phase of the arbitration process, a great deal of wasted time and expense can be avoided if facts are revealed demonstrating evident partiality or bias on the part of the proposed arbitrators.

In *Commonwealth Coatings Corp. v Continental Casualty Co.*,[237] the Supreme Court stated that it is far better that the relationship be disclosed at the outset, when the parties are free to reject the arbitrator or accept him with knowledge of the relationship and continuing faith in his objectivity, than to have the relationship come to light after the arbitration, when a suspicious or disgruntled party can seize on it as a pretext for invalidating the award.[238]

Courts have applied the stricter standard of "reasonable impression of partiality" in instances where a party seeks to vacate an arbitration award based on non-disclosure of a potential conflict by an arbitrator as opposed to a claim of actual arbitrator bias.

The Ninth Circuit, in *Schmitz v Zilveti*,[239] held: "The policies of 9 U.S.C. - Section 10 also support the notion that the standard for nondisclosure cases should differ from that used in actual bias case. In a nondisclosure case, the integrity of the process by which arbitrators are chosen is at issue.

Showing a "reasonable impression of partiality" is sufficient in a nondisclosure case because the policy of section 10(a)(2) instructs that the parties should choose their arbitrators intelligently. The parties can choose their arbitrators intelligently only when facts showing potential partiality are disclosed. Whether the arbitrators' decision itself is faulty is not necessarily relevant. But in an actual bias determination, the integrity of the arbitrators' decision is directly at issue.

That a reasonable impression of partiality is present does not mean the arbitration award was the product of impropriety."[240] Accordingly, parties to an arbitration should obtain as complete a disclosure as possible from the proposed arbitrators since, as the courts have noted, it is primarily the parties and not the courts that are tasked with judging the partiality of the arbitrators.[241]

[237] *Commonwealth Coatings Corp. v Continental Casualty Co.* 393 U.S. 145 (1968).

[238] *Commonwealth Coatings Corp. v Continental Casualty Co.* 393 U.S. 145 (1968) at 151. (White, J. and Marshall, J., concurring).

[239] *Schmitz v Zilveti* 20 F.3d 1043 (9th Cir. 1994).

[240] *Schmitz v Zilveti* 20 F.3d 1043 (9th Cir. 1994) at 1047 (citation omitted).

[241] *Commonwealth Coatings Corp. v Continental Casualty Co.* 393 U.S. 145 (1968) at 151. (White, J. and Marshall, J., concurring) and *Schmitz v Zilveti* 20 F.3d 1043 (9th Cir. 1994) at 1048.

Parties should seek full disclosure from arbitrator candidates and seek the disqualification of the arbitrator as soon as possible after the determination is made that evident partiality exists or the arbitrator failed to meet some other qualification.

Finally, failure to timely seek the disqualification may result in a waiver of the party's ability to raise the arbitrator's lack of qualifications.[242]

Overall, it can be concluded that a party is frequently best served by first raising the qualification issue within the arbitration proceeding. If the party determines, however, that a fair hearing on this issue cannot be had within the arbitration proceeding, or the panel refuses to address the issue, then that party should seriously consider filing the appropriate motion to disqualify with the court. The party bringing the disqualification motion should recognize that the courts are reluctant to entangle themselves in matters that the parties agreed to arbitrate.

Additionally, intervention on the qualification issue may slow down and increase the expense of resolving the dispute.

Nevertheless, a motion to disqualify at the outset of the arbitration lessens the possibility that even greater amounts of time and expense will be incurred if an arbitrator's lack of qualifications causes an award to be vacated. The successful motion to disqualify should clearly demonstrate that a contractual qualification prerequisite has not been met or that absent the disqualification of the challenged arbitrator, the arbitration would proceed in contravention of fundamental contract law on equitable principles.

4.4.17.3 The Question of Biased Arbitrators

Arbitration clauses provide a method for companies to settle business disputes without expending the amount of time and resources required in judicial proceedings. When an arbitration clause is invoked, a neutral third party takes on the role of adjudicator, and the parties defer to the unbiased decision of that neutral.

Sometimes what is "unbiased" becomes more uncertain when parties contract for the right to appoint their own arbitrators.

In the USA *Trustmark Ins. Co. v John Hancock Life Ins. Co.*[243] stands for the principle that the Seventh Circuit will relax the impartiality standard to which they hold party appointed arbitrators, especially compared to the standard for federal judges.

---

[242] *York Research Corp. v Harris Landgarten*, 927 F.2d 119 (2d Cir. 1991). *United States v Int'l Bhd. of Teamsters*, 814 F. Supp. 1165 (S.D.N.Y. 1993). *San Carb Opera Co. v Conley*, 72 F. Supp. 825 (S.D.N.Y. 1946), aff'd, 163 F.2d 310 (2d Cir. 1947). *Cecil v Bank of Am. Nat'l Trust & Sav. Ass'n*, 236 P.2d 408 (Cal. Ct. App. 1951). *Johnson v Korn*, 117 S.W.2d 514 (Tex. Civ. App. 1938).

[243] *Trustmark Ins. Co. v. John Hancock Life Ins. Co.*, 631 F.3d 869 (7th Cir. 2011), cert. denied, 79 U.S.L.W. 3641 (U.S. May 16, 2011) (No. 10-1213); Koennig (2012), p. 265.

In *Trustmark Ins. Co. v John Hancock Life Ins. Co.*[244] plaintiff, Trustmark Insurance Company (Trustmark), contracted with Defendant, John Hancock Life Insurance Company (John Hancock), to provide reinsurance coverage for risks underwritten by John Hancock. A disagreement arose between the parties regarding a term in the contract language and its impact on the scope of Trustmark's duty to reinsure. Pursuant to the arbitration clause in the parties' contract, the dispute went to arbitration before a three-member panel. John Hancock selected Mark Gurevitz as its party-appointed arbitrator.

The panel ruled in favor of John Hancock and construed the contract in favor of John Hancock's interpretation of Trustmark's duties.[245]

The dispute between the parties did not end, however, with the initial award. John Hancock billed Trustmark according to its understanding of the arbitral award, but Trustmark refused to pay. John Hancock proceeded to arbitration again to collect payment from Trustmark. In response, Trustmark argued John Hancock fraudulently failed to disclose documents during discovery in the first arbitration, leading to an award in John Hancock's favor. John Hancock again named Mark Gurevitz as its party-appointed arbitrator, while Trustmark selected a different arbitrator than in the first proceeding. Similar to the first arbitration, the two party-appointed arbitrators selected a third, neutral arbitrator to complete the three-member panel.

The panel considered how much deference it should give the first arbitration award. In doing so, the arbitrators necessarily began by determining the effect of a confidentiality agreement signed by the parties during the first arbitration. The confidentiality agreement prohibited the parties and arbitrators from disclosing the evidence, proceedings, and award of the first arbitration. The parties disagreed as to whether the agreement applied to disclosure of the prior proceedings to the parties' lawyers and future arbitrators.

Ultimately, the panel interpreted the agreement to permit disclosures to the lawyers and arbitrators involved.

Before the arbitration panel could hold a hearing on the merits, Trustmark filed suit in federal district court requesting an injunction of any further arbitration while Gurevitz remained on the panel.

Trustmark argued that Gurevitz was not a "disinterested" arbitrator because he was aware of what took place in the first arbitration.[246] Trustmark also argued the second arbitration panel should be enjoined from ruling on disputes arising out of the confidentiality agreement, which did not itself contain an arbitration clause.

Siding with Trustmark, the court held that Gurevitz was not "disinterested" due to his knowledge of the first arbitration. The court further noted that Gurevitz was a possible fact witness with respect to the first arbitration, because of his prior

[244] *Trustmark Ins. Co. v. John Hancock Life Ins. Co.*, 631 F.3d 869 (7th Cir. 2011), cert. denied, 79 U.S.L.W. 3641 (U.S. May 16, 2011) (No. 10-1213); Koennig (2012), p. 265.

[245] Koennig (2012), p. 266.

[246] Koennig (2012), p. 267.

knowledge. Accordingly, the district court prohibited the second arbitration panel from considering the first arbitration award.

John Hancock appealed to the U.S. Court of Appeals for the Seventh Circuit. The Seventh Circuit reversed the decision of the district court, striking down the injunction. In addition to overturning the injunction, the court overturned the district court's decision on the merits.

The court held that Gurevitz was indeed a disinterested arbitrator because his knowledge of the first arbitration did not amount to a financial or other personal stake in the outcome.

Finally, the court held that the current panel "[was] entitled to follow its own view about the meaning of the confidentiality agreement" when, as in this case, "the parties did agree to arbitrate their disputes about reinsurance."

The Seventh Circuit, for the first time at the federal appellate level, held that prior knowledge about a dispute is not grounds for disqualifying a party-appointed arbitrator for partiality.[247]

4.4.17.4 Impartiality Standards for Arbitrators: Legal Background

The U.S.A. court system employs a "liberal federal policy" in favor of arbitration agreements.[248] This favorable treatment is compromised when the honesty and fairness of an arbitrator are called into question. When a party is dissatisfied with the conduct of an arbitrator, it can challenge the participation of that arbitrator prior to or after an award. Before an arbitrator or arbitration panel orders an award, a party may attempt to enjoin the proceeding.

After an award has been made, a party may move to set aside or vacate the award under § 10 of the FAA which provides for vacation of arbitration awards when, upon the application of a party, a court finds "evident partiality" on the part of the arbitrator. However, this standard of impartiality is subject to agreement between the parties. Once it has been determined that the parties agreed to arbitrate the dispute, arbitrators enjoy a great deal of autonomy during the proceedings, and may generally resolve procedural questions as they see fit.[249]

4.4.17.5 Representative Case Law

In 1968, the U.S.A. Supreme Court interpreted § 10(a)(2) of the FAA with respect to Congress' expectations of what "evident partiality" meant for arbitrators.

---

[247] Koennig (2012), p. 267.

[248] *Moses H. Cone Memorial Hosp. v Mercury Const. Co.*, 460 U.S. 1, 24 (1983); Blum (1999), p. 179 ("[C]ourts look with favor on arbitration proceedings and make every presumption in favor of the validity of awards . . . .").

[249] Koennig (2012), p. 269.

Section 10(a)(2) permits federal courts to vacate arbitration awards when an arbitrator's conduct is corrupt or evidently partial to one party.

In *Commonwealth Coatings Corp. v Continental Casualty Co.*,[250] the issue before the Court was whether the impartiality requirements of a judge applied to a neutral arbitrator in a tripartite panel. The neutral arbitrator failed to disclose prior business dealings he had with one of the parties prior to the arbitration, and then ruled in favor of that party. The arbitrator had a "repeated and significant" business relationship with one party over a 5-year period, but had not conducted any business within 1 year of the arbitration proceeding. The business dealings included work on projects involved in the lawsuit.

In a plurality decision, the U.S.A. Supreme Court reversed the lower court's decision to uphold the arbitration award. The Court applied the impartiality standards for federal judges, reasoning that, on the same facts, a judge would be subject to a challenge to his partiality. The Court analogized the facts in *Commonwealth Coatings*[251]to *Tumey v State*[252] a Supreme Court case where a judgment was set aside for a judge's undisclosed prior business dealings with one of the parties.

In *Tumey v State*,[253] the Court held that a decision should be set aside if a federal judge held even "the slightest pecuniary interest." The *Commonwealth Coatings*[254] court ruled that the same standard extended to arbitrators, suggesting that arbitrators be required to disclose any dealings that would give an "impression of possible bias" in order to avoid giving "even the appearance of bias."[255]

The strong federal policy in favor of arbitration has affected the breadth of powers bestowed on arbitrators in an expansive way. Once it is determined by a court (or otherwise agreed by the parties) that a dispute is arbitrable, the appointed arbitrator or panel of arbitrators can decide most questions that arise on the way to their final disposition and award.

These decisions include contract interpretation, procedural questions, and the preclusive effect of earlier awards.

In *Trustmark*,[256] the Seventh Circuit applied these rules to a situation where an arbitration panel, in order to reach the merits, interpreted a confidentiality agreement signed during a prior arbitration.

The Seventh Circuit of the U.S.A. Court of Appeals stated that, because a judge cannot be disqualified based on his prior knowledge of a controversy and because it takes more to disqualify an arbitrator than to disqualify a judge, party-appointed arbitrators may proceed in their capacities despite having prior knowledge about a

[250] *Commonwealth Coatings Corp. v Continental Cas. Co.*, 393 U.S. 145 (1968).

[251] *Commonwealth Coatings Corp. v Continental Cas. Co.*, 393 U.S. 145 (1968).

[252] *Tumey v. State*, 273 U.S. 510, 525 (1927).

[253] *Tumey v. State*, 273 U.S. 510, 525 (1927).

[254] *Commonwealth Coatings Corp. v Continental Cas. Co.*, 393 U.S. 145 (1968).

[255] Koennig (2012), p. 269.

[256] *Trustmark Ins. Co. v. John Hancock Life Ins. Co.*, 631 F.3d 869 (7th Cir. 2011), cert. denied, 79 U.S.L.W. 3641 (U.S. May 16, 2011) (No. 10-1213); Koennig (2012), p. 276.

controversy and stressed the importance of the parties' contractual choices not only to avoid to arbitrate and avoid federal court but also to self-appoint arbitrators. It noted that arbitrators can decide procedural questions during arbitration proceedings including the preclusive effect of an earlier award. Finally, the Seventh Circuit stated that, in determining whether or not to vacate an arbitration award, a court should not look at whether the arbitrators erred in their interpretation of an agreement, but that they interpreted it at all, and empowered the current arbitration panel to interpret the confidentiality agreement as it saw fit, because interpreting such an agreement was within the scope of their powers as arbitrators.[257]

4.4.17.6 Comment

Trustmark's[258] importance arises from the analysis which the Seventh Circuit acknowledged was not essential to its decision on the merits.

Trustmark[259] held that an arbitrator should not be disqualified for lack of the requisite impartiality because of specific knowledge gained in a prior arbitration between the same parties. In doing so, the Seventh Circuit continued a trend of distinguishing between the standards of partiality between a federal judge and an arbitrator.

This decision is favorable to arbitrators in the reinsurance industry and other similarly specialized industries where repeat arbitrators are common.

The court also construed the parties' arbitration clause broadly to vest considerable power in the second arbitration panel. Even when the same issue remained unchanged between the first and second arbitration, a member of the second panel was permitted to not only remain on the panel, but also to disclose privileged information from the first arbitration to the other two panel members. This result underlines the concept that arbitration is not as secretive and confidential as parties may believe.[260]

In many ways, the arbitration in Trustmark[261] was standard fare for the reinsurance industry. Reinsurance agreements normally contain arbitration clauses because of the likelihood that the two parties will need to continue doing business together in the future. Commonly, a reinsurance arbitration clause requires

[257] Koennig (2012), p. 274.

[258] Trustmark Ins. Co. v. John Hancock Life Ins. Co., 631 F.3d 869 (7th Cir. 2011), cert. denied, 79 U.S.L.W. 3641 (U.S. May 16, 2011) (No. 10-1213); Koennig (2012), p. 276.

[259] Trustmark Ins. Co. v. John Hancock Life Ins. Co., 631 F.3d 869 (7th Cir. 2011), cert. denied, 79 U.S.L.W. 3641 (U.S. May 16, 2011) (No. 10-1213); Koennig (2012), p. 276.

[260] Koennig (2012), p. 276.

[261] Trustmark Ins. Co. v. John Hancock Life Ins. Co., 631 F.3d 869 (7th Cir. 2011), cert. denied, 79 U.S.L.W. 3641 (U.S. May 16, 2011) (No. 10-1213); Koennig (2012), p. 276.

arbitration of all issues related to a reinsurance agreement. The scope of reinsurance arbitration clauses are often construed broadly, as in Trustmark.[262]

In addition to scope, another provision commonly found in reinsurance arbitration clauses is the selection procedure for picking the arbitration panel.

In Trustmark,[263] the parties bargained for the power to appoint one arbitrator each with the third, neutral umpire to be selected by the two party-appointed arbitrators. Arbitration awards are final and binding, but may be vacated if a court finds that an arbitrator displayed evident partiality. As an alternative, parties may alter this standard by contract.

In Trustmark,[264] the parties decided that all arbitrators had to be "disinterested." However, the question left open by the Seventh Circuit is how it would view conduct of a party-appointed arbitrator that would require judicial recusal, but falls somewhere between sufficient partiality to require recusal and an impartiality limit imposed by statute or contract.

The open question left by the Seventh Circuit could prove problematic in future cases because the dispute in Trustmark[265] is common in reinsurance The autonomy provided to parties to set their own standard of impartiality is necessary in a specialized industry like reinsurance, where parties often seek arbitrators with knowledge of industry customs and practices.

For the Merit trade-off theory to be beneficial, parties must be able to make contractual concessions with regard to the statutory standard of partiality. It is important for courts to promote party-defined standards for arbitrator impartiality. This autonomy allows parties to account for prior knowledge that abounds in reinsurance arbitration by imposing looser grounds for disqualification.

If future decisions follow the scheme of Trustmark,[266] where the court does not apply a party-created standard of impartiality to the facts, reinsurance companies will not be able to predict how the Seventh Circuit will treat the conduct of the companies' party-appointed arbitrators.

A solution to this problem is for the Seventh Circuit to adopt the reasonable person standard used in the Second Circuit.[267] This standard would permit the court to shift away from its focus on the judicial standard of impartiality and focus more

[262] Trustmark Ins. Co. v. John Hancock Life Ins. Co., 631 F.3d 869 (7th Cir. 2011), cert. denied, 79 U.S.L.W. 3641 (U.S. May 16, 2011) (No. 10-1213); Koennig (2012), p. 276.

[263] Trustmark Ins. Co. v. John Hancock Life Ins. Co., 631 F.3d 869 (7th Cir. 2011), cert. denied, 79 U.S.L.W. 3641 (U.S. May 16, 2011) (No. 10-1213); Koennig (2012), p. 276.

[264] Trustmark Ins. Co. v. John Hancock Life Ins. Co., 631 F.3d 869 (7th Cir. 2011), cert. denied, 79 U.S.L.W. 3641 (U.S. May 16, 2011) (No. 10-1213); Koennig (2012), p. 276.

[265] Trustmark Ins. Co. v. John Hancock Life Ins. Co., 631 F.3d 869 (7th Cir. 2011), cert. denied, 79 U.S.L.W. 3641 (U.S. May 16, 2011) (No. 10-1213); Koennig (2012), p. 276.

[266] Trustmark Ins. Co. v. John Hancock Life Ins. Co., 631 F.3d 869 (7th Cir. 2011), cert. denied, 79 U.S.L.W. 3641 (U.S. May 16, 2011) (No. 10-1213); Koennig (2012), p. 276.

[267] Morelite Const. Corp. v N.Y. City Council Carpenters Benefit Funds, 748 F.2d 79 (2d Cir. 1984) (evident partiality is found where "a reasonable person would have to conclude that an arbitrator was partial to one party to the arbitration").

on the conduct of the arbitrator. The standard would only need to be utilized in cases where the parties did not otherwise agree to a different standard. This problem is exacerbated when, as in Trustmark,[268] the second panel has the power to permit the knowledge to flow to the other two non-repeat arbitrators.

Even if the Second Circuit's rule is a more appropriate way to evaluate arbitrator partiality, applying the rule in Trustmark[269] would have produced an unfair result for John Hancock that the Seventh Circuit seemed determined to avoid.

For arbitrators in the reinsurance industry, Trustmark[270] is good news: the Seventh Circuit eliminated another situation in which party-appointed arbitrators may be found inappropriately partial. This case should also teach commercial parties to take full advantage of the impartiality standard in the arbitration clause, especially if they bargain for the power to appoint their own arbitrator.

Trustmark[271] did not appoint a repeat party-appointed arbitrator, and no amount of complaining to the Seventh Circuit redeemed the company's mistake. As reinsurance companies continue to contract for such a specific, tailored standard of impartiality for arbitrators, Trustmark[272] does not provide much more certainty regarding how a court will apply the language the parties agreed to in their contract.

However, at least in the Seventh Circuit, companies can be certain that if a party-appointed arbitrator would satisfy the impartiality requirements of a federal judge, he will be permitted to remain on a panel.[273]

The second non-essential holding made by the Seventh Circuit in Trustmark[274] permitted the second arbitration panel to construe the confidentiality agreement signed in the first arbitration.

This decision opens the door for a signatory to the confidentiality agreement from the first arbitration, to disclose his knowledge of the first arbitration to his two fellow arbitrators on the second panel.

The holding exemplifies the gap between the privacy expectations of arbitrating parties and the reality of that privacy. While parties often turn to arbitration for the very purpose of confidentiality, they must still contract for it because it is generally not required by law. Even when the parties contract for confidentiality, courts may still find reasons to not enforce the agreement, such as unconscionability, waiver, or

[268] Trustmark Ins. Co. v. John Hancock Life Ins. Co., 631 F.3d 869 (7th Cir. 2011), cert. denied, 79 U.S.L.W. 3641 (U.S. May 16, 2011) (No. 10-1213); Koennig (2012), p. 276.

[269] Trustmark Ins. Co. v. John Hancock Life Ins. Co., 631 F.3d 869 (7th Cir. 2011), cert. denied, 79 U.S.L.W. 3641 (U.S. May 16, 2011) (No. 10-1213); Koennig (2012), p. 276.

[270] Trustmark Ins. Co. v. John Hancock Life Ins. Co., 631 F.3d 869 (7th Cir. 2011), cert. denied, 79 U.S.L.W. 3641 (U.S. May 16, 2011) (No. 10-1213); Koennig (2012), p. 276.

[271] Trustmark Ins. Co. v. John Hancock Life Ins. Co., 631 F.3d 869 (7th Cir. 2011), cert. denied, 79 U.S.L.W. 3641 (U.S. May 16, 2011) (No. 10-1213); Koennig (2012), p. 276.

[272] Trustmark Ins. Co. v. John Hancock Life Ins. Co., 631 F.3d 869 (7th Cir. 2011), cert. denied, 79 U.S.L.W. 3641 (U.S. May 16, 2011) (No. 10-1213); Koennig (2012), p. 276.

[273] Koennig (2012), p. 278.

[274] Trustmark Ins. Co. v. John Hancock Life Ins. Co., 631 F.3d 869 (7th Cir. 2011), cert. denied, 79 U.S.L.W. 3641 (U.S. May 16, 2011) (No. 10-1213); Koennig (2012), p. 276.

when the subject matter of an award pertains to public health or safety. Additionally, information from arbitrations may become public through discovery and trial in subsequent judicial proceedings

Trustmark[275] lacks an abundance of guidance as to why the Seventh Circuit decided to permit disclosure of the information from the first arbitration. Writing for the majority, Judge Easterbrook spelled out several rules about the broad powers of arbitrators to conduct arbitrations as they see fit, but gave little justification for allowing the second panel to ignore the confidentiality agreement. If the Seventh Circuit held that Gurevitz' prior knowledge was not a disqualifying factor, then permitting the other two arbitrators to also obtain such knowledge would do no further harm. In fact, placing all three arbitrators on the same footing would improve the ability of the panel to consider the first award's validity. If the parties agreed to arbitrate disputes arising out of the reinsurance agreement, then they probably did so expecting to be able to quickly deal with disputes and move on with their business together. Extending the confidentiality agreement to the other two panel members was therefore in the best interest of the parties if doing so streamlined the process.[276]

4.4.17.7 Conclusions

In Trustmark,[277] the Seventh Circuit allowed an arbitration to recommence when it reversed the district court's grant of an injunction to stay arbitration. This allowed parties to a reinsurance agreement to continue resolving a dispute using a method to which they originally agreed.

Taking its opinion a step further, the Seventh Circuit concluded by empowering the newly-reinstated arbitration panel with the authority to determine their own view of a confidentiality agreement signed by the parties during the preceding arbitration.

The holding confirms that the Seventh Circuit will permit a party-appointed arbitrator to remain on a panel despite allegations of partiality, as long as recusal would not be required of a federal judge in a judicial proceeding. Significantly, an already small pool of reinsurance arbitrators will not be narrowed further by disqualifications for prior knowledge of a dispute. The Seventh Circuit infringed upon the privacy expectations of the parties but made a logical and necessary decision to permit construal of the confidentiality agreement by the second panel.[278]

---

[275] Trustmark Ins. Co. v. John Hancock Life Ins. Co., 631 F.3d 869 (7th Cir. 2011), cert. denied, 79 U.S.L.W. 3641 (U.S. May 16, 2011) (No. 10-1213); Koennig (2012), p. 276.

[276] Koennig (2012), p. 279.

[277] Trustmark Ins. Co. v. John Hancock Life Ins. Co., 631 F.3d 869 (7th Cir. 2011), cert. denied, 79 U.S.L.W. 3641 (U.S. May 16, 2011) (No. 10-1213); Koennig (2012), p. 279.

[278] Koennig (2012), p. 278.

4.5 Jurisdiction of Courts

The Arbitration Act 1996 provides expressly for specific ways in which assistance may be sought from the High Court, for example by way of application to enforce a peremptory order made by an arbitration tribunal; or to secure the attendance of witnesses or to preserve evidence (including the inspection, photographing, custody or detention of property, or ordering that samples be taken from or experiments be conducted upon such property); or the granting of interim injunctions; or the determination of preliminary issues of law; or the removal of arbitrators and the filling of any vacancies in the tribunal; or appeals from the awards of arbitrators.

A rather more difficult question is whether, as a matter of common law, the court possesses inherent jurisdiction of a general or other supervisory nature.

In The Bremer Vulkan,[279] the House of Lords accepted in principle that the court had power to intervene in certain circumstances by way of injunction to restrain a reference, but there are a number of conditions which must be met before the court can be asked to intervene. The wording of section l (c) of the Act is that "in matters governed by this Part the court should not intervene except as provided by this Part".

The question arises, therefore, as to whether the Act removes any inherent jurisdiction of the court to make Orders otherwise than as allowed by the Act or whether it merely cautions the court to intervene only in exceptional cases.

In ValeDo Rio Doce Navegacao SA v Shanghai Bao Steel Ocean Shipping Co. Ltd (t/a Baosteel Ocean Shipping Co.)[280] and subsequent cases—including Hiscox Underwriting Ltd v Dickson Manchester & Co. Ltd[281] the court took the view that the court possessed an inherent jurisdiction in relation to matters not provided for by the Act.

In each case, however, the court emphasised that section l (c) is to be taken seriously and it will only be in very exceptional circumstances that the court will exercise its inherent jurisdiction if the Act does not expressly give the court the power to make an order. Section 37(1) of the Supreme Court Act 1981 is also relevant in this context as, independent of the provisions of the Arbitration Act 1996, it gives the High Court the power to grant an injunction or appoint a receiver in all cases in which it appears convenient to do so.[282]

[279] The Bremer Vulkan [1981] AC 909.

[280] ValeDo Rio Doce Navegacao SA v. Shanghai Bao Steel Ocean Shipping Co. Ltd (t/a Baosteel Ocean Shipping Co.) [2000] 2 All ER (Comm) 70.

[281] Hiscox Underwriting Ltd v. Dickson Manchester & Co. Ltd [2004] EWHC 479 (Comm).

[282] XL Insurance Ltd v. Owens Corning [2000] 2 Lloyd's Rep 500).

4.5.1 Choice of Law in Reinsurance Arbitration Disputes

Most reinsurance agreements constitute contracts involving interstate commerce and thus fall within the ambit of the FAA. For all contracts covered by the FAA, federal "common" law governs questions of the interpretation, construction, validity, revocability and enforceability of the contractual arbitration provisions. Federal law, however, directs a court to the relevant state law to determine whether the parties in fact have agreed to arbitrate their disputes.[283]

A number of different issues arise in relation to choice of law in the context of reinsurance arbitrations. The arbitrators must determine the law governing the agreement to submit the dispute to arbitration, the law governing the reference to arbitration, the law governing the arbitral proceedings and the law governing the substance of the dispute.[284]

4.5.2 The Law Governing the Agreement to Submit the Dispute to Arbitration

The law governing the arbitration agreement may not necessarily be the same as the law which governs the rest of the contract. The law which governs the arbitration agreement will be used to help determine issues such as the question whether the agreement to arbitrate is valid; whether the interpretation of the arbitration agreement and in particular whether the arbitrator has jurisdiction over certain issues; or whether an agreement to arbitrate has been frustrated; or whether the law governing the arbitration agreement will be applied to decide whether there has been an agreement as to curial law.

Notwithstanding our statement above that law governing the arbitration agreement may not necessarily be the same as the law which governs the rest of the contract, nonetheless, often an arbitration clause will be governed by the same law as that which governs the contract of which it forms part. In exceptional cases the law may differ.

In Deutsche Schachtbau und Tiefbohrgesellschaft MbH v Ras Al Khaimah National Oil[285] an arbitration agreement providing for arbitration in Geneva, was governed by Swiss law notwithstanding that the contract which was to be performed in Ras Al Khaimah had been held by the arbitral tribunal to be governed by general principles of law.[286]

---

[283] Hummer (1996).

[284] Cox et al. (2006).

[285] Deutsche Schachtbau und Tiefbohrgesellschaft MbH v Ras Al Khaimah National Oil [1990]1 AC 295.

[286] Cox et al. (2006).

Thus, although usually an arbitration agreement in reinsurance contracts will be governed by the law applicable to the contract it is contained in, determined in accordance with the relevant choice of law regime, this will not be the case where the underlying contract is governed by law X but provides for arbitration in state Y which may be chosen as neutral territory.[287]

In the USA most reinsurance agreements constitute contracts involve interstate commerce and thus fall within the ambit of the FAA.[288] For all contracts covered by the FAA,[289] federal "common" law governs questions of the interpretation, construction, validity, revocability and enforceability of the contractual arbitration provisions.[290]

Federal law, however, directs a court to the relevant state law to determine whether the parties in fact have agreed to arbitrate their disputes.[291] At times, the interplay between the McCarran-Ferguson Act[292] and the FAA[293] creates issues unique to the insurance and reinsurance industries. Some courts, notably those in New York, interpret their state's legislative framework for handling the affairs of insolvent insurers and reinsurers as vesting exclusive jurisdiction in that area in the state court responsible for overseeing the liquidation or rehabilitation.[294] Under this reasoning, the McCarran-Ferguson Act[295] bars application of FAA[296] and, accordingly, enforcement of arbitration provisions.[297]

---

[287] In such a case the presumption that the agreement to arbitrate will be governed by the same law as the law of the arbitration will most likely outweigh any other presumption; Cox et al. (2006).

[288] 9 U.S.C. § 1 et seq. Duryee v Am. Druggists' Ins. Co., No. C2-92-931 (S.D. Ohio May 10, 1993), reprinted in Mealey's Litig. Rep.: Reins., Vol. 4, No. 2, at A-1 (May 26, 1993); Hummer (1996), p. 228.

[289] 9 U.S.C. § 1 et seq. Stephens v Am. Int'l Ins. Co., No. 91 CIV 6245, 1994 WL 414374 (S.D. N.Y. Aug. 5, 1994). Duryee v Am. Druggists' Ins. Co., No. C2-92-931 (S.D. Ohio May 10, 1993), reprinted in Mealey's Litig. Rep.: Reins., Vol. 4, No. 2, at A-1 (May 26, 1993); Hummer (1996), p. 228.

[290] Coenen v R.W. Pressprich & Co., 453 F.2d 1209, 1211 (2d Cir.), cert. denied, 406 U.S. 949 (1972). accordingly Gen. Sec. Assurance Co. v Capital Assurance Co., No. 110807/93 (N.Y. Sup. Ct., N.Y. Co., IAS Part 19, June 8, 1994), reprinted in Mealey's Litig. Rep.: Reins., Vol. 5, No. 6, at C1 (July 27, 1994). Old Republic Ins. Co. v Lanier, 644 So.2d 1258 (Ala. 1994); Hummer (1996), p. 228.

[291] Progressive Casualty Ins. Co. v C.A. Reaseguradora Nacional de Venezuela, 991 F.2d 42 (2d Cir. 1993).

[292] 15 U.S.C. § 1012(b).

[293] 9 U.S.C. § 1 et seq. Stephens v Am. Int'l Ins. Co., No. 91 CIV 6245, 1994 WL 414374 (S.D. N.Y. Aug. 5, 1994). Duryee v Am. Druggists' Ins. Co., No. C2-92-931 (S.D. Ohio May 10, 1993), reprinted in Mealey's Litig. Rep.: Reins., Vol. 4, No. 2, at A-1 (May 26, 1993); Hummer (1996), p. 228.

[294] Hummer (1996), pp. 228–229.

[295] 15 U.S.C. § 1012(b).

[296] 9 U.S.C. § 1 et seq. Duryee v Am. Druggists' Ins. Co., No. C2-92-931 (S.D. Ohio May 10, 1993), reprinted in Mealey's Litig. Rep.: Reins., Vol. 4, No. 2, at A-1 (May 26, 1993); Hummer (1996), p. 228.

[297] Union Indem. Ins. Co. v Am. Centennial Ins. Co., 521 N.Y.S. 2d 617 (N.Y. Sup.Ct. N.Y. Cty. 1987). Cf. Gerling-Konzern Globale Rueckversicherungs-Ag v Selcke, No. 93 C4439, 1993 WL

Courts in other states, which do not have such restrictive legislative schemes, have enforced arbitration agreements and either compelled liquidators or rehabilitators to arbitrate or enforced demands by liquidators to arbitrate.[298] Courts also have relied on the McCarran-Ferguson Act[299] to uphold state statutes or common law doctrines that do not permit insurance or reinsurance agreements to contain arbitration provisions.[300] Since the FAA[301] does not confer on a federal question of jurisdiction, absent some other basis for federal jurisdiction disputes over an arbitration clause must be litigated in state court.[302] Where federal jurisdiction is present, the general federal venue rules apply.[303]

4.5.3 The Law Governing the Reference to Arbitration

In theory, there can be a distinction between the agreement to arbitrate and the actual reference to arbitration which constitutes a contract in its own right. Again in theory, at least, that contract is capable of having its own law. However, in practice it will most likely be governed by the same law.[304]

4.5.3.1 The Law Governing the Arbitral Proceedings

The law governing the arbitral proceedings, or else curial law, will govern procedural aspects of the arbitration, such as appointment of arbitrators, the conduct of

443404 (N.D. Ill. Oct. 29, 1993) (abstaining from deciding case in which reinsurer sought to compel arbitration of disputes with liquidator of insolvent insurance company); Hummer (1996), pp. 228–229.

[298] Selcke v New England Ins. Co., 995 F.2d 688 (7th Cir.). Capitol Life Ins. Co. v Gallagher, 839 F. Supp. 767 (D. Colo. 1993), aff'd, 47 F.3d 1178 (10th Cir. 1995). Costle v Fremont Indem. Co., 839 F. Supp. 265 (D. Vt. 1993). Ainsworth v Allstate Ins. Co., 634 F. Supp. 52 (W.D. Mo. 1985); In the Matter of the Liquidation of Integrity Ins. Co.: Arkwright Mut. Ins. Co. in Liquidation, No. C-70-95 (N.J. App. July 31, 1995), reprinted in Mealey's Litig. Rep.: Reins., Vol. 6, No. 8, at A-1 (Aug. 20, 1995); Hummer (1996), p. 229.

[299] 15 U.S.C. § 1012(b).

[300] Mut. Reins. Bureau v Great Plains Mut. Ins. Co., 969 F.2d 931 (10th Cir.), cert. denied, 113 S. Ct. 604 (1992). Federated Rural Elec. Ins. Co. v Nationwide Mut. Ins. Co., 874 F. Supp. 1204 (D. Kan. 1995). Hummer (1996), pp. 228–236, 229.

[301] 9 U.S.C. § 1 et seq. Duryee v Am. Druggists' Ins. Co., No. C2-92-931 (S.D. Ohio May 10, 1993), reprinted in Mealey's Litig. Rep.: Reins., Vol. 4, No. 2, at A-1 (May 26, 1993); Hummer (1996), p. 228.

[302] Harry Hoffman Printing Inc. v Graphic Communications Int'l Union Local 261, 912 F.2d 608, 611 (2d Cir. 1990). Wisconsin Comm'r of Ins. v California Reins. Management Corp., 819 F. Supp. 797, 802 (E.D. Wis. 1993); Hummer (1996), p. 229.

[303] Constitution Reins. Corp. v Stonewall Ins. Co., 872 F. Supp. 1247 (S.D. N.Y. 1995); Hummer (1996), p. 229.

[304] Cox et al. (2006).

the proceedings and challenge to the award. With regards to English law, the application of the Arbitration Act 1996 depends on a number of factual questions, mostly whether the seat of arbitration is England. The juridical seat of the arbitration is not necessarily the place where arbitration will physically take place. In the absence of an express designation by the parties and the tribunal, courts will determine the seat of the arbitration.

In doing so, the courts will take into account the parties agreement and any other relevant circumstances, such as any connections with one or more particular countries in relation to the parties, the dispute, the proposed arbitral procedures or the issue of the future award. If the seat of the arbitration is England, the Arbitration Act 1996 will apply in it alongside the various procedural rules contained in it, some of which are mandatory[305] and some are non-mandatory.[306]

Parties may contract out of the non-mandatory provisions, if they have agreed on such an opt out in their arbitration agreement,[307] or if they have agreed to arbitrate in accordance with the rules of an arbitral institution and in which case such rules—to the extent that they are inconsistent with non-mandatory provisions of the Arbitration Act 1996—will apply, or if they have chosen a different curial law.

With regards to the case where a different curial law than English law is chosen, such a choice will incorporate any rules of that law which are inconsistent with the non-mandatory provisions of the Arbitration Act 1996.[308] If the seat of the arbitration is not England, the Arbitration Act 1996 has only limited application, whether or not the parties have chosen English law as the curial law.

Certain provisions apply regardless of the seat of the arbitration namely, those relating to the stay of proceedings and the enforcement of the arbitral awards.[309]

There are also certain procedures exercisable by the English court in relation to foreign arbitrations—such as the power to grant interim injunctions—where the English courts can refuse to act if there is no necessary link with the domestic jurisdiction. With regards to the separability of the arbitral agreement,[310] this

[305] Such as the provisions relating to the courts' powers to set aside or remit an award.

[306] Such as the provisions relating to the power to appeal on questions of law.

[307] In XL Insurance Ltd v Owens Corning [2000]2 Lloyd's Rep. 500 the parties had agreed to arbitrate in London but had excluded sections 45 and 69 of the English Arbitration Act 1996 from applying.

[308] This case will arise where England is the seat of the arbitration but the parties have expressly chosen a different curial law. In the absence of an express agreement or strong implication to this effect, the inference that the parties—when contracting to arbitrate in a particular place—consented to having the arbitral process governed by the law of that place is "irresistible" (Channel Tunnel Group Ltd v Balfour Beatty [1991]1 All ER 127, Sumitomo Heavy Industries Ltd v Oil and Natural Gas Commission [1994]1 Lloyd's Rep 219). This will usually be the case even if the law governing the arbitration agreement is different (James Miller and Partners Ltd v Whitworth Street Estates (Manchester) Ltd [1970] AC 583); Cox et al. (2006).

[309] Sections 9–11 and 66 of the English Arbitration Act 1996.

[310] Section 7 of the English Arbitration Act 1996.

provision applies where English law is the law applicable to the arbitration agreement, regardless of the seat of the arbitration.[311]

4.5.3.2 The Law Governing the Substance of the Dispute

Where the seat of the arbitration is England, and unless the parties have agreed otherwise, section 46 of the Arbitration Act 1996 sets out the approach which the arbitrators should take to determine the standards by which the merits of the dispute should be judged.[312]

4.5.3.2.1 Express Choice of Law

The parties are free to agree the law applicable to the dispute. In contracts, the will of the parties is accorded substantial pre-eminence. Unsurprisingly the same respect for party autonomy is accorded in the context of arbitration, itself a process founded on the consent and agreement of the parties.[313] However even this simple first step may be more complex than what it appears to be.

Whether the parties are free to choose any law is an issue of considerable importance in an insurance and reinsurance context.

Whereas under the Rome Convention party autonomy is given primary importance under article 3, if the contract is an insurance contract to which the insurance directives apply, the parties freedom to choose the applicable law may well be curtailed. Whether by choosing to arbitrate the parties have contracted out of those provisions, depends on the source of the parties autonomy.

In other words, the issue is whether the source of the parties ability to choose the law governing their contract is simply based upon their will or whether the parties autonomy is confined to selecting from amongst the options offered by a particular system of law. If the latter is the case, then the issue is which law is the law applying to reinsurance arbitrations.

For many reasons, the respect given to party autonomy should prevail: for once, in England, the special conflict rule for arbitration set out in section 46(1) of the 1996 Arbitration Act appears to make the obligation absolute.

Secondly, due to the universal acceptance of party autonomy, party autonomy operates as a right in itself.

However there may be an exception for the application of mandatory rules that are contrary to international public policy. Although the arbitrator is not a state organ bound to apply mandatory rules, his duty to enable awards to be enforceable

[311] Cox et al. (2006).

[312] Cox et al. (2006).

[313] Cox et al. (2006).

as well as to support the whole system of arbitration ought to require him, at the least, not to apply any rules contrary to public policy.[314]

Parties are generally free to agree the law applicable to the dispute. As per section 46(1)(b) of the Arbitration Act 1996, parties are free to choose to apply such other considerations as are agreed by them or determined by the tribunal. Thus, parties can agree to incorporate equity clauses of honourable engagement or else amiable compositeur provisions, or they max choose to adopt a version of the so-called *lex mercatoria*, for example the UNIDROIT principles of international commercial contracts.[315]

4.5.3.2.2 No Express or Implied Choice of Law

Where no express choice of law exists, the question becomes even more complex. The tribunal will apply the law determined by the conflict of laws rules that it considers applicable.

In England, section 46(3) of the Arbitration Act 1996 gives the general discretion to apply any conflict of law rule, not necessarily the rules of a particular country.

However, section 46(3) of the Arbitration Act 1996 does not allow the arbitrators to apply directly whatever law they think appropriate but to choose what conflict of law rule to apply and then apply that rule so as to find the applicable law.

Also, it should be noted that section 46(3) of the Arbitration Act 1996 refers to the arbitrators applying the conflict of law rules which it considers applicable, note not appropriate. Thus, the question arises again as to whether the arbitrators will be required to determine the regime which would apply or whether their discretion is wider.

Traditionally the choice of law process constitutes an attempt to localise a legal issue in a national legal system. By contrast, the power of the arbitral tribunal to determine the rules to apply to the merits of the dispute can be considered an extension to the principle of party autonomy. Arbitrators are under a duty to the parties and their way to determine the applicable law should be focused and based on that.

In England, section 46(3) of the Arbitration Act 1996 gives a general discretion to apply any conflict of law rule, not necessarily the rules of a particular country. Arbitrators should be wary of assuming that solutions adopted within the EU are a safe guide to the determination of applicable conflict rules for a dispute where the parties and subject-matter are outside the EU.

Thus, overall we note that it is possible for a reinsurance contract to have a different applicable law, depending on whether or not there is an arbitration clause. It is important to bear in mind that through the impact on the choice of law issues,

---

[314] Cox et al. (2006).

[315] Cox et al. (2006).

an agreement to arbitrate may also affect the parties' substantive rights and liabilities.[316]

The law applicable to an arbitration clause is to be ascertained by common law principles rather than under Rome I.[317] The common law leans towards a finding that a choice of law for the reinsurance agreement extends also to the arbitration clause and conversely Rome I specifically states in Recital 12 that a choice of tribunal indicates a choice of law in respect of the substantive contract. Whether "tribunal" includes an arbitral tribunal is a matter of some doubt, but the latter point is largely irrelevant because where there is an operative arbitration clause, the law applicable to the substantive dispute is governed by entirely different principles.[318]

Section 46 (1) of the Arbitration Act 1996 requires the arbitrators to apply the law chosen by the parties to the substance of the dispute, and this means in accordance with section 46(2) the substantive law and not conflict of laws rules, so renvoi is excluded. This reflects the principle in Rome I article 3.1 that the parties may choose the applicable law and that their choice is paramount.

Regarding reinsurance agreements, if no choice of law is made under Rome I and article 4(1) the rule of the law of the country of habitual residence of the reinsurer applies. In reinsurance arbitration though, the arbitrator must determine the conflict of laws rules which should apply, ascertain the applicable law under those choice-of-law rules and then apply the substantive principles of the applicable law. However, Rome I is unlikely to be of any real importance when an arbitration clause has been inserted into the reinsurance agreement, which is often the case. No doubt, the arbitrators must apply the chosen law if one exists, but may also be empowered to apply a system of law not recognized by Rome I and in the absence of agreement on the applicable law they can also decide—by adopting a different system of applicable law rules—that Rome I has no relevance at all.[319]

4.6 Conclusions

Arbitration clauses in reinsurance contracts are commonly included and favoured by parties. Cedent companies and reinsurers may draft arbitration clauses as they desire. English as well as German law, do not impose restrictions regarding the use of arbitration clauses English courts have held that general words of incorporation were not sufficient to incorporate an arbitration clause into the reinsurance in the absence of an express intention.[320] Following Excess Insurance Company v Mander[321] it is supported in English law that the arbitration clauses had not been

[316] Cox et al. (2006).

[317] Merkin (2009), pp. 69, 75.

[318] Merkin (2009), pp. 69, 75.

[319] Merkin (2009), pp. 69, 75.

[320] Equitas & Ors v Trygg Hansa Dec. 1997 (unreported).

[321] Excess Insurance Company v Mander [1995] L.R.L.R. 385.

incorporated in to the reinsurance contract by means of mere reference. The policy favouring arbitration does not supplant the intent of the parties as the primary factor in determining the scope of an arbitration clause.[322] A narrowly drawn arbitration clause will render only the specific issues within its scope arbitrable.[323] Broadly-worded arbitration clauses will also normally be construed to encompass extra-contractual Claims, such as fraud in the inducement.[324] Although there is no difference between litigation and arbitration because in each proceeding, a neutral third party decides the dispute between the parties and issues a binding decision, procedurally there are dramatic differences. Reinsurance contracts have arbitration clauses as arbitration has been the traditional method of dispute resolution for reinsurance disputes for many decades. Difficulties arise, however, when the parties' intentions regarding the scope of arbitration are not clearly expressed in the reinsurance agreement. In the U.S.A. the pondering view is that any doubt concerning the scope of arbitrable issues should be resolved in favour of arbitration.[325] Recent decisions also demonstrate the tendency to support the conclusion of the existence of the intent to arbitrate, in simple phrases purporting so.[326] The most popular defence to arbitration is the allegation that the arbitration clause is not broad enough to encompass the dispute at issue. Arbitration clauses use various phrases to define the scope of arbitrable issues. The clauses usually refer to disputes arising under this agreement or arising out of or relating to the agreement. Courts may construe differently these very similar phrases. In addition, a party's own conduct may preclude it from exercising its right to pursue arbitration. Litigation has also resulted from ambiguity over whether arbitration agreements under separate contracts underlying larger reinsurance programs call for consolidated or class arbitration as opposed to separate arbitrations. The clear trend among courts is to

[322] S.A. Mineracao da Trindade Samitri v Utab, Int'l, Inc., 745 F.2d 190, 193 (2d Cir. 1984). Futter v Guthrie, 565 F.2d 259, 261 (2d Cir. 1977). Lukens Steel Co. v United Steelworkers of Am. (AFL-CIO), 989 F.2d 668, 672 (3d Cir. 1993) [quoting F. Harkins Co. v Waldinger Corp., 796 F.2d 657, 660 (3d Cir. 1986), cert. denied, 479 U.S. 1059 (1987)]. Shearson Lehman Hutton, Inc. v Wagoner, 944 E2d 114, 121 (2d Cir. 1991). Seaboard Coast Line RR. Co. v Trailer Train Co., 690 F.2d 1343, 1352 (11th Cir. 1982). Syufy Enterprises v North Cal State Ass'n ofl.AT.S.E Locals, 631 E2d 124, 126 (9th Cir. 1980), cert. denied, 451 U.S. 983 (1981). AfecdW S.PA. v Necchi Sewing Machine Sales Corp., 348 F.2d 693, 696 (2d Cir. 1965), cert. denied, 383 U.S. 909 (1966); Ostrager and Vyskocil (1996), §§ 14-01, 14-4, 14-5.

[323] McDonnell Douglas Finance Corp. v Pennsylvania Power & Light Co., 858 E2d 825, 832 (2d Cir. 1988). Associated Brich Mason Contractors of Greater N.Y, Inc. v Harrington, 820 F.2d 31, 35 (2d Cir. 1987). Prudential Lines, Inc. v Exxon Corp., Associated Indemnity Corp. v Home Insurance Co., 19 F.3d 1432 (6th Cir. 1994)704 F.2d 59, 64 (2d Cir. 1983). Äodbrfafe Village Inc. v Public Serv. Employees Union, LocalNo. 80,605 F.2d 1290, 1295 (2d Cir. 1979); Ostrager and Vyskocil (1996), §§ 14-01, 14-6, 14-7.

[324] Prima Paint Corp. v Flood & Conklin Manufacturing Co., 388 U.S. 395.

[325] Moses H Cone Memorial Hospital v Mercury Constr. Corp. 460 US 1 (1983).

[326] Hartford Accident and Indemnity Co. v Swiss Reinsurance Co. of America, 246 F.3d 219 (2d Cir. 2001): Security Life Insurance Co. of America v Hannover Life Reinsurance Co. of America, 2001 WL 392412 (D. Minn.)

defer to arbitrators the question of consolidation, finding that the question is procedural. Notwithstanding the above remarks, many arbitration clauses need clarity.

The importance of the arbitration panel's qualifications and the process of selecting an arbitrator and umpire are matters of great concern in any reinsurance arbitration. The reinsurance industry elects to submit its disputes to arbitration so that a panel of industry experts can resolve the issues involved through a process that is generally less time consuming, expensive and formal than traditional court proceedings. The court may, on the application of any party to arbitral proceedings, remove an arbitrator when there are justifiable doubts as to its impartiality, or he does not possess the qualifications required by the arbitration agreement, or he is physically or mentally incapable of conducting the proceedings or that there are justifiable doubts as to his capacity to do so or has refused or failed to conduct the proceedings properly or to use all reasonable despatch in conducting the proceedings or in making an award.

The courts appear to be split on the issue of when a party seeking to challenge the qualifications of an arbitrator should bring such a challenge. A significant number have held that a challenge to an arbitrator's qualifications can only be made after the arbitration is concluded and must be brought in the context of a motion to vacate the arbitration award.[327] Other courts have recognized that if a provision of the contract dealing with arbitration qualification has not been met, a condition precedent to the commencement of the arbitration may be lacking and the arbitrator's qualifications and appointment may be challenged.[328] Trustmark[329] whereby it was held that an arbitrator should not be disqualified for lack of the requisite impartiality because of specific knowledge gained in a prior arbitration between the same parties is a decision favorable to arbitrators in the reinsurance industry and other similarly

[327] Aviall, Inc. v Ryder Sys., Inc., 110 F.3d 892 (2d Cir. 1997). Florasynth, Inc. v Pickholz, 750 F.2d 171 (2d Cir. 1984). In Re Michaels v Mariforum Shipping, S.A., 624 F.2d 411 (2d Cir. 1980). Sanko S.S. Co. Ltd. v Cook Indus. Inc., 495 F.2d 1260 (2d Cir. 1973). Old Republic Ins. Co. v Meadows Indem. Co., 870 F. Supp. 210 (N.D Ill. 1994). Corporate Printing Co. Inc. v New York Typographical Union No. 6, 601 F. Supp 323 (S.D.N.Y. 1984). Marc Rich & Co., A.G. v Transmarine Seaways Corp. of Monrovia, 443 F. Supp. 386 (S.D.N.Y. 1978). Andarko Petroleum Corp. v Panhandle Eastern Corp., (No.87381 Del. Ch. Sept. 21, 1987), aff'd, 545 A.2d 1171 (Del. 1988).

[328] Argonaut Midwest Ins. Co. v General Reinsurance Corp., 1998 U.S. Dist. LEXIS 12497, 1998 WL4142 (N.D. Ill. Aug. 6, 1998). In Re Certain Underwriters at Lloyd's, London v Continental Cas. Co., 1997 U.S. Dist. LEXIS 11934, 1997 WL 461035 (N.D. Ill. Aug. 11, 1997) (mem. and order). Fremont Indemn. Co. v Assicurazoni Generali SpA, No. CV94-7908 (C.D. Cal., Mar. 7, 1995) (order). Fireman's Fund Ins. Co. v Sorema North American Reinsurance Co., No. C94-3617SC (N.D. Cal., Feb. 8, 1995) (order). Evanston Ins. Co. v Kansa Gen. Int'l Ins. Co., No. 94C4957 (N.D. Ill. Oct. 17, 1994 and Jan. 13, 1995) (mems. and orders). Int'l Ins. Co. v Certain Underwriters at Lloyd's, London, No. 1:88-CV-09838 (N.D. Ill. Dec. 30, 1992) (order). Metropolitan Property & Cas. Ins. Co. v J.C. Penny Cas. Ins. Co., 780 F. Supp. 885 (D. Conn. 1991). Third Nat'l Bank In Nashville v Wedge Group, Inc., 749 F, Supp. 851 (M.D. Tenn. 1990).

[329] Trustmark Ins. Co. v. John Hancock Life Ins. Co., 631 F.3d 869 (7th Cir. 2011), cert. denied, 79 U.S.L.W. 3641 (U.S. May 16, 2011) (No. 10-1213); Koennig (2012), p. 276.

specialised industries. However, it has been supported that the adoption of the reasonable person standard which permits the court to shift away from its focus on the judicial standard of impartiality and focus more on the conduct of the arbitrator is tentatively a good solution.

References

Bank JF, Winters P (1989) Reinsurance arbitration: a U.S. perspective. J Insur Reg 7:323

Barlow Lyde and Gilbert LLP (2009) Reinsurance practice and the law. Informa, London

Blum GL (1999) Setting aside arbitration award on ground of interest or bias of arbitrators—commercial, business, or real estate transactions. ALR 67:179

Chiafullo LA, Cruz-Brown KA, Rourke-Hugener J, Monahan JC, Rush DE (2007) Recent developments in excess insurance, surplus lines insurance and reinsurance law. Tort Trial Insur Pract Law J 42:435

Cox R, Merrett L, Smith M (2006) Private international law of reinsurance and insurance. Informa, London

DiUbaldo RW (2008) Evolving issues in reinsurance disputes: the power of arbitrators. Fordham Urban Law J 35:83–106

Hammesfahr RW, Wright SW (1994) The law of reinsurance claims. Andrews Professional Books, Westtown

Hummer P (1996) Reinsurance arbitrations from start to finish: a practitioner's guide. Def Couns 63:228–236

Holmes EM, Sutin LA (1996) Holmes' Appleman on insurance 2d, vol 14. Lexis, Los Angeles

Kanefsky EP, Diubaldo RW (2009) Notable 2009 U.S. reinsurance arbitration decisions. Insur Reinsur Rev. www.edwardswildman.com/insights/PublicationDetail.aspx?publication=1914

Kareken MC, Soderstrom RS, Duffy MJ (2000) Challenging the qualifications of the reinsurance arbitrator. FICC Q 50(2):141

Koennig C (2012) If we could, then so can you: the seventh circuit resurrects its judge versus arbitrator analogy to reinstate a repeat arbitrator. J Disp Resolut 2012:265

McDonald JJ (2001) Reinsurance arbitration 2001: will the new ways cripple arbitration? Def Couns J 68:328–338

Merkin R (2009) The Rome I regulation and reinsurance. J Priv Int Law 5(1):69

Ostrager BR, Vyskocil MC (1996) Modern reinsurance law and practice. Glasser Legal Works, Little Falls

Schiffer L (2006) Expert commentary: reinsurance – arbitration: a primer. IRMI, USA

Thomas JE et al (eds) (2011) New Appleman insurance law practice guide, vol 4, Separate lines of insurance. Lexis, Los Angeles

Thomas JE, Lyons S (eds) (2012) New Appleman on insurance law – library edition, vol 7, Property insurance (chapters 71–79 §§ 71.01–79.06). Lexis Nexis, Los Angeles

The Reinsurance Arbitration Proceedings

Reinsurance arbitration proceedings are commonly conducted in a way similar to a hearing before the state courts. However, differentiating factors are *inter alia* the constitution of the arbitral panel by knowledgeable industry experts, as well as the speed, confidentiality and no precedential character of the arbitral proceedings. Arbitrators are subject to a general to act fairly and impartially as between the parties. The court has a subsidiary power to order compliance with a peremptory order made by a tribunal. The party aggrieved may seek from a court an order compelling arbitration. Arbitration agreements will be consolidated if parties or tribunals decide so. Reinsurance arbitral agreements are fully enforced by the courts.

5.1 Procedure at the Hearing

It is common, in reinsurance arbitrations, for the parties to conduct proceedings in a form similar to a hearing before the Commercial Court. Such a traditional procedure usually involves the following steps[1]:

1. Counsel for the claimant produces an agreed list of issues, a detailed chronology of events and a *dramatis personae* which lists all the relevant persons and any non-contentious information regarding such persons.
2. Counsel for the claimant may then make an opening statement which could, according to the circumstances, be either fairly brief or fairly lengthy. Its purpose is to provide the panel with a background to the dispute, take them through the detailed chronology and, where necessary, refer them to the list of key witnesses and any relevant documents in the core bundle (a bundle

[1] Barlow Lyde and Gilbert LLP (2009), p. 26-12.

K. Noussia, *Reinsurance Arbitrations*, DOI 10.1007/978-3-642-45146-1_5,

containing key documents, typically including the slip, wording, the most important correspondence, etc.).

3. Counsel for the claimant may then call his first witness whom he will examine in chief. The witness may have previously provided a Statement of his evidence which counsel may seek to tender as evidence in chief, or he may choose to take the witness through his Statement. It is increasingly the tendency to ask a witness who has given a written Statement only to confirm that the Statement is authentic, and then to allow cross-examination by the opposing party's counsel.
4. Counsel for the respondent may then cross-examine the claimant's first witness and seek to obtain some concessions on his evidence which assist the respondent's case. He will also seek to attack the credibility of the witness, so that the panel are inclined to reject his evidence either on the basis that the witness is biased or has an interest in the outcome of the proceedings, or perhaps on the basis that his evidence is unreliable.
5. The claimant's counsel is then in a position to re-examine the witness for the purpose of rehabilitating his evidence and restoring his credibility in the eyes of the panel.
6. Counsel for the claimant may then call further witnesses, whether they be witnesses of fact or expert witnesses.
7. Once counsel for the claimant has finished calling his evidence, counsel for the respondent (after making an opening Statement) calls his witnesses (both factual and expert), who in turn are cross-examined and then re- examined. Generally speaking, witnesses of fact will, as appropriate, be taken to various relevant documents and questioned on them. Expert witnesses will be taken through their expert reports, if any, and asked to justify their conclusions, or to consider the opposing expert's views and to comment upon them.
8. At the conclusion of the evidence, counsel for the respondent and then counsel for the claimant make their closing Speeches. The purpose of the closing speeches is to draw together the evidence which has been given before the panel to place particular emphasis upon evidence favourable to a party's case and to draw to the attention of the panel weaknesses in the arguments and evidence put forward by the opposing party. Counsel's closing speeches may be accompanied by written submissions, and in some cases only written submissions may be presented. The disadvantage of proceeding without final speeches is that it denies the panel the opportunity of raising questions with counsel and thus focusing their minds upon the issues in dispute and the relative weight which they will attach to each party's arguments.[2]

It is of the essence of an arbitration that it is a means of private dispute resolution. Therefore, restrictions are placed upon those who may attend the hearing.

[2] Barlow Lyde and Gilbert LLP (2009), pp. 26-12–26-14.

Naturally the parties to the arbitration are entitled to attend with their legal representatives, the arbitration panel, the witnesses, factual and expert, and any person charged with preparation of the transcript.

Strictly speaking, no third party—even one who may have an interest in the outcome of the proceedings—has any right or standing to appear at or attend the hearing.

There have been occasions where, in an arbitration, by the consent of the parties and the arbitration panel, a third party has been allowed to attend, but no doubt the third party would ordinarily be bound by an express or implied agreement not to disclose confidential information obtained by his attendance. For example, in a dispute between a reinsured and a reinsurer, the reinsurance broker may have an interest in hearing the evidence given before the arbitration panel, because the outcome of the dispute may result in his becoming involved in subsequent litigation.[3]

Notwithstanding the above, the English Arbitration Act 1996 expressly authorises the arbitrators (subject to the parties' agreement) to decide whether and to what extent the tribunal should itself take the initiative in ascertaining the facts and the law: section 34(2)(g).

Alternatively, the parties (as in a continental arbitration) may elect to adopt an inquisitorial approach.

Generally speaking, this involves the arbitrator taking a far more active role in the proceedings, whether it be in terms of deciding what procedure he will adopt, whether he will accept expert evidence, whether witnesses will be invited to attend the hearing and whether the arbitrator will ask questions of the witnesses before they are questioned by the parties.

Typically, in a continental arbitration the arbitrator's primary function is to ascertain the truth by whatever means are within his power. Unlike the English system, the arbitrator in a "continental system" has no power to compel witnesses to attend or give evidence, nor has he the power to require that evidence be given under oath or affirmation.[4]

5.1.1 Ensuring Procedural Justice in Arbitrations

The Arbitration Act 1996 redefines the relationship between arbitrators and the courts. The arbitrators are the prime movers for the purpose of ensuring procedural justice and enjoy extended powers. As a corollary, the court's powers have been restricted to a subsidiary, supporting role. The procedure for making applications to the court in circumstances where the court is empowered to intervene in the arbitral

[3] Barlow Lyde and Gilbert LLP (2009), pp. 26-6, 26-12–26-14.

[4] Barlow Lyde and Gilbert LLP (2009), pp. 26-6, 26-12–26-14.

process is governed by Part 62 of the Civil Procedure Rules which sets out a comprehensive code in this respect.[5]

5.1.2 General Duty of Arbitrators

Arbitrators are subject to a general duty imposed by section 33 of the Arbitration Act 1996 to act fairly and impartially as between the parties, giving each party a reasonable opportunity of putting his case and dealing with his opponent's case, and to adopt procedures suitable to the circumstances of the particular case, avoiding unnecessary delay or expense, so as to provide a fair means for the resolution of the matters falling to be determined. Subject to compliance with this overriding principle, and subject also to the contrary agreement of the parties, the Arbitration Act 1996 confers further specific powers on the arbitrators.[6]

5.1.3 Powers of the Court

During the proceedings, the powers of the court are fairly limited. The general principle expressed by section 1 (c) of the Arbitration Act 1996 is that the court should not intervene in arbitrations except to the extent provided by the Arbitration Act 1996 itself.

5.1.4 Enforcement of Peremptory Orders

The court has a subsidiary power to order compliance with a peremptory order made by a tribunal. An application for a court order may be made by the tribunal or by a party to the arbitral proceedings with the permission of the tribunal and upon notice to the other parties.

Section 43 of the Arbitration Act 1996 provides that (with the permission of the tribunal or the agreement of the parties) a party to arbitral proceedings may apply to the court to exercise the same powers as are available to the court in relation to judicial proceedings, the issue of subpoenas to compel a party to attend an arbitral hearing to give evidence (*subpoena ad testificandum*) or to produce documents (*subpoena duces tecum*).

[5] Barlow Lyde and Gilbert LLP (2009), pp. 26-7, 26-15; A detailed discussion of the procedural rules would, however, go beyond the scope of this monograph.

[6] Barlow Lyde and Gilbert LLP (2009), pp. 26.7.3, 26-16.

This procedure is only available if the witness in question is in the UK and the arbitral proceedings are being conducted in England, Wales, or Northern Ireland. If the witness is outside the jurisdiction, an application may be made to the court to arrange for his or her evidence to be given on deposition.

5.1.5 Injunctions and Similar Orders

Subject to any contrary agreement by the parties, section 44 gives the court powers similar to those conferred upon the tribunal by section 38, together with certain ancillary powers which it would not normally be open to the parties to confer upon arbitrators simply by agreement, such as the power to authorise any person to enter any premises in the possession or control of a party to the arbitration for purposes of the preservation of evidence, the power to order the sale of any goods which are the subject of the arbitral proceedings, and the power to grant an interim injunction or to appoint a receiver.

As regards the power to grant injunctions [section 44(2) (c)], the court in *Hiscox Underwriting Ltd v Dickson Manchester & Co Ltd*[7] confirmed that the power is a general one and is not limited to making orders relating to the preservation of evidence or assets.

The decision of Cooke J. also establishes that in cases of urgency, when, exceptionally, a party is allowed to apply to the court for assistance without the agreement of the tribunal or the other parties to the arbitration, the court is not limited to injunctive orders for the preservation of evidence or assets, notwithstanding the apparently limiting words of section 44(3).

The subsidiary nature of the court's powers is once again emphasised by certain pre-conditions the court's powers must not have been excluded by agreement of the parties, unless the case is one of urgency, the court shall act only on the application of one of the parties, made with the permission of the tribunal or the agreement in writing of all the other parties, and m any case, the court shall act only if or to the extent that the arbitral tribunal has no power with regard to the relevant matters, or is unable for the time being to act effectively.

5.1.6 Determination of Preliminary Points of Law

Section 45 of the Arbitration Act 1996 states (subject to any contrary agreement) the parties' rights under the previous arbitration regime to refer a question of English law to the court for a preliminary ruling.

[7] *Hiscox Underwriting Ltd v Dickson Manchester & Co Ltd* [2004] EWHC 479 (Comm).

The court must be satisfied that the question substantially affects the rights of one or more of the parties and an application for the preliminary determination of a point of law will not be considered by the court unless it is made either with the agreement of all the other parties to the arbitral proceedings, or with the permission of the tribunal.

In the latter case, the court must further be satisfied that the determination of the issue is likely to produce substantial savings in costs and that the application was made without delay.

The parties may agree to exclude the court's jurisdiction under section 45. Any decision given by the court pursuant to section 45 shall be treated as a judgment of the court for the purposes of an appeal.

The Arbitration Act 1996 lays down further detailed rules in connection with these matters, which generally follow the same regime as that which applies to appeals from arbitration awards.

5.1.7 Staying Court Proceedings

5.1.7.1 Scott v Avery Clauses

"Scott v Avery" clauses take their name from a leading case in which their validity was considered by the court, *Scott v Avery.*[8] They take the form of an arbitration clause which also stipulates that an arbitration award is a condition precedent to the enforcement of any rights under the contract. In such circumstances there is no cause of action under the contract until a favourable award has been obtained by a party. There may, therefore, be a term of the contract that no action should be brought until the arbitration has been conducted and an award made, or a provision to the effect that the obligation of the defendant is to meet only sums awarded by arbitrators. It is important to note that court proceedings brought before an award has been obtained are not null and void. The existence of the *Scott* v *Avery* clause would, however, provide a defence to any such proceedings.

A "Scott v Avery" clause will be automatically overriden where the court refuses to stay judicial proceedings in favour of arbitration. The conduct of the defendant may also disentitle him from relying upon the clause, e.g. by his serving a defence on the merits in the action without pleading the clause specifically, or by instituting legal proceedings of his own. It is also possible that, where the agreement to arbitrate has ceased to exist or cannot otherwise be implemented, there is no subject matter for the condition precedent contained in the *Scott* v *Avery* clause, although the position is not clear-cut.

---

[8] *Scott v Avery* (1856) 5 HL Gas 811.

In *Alfred C Toepfer International GmbH v. Societe Cargill France*,[9] the court held that a *Scott* v *Avery* clause could not apply to injunctive proceedings commenced with the aim of enforcing the clause itself.

5.1.7.2 Stay for Arbitration

It is a general principle of English law that parties should be held to their agreements, including agreements to refer their disputes to arbitration. On the other hand, it is not possible for the courts' jurisdiction to be ousted completely by the parties to a dispute, whether by an arbitration agreement or by any other means.

The Arbitration Act 1996 therefore, provides a mechanism for the stay of judicial proceedings brought in contravention of an arbitration agreement. Such proceedings are not null and void and, as a matter of practicality, a court action may be instituted in breach of an arbitration agreement and continued until such time as an application is heard by the court for those proceedings to be stayed.

If a defendant to such proceedings decides, notwithstanding an applicable arbitration agreement, that the dispute may as well be resolved by the state court rather than by an arbitral tribunal, he need do nothing other than participate without objection in the court proceedings.

5.1.8 "Domestic" and "Non-domestic" Arbitration Agreements

Historically, English law on arbitration has distinguished between "domestic" and "non-domestic" arbitration agreements. In the reinsurance context, many arbitrations are likely to be non-domestic. It is common for at least one party in a large subscription market to be domiciled elsewhere than in the UK. Perhaps surprisingly, the participation of foreign Names in a Lloyd's syndicate can entail the consequence that any arbitration involving that syndicate will be considered non-domestic.

In *Hume v AA Mutual International Insurance Company Ltd*,[10] the court had to interpret arbitration provisions involving a reinsured Lloyd's syndicate and various reinsurers under several contracts. The court found that, on a strict analysis, separate contracts had been made between each member of the reinsured syndicate on the one hand, and the members of each reinsuring syndicate or corporate reinsurer on the other. This analytical position did not, however, make commercial sense and the court held that, on their true construction, the arbitration clauses contemplated, at most, an arbitration proceeding, between the reinsured syndicate and each reinsurer. Since some members of the reinsured syndicate were nationals of, or habitually resident in, states other than the UK, the arbitration agreement was

---

[9] *Alfred C Toepfer International GmbH v Societe Cargill France* [1998] 1 Lloyd's Rep 379 (CA).

[10] *Hume v AA Mutual International Insurance Company Ltd* [1996] LRLR 19 (QB Com Ct).

a non-domestic one and was, accordingly, subject to a mandatory stay under section 1 of the Arbitration Act 1975. If the criteria of section 9 of the Arbitration Act 1996 are fulfilled, the court must stay any legal proceedings brought in contravention of an arbitration agreement. Section 9(4) of the Arbitration Act 1996 provides that the court shall grant a stay unless satisfied that the arbitration agreement is null and void, inoperative, or incapable of being performed. The burden of proving the applicability of any of these grounds probably lies on the party opposing the stay.[11]

5.1.9 Arbitration and the Service of Suit Clause

There is an apparent conflict between the wordings of the typically broad arbitration clause and the service of suit clause customarily contained in reinsurance treaties (and some types of insurance contracts) between the London market and U.S.A. entities. The arbitration clause, depending on its breadth, is likely to require that a given dispute under the treaty be submitted to arbitration.

By contrast, the service of suit clause typically states that "in the event of the failure of reinsurers hereon to pay any amount claimed to be due hereunder, reinsurers hereon, at the request of the reinsured, will submit to the jurisdiction of any court of competent jurisdiction within the United States." The apparent conflict between these clauses has emerged with some frequency at the outset of disputes when the reinsured, relying on the service of suit clause, files a lawsuit to recover alleged "amounts claimed to be due," and the reinsurer, relying on the arbitration clause, moves to stay the lawsuit and to compel arbitration.

Most courts in the U.S.A., construing this issue have looked behind the wording of the service of suit clause to hold that the dispute must be arbitrated pursuant to an otherwise binding arbitration clause.[12]

According to these courts, the apparent inconsistency between the two clauses is not real. They interpret the phrase "failure to pay any amount claimed to be due" in the service of suit clause to refer only to a failure to pay any amount due under an arbitration award. The courts have further explained that the purpose of the service of suit clause is merely to help U.S.A. ceding companies to enforce payment of arbitration awards by foreign reinsurers.

A ruling to the contrary was rendered last year by a Missouri state appellate court in *Transit Casualty Co. in Receivership v Certain Underwriters at Lloyd's of London*,[13] which concerned the arbitrability of a claim that Lloyd's had failed to make reinsurance payments.

---

[11] Barlow Lyde and Gilbert LLP (2009), pp. 26-8, 26-17–26-22.

[12] Cases resolving the apparent conflict between arbitration clauses and service of suit clauses in favor of arbitration such as e.g. *Hart v Orion Ins. Co.*, 453 F.2d 1358, 1361 (10th Cir. 1971); Maloney et al. (2000), p. 480.

[13] *Transit Cas. Co. v Certain Underwriters at Lloyd's of London*, 963 S.W.2d 392 (Mo. Ct. App. 1998).

In denying Lloyd's motion to stay litigation and to compel arbitration, the court found that the service of suit clause, by its terms, was limited to claims alleging failure of the reinsurer to pay, and was thus more specific than the broad arbitration clause requiring arbitration of all disputes.

It then applied the rule of contract construction favoring the specific over the general.

The court also applied the doctrine of *contra proferentem* to construe the service of suit clause against its drafters, Lloyd's.[14] The court further claimed to harmonize the clauses by finding that arbitration would still be required for all disputes except those for failure to pay.

Transit Casualty[15] attempts to carve out an exception to arbitration that many reinsurers would have little reason to expect. In order to avoid such surprises, the parties may consider wording revisions that preserve the right to arbitrate, even where sums are claimed to be due that would otherwise trigger a service of suit clause.[16]

5.1.10 Pre-answer Security

Another concern for foreign reinsurers in disputes with American insurers is pre-answer security. Approximately 40 states have statutes requiring unauthorized, alien insurers to post a bond prior to their answering in proceedings brought against them under their insurance policies.

Several states, including the important commercial jurisdictions of Florida and Pennsylvania, specifically exclude reinsurance from the scope of their statutes. Where no such exclusion exists, courts have required reinsurers to post security under the statutes, even when the merits are being decided in arbitration.[17]

In 1997, the Illinois legislature amended that state's pre-answer security statute to apply specifically to reinsurance arbitrations.[18]

In *Continental Casualty Co. v Certain Underwriters at Lloyd's*,[19] a U.S.A. ceding company, Continental, was engaged in arbitration against certain Lloyd's syndicates and London market companies (the respondents). When the

[14] The applicability of the *contra proferentem* doctrine to reinsurance contracts is subject to debate among U.S. courts.; Maloney et al. (2000), p. 481.

[15] *Transit Cas. Co. v Certain Underwriters at Lloyd's of London*, 963 S.W.2d 392 (Mo. Ct. App. 1998); The applicability of the *contra proferentem* doctrine to reinsurance contracts is subject to debate among U.S. courts.; Maloney et al. (2000), p. 481.

[16] Maloney et al. (2000), p. 481.

[17] *American Centennial Ins. Co. v Seguros La Republica, S.A.*, 1992 WL 162770 (S.D.N.Y. 1992).

[18] 215 Ill. Comp. Stat. Ann. 5/123 (West 1997).

[19] *Continental Cas. Co. v Certain Underwriters at Lloyd's of London*, Nos. C-92-4094 and C-98-3145 (N.D. Cal. Nov. 30, 1998), *reported in* 9 Mealey's Litig. Rep. Reins. 15, (Dec. 10, 1998).

respondents named their arbitrator, Continental moved for pre-arbitration security under the Illinois statute in the California federal district court that had previously compelled arbitration.

The first issue addressed by the district court was whether it had authority to grant preliminary injunctive relief under the Convention. The court ruled that it did, following the Second Circuit's decision in *Borden, Inc. v Meiji Milk Products Co.*[20]

However, the court rejected Continental's argument that the Illinois pre-answer security statute left the court with no discretion in ordering security, finding instead that equity jurisdiction invested the court with broad discretion in fashioning injunctive relief.[21]

The court then determined the central issue of whether the parties had intended Illinois law, and thus the statute, to govern their arbitration. The reinsurance treaty did not address choice of law, but contained a typical arbitration clause providing that the arbitrators would settle the dispute in "an equitable rather than a strictly legal way" and "abstain from following the strict rule of law."

The court characterized these provisions as a "choice of no law" clause, and held that issues relating to application of the Illinois pre-answer security statute should thus be decided by the arbitrators.

The court rejected Continental's argument that the parties implicitly intended Illinois law to apply when they designated Chicago as the place of arbitration, finding that the parties' express decision not to apply the strict rule of law negated any inference that the parties intended to apply Illinois law.[22]

5.1.11 Organisational Meeting

This is a preliminary meeting attended by representatives of all parties, at which the panel of arbitrators outlines the procedures to be used.

These will include:

1. Confidentiality of the proceedings,
2. If and when ex parte communications will be allowed,
3. Discovery issues,
4. Briefing schedules and
5. Whether witnesses and expert witnesses will be used at the hearing.

---

[20] *Borden, Inc. v Meiji Milk Prod. Co.*, 919 F.2d 822, 826 (2d Cir. 1991).

[21] Maloney et al. (2000), p. 487.

[22] Maloney et al. (2000), p. 487.

5.1.12 Hearing

After discovery has been completed and pre-hearing briefs exchanged, the actual hearing before the panel arbitrators will commence. Depending on the agreed on procedures, the hearing itself will be very informal and will likely involve a good deal of discussions between the parties and the panel.

5.1.13 Post-hearing Issues

After the hearing, briefs may be submitted if agreed on and necessary, for instance, when complex issues are involved. Once the award is given by the arbitrators, an additional step may include a court application for confirmation of the award or to seek to vacate of the award.

These steps make up the main issues in an arbitration proceeding. While finer detail may be added by agreement of the parties, any formal arbitration proceeding will have some semblance of the above steps.

In September 1999, the Reinsurance Dispute Resolution Task Force of the Reinsurance Association of America released its recommended "Procedures for the Resolution of U.S.A. Insurance and Reinsurance Disputes," the purpose of which is to formalize the insurance and reinsurancc disputc process.

5.1.14 Enforceability of the Arbitration Agreement

The FAA authorizes "a party aggrieved by the alleged failure, neglect or refusal of another" to comply with an arbitration agreement to seek a court order compelling arbitration.[23] Arbitration agreements will be enforced by the courts.

Under the FAA, if the parties have agreed to arbitrate, and if the dispute in question falls within the scope of the agreement, either party may obtain a stay of court proceedings in favour of arbitration and an order requiring the other party to submit to arbitration.

Conversely, in the absence of an agreement to arbitrate, neither party to a dispute can be deprived of the opportunity to litigate and forced into arbitration. Procedural aspects of arbitration agreements will be enforced as strictly as substantive aspects.[24]

The New York Convention is the primary mechanism governing the recognition and enforcement of foreign arbitral awards. The United States is a signatory to the Convention and enacted implementing legislation in 1970. The New York

---

[23] 9 U.S.C. §4.

[24] Holmes and Sutin (1996), p. 556.

Convention applies to arbitration agreements or awards involving a commercial relationship between at least two citizens of countries subscribing to the New York Convention or between citizens of the United States where there exists some reasonable connection with one or more foreign states.

The federal courts are assigned original jurisdiction over actions within the terms of the Convention. A state court action falling within the New York Convention can be removed to federal court. The federal court is required to compel arbitration unless it determines that the arbitration agreement is "null and void, inoperative or incapable of being performed".[25]

A principal disadvantage of arbitration is that, because only the ceding insurer and the reinsurer have contracted to arbitrate, non-parties generally may not be brought into the arbitration. Thus, arbitration alone may not be capable of providing complete relief in situations involving possible liability on the part of intermediaries or managing general agents.[26]

On another tone, the fact that the reinsurer might have a claim against a second insurer for indemnification or some other remedy would not prevent enforcement of the ceding insurer's right to compel arbitration under the reinsurance agreement without joinder of the second reinsurer.[27] Compelling circumstances can authorize a non-signatory to an arbitration agreement invoke its provisions.[28]

Arbitration panels generally have wide latitude in the type of award they can grant. However, the arbitration panel should make sure that the award issued is correct as there may be difficulty to modify an award, except to correct technical mistakes. An arbitration panel is not required to state its reasoning or provide any analysis for its conclusion, although some decisions do set forth the reasoning.[29]

Reinsurance arbitration panels usually issue a written decision articulating the award. In the USA an arbitration panel need not set forth the rationale supporting its award unless the parties arbitration agreement requires them to do so.[30]

The increasing complexity of the disputes and the increased amount in moneys at issue, have blurred some of the distinctions between arbitration and litigation.

However, there is one salient feature of arbitration that is largely ignored in weighing the relative merits of either forum: an arbitration's virtual unassailability. Under U.S.A. law, there is virtually no recourse for a losing party in an arbitration. The standards to overturn an arbitration are narrow and circumscribed. No arbitration record is kept, so no record can be referenced in the event of an appeal.[31]

[25] United Nations Convention on the Recognition and Enforcement of Foreign Arbitral Awards, art. II.3.

[26] Holmes and Sutin (1996), pp. 557–558.

[27] *Hamilton Life Ins. Co. of New York v Republic Nat. Life Ins. Co.*, 291 F. Supp. 225 (S.D.N. Y.1968); Holmes and Sutin (1996), p. 563.

[28] *Gulf Guar. Life Ins. Co., v Connecticut Gen. Life Ins.*, 957 F. Supp. 839 (S.D. Miss. 1997); Holmes and Sutin (1996), p. 563.

[29] Hammesfahr and Wright (1994), pp. 308–311.

[30] Thomas et al. (2011), § 40-27.

[31] Hosack and Kline (1998), p. 108.

The arbitration decision-making process is closed and generally not under any outside scrutiny. The general American practice for arbitration panels in rendering awards is to not specify the bases for such award. Therefore, an aggrieved party in an arbitration has little or no recourse to overturn an award on appeal.[32]

An example of this concept is reflected in the decision of the Ninth Circuit in *Michigan Mutual Insurance Company and Others v Unigard Security Insurance Company*[33] where the reinsurance arbitration award was upheld that granted certain retrocessionaires (reinsurers of reinsurers) relief beyond what they requested in the underlying arbitration.

In *Michigan Mutual Insurance Company and Others v Unigard Security Insurance Company*[34] the arbitration panel granted rescission to retrocessionaires without requiring them to return the premium to the reinsurer. On appeal, the reinsurers contended that the award was inherently unfair because it gave retrocessionaires more than what they actually requested at arbitration.

In its decision, the Ninth Circuit noted the anomaly of the panel's award, as its effect was to put retrocessionaires in a better position than the one in which they would have been had the panel awarded the contract rescission requested by retrocessionaires, but stated that they could not conclude that the arbitrator's award was either completely irrational or a manifest disregard of the law.

It also noted that the arbitration clause of the retrocessional agreement gave the panel wide lateral to resolve disputes between the parties and that the contract provided that the parties had to submit "any" dispute to arbitration with no limitation placed on the panel.

The decision in *Michigan Mutual Insurance Company and Others v Unigard Security Insurance Company*[35] demonstrates the extent to which a court will go to reaffirm an arbitration award. The governing standard for an award is that it not be "completely irrational" or be a "manifest disregard of the law".

In practice, it is virtually impossible to overturn an arbitration award. Further, no real appellate rights exist. For title insurers, this unfamiliar process can cause great difficulties. The arbitration panel's likely ignorance of title insurance law, in combination with an unfamiliar procedure, may daunt title insurers, whose previous reinsurance experience, if it existed at all, consisted of cordial relationships among fellow title insurers in which disputes were rarely arbitrated.[36]

[32] Hosack and Kline (1998), p. 109.

[33] *Michigan Mutual Insurance Company and Others v Unigard Security Insurance Company*, 44 F.3d 826 (9th Cir. 1995).

[34] *Michigan Mutual Insurance Company and Others v Unigard Security Insurance Company*, 44 F.3d 826 (9th Cir. 1995).

[35] *Michigan Mutual Insurance Company and Others v Unigard Security Insurance Company*, 44 F.3d 826 (9th Cir. 1995).

[36] Hosack and Kline (1998), p. 109.

In addition, several decisions illustrate that courts continue to adhere to the strong presumption in favour of enforcing arbitration agreements, even where one of the parties to the dispute is a non-signatory to the relevant arbitration agreement.

In the most notable decision, *Arthur Andersen LLP, et al. v. Carlisle, et al.*,[37] the U.S. Supreme Court resolved a split among federal circuit courts and held that a non-signatory to an arbitration agreement has standing to stay an action in favour of arbitration under Section 3 of the FAA, so long as the governing state law allows a contract to be enforced by or against non-signatories to a contract based upon principles of assumption, piercing the corporate veil, alter ego, incorporation by reference, third-party beneficiary theories, waiver and/or equitable estoppel. The Supreme Court found that the Sixth Circuit's ruling that non-signatories to an arbitration agreement are categorically barred from such relief under the FAA was in clear error.

Similarly, in *Cooke & Partners, Ltd. v. Certain Underwriters at Lloyd's, London*,[38] the U.S. District Court for the Southern District of New York compelled the assignee (Cooke) of a Liquidator's claims to arbitrate its disputes with the reinsurers of the liquidated company, finding that there was a clear connection between Cooke's claims and the reinsurance contracts containing the subject arbitration clauses.

In so holding, the District Court rejected Cooke's argument that it was exempt from arbitration, finding that the defendant's inability to compel the Liquidator to arbitrate did not preclude the arbitration of Cooke's claims, as the contract providing for the assignment was silent on this issue.

Finally, addressing the reverse scenario, a federal court in New York held, in *Utopia Studios Ltd. v. Earth Tech Inc.*,[39] that a signatory to an agreement containing an arbitration clause can compel a nonsignatory to arbitrate where the nonsignatory enters into a separate contract that incorporates that clause.[40]

5.1.15 Enforcing a Reinsurance Arbitration Provision

The traditional reinsurance relationship has undergone significant change.[41] Given the significant change in the industry, it is logical that the use of arbitration also is, to a certain degree, under siege.

There are a number of cases in which parties to a reinsurance treaty have attempted to avoid arbitration when there was, at a minimum, an implied intent to

[37] *Arthur Andersen LLP, et al. v. Carlisle, et al.*, 129 S.Ct. 1896 (2009).

[38] *Cooke & Partners, Ltd. v. Certain Underwriters at Lloyd's, London*, No. 08 Civ. 3435 (S.D.N.Y. Mar. 26, 2009).

[39] *Utopia Studios Ltd. v. Earth Tech Inc.*, No. 08-cv-3515 (E.D.N.Y. April 20, 2009).

[40] Kanefsky and Diubaldo (2009), p. 9.

[41] Monin and Brady (1996), p. 219; McDonald (2001), p. 332.

arbitrate disputes. These cases are interesting because they essentially turn on whether the language "arbitration clause" found in the slip agreement was legally sufficient to compel arbitration. Assuming a dispute and one of the parties commencing suit in a state court, what options are available for the party seeking to enforce the arbitration provision?

5.1.15.1 Statutory Authority

In a dispute over the enforcement of an arbitration clause and to avoid litigation, one must examine the FAA and perhaps the New York Convention[42] along with its implementing statute.[43]

The FAA and the New York Convention require a court to enforce the parties' agreement to arbitrate. A dispute over arbitration is subject to the New York Convention when one of the parties to the agreement is a foreign company, and the country of the foreign company is a signatory to the convention. The FAA may also apply to an action brought under the convention, according to Section 208 of the implementing statute, "to the extent that [it] is not in conflict with the [convention's implementing legislation] as ratified by the United States."

There are a number of provisions of the FAA that are relevant when analyzing an arbitration dispute.

First, Section 205 of the implementing statute will allow the parties to remove the case to federal court.[44]

Section 3 of the FAA stays court proceedings when the issues in the case are subject to arbitration.[45]

---

[42] 3 U.S.T. 2517 (entered into for the United States on December 30, 1970) and 9 U.S.C. Section 205.

[43] 9 U.S.C. Section 201 et seq.

[44] Where the subject matter of an action or proceeding pending in a state court relates to an arbitration agreement or award falling under the convention, the defendant or the defendants may, at any time before the trial thereof, remove such action or proceeding to the district court of the United States for the district and division embracing the place where the action or proceeding is pending. The procedure for removal of causes otherwise provided by law shall apply, except that the ground for removal provided in this section need not appear on the face of the complaint but may be shown in the petition for removal. For the purposes of Chap. 1 of this title any action or proceeding removed under this section shall be deemed to have been brought in the district court to which it is removed; McDonald (2001), p. 333.

[45] It provides, in relevant part that if a suit or proceeding be brought in any of the courts of the United States upon any issue referable to arbitration under an agreement in writing for such arbitration, the court in which such suit is pending, upon being satisfied that the issue involved in such suit or proceeding is referable to arbitration under such an agreement, shall on application of one of the parties stay the trial of the action until such arbitration has been had in accordance with the terms of the agreement, providing the applicant for the stay is not in default in proceeding with such arbitration; McDonald (2001), p. 333.

Another provision of the FAA permits a party to enforce an arbitration agreement by petitioning a United States court for an order to compel arbitration.

Section 4 provides, in relevant part that a party aggrieved by the alleged failure, neglect, or refusal of another to arbitrate under a written agreement for arbitration may petition any United States district court which, save for such agreement, would have jurisdiction under Title 28, in a civil action or in admiralty of the subject matter of a suit arising out of the controversy between the parties, for an order directing that such arbitration proceed in the manner provided for in such agreement. Five days' notice in writing of such application shall be served upon the party in default. Service thereof shall be made in the manner provided by the Federal Rules of Civil Procedure.

The court shall hear the parties, and upon being satisfied that the making of the agreement for arbitration or the failure to comply therewith is not in issue, the court shall make an order directing the parties to proceed to arbitration in accordance with the terms of the agreement. The hearing and proceedings, under such agreement, shall be within the district in which the petition for an order directing such arbitration is filed.

If the making of the arbitration agreement or the failure, neglect, or refusal to perform the same be in issue, the court shall proceed summarily to the trial thereof.

If no jury trial be demanded by the party alleged to be in default, or if the matter in dispute is within admiralty jurisdiction, the court shall hear and determine such issue.

Where such an issue is raised, the party alleged to be in default may, except in cases of admiralty, on or before the return day of the notice of application, demand a jury trial of such issue, and upon such demand the court shall make an order referring the issue or issues to a jury in the manner provided by the Federal Rules of Civil Procedure, or may specially call a jury for that purpose.

If the jury find that no agreement in writing for arbitration was made or that there is no default in proceeding thereunder, the proceeding shall be dismissed. If the jury find that an agreement for arbitration was made in writing and that there is a default in proceeding there under, the court shall make an order summarily directing the parties to proceed with the arbitration in accordance with the terms thereof.[46]

Also relevant to an arbitration dispute is Section 5 of the FAA, which directs the appointment of arbitrators or an umpire and which states that if in the agreement provision be made for a method of naming or appointing an arbitrator or arbitrators or an umpire, such method shall be followed; but if no method be provided therein, or if a method be provided and any party thereto shall fail to avail himself of such method, or if for any other reason there shall be a lapse in the naming of an arbitrator or arbitrators or umpire, or in filling a vacancy, then upon the application of either party to the controversy the court shall designate and appoint an arbitrator or arbitrators or umpire, as the case may require, who shall act under the said agreement with the same force and effect as if he or they had been specifically

[46] McDonald (2001), p. 334.

named therein; and unless otherwise provided in the agreement the arbitration shall be by a single arbitrator.[47]

Finally, Section 7 of the FAA is important as it provides, in relevant part that the arbitrators selected either as prescribed in this title or otherwise, or a majority of them, may summon in writing any person to attend before them or any of them as a witness and in a proper case to bring with him or them any book, record, document, or paper which may be deemed material as evidence in the case. The fees for such attendance shall be the same as the fees of witnesses before masters of the United States courts.

Said summons shall issue in the name of the arbitrator or arbitrators, or a majority of them, and shall be signed by the arbitrators, or a majority of them, and shall be directed to the said person and shall be served in the same manner as subpoenas to appear and testify before the court; if any person or persons so summoned to testify shall refuse or neglect to obey said summons, upon petition the United States district court for the district in which such arbitrators, or a majority of them, are sitting may compel the attendance of such person or persons before said arbitrator or arbitrators, or punish said person or persons for contempt in the same manner provided by law for securing the attendance of witnesses or their punishment for neglect or refusal to attend in the courts of the U.S.A. These provisions of the FAA are important and should be examined when analyzing a dispute over the enforcement of an arbitration clause.[48]

Courts can also enforce an arbitration panel's interim orders. Judicial review of an arbitration award is generally appropriate only where the award is final. An interim award is sufficiently final if it finally and definitely disposes of a separate independent claim even though it does not dispose of all the claims that were submitted to arbitration.[49]

5.1.15.2 Case Law

In *North Carolina League of Municipalities v Clarendon National Insurance Co.*[50] a federal district court addressed the issue whether the phrase "arbitration clause" in the placement slips was sufficient to show an intent to arbitrate. Both parties had accepted the placement slips without reservation, and a treaty containing the full language of the terms of any arbitration also had been circulated between the parties. However, the treaty was never signed.

---

[47] McDonald (2001), p. 334.

[48] McDonald (2001), p. 335.

[49] *Century Indem. Co v Certain Underwriters at Lloyd's London*, No 11 Civ. 1040 (RJS), 2012 U.S.Dist. LEXIS 4237, at *11–12 (S.D.N.Y. Jan. 10, 2012); Thomas and Lyons (2012), pp. 77–129.

[50] *North Carolina League of Municipalities v Clarendon National Insurance Co.* 733 F. Supp. 1009 (E.D. N.C. 1990).

Placing great emphasis and weight on the custom of the reinsurance industry, the court concluded it was the industry custom to use abbreviated terms in placement slips. It held that the phrase "arbitration clause" was enough to compel arbitration, concluding that industry custom conclusively established an intent to arbitrate.

In support of its decision, the court noted extrinsic evidence, including the failure by either party to modify the arbitration agreement. The court did not look to the language of the treaty. Instead, it found the phrase "arbitration clause" in the placement slips dispositive on the issue of arbitration.

The court's decision was both proper and logical because it was based on the nature of the reinsurance industry. Its reliance on the custom of the industry is also consistent with the approach taken by arbitrators. The decision is consistent with that of other courts faced with the same issue.

Allianz Life Insurance Co. of North America v American Phoenix Life and Reassurance Co.[51] is one of a handful of cases filed as a result of what has been dubbed "Unicover." According to the Allianz court, "The Unicover Pool consists of a book of risk ceded by a large number of retail workers' compensation insurers." The plaintiff, Allianz, was the retrocessionaire of American Phoenix, Phoenix Home Life Mutual Insurance Co. and Sun Life Assurance Co. of Canada. These parties entered into three separate contracts for retrocessional coverage. All three contracts contemplated that disputes over the terms of the agreement would be resolved by arbitration. The written agreements between the parties were in the placements slips. The slips were silent on the issue of arbitrating disputes except they contained the single phrase "arbitration clause." When a dispute arose, Allianz sued the retrocedents in Minnesota state court, seeking rescission of the contract and damages. The case was removed to the U.S. District Court for Minnesota, and the retrocedents sought to compel arbitration based on the inclusion of "arbitration clause" in the placement slips. In their motion to dismiss and/or compel arbitration, the retrocedents asserted reinsurance industry custom and practice. They pointed out that the governing placement slips resulted from a series of negotiations between the parties in which Allianz never objected to the inclusion of "arbitration clause" in the placement slips, and that it repeatedly reviewed and ratified these slips. Allianz argued that the words "arbitration clause" merely evidenced the parties agreement to agree and, as such, was not an enforceable arbitration agreement. The retrocedents also relied on the FAA and the Arbitral Awards Convention, noting the U.S. Supreme Court's emphasis on the strong federal policy in favour of arbitration.[52] The retrocedents position that "arbitration clause" indicates the

---

[51] *Allianz Life Insurance Co. of North America v American Phoenix Life and Reassurance Co.* 2000 U.S. Dist. Lexis 7216 (D. Minn.).

[52] *Moses H. Cone Mem'l Hosp. v Mercury Constr. Corp.*, 460 U.S. 1, 24 (1983), aff'g 656 F.2d 933 (4th Cir. 1981), rehearing denied, 664 F.2d 936 (4th Cir. 1981) stating that any doubts concerning the scope of arbitrable issues should be resolved in favour of arbitration. *AT&T Technologies Inc. v Communications Workers of Am.*, 475 U.S. 643, 650 (1986), vacating and remanding 751 F.2d 203 (7th Cir. 1984) and stating that where contract contains arbitration clause, there is presumption of arbitrability. *Allied-Bruce Terminix Cos. v Dobson*, 513 U.S. 265,

parties intent to resolve disputes through arbitration also finds support in English decisions. In *Hobbs Padgett & Co. (Reinsurance) Ltd. v JC Kirkland, Lloyd's*[53] the English court was faced with an issue similar to that in *Allianz Life Insurance Co. of North America v American Phoenix Life and Reassurance Co.*,[54] having to decide whether the inclusion of the phrase "suitable arbitration clause" in a reinsurance broker agreement required that the matter be submitted to arbitration. Like in *Allianz Life Insurance Co. of North America v American Phoenix Life and Reassurance Co.*,[55] the party opposing arbitration argued that the parties had never agreed on a suitable arbitration clause, and therefore the clause merely represented an agreement to agree. That party went a step further, arguing that because the contract contained a phrase not yet agreed on, there was no valid contract.

The court rejected this argument outright, pointing out the inconsistency in the party's position: it was suing on the very document it claimed did not constitute a valid and binding contract. Another argument raised in Hobbs Padgett by the party opposing arbitration was that the arbitration clause was meaningless and therefore could be ignored. The court also rejected this argument, noting the impossibility of saying that there can be no suitable arbitration clause.

The court stated that the mere "fact that the clause is very short does not . . . make it any less meaningful," and it concluded: "'Suitable arbitration clause' means that these parties have agreed that, if any dispute arises between them under the contract, including any dispute as to the meaning of the contract, that dispute should be referred to arbitration rather than the courts."

In the *Allianz Life Insurance Co. of North America v American Phoenix Life and Reassurance Co.*[56] case, the parties opposing argued that even if the court did not dismiss the action, it must stay the litigation pending resolution of the arbitration, because Section 3 of the FAA mandates that litigation must be stayed where the parties agreed in writing to arbitrate.[57]

---

270 (1995), rev'g 628 So.2d 354 (Ala. 1993) (whereby it was stated that the FAA was enacted to overcome corts' refusal to enforce agreements to arbitrate; *Mitsubishi Motors Corp. v Soler Chrysler-Plymouth Inc.*, 473 U.S. 614, 631 (1985), aff'g in part, rev'g in part 723 F.2d 155 (1st Cir. 1983) where it was held that the policy in favor of arbitration applies with special force in international commerce (opinion on remand, 814 F.2d 844 (1st Cir. 1987). Minnesota law also requires deference to arbitration clauses; See *Niazi v St. Paul Mercury Ins. Co.*, 121 N.W.2d 349, 355 (Minn. 1963) (where the arbitration has been looked on with favour in state and *Brothers Jurewicz Inc. v Atari Inc.*, 296 N.W.2d 422, 427 (Minn. 1980) where the arbitration was accorded "preferred status".

[53] *Hobbs Padgett & Co. (Reinsurance) Ltd. v JC Kirkland, Lloyd's* 2 Lloyd's Rep. 547 (1969).

[54] *Allianz Life Insurance Co. of North America v American Phoenix Life and Reassurance Co.* 2000 U.S. Dist. Lexis 7216 (D. Minn.).

[55] *Allianz Life Insurance Co. of North America v American Phoenix Life and Reassurance Co.* 2000 U.S. Dist. Lexis 7216 (D. Minn.).

[56] *Allianz Life Insurance Co. of North America v American Phoenix Life and Reassurance Co.* 2000 U.S. Dist. Lexis 7216 (D. Minn.).

[57] *Contracting Northwest Inc. v City of Fredericksburg*, 713 F.2d 382, 387 (8th Cir. 1983).

In its decision, the Allianz court noted that the motion to compel arbitration was unlike any other it had decided before because the arbitration agreement sought to be enforced consisted only of the phrase "arbitration clause." As in Clarendon, the court felt the phrase "arbitration clause," though sparse, it had significant meaning in the reinsurance industry. The court concluded that based on the customs and practices of the industry, the phrase "arbitration clause" had considerable meaning.

In contrast with the above cases, in *Frank B. Hall Inc. v Colorado School Districts Self-Insurance Pool*,[58] at least one court did not compel arbitration based on the phrase "arbitration clause." In a coverage dispute between the reinsured and its reinsurers, the reinsured sought coverage on all its buildings damaged by a major hail storm. The reinsurers denied coverage, arguing that all the property at issue was written on a per risk basis and per building basis, therefore the reinsureds self-insured retention applied to each building. In a lawsuit filed by the reinsureds, the reinsurers sought to compel arbitration based on "arbitration clause" in the placement slip.

However, the court did not order arbitration in this case. Although the court conceded that certain terms of the arbitration could be supplied from the Uniform Arbitration Act or the FAA, these acts, even coupled with the custom of the industry, could not be used to delineate the scope of arbitration agreed on by the parties. To order arbitration would be to write the agreement, the court stated.

This decision illustrates the potential danger reinsurers and reinsureds face when confronted with litigation over issues steeped in the customs and practices of the reinsurance industry. For instance, the court may decide the case on pure legal principles and thereby reach a decision that defeats the original intent of the parties.

Would this have happened, far ago in the past? Probably not, because it is unlikely that any litigation, would have been commenced at that time. However, the reality of today's reinsurance relationship is that litigation is no longer considered the last resort. Until the reinsurance industry reacts to this change in posture, there will continue to be attempts to avoid arbitration.[59]

In *Connecticut General Life Insurance. Co. v Sun Life Insurance Co. of Canada*,[60] the Seventh Circuit addressed the issue of when a federal district court has the authority to order consolidation of arbitration proceedings before a single arbitral panel. It involved a reinsurance contract between two overlapping sets of insurance companies. The contract was negotiated on behalf of the insurers by Unicover, described in the contract as their "manager." Unicover, an intermediary in the workers' compensation reinsurance market, although not an insurance company, issued reinsurance contracts to insurance companies (the retrocedents in this case) and then assigned these contracts to other insurance companies (the

[58] *Frank B. Hall Inc. v Colorado School Districts Self-Insurance Pool* No. 92-CV-225 (Colo. Dist. Ct. March 26, 1993).

[59] McDonald (2001), pp. 336–338.

[60] *Connecticut General Life Insurance. Co. v Sun Life Insurance Co. of Canada* 210 F.3d 771 (7th Cir. 2000).

retrocessionaires). The assignees bore the risk created by the contracts, but they also received the premiums. Based on the arbitration clause in the contract, the reinsurers served a demand for arbitration on Unicover and its insurers. Four of the latter responded by filing their own demands, each seeking a separate arbitration between itself, on the one hand, and Sun and Phoenix, on the other. Each of the six companies filed a motion in the federal district court in the Northern District of Illinois, which was prescribed by the arbitration provision of the contract, pursuant to Section 4 of the FAA.

The district court denied the reinsurers' motion for a single arbitration and granted the insurers' motions for separate arbitrations. None of the parties contended that the issue of one versus many in number arbitrations is for the arbitrators rather than the court to decide. Nor did the arbitration provision in the contract address the question of who makes this decision. The insurers maintained that case law provided a federal district court cannot grant a motion to consolidate separate arbitration proceedings unless the contract on which the arbitration is founded expressly authorizes consolidation.

But the Seventh Circuit concluded that under certain circumstances, a court can consolidate cases before it, no matter whether the parties agreed, holding that a court cannot consolidate an arbitration proceeding in defiance of the parties' wishes or contractual undertakings, but at the same time a court cannot interfere in the arbitrators' procedures beyond the very limited extent permitted by Sections 9 and 10 of the FAA.

But the court could not see any reason why it should place its thumb on the scale, insisting that it be "clear," rather than merely more likely than not, that the parties intended consolidation. It is not as if consolidation of arbitration proceedings were somehow disfavoured; quite the contrary, the same considerations of adjudicative economy that argue in favour of consolidating closely related court cases argue for consolidating closely related arbitrations.

To repeat, the court has no power to order such consolidation if the parties' contract does not authorize it. But in deciding whether the contract does authorize it the court may resort to the usual methods of contract interpretation, just as courts do in interpreting other provisions in an arbitration clause.[61] Although the court found no textual inferences in the agreements to be conclusively in favour of consolidation, it favoured consolidation based on practical considerations.

The court concluded that litigating identical disputes before different arbitration panels is "a formula for duplication of effort and a fertile source of disputes over esoteric issues in the law of *res judicata*." If separate arbitrations were ordered and the reinsurers lose the first arbitration, will the decision by that arbitration panel have res judicata or collateral estoppel effect in the other arbitrations, the court asked. What if the first order is confirmed first? What if the second order is confirmed first? If the reinsurers win, this would only bind the insurer involved in

[61] *Connecticut General Life Insurance. Co. v Sun Life Insurance Co. of Canada* 210 F.3d 771 (7th Cir. 2000) at *774; McDonald (2001), pp. 336–338.

the particular arbitration-unless the insurers are deemed to be in privity with each other because of the common agency of Unicover.

The court concluded that all these problems are avoided by interpreting the contract to allow the reinsurers to demand a single arbitration, provided there is a single dispute, as appeared to be the case. However, the court stated, if there were more than one dispute, severance would be possible.[62]

In *Hartford Accident and Indemnity Co. v. Swiss Reinsurance Co. of America,*[63] the court applied a broad standard for arbitration and held that claims yet to be submitted by the insurer to the reinsurer may be joined in the arbitration of pending disputes. Since each claim made to the reinsurer involved a similar calculation, the court stated, common arbitration potentially could resolve each dispute.

In *Security Life Insurance Co. of America v Hannover Life Reinsurance Co. of America*[64] the court considered contradictory language in the reinsurance contract. On the one hand, the contract stated that "arbitration is the sole remedy for disputes arising under this agreement." On the other hand, the contract noted that either party "may request arbitration," and a service of suit clause provided that the parties must submit to the "jurisdiction of any court of competent jurisdiction." Sorting it out, the court stayed the proceeding and ordered the parties to submit to arbitration.

The court noted that the reinsurance contracts fell within the protection of the FAA and stated that it was its practice to stay litigation when the parties have agreed to arbitrate.[65]

5.1.15.3 Pre-arbitration Injunctive Relief

Even when parties have agreed to arbitrate their disputes, they may find themselves in court prior to the arbitration. Parties may, for example, seek injunctive relief in order to maintain the status quo or to prohibit certain activity pending the arbitration. Such pre-arbitration injunctive relief was sought in a case arising out of the departure of Maurice Greenberg as CEO of AIG.

In *National Union Fire Insurance Co. of Pittsburgh v Starr Technical Risks Agency,*[66] the parties seeking the injunction were all affiliates of the AIG insurance group of companies. Their managing general agent was C. V. Starr & Co., which acted through its subsidiaries, including Starr Technical Risks Agency. Conflict arose among the parties after Mr. Greenberg left AIG. Despite his departure, it was

---

[62] *Connecticut General Life Insurance. Co. v Sun Life Insurance Co. of Canada* 210 F.3d 771 (7th Cir. 2000); McDonald (2001), pp. 336–338.

[63] *Hartford Accident and Indemnity Co. v. Swiss Reinsurance Co. of America*, 246 F.3d 219 (2d Cir. 2001).

[64] *Security Life Insurance Co. of America v Hannover Life Reinsurance Co. of America*, 2001 WL 392412 (D. Minn.).

[65] McDonald (2001), p. 339.

[66] *National Union Fire Insurance Co. of Pittsburgh v Starr Technical Risks Agency*, No. 600263/06, 2006 WL 304746 (N.Y. Sup. Ct. Feb. 8, 2006).

alleged that Mr. Greenberg still had significant control of C.V. Starr and that this control was being misused. Under Mr. Greenberg's alleged control, Starr Tech, still serving as AIG's managing agent, entered into a reinsurance agreement with National Indemnity Company ("NICO") whereby NICO would reinsure various risks ceded by AIG. This resulted in a "reduction in premiums" which would otherwise be paid to AIG.[67] AIG complained that this agreement was a "product of self-dealing by Greenberg,"[68] and the practical effect of the agreement was to "siphon premiums away from AIG" and towards NICO.[69] The act also allegedly tarnished AIG's business reputation because AIG had promised to other companies the business ceded to NICO.[70] As the parties proceeded to arbitration, AIG asked the court for an injunction, which the court granted.

In reviewing the requirements for an injunction, the court was satisfied that AIG was at risk of "irreparable reputational harm" if the injunction was not granted and if Starr Tech was allowed to "funnel large amounts of reinsurance premiums" away from AIG.[71]

The court also ruled that an injunction was needed "to ensure that an ultimate arbitration award is not rendered ineffectual."[72]

The court was concerned that "[b]y the time an award is issued at the conclusion of arbitration, AIG may no longer be capable of doing business with the reinsurers to whom it made promises" regarding reinsurance business.[73] As part of the preliminary injunction, it was ordered that "Starr Tech may not enter into, or perform, any contract of reinsurance with NICO, on behalf of AIG."[74]

---

[67] *National Union Fire Insurance Co. of Pittsburgh v Starr Technical Risks Agency*, No. 600263/06, 2006 WL 304746 (N.Y. Sup. Ct. Feb. 8, 2006) at *2.

[68] *National Union Fire Insurance Co. of Pittsburgh v Starr Technical Risks Agency*, No. 600263/06, 2006 WL 304746 (N.Y. Sup. Ct. Feb. 8, 2006) at *2.

[69] *National Union Fire Insurance Co. of Pittsburgh v Starr Technical Risks Agency*, No. 600263/06, 2006 WL 304746 (N.Y. Sup. Ct. Feb. 8, 2006) at *2.

[70] *National Union Fire Insurance Co. of Pittsburgh v Starr Technical Risks Agency*, No. 600263/06, 2006 WL 304746 (N.Y. Sup. Ct. Feb. 8, 2006) at *4.

[71] *National Union Fire Insurance Co. of Pittsburgh v Starr Technical Risks Agency*, No. 600263/06, 2006 WL 304746 (N.Y. Sup. Ct. Feb. 8, 2006) at *5.

[72] *National Union Fire Insurance Co. of Pittsburgh v Starr Technical Risks Agency*, No. 600263/06, 2006 WL 304746 (N.Y. Sup. Ct. Feb. 8, 2006) at *5.

[73] *National Union Fire Insurance Co. of Pittsburgh v Starr Technical Risks Agency*, No. 600263/06, 2006 WL 304746 (N.Y. Sup. Ct. Feb. 8, 2006) at *5.

[74] *National Union Fire Insurance Co. of Pittsburgh v Starr Technical Risks Agency*, No. 600263/06, 2006 WL 304746 (N.Y. Sup. Ct. Feb. 8, 2006) at *5; Chiafullo et al. (2007), pp. 469–470.

5.2 Salient Differences Between the U.S. and English Arbitration Systems

As the preceding discussion may have made apparent, there are several significant differences between reinsurance arbitration in England and reinsurance arbitration in the USA. Most importantly, the panel's award is very difficult to overturn in the USA. A reviewing court may disagree profoundly and repeatedly with the arbitration panel's reasoning and award but cannot vacate the award for that reason.

In addition, USA reinsurance arbitration panels typically do not view themselves as being bound to follow the law of a particular jurisdiction. Rather, while they may take the law into account, they are just as likely to draw upon reinsurance custom and practice, as well as their own experience, as they consider the facts and reach their decision.

Not least, it is noted that party-appointed arbitrators in the USA are generally not viewed as being entirely neutral panellists.

It is common practice for a party, i.e. more likely its counsel, to discuss in broad outline the nature of the dispute with a prospective arbitrator prior to appointing him. In general terms, the goal is not to secure a commitment from the arbitrator that he will vote in his party's favour, but simply that he understands the party's position and is not uncomfortable with it (subject, of course to receiving further evidence as the case develops).

It is also common practice for the parties to be allowed *ex parte* communications with their respective party-appointed arbitrators throughout some period of the case. Under such circumstances, the USA courts have recognised that party-appointed arbitrators are generally not held to the same absolute neutrality as may be expected and required of the umpire.[75]

5.3 Consolidation of Arbitration Proceedings

Due to its efficient and cost-effective nature, arbitration is often the preferred approach for resolving reinsurance and other complex business disputes. For this reason, reinsurance contracts, as well as many other commercial agreements, often contain arbitration clauses requiring that any and all disputes arising under the contract be resolves by arbitration.[76]

Arbitration is a creature of contract, and the powers that arbitrators possess originate from the parties, who agree to confer specific powers on the arbitrators—either through an arbitration clause in the contract or through a separate agreement.[77]

[75] *Merit Ins. Co v Leatherby Ins. Co.*, 714 F.2d 673,679 (7th Cir. 1983); Barlow Lyde and Gilbert LLP (2009), pp. 941–942.

[76] DiUbaldo (2008), p. 83.

[77] DiUbaldo (2008), p. 83.

Typically, arbitration clauses found in reinsurance agreements confer broad power on arbitrators with respect to certain procedural or substantive issues. Where an arbitration clause enumerates specific powers to arbitrators, it is rare that parties challenge an exercise of those powers. Parties often challenge an arbitrator's actions, however, where an arbitrator acts in a manner not provided for in the contract.[78] As case law also suggests, courts often struggle to grasp the extent of arbitral powers pursuant to the interplay between arbitration agreements contained in reinsurance contracts, industry custom and practice, and the FAA. The result has been contradictory and often inconsistent decisions in this area of the law.

Historically, courts have become involved in disputes over arbitration consolidation, and reinsurance arbitrations in particular either when one party to multiple arbitrations refuses to proceed with a single consolidated proceeding covering multiple disputes and its adversary seeks a court order compelling the resisting party to participate in the consolidated arbitration, or when the party opposing consolidation files a federal court action seeking an order precluding its opponent from continuing with a consolidated arbitration proceeding.

Case law has favoured consolidation at times and at other times not. In *Compania Espanola de Petroleos S.A. v Nereus Shipping S.A.*[79] the Second Circuit held that there would be no legitimate prejudice suffered from consolidation. However, this ruling was rejected in *Wyerhaeuser Co v Western Seas Shipping Co*[80] where it was held that neither the FAA nor the Federal Rules of Civil Procedure provided federal courts with the authority to order consolidation where one or more parties did not consent. For years it was settled that under the FAA courts would simply enforce arbitration agreements and that were such agreements were silent on consolidation, courts did not have authority to order consolidation even if this seemed more practical. However, since the rulings in *Howsam v Dean Witer Reynolds Inc.*[81] and *Green Tree Financial Corp v Bazzle*,[82] federal courts are required to stay out of the consolidated business issue and leave this to arbitral tribunals. After *Howsam v Dean Witer Reynolds Inc.*[83] and *Green Tree Financial Corp v Bazzle*,[84] several of the US Courts of Appeals revised prior ruling on the role federal courts should play in resolving disputes over arbitral consolidation and in effect sent consolidation disputes back to arbitrators. This is even more happening because consolidation is being viewed rather as a question of procedure and not one of arbitrability and hence courts are refusing to rule on disputes over the propriety of consolidated proceedings. This uniform approach has not helped cedents or reinsurers. There is at first the issue of which arbitrators get to decide the issue.

[78] DiUbaldo (2008), p. 83.

[79] *Compania Espanola de Petroleos S.A. v Nereus Shipping S.A.*, 527 F2d 966 (2d Cir. 1975).

[80] *Wyerhaeuser Co v Western Seas Shipping Co* 743 F.2d 635 (9th Cir. 1984).

[81] *Howsam v Dean Witer Reynolds Inc.*537 US 79 (2002).

[82] *Green Tree Financial Corp v Bazzle* 539 US 444 (2003).

[83] *Howsam v Dean Witer Reynolds Inc.*537 US 79 (2002).

[84] *Green Tree Financial Corp v Bazzle* 539 US 444 (2003).

The case of *Argonaut Ins. Co. v Century Indemn. Co*,[85] highlighted that there may be a quagmire on who decides the consolidation issue. A good resolution requires parties to act swiftly and as *Argonaut Ins. Co. v Century Indemn. Co*[86] highlighted the return of the consolidation issue to arbitrators is neither swift nor good a solution at all. As arbitrators are not bound by precedent or procedural rules there is little help they can get and the matter is best left to the sensible sense of arbitrators and parties. Arbitrators could look to the contractual provisions and parties intention or apply their retinal discretion. Yet this is no safe or stable solution, as consolidation rulings could potentially in such cases be subject to challenge where arbitrators will have exceeded their authority.

5.4 Critique

Case law illustrates that courts will show great deference to the authority conferred to arbitrators by the FAA with respect to many procedural issues.

Nonetheless a great deal of inconsistency remains in the judicial interpretation of certain arbitral powers.

The resolution of disputes between parties involving the power of arbitrators with respect to consolidation can often impact whether parties will prevail in a current or future arbitration between them.

Moreover, the determination of issues such as consolidation and the enforceability of hold harmless agreements can have a substantial effect on the cost-effectiveness and overall efficiency of arbitration—reasons that parties seek to arbitrate their commercial disputes in the first place.[87]

The common adjudication of multi-party disputes prevents inconsistent findings, assists time management and allows for efficient utilisation of resources. Unlike litigation, where the mere lack of an agreement is no preclusion, for consolidating disputes amongst all related parties, consolidation of arbitration proceedings is not as routinely possible, as it is in litigation.

The obvious theoretical impediment for consolidating arbitral proceedings is that dispute resolution through arbitration is founded on the consent of parties meaning thereby that absent consent, arbitration proceedings ought to only be conducted between parties to the arbitration agreement.

In practice, however, this theoretical impediment has not tied the hands of all courts, which, recognising the practicality of consolidated or common proceedings, have gone beyond the scope of the arbitral clause and consolidated disputes.[88]

---

[85] *Argonaut Ins. Co. v Century Indemn. Co* 2007 US Dist. LEXIS 65863.

[86] *Argonaut Ins. Co. v Century Indemn. Co* 2007 US Dist. LEXIS 65863.

[87] DiUbaldo (2008), pp. 105–107.

[88] Tong Chun Fai and Dewan (2009), pp. 70–71.

The issue of multi-party arbitral adjudication or consolidation of multi-party disputes is important for both the claimant and respondent. For example, an insurance contract may be reinsured by not one but a number of re-insurers who may have a dispute resolution clause providing for arbitration with the insurer but may not have a provision which allows for multi-party dispute resolution of a claim relates to a single cause of action.[89]

The issue arises when the arbitration clause is silent on the matter of consolidation. Even though a generalised statement of the law is that if not founded on the consent then the law has not stepped in to enforce consolidation, it is possible for parties to be subject to consolidation if the governing law the arbitral rules or the applicable law in the seat of arbitration allow for consolidation or if the courts in a particular jurisdiction direct consolidation even without the consent of parties. Except for court directed consolidation, the remaining may be deemed to be cases of implied consent even though it is quite possible that the choices were made without considering the issue of consolidation.[90]

Reinsurance disputes often come in groups. In such cases, consolidation of those disputes in a single arbitration can make sense.[91] Thus, the issue of whether multiple disputes among related parties should be consolidated often arises in reinsurance arbitrations.[92] Reinsurers and cedents can agree to consolidate their disputes. But parties do not often agree that consolidation is appropriate.[93]

There are potential advantages and disadvantages posed by the consolidation of arbitration proceedings.

On the one hand consolidation may prevent inconsistent and conflicting decisions, provide arbitrators with a more solid understanding of the issues involved in arbitration disputes and promote more efficient and cost effective dispute resolution.

On the other hand consolidation may be more expensive for a party only peripherally involved in a series of complex disputes, or create a risk that the panel's decision will be tainted by facts irrelevant to the dispute and raise additional confidentiality concerns, or it may be difficult to restructure an arbitration proceeding to accommodate the rights of additional parties or related disputes. Thus, contracting parties should carefully consider whether to include consolidation and joinder provisions in the arbitration agreement or request consolidation once arbitration has commenced.[94]

---

[89] Tong Chun Fai and Dewan (2009), p. 72; Grais (2007), p. 18-5.

[90] Tong Chun Fai and Dewan (2009), p. 74.

[91] Ludwig and Chester (2008), p. 1.

[92] *Local 1351 Int'l Longshoremens Ass'n v Sea-Land Serv., Inc.*, 214 F.3d 566, 570–571 (5th Cir. 2000) noting that the FAA 1925 only grants the district court the power to enforce consolidation if it is expressly provided for in the contract. *Accord Champ v Siegel Trading Co.*, 55 F. 3d 269, 275–275 (7th Cir. 1995). DiUbaldo (2008), p. 84.

[93] Ludwig and Chester (2008), p. 1.

[94] Thomas et al. (2011), § 40-22.

Until recently, the majority of case law has not supported consolidation, absent specific language in the parties' contract.[95] The majority of federal courts to consider the issue of consolidation have held that a court may not order the consolidation of arbitration proceedings arising under separate agreements to arbitrate without the consent of the parties.[96]

In reaching its decision in *Government of U.K. of Gr. Brit. v Boeing Co.*,[97] the Second Circuit reversed its prior view articulated in *Compania Espanola de Petroleos S.A v Nereus Sbipping, S.A.*,[98] The Second Circuit noted that *Compania Espanola de Petroleos S.A v Nereus Sbipping, S.A.*,[99] was premised on the liberal purposes of the FAA, but that subsequent Supreme Court cases had undermined that premise. The Second Circuit also held that *Government of U.K. of Gr. Brit. v Boeing Co.*,[100] left intact the court's equitable powers to order consolidation.[101]

The issue of whether multiple disputes among related parties should be consolidated often arises in reinsurance arbitrations, where many contracts involve several reinsurers sharing a certain risk ceded to them by a single insurer, known also as a cedent. In the past, the majority of case law has not supported consolidation, absent specific language in the parties' contract.[102] A party seeking to enforce consolidation in an arbitration agreement may petition the court to do so pursuant to section 4 of the FAA, which provides that "a party aggrieved by the alleged failure, neglect or refusal of another to arbitrate under a written agreement for arbitration may petition any U.S. district court for an order directing that such arbitration proceed in the manner provided for in such agreement."[103] Although the language of this statute seems clear, courts have interpreted it in a variety of ways. Early interpretation of section 4 held that an arbitration panel lacked the authority to order consolidation.

In the USA most reinsurance agreements arise in interstate commerce and are governed by the FAA which is silent on consolidation. Until recently, courts

---

[95] *Local 1351 Int'l Longshoremens Ass'n v Sea-Land Serv., Inc.*, 214 F.3d 566, 570–571 (5th Cir. 2000) noting that the FAA 1925 only grants the district court the power to enforce consolidation if it is expressly provided for in the contract. *Accord Champ v Siegel Trading Co.*, 55 F. 3d 269, 275–275 (7th Cir. 1995). DiUbaldo (2008), p. 84.

[96] *Government of U.K. of Gr. Brit. v Boeing Co.*, 998 F.2d 68 (2d Cir. 1993).

[97] *Government of U.K. of Gr. Brit. v Boeing Co.*, 998 F.2d 68 (2d Cir. 1993).

[98] *Compania Espanola de Petroleos S.A v Nereus Shipping, S.A.*, 527 E2d 966 (2d Cir. 1975), cert. denied 426 U.S. 936 (1976).

[99] *Compania Espanola de Petroleos S.A v Nereus Shipping, S.A.*, 527 E2d 966 (2d Cir. 1975), cert. denied 426 U.S. 936 (1976).

[100] *Government of U.K. of Gr. Brit. v Boeing Co.*, 998 F.2d 68 (2d Cir. 1993).

[101] Ostrager and Vyskocil (1996), §§14-04, 14-43, 14-44.

[102] *Local 1351 Int'l Longshorements Ass'n v Sea-Land Serv. Inc.*, 214 F.3d 566, 570–571 (5th Cir. 2000). *Accord Champ. v Siegel Trading Co.*, 55 F.3d 269, 274–275 (7th Cir. 1995) .*U.K. v Boeing Co.*, 998 F.2d 68,69 (2d Cir. 1993). *Am. Centennial Ins. Co. v Nat'l Cas. Co.*, 951 F.2d 107,108 (6th Cir. 1991); DiUbaldo (2008), p. 84.

[103] 9 U.S.C.A. §4.

determined whether arbitrations involving multiple contracts, parties, or claims could be consolidated. They routinely denied such requests absent express contractual provisions providing for consolidation, despite equitable or public policy considerations favoring consolidation.[104]

In *Stolt-Nielsen S.A v Animal Feeds Int 'l Corp.* ("*Stolt-Nielsen*"),[105] the Supreme Court considered whether an arbitration panel may order class arbitration where an arbitration clause is silent on that issue. In a five-to-three decision, the Court held that the FAA does not permit imposing class arbitration unless there is a contractual basis for concluding that the parties agreed to do so.?

Since the decision was issued, there has been extensive commentary on the impact this decision will have on consolidated arbitrations. While it is clear that the effect of the decision will be widespread and varied—from who decides the issue to what contractual basis is necessary to find the parties agreed to consolidation—exactly how these changes will play out is not.[106]

In *Markel International Insurance Co. v Westchester Fire Insurance Co.*,[107] Westchester demanded a consolidated arbitration with respect to two reinsurance agreements issued to it by a combination of various reinsurers. In response to Westchester's demand for consolidated arbitration, the reinsurers moved to compel separate arbitration proceedings. The court observed that the "reinsurance contracts are multi-layered and had different terms of years, but contain substantially similar arbitration clauses," which were silent with respect to the issue of consolidation. Westchester cross-moved to commence a single arbitration for the purposes of determining the consolidation issue.

The court held that it was for the arbitrator to decide whether there should be a consolidated arbitration proceeding, and ordered that a single arbitration panel be constituted for the purpose of making the decision. The court stated that principles

[104] For example, in *Government of U.K. of Gr. Brit, v Boeing Co*, 998 H.2d 68 (2d Cir.1993) abrogated by *Green Tree Fin. Corp v Bazzle*, 539 U.S. 444 (2003) as recognized in *Stoh-Nielson SA v Ammal Feeds Intern, Corp.*, 548 FJd 85, 100 (2008), the Second Circuit refused to consolidate arbitrations of two disputes arising from a single incident without the full consent of the parties even though the contracts and issues were identical and there were clear efficiencies in consolidation. Boeing thus reversed the Second Circuit's original view that the FAA conferred upon the Federal Court the power to order consolidation of arbitration proceedings. *Compania Espanola de Peiroleos, S.A. ν Nereus Shipping*. S.A., 527 F.2d 966 (2d Cir. 1975). The majority of Federal Circuit Courts of Appeal considering the issue of consolidation had held that a court could not order the consolidation of arbitration proceedings arising under separate agreements without the consent of the parties. *Del Webb Construction v Richardson Hospital Authority*. 823 F.2d 145 (5th Cir. 1987). One notable exception is in the First Circuit which ruled in New England Energy ν Keystone Shipping Co, 855 F.2d 1.5 (1st Cir. 1988), *cert, denied*, 489 U.S. 1077 (1989). that where Massachusetts law governed, the Massachusetts Arbitration Act provisions expressly providing for consolidation were not inconsistent with the FAA and thus were not preempted; King and Matosky (2011), p. 70.

[105] *Stolt-Nielsen S.A v Animal Feeds Int'l Corp.* ("*Stolt-Nielsen*"), 130 S.Ct.1758 (2010).

[106] Dotseth and Loynes (2011), p. 362.

[107] *Markel International Insurance Co. v Westchester Fire Insurance Co.*, 442 F. Supp.2d 200 (D. N.J. 2006).

of efficiency strongly favor a single arbitration panel's determination of whether consolidation is appropriate under the agreements that make up the Reinsurance Program.

Requiring multiple panels to decide the question of consolidated arbitration, would likely result in strategic behavior that would only serve to frustrate a resolution of the parties' dispute. For instance, the parties might seek a determination from a particular panel on the consolidation issue so as to bind later panels to that decision or panels may reach conflicting decision about consolidation which will ultimately require a district court to decide which panel's interpretation of the agreement was correct.

In other words, courts would have to engage in exactly the type of activity the Supreme Court wanted to leave to the arbitrators.[108] The reinsurers argued that the court should order a separate arbitration for each contract. The court, however, questioned whether multiple arbitration panels would raise efficiency concerns. In its decision, the court cited *Certain Underwriters at Lloyd's, London v Cravens Dargan & Co.*,[109] a California federal district court case with a similar outcome.

A sample consolidation clause in a reinsurance contract may appear as follows: "If more than one reinsurer is involved in an arbitration, where there are common questions of law or fact and a possibility of conflicting awards or inconsistent results, all such reinsurers will constitute and act as one party for purpose of this clause."[110]

A party seeking to enforce consolidation in an arbitration agreement may petition the court to do so pursuant to section 4 of the FAA 1925 which provides that: "...a party aggrieved by the alleged failure, neglect or refusal of another to arbitrate under a written agreement for arbitration may petition any United States district court ... for an order directing that such arbitration proceed in the manner provided for in such agreement."[111]

Although the language of this statute seems clear, courts have interpreted it in a variety of ways. Early interpretations of section 4 of the FAA 1925 held that an arbitration panel lacked the authority to order consolidation.

In *Del E. Webb Construction v Richardson Hospital Authority*[112] the Fifth Circuit held that, under section 4 of the FAA 1925, the question of consolidation was for the district court, as only courts may determine whether the contract provides for consolidated arbitration, which should be a question free of the underlying facts. Moreover, the Fifth Circuit stated that it is unclear how separate arbitrations could be consolidated by one of the arbitrators and that, in short and as per § 4 of the FAA 1925, the sole question for the district court was whether there

[108] Ten Cate (2004), p. 150.

[109] *Certain Underwriters at Lloyd's, London v Cravens Dargan & Co.*, No. CV 05-4266, 2005 U.S. Dist. LEXIS 39724 (C.D. Cal. Aug. 11, 2005), aff'd 197 Fed Appx. 645 (9th Cir. 2006).

[110] DiUbaldo (2008), p. 85.

[111] 9 U.S.C.A. § 4.

[112] *Del E. Webb Construction v Richardson Hospital Authority* 823 F.2d 145, (5th Cir. 1987).

existed a written agreement among the parties providing for consolidated arbitration.[113]

In spite of the ruling of the Fifth Circuit in *Del E. Webb Construction v Richardson Hospital Authority*[114] that under Section 4 of the FAA the question for consolidation is for the district court to determine is based on the existence or not of a written agreement among the parties providing for a consolidated arbitration,[115] and the ruling in *Howsam v Dean Witter Reynolds Inc.*,[116] whereby the court held that issues of procedural arbitrability, i.e. whether prerequisites such as time limits, notice, laches, estoppel, and other conditions precedent to an obligation to arbitrate have been met, are for the arbitrators to decide, in general case law has cemented an arbitrators powers with respect to consolidation.[117] Hence, it appears that the case law has tended to resolve the consolidation issue in favour of preserving that power for arbitrators.[118]

Of the most important case law on the consolidation of arbitration disputes was *Vigo Steamship Co v Marship Corporation of Monrovia*[119] whereby it was ruled that consolidation of two arbitration proceedings under New York law was appropriate. The case also discussed consolidation under federal law and thus laid out a rationale later adopted by federal courts facing disputes over arbitration consolidation under the FAA.

In *Re Matter Of Arbitration Between Chilean Nitrate & Iodine Sales And Intermarine Corp.*[120] the district court saw no legal reason why two arbitrations should not and cannot be consolidated. In *Lavino Shipping Co v Santa Cecilia Co*[121] the court allowed consolidation because the issues were identical and there was no prejudice to the party opposing consolidation.

---

[113] *Del E. Webb Construction v Richardson Hospital Authority* 823 F.2d 145, 150 (5th Cir. 1987); DiUbaldo (2008), p. 85.

[114] *Del E. Webb Construction v Richardson Hospital Authority* 823 F.2d 145 (5th Cir. 1987); DiUbaldo (2008), p. 85.

[115] *Del E. Webb Construction v Richardson Hospital Authority* 823 F.2d 145, at *150 s (5th Cir. 1987); DiUbaldo (2008), p. 85.

[116] *Howsam v Dean Witter Reynolds Inc.*, 537 US 79, (2002).

[117] *Howsam v Dean Witter Reynolds Inc.*, 537 US 79, at *85 (2002). *Shaw's Supermarkets Inc. v United Food and Commercial Workers Union, Local 791*, 321 F.3d at *225. *Employers Insurance of Wasau v First State Insurance Group*, 324 F. Supp. 2d at *336. *Certain Underwriters at Lloyds v Century Indemnity Co.*, 2005 U.S. Dist. LEXIS 16675 at *6–8. *Certain Underwriters at Lloyds v Cravens Dargan & Co*, 197 F. App'x 645, 647 (9th Cir. 2006); *Employers Ins. Co of Wasau v Century Ind. Co.*, 443 F.3d 573, 577–578 (7th Cir. 2006). *Allstate Ins. Co. v Global Reinsurance Corp.*, No 06 Civ. 4419, 2006 WL 2289999, at *1 (S.D.N.Y. Aug. 8, 2006); *Certain Underwriters at Lloyds London v Westchester Fire Ins.*, 489 F.3d 580, 585–586 (3d Cir. 2007). *Dockser v Schwartzberg*, 433 F.3d 421, 427 (4th Cir. 2006); DiUbaldo (2008), pp. 86–88.

[118] DiUbaldo (2008), p. 88.

[119] *Vigo Steamship Co v Marship Corporation of Monrovia* 26 NY 2d 157, 400 US 819 (1970).

[120] *Re Matter of Arbitration between Chilean Nitrate & Iodine Sales and Intermarine Corp.* No. 71 Civ. 2348 HRT 1972 AMC 2460 (SDNY 1971).

[121] *Lavino Shipping Co. v Santa Cecilia Co.* No 72 Civ. 3097, 1972 AMC 2454 (SDNY 1972).

In *Compania Espanola de Petroleos SA v Nereus Shipping SA*[122] consolidation was held as clearly proper to be ordered by the district court. The Second Circuit explained that Nereus would suffer no legitimate prejudice from consolidation and also stated that the liberal purposes of the FAA 1925 clearly require the act to be interpreted so as to permit and even encourage the consolidation of arbitration proceedings in proper cases.[123]

Other courts have held that consolidation was only appropriate with the parties' consent or if the contract expressly provided for consolidation.

Thus, in *Weyerhaeuser Co v Western Seas Shipping Co.*,[124] the reasoning of *Compania Espanola de Petroleos SA v Nereus Shipping SA*[125] was rejected.[126] Following *Weyerhaeuser Co v Western Seas Shipping Co.*,[127] in 1989, in *Volt Info. Scis., Inc. v Bd. of Trs. of Stanford Univ.*,[128] it was held that, the district courts do not have the power under the FAA 1925 to consolidate arbitrations absent the parties' consent.[129]

However, a new line of cases, has emerged from the Supreme court's decision in *Howsam v Dean Witter Reynolds, Inc.*[130] in which the court held that "issues of procedural arbitrability", i.e., whether prerequisites such as time limits, notice, laches, estoppel, and other conditions precedent to an obligation to arbitrate have been met, are for the arbitrators to decide and, thus, procedural questions which grow out of the dispute and bear on its final disposition, are presumptively not for the judge, but for an arbitrator, to decide.[131]

Post *Howsam v Dean Witter Reynolds, Inc.*[132] decisions have interpreted consolidation as a procedural issue best left in the hands of arbitrators.[133]

To mention only a few representative court rulings, in *Shaw's Supermarkets, Inc. v United Food & Commercial Workers Union, Local* 791[134] the First Circuit held that the issue of whether multiple grievances before the American Arbitration

---

[122] *Compania Espanola de Petroleos SA v Nereus Shipping SA* 527 F2d 966 (2d Cir. 1975)426 US 936 (1976).

[123] Ludwig and Chester (2008), pp. 1–7.

[124] *Weyerhaeuser Co v Western Seas Shipping Co.*, 743 F2d 635 (9th Cir, 1984).

[125] *Compania Espanola de Petroleos SA v Nereus Shipping SA* 527 F2d 966 (2d Cir. 1975)426 US 936 (1976).

[126] Ludwig and Chester (2008), p. 8.

[127] *Weyerhaeuser Co v Western Seas Shipping Co.*, 743 F2d 635 (9th Cir, 1984).

[128] *Volt Info. Scis., Inc. v Bd. of Trs. of Stanford Univ.*, 489 U.S. 468, (1989).

[129] *Volt Info. Scis., Inc. v Bd. of Trs. of Stanford Univ.*, 489 U.S. 468, 476 (1989).

[130] *Howsam v Dean Witter Reynolds, Inc.* 537 U.S. 79, (2002).

[131] *Howsam v Dean Witter Reynolds, Inc.* 537 U.S. 79, 84–85, (2002) at 84 , quoting *John Wiley & Sons, Inc. v Livingston*, 376 U.S. 543, 557 (1964).

[132] *Howsam v Dean Witter Reynolds, Inc.* 537 U.S. 79, (2002).

[133] *Certain Underwriters at Lloyd's v Cravens Dargan & Co.*, 197 F. App'x 645, (9th Cir. 2006); DiUbaldo (2008), p. 86.

[134] *Shaw s Supermarkets, Inc. v United Food and Commercial Workers Union, Local 791*, 321 F.3d 251 (1st Cir. 2003).

Association should be consolidated into a single proceeding was for the arbitrator, not the court, to decide.[135] In ruling so, the First Circuit had relied on the Supreme court's decision in *Green Tree Financial Corp. v Bazzle*[136] where the court had to consider whether an arbitration panel can address disputes arising under identical arbitration provisions in contracts between a commercial lender and several of its clients in class arbitration[137] and the South Carolina Supreme court had interpreted the arbitration provisions as permitting class arbitration. Overruling the South Carolina Supreme Court, the Supreme Court held that the arbitral tribunal, and not the court, had the requisite authority to decide whether class arbitration was appropriate.[138] Thus, it was held that arbitrators are well situated to answer decide procedural questions and issues of contract interpretation.[139]

In *Employers Ins. Co. of Wausau v Century Indem. Co.*[140] 2004 the United States District court for the District of Massachusetts cited *Shaw's Supermarkets, Inc. v United Food & Commercial Workers Union, Local* 791[141] and noted that under *Howsam v Dean Witter Reynolds, Inc.*[142] consolidation is a procedural matter for the arbitrator.[143]

Several federal district courts have also, in multiple occasions held that consolidation was an issue of contract interpretation and of arbitration procedure matters that parties would expect arbitrators to decide.[144]

In *Certain Underwriters at Lloyd's v Century Indemnity Co.*,[145] the Eastern District of Pennsylvania refused to consolidate multiple arbitrations brought by members of a reinsurance program against their reinsurer, Lloyd's, because the reinsurance contracts at issue did not explicitly provide for consolidation. The program members did not move the court to compel consolidation of multiple arbitrations, but rather initially submitted a single demand for arbitration against Lloyd's. Lloyd's challenged this procedure, arguing that it had not consented to consolidation and that the reinsurance contracts did not provide for this option for resolving disputes between the parties. The court held that, although the program members did not seek an order consolidating the disputes, there was no contractual

---

[135] *Shaw's Supermarkets, Inc. v United Food and Commercial Workers Union, Local 791*, 321 F.3d 251 (1st Cir. 2003) at 255.

[136] *Green Tree Financial Corp. v Bazzle* 539 U.S. 444, (2003).

[137] *Green Tree Financial Corp. v Bazzle* 539 U.S. 444, (2003), at 447.

[138] *Green Tree Financial Corp. v Bazzle* 539 U.S. 444, (2003), at 454.

[139] *Green Tree Financial Corp. v Bazzle* 539 U.S. 444, (2003), at 452–453; DiUbaldo (2008), p. 86.

[140] *Employers Ins. Co. of Wausau v Century Indem. Co.*, 443 F.3d, 573 (7th Cir. 2006).

[141] *Shaw's Supermarkets, Inc. v United Food and Commercial Workers Union, Local 791*, 321 F.3d 251 (1st Cir. 2003).

[142] *Howsam v Dean Witter Reynolds, Inc.* 537 U.S. 79, (2002).

[143] *Employers Ins. Co. of Wausau v Century Indem. Co.* 324 F. Supp. 2d at 336.

[144] *Certain Underwriters at Lloyd's v Cravens Dargan & Co.*, No. 05-2809, 2005 U.S. Dist. LEXIS 16675, at *6–8 (E.D. Pa. Aug. 1, 2005).

[145] *Certain Underwriters at Lloyd's v Century Indemnity Co.* 2005 U.S. Dist. LEXIS 16675.

language supporting consolidation and, even if there was, such a request must be directed towards the arbitration panel.[146]

Over the last 3 years, courts appear to have erased whatever doubts remained as to whether consolidation is an issue properly left to arbitrators. As stated already above, in *Employers Ins. Co. of Wasau v Century Indem. Co.*[147] the Seventh Circuit held that consolidation is a matter that arbitration panels are well suited to address. In *Certain Underwriters at Lloyd's v Cravens Dargan* & Co.,[148] the Ninth Circuit, noted that under the FAA 1925 "courts may only decide certain gateway matters, such as whether the parties have a valid arbitration agreement at all or whether a concededly binding arbitration clause applies to a certain type of controversy."[149]

In *Re Allstate Insurance Co.*[150] the court ordered a panel of arbitrators to decide whether disputes arising from two reinsurance contracts should be consolidated and noted that "submitting the question of consolidation to an arbitration panel comports with the strong federal policy favouring out-of-court resolution of arbitrable controversies."[151]

In *Certain Underwriters at Lloyd's London v Westchester Fire Ins.*,[152] the Third Circuit held that the issue of consolidated or separate arbitration proceedings concerns matters of contract interpretation, not arbitrability, and thus was an issue for arbitrators to decide.[153]

Although the law is becoming more settled in this area, practical problems remain. For example, a dispute between the same parties involving several reinsurance contracts with arbitration agreements may result in the formation of multiple arbitration panels—before the consolidation issue is either raised by one of the parties or decided by a given panel. In such a situation, lack of clarity as to which arbitrators have the authority to address the issue may lead to additional disputes. Moreover parties could subject themselves to conflicting decisions from different panels.

As the Seventh Circuit stated in *Connecticut General Life Insurance Co. v Sun Life Assurance Co of Canada*[154]: "Arbitral panels are *ad hoc*, making it difficult to coordinate their decision on such a question. And there are no contractual or

---

[146] *Certain Underwriters at Lloyd's v Century Indemnity Co.* 2005 U.S. Dist. LEXIS 16675, at *8.

[147] *Employers Ins. Co. of Wasau v Century Indem. Co.*, 443 F. 3d, (7th Cir. 2006).

[148] *Certain Underwriters at Lloyd's v Cravens Dargan & Co.* (2005) 197 F., 646.

[149] *Certain Underwriters at Lloyd's v Cravens Dargan & Co.* (2005) 197 F., 646, 647; DiUbaldo (2008), p. 88.

[150] *Re Allstate Insurance Co.* No. 06 Civ. 4419 (DAB), 2006 WL 2289999, (S.D.N.Y. Aug. 8, 2006).

[151] *Re Allstate Insurance Co.* No. 06 Civ. 4419 (DAB), 2006 WL 2289999, at *1 (S.D.N.Y. Aug. 8, 2006); DiUbaldo (2008), p. 88.

[152] *Certain Underwriters at Lloyd's London v Westchester Fire Ins.*, 489 F.3d 580, (3d Cir. 2007).

[153] *Certain Underwriters at Lloyd's London v Westchester Fire Ins.*, 489 F.3d 580, 585–586 (3d Cir. 2007).

[154] *Connecticut General Life Insurance Co. v Sun Life Assurance Co of Canada* 210 F.3d 771 (7th Cir. 2000); DiUbaldo (2008), p. 89.

statutory provisions for transferring cases between panels, should multiple arbitrations be commenced when the contract envisaged a single consolidated one."[155] As such, consolidation remains an issue of which arbitrators, practitioners, insurers, reinsurers, and other commercial entities should be wary.[156]

Based on the cases discussed above, it appears that the consolidation issue has now been resolved in favour of preserving that power for arbitrators. Indeed, the First, Third, Fourth, Seventh, and Ninth Circuits, as well as the Second Circuit, have held that this issue is properly left for arbitrators to decide. Moreover, courts, are being now extremely wary of imposing their own views of efficiency in arbitral disputes, thus interfering with parties' agreements to arbitrate.

The Supreme court decisions in *Howsam v Dean Witter Reynolds, Inc.*[157] and in *Green Tree Financial Corp. v Bazzle*,[158] have provided courts addressing this issue with ample precedent[159] and it is now made clear by several of the USA courts of Appeal that federal courts should stay out of the fray on the issue of consolidation, as the latter is now characterised mainly as an issue of procedure rather than one of arbitrability.

However, this uniform approach has not resulted in clarity for cedents or reinsurers and several issues remain open. For once, an open issue is which arbitrators should decide consolidation. Arbitrators exist only in relation to specific arbitration demands, while judges have certain dockets. And there is also the issue of different panels deciding differently on the issue of consolidation of arbitration. Case law and common sense are the only guides to the parties in such situations.

This problem arose also in *Argonaut Ins. Co v Century Indem. Co.*[160] Again the court concluded that it had no authority to decide even which panel should decide on the dispute which had arisen over the consolidation of four arbitrations and ordered all four arbitrations to proceed whilst encouraging the sophisticated business litigants to come with a sensible conclusion and stating that—absent a consensual result—it would be up to the arbitration panels to agree on a solution.[161] The decision in *Argonaut Ins. Co v Century Indem. Co.*,[162] illustrates, not least, that simply throwing the issue back to the arbitrators does not help the better and more efficient resolution of businesses.[163]

---

[155] *Connecticut General Life Insurance Co. v Sun Life Assurance Co of Canada* 210 F.3d 771, at *773 (7th Cir. 2000); DiUbaldo (2008), p. 89.

[156] DiUbaldo (2008), p. 89.

[157] *Howsam v Dean Witter Reynolds, Inc.* 537 U.S. 79, (2002).

[158] *Green Tree Financial Corp. v Bazzle* 539 U.S. 444, (2003).

[159] DiUbaldo (2008), pp. 88–89.

[160] *Argonaut Ins. Co v Century Indem. Co.* CA No. 05-5355, 2007 US Dist. LEXIS 65863 (ED Pa Sept. 6, 2007).

[161] *Argonaut Ins. Co v Century Indem. Co.* CA No. 05-5355, 2007 US Dist. LEXIS 65863 (ED Pa Sept. 6, 2007), at *17.

[162] *Argonaut Ins. Co v Century Indem. Co.* CA No. 05-5355, 2007 US Dist. LEXIS 65863 (ED Pa Sept. 6, 2007).

[163] Ludwig and Chester (2008), pp. 25–29.

A solution to this quagmire would be to urge arbitrators to look to the parties contract and apply contractual terms to consolidation disputes. In the absence of express wording permitting consolidation, consolidation should still be allowed based on implicit terms into the parties contracts.

Cases such as *Connecticut General Life Ins. Co v Sun Life Assurance Co of Canada*[164] and *Hartford Accident and Indem. Co. v Swiss Reinsurance America Corp.*[165] have shown that the mere failure of a contract to address consolidation does not automatically equate with the denial of a consolidation motion and thus, contractual consolidation techniques can be used by parties and arbitrators to justify consolidation even where a contract is silent on the issue.[166]

5.5 Existing Panel Approach

In *Dorinco Reinsurance Co. v Ace American Insurance Co.*,[167] 35 the Court rejected the *Markel International Insurance Co. v Westchester Fire Insurance Co.*[168] approach (i.e. empanelling arbitrators specifically for the purpose of considering consolidation), which was expressly based on "principles of efficiency," as beyond the court's authority and observed that the jurisdictional difficulty of entertaining consideration of 'principals of efficiency' to resolve the question of which panel(s) should decide consolidation is that it involves the Court, and not arbitrators, in the interpretation of the arbitration provision.[169]

The reinsurers sought to have the question of consolidation directed to eight separate panels, whereas the reinsured sought to direct the question to two panels according to its two arbitration demands. The court rejected the reinsurers' approach, noting that the problem presented is that if more than a single panel of arbitrators per occurrence is appointed and any one panel decides that separate panels are warranted, a consolidated panel is necessarily precluded. The principal at stake is not just one of efficiency, but one of preserving the arbitrators' ability to actually decide the question. It found, instead, that ordering the parties to submit the

---

[164] *Connecticut General Life Ins. Co v Sun Life Assurance Co of Canada* 210 F3d, 771, (7th Cir. 2000), whereby consolidation was ordered at least in part under an implied agreement; Ludwig and Chester (2008), p. 31.

[165] *Hartford Accident and Indem. Co. v Swiss Reinsurance America Corp.* 246 F3d 219 (2d Cir. 2001) whereby consolidation was allowed even where the contract itself did not clearly resolve the issue of consolidation; Ludwig and Chester (2008), pp. 31–32.

[166] Ludwig and Chester (2008), pp. 30–32.

[167] *Dorinco Reinsurance Co. v Ace American Insurance Co*, No. 07-12622, 2008 U.S. Dist. LEXIS 4593(E.D. Mich. Jan. 23, 2008).

[168] *Markel International Insurance Co. v Westchester Fire Insurance Co.*, 442 F. Supp.2d 200 (D. N.J. 2006).

[169] *Dorinco Reinsurance Co. v Ace American Insurance Co*, No. 07-12622, 2008 U.S. Dist. LEXIS 4593(E.D. Mich. Jan. 23, 2008) at 29, 30.

question to the panels in the two arbitrations demanded by the reinsured would advance the principal that it is arbitrators that should determine the structure of the parties' arbitration absent clear guidance in the parties' contract.

In *Aegis Security Insurance Co. v Philadelphia Contributionship*,[170] Aegis was covered by two successive reinsurance treaties. The contributionship participated in the 2002 Treaty, but not the 2001 Treaty. The treaties contained identical arbitration clauses. Disputes arose and in 2004, Aegis commenced arbitration against a Lloyd's syndicate under the 2002 Treaty (the "2004 Arbitration"). Subsequently, another reinsurer demanded arbitration against Aegis based on both the 2001 Treaty and the 2002 Treaty, eventually agreeing to consolidate its claims into the 2004 Arbitration. Additional reinsurers later intervened in the 2004 Arbitration. In early 2005, the contributorship demanded arbitration against Aegis (the "2005 Arbitration") in response, another certificate. As part of the second task, the assembled panel would determine the procedures for the consolidated or non-consolidated arbitrations, including whether the two disputes, if not consolidated, nevertheless would be considered by the single panel. The treaties also contained a provision regarding consolidated arbitration, although it did not figure into the court's discussion of its reasoning. In particular, the treaties provided that if more than one reinsurer is involved in arbitration where there are common questions of law and fact and a possibility of conflicting awards or inconsistent results, all such reinsurers shall constitute and act as one party for the purposes of the Article [i.e., the arbitration agreement]. Aegis demanded that the contributorship consolidate its claims into the 2004 Arbitration. When the contributorship refused, Aegis filed a petition to compel consolidated arbitration. Aegis later amended its petition to request an order, directing the contributorship to submit before the 2004 Arbitration panel the question whether the contributorship's claims should be consolidated into the 2004 Arbitration. Aegis argued that the contributorship had failed to arbitrate and thus should be compelled to arbitrate before the 2004 panel. The contributorship argued that, instead, Aegis should be compelled to arbitrate before the 2005 panel. Each party denied that it had refused to arbitrate but asserted, rather, that it had actively sought to arbitrate in its chosen forum.

The court held that the contributorship had refused to arbitrate a dispute covered by the arbitration agreement—whether or not its claims ought to be consolidated into the 2004 Arbitration. On this basis, the court held that it had jurisdiction under the FAA to compel the contributorship to participate in the 2004 Arbitration for a determination of the consolidation issue before the earliest constituted panel.

---

[170] *Aegis Security Insurance Co. v Philadelphia Contributionship*, 416 F. Supp.2d 303 (M.D. Pa. 2005). 40.

5.5.1 Critique

The courts have not provided clear direction as to how the parties or arbitrators are supposed to proceed following a ruling that consolidation is an issue for the arbitrators to resolve.

To the extent one may be extracted, the guiding principle appears to be that the courts will consider not only the parties' substantive rights but also (and often primarily) the procedural posture of each case. Indeed, in some jurisdictions it is clear that parties who disagree on consolidation will need to engage in procedural skirmishes in an effort to best assert their position on consolidation.

As we have seen, the courts' approaches in referring the consolidation question to arbitrators have been various, but their case-specific decisions provide grist for practical and substantive arguments on every side of the issue.[171]

5.6 Discovery

The nature and extent of discovery available in reinsurance arbitrations varies widely. Although arbitration clauses do not address the arbitrator's authority to resolve discovery disputes, it is commonly recognised that arbitrators have the authority to resolve procedural disputes, including the scope and nature of permissible discovery.

It is sometimes argued that the limited degree of "discovery" available in an arbitration proceeding is one of its chief virtues, since it permits much less expensive proceedings. This is true if ignorance can be considered inexpensive. It is, perhaps, more accurate to say that one of the chief virtues of arbitration is the ability of the arbitral panel in all three jurisdictions to control the collection of evidence for use at the arbitral hearing in a manner that respects the balance between cost and effectiveness.

In the first instance, most of the evidence relevant to a proceeding will often be in the hands, or at least within the reach, of only one of the parties.

Under U.S.A. law, the arbitrators, upon request and within their discretion, may order the production of documents or persons within the reach of a party, and may enforce their order by the indirect, but by no means ineffective mechanism of drawing negative inferences from the failure of any party to produce records or witnesses as ordered. Accessibility of non-party witnesses is a more difficult problem.

The FAA provides that "a panel of arbitrators may take advantage of the subpoena power of the federal court in the jurisdiction in which it is sitting, and on petition to the federal court, have any contempt for such subpoenas punished." It is clear, however, in American law, that automatic recourse to Federal Rules of Civil

[171] King and Matosky (2011).

Procedure discovery mechanisms is not available in arbitration simply at the behest of the parties. The entire scope of discovery is subject to the control of the arbitrators and vests only secondarily in the courts. On the other hand, American courts will not automatically accede to the arbitrators' request for assistance, and may demand a showing of necessity or special circumstance.'[172]

5.6.1 Contractual Limitations Are Enforceable

When an arbitration agreement either provides for or limits discovery, the agreement itself may conclusively determine the scope of discovery available in arbitration. In such a case, the arbitrators can exert no more control over the parties in discovery than that which the parties, through their agreement, granted to the arbitrators.[173] Similarly, parties cannot complain of an arbitrator's decision either to order or to refuse to order discovery if they granted the arbitrator discretion over discovery in the arbitration agreement.[174]

5.6.2 Discovery Under the FAA

Under Section 7 of the FAA[175] arbitrators have broad powers to issue subpoenas and subpoenas *duces tecum*, if the evidence sought for the hearing is material to the proceedings. The FAA[176] does not however specifically address the arbitrator's power to require non-parties to submit to pre-hearing discovery.[177]

Arbitration agreements typically do not specify or restrict the scope of discovery. In these circumstances, the scope of an arbitrator's power to order discovery is determined solely by the FAA,[178] which states[179]: "[A]rbitrators . . . may summon in writing any person to attend before them or any of them as a witness and in a proper case to bring with him or them any book, record, document, or paper which may be deemed material as evidence in the case. . . . [I]f any person or persons so summoned to testify shall refuse or neglect to obey said summons, upon petition to

[172] Milligan-Wbyte and Cannon Veed (1989), p. 120.

[173] *Integrity Inc. Co. v Am. Centennial Ins. Co.*, 885 F. Supp. 69, at *71 (S.D.N.Y. 1995); Hummer (1996), p. 232.

[174] *Laschco Inc. v Ericksoil*, 700 F. Supp. 960, 963 (N.D. Ill. 1998); Hummer (1996), p. 232.

[175] FAA 9 U.S.C.A. § 7.

[176] FAA 9 U.S.C.A. § 7.

[177] Thomas et al. (2011), § 40-25.

[178] *Integrity Inc. Co. v Am. Centennial Ins. Co.*, 885 F. Supp. 69, at *71 (S.D.N.Y. 1995); Hummer (1996), p. 232.

[179] 9 U.S.C. §7.

the United States district court for the district in which such arbitrators, or a majority of them, are sitting may compel the attendance of such person or persons before said arbitrator or arbitrators, or punish said person or persons for contempt in the same manner provided by law for securing the attendance of witnesses or their punishment for neglect or refusal to attend in the courts of the United States."

Given this plain language, courts have upheld an arbitrator's power to summon witnesses, even non-party witnesses, to appear at the arbitration hearing or to bring documents with them to the hearing.[180] The FAA, however, has no express provision to provide for prehearing discovery.[181]

Although the FAA speaks only to the authority of an arbitrator, to compel witnesses to appear at the arbitration or to bring documents with them, courts generally have held that arbitrators also have the authority to compel discovery between the parties, including prehearing document production or appearances of parties at depositions before the hearing.

Many of the cases recognizing the authority of an arbitrator to compel discovery arise in the context of an ancillary arbitration proceeding, that is, ancillary to a civil action that has been stayed pending arbitration under the authority of the FAA. In these cases, courts have rejected requests to proceed with discovery in the stayed litigation and reason that if discovery were permitted to proceed both in the courts and in arbitration, this would be wasteful "dual discovery" and contrary to the purpose of arbitration as an efficient alternative to litigation. Dual discovery generally is permitted only where the party requesting it can show exceptional circumstances warranting the expense.[182]

5.6.3 Non-party Discovery

Arbitration at times involves discovery on a scale similar to that of litigation. Arbitration panels frequently take an active role by issuing subpoenas and other requests for documents and depositions. However, based on several federal courts of appeal decisions, parties in foreign arbitrations should not expect U.S. federal court assistance in enforcing such subpoenas.

Perhaps no issue involving the power of arbitrators has been the subject of more debate over the past few years than non-party discovery.

Section 7 of the FAA 1925 provides, among other things, that "arbitrators . . . or a majority of them, may summon in writing any person to attend before them or any of them as a witness and in proper case to bring with him or them any book, record, document, or paper which may be deemed material as evidence in the case" and

---

[180] *Hires Parts Serv. v NCR Corp.*, 859 F. Supp. 349, 353 (N.D. Ind. 1994); Hummer (1996), p. 232.

[181] Hummer (1996), p. 232.

[182] Hummer (1996), p. 233.

further states that an arbitral subpoena "shall be served in the same manner as subpoenas to appear and testify before the court."[183]

While this language is fairly straightforward on its face, courts have struggled to balance the discovery powers available to arbitrators under the FAA 1925 with the goals of arbitration, i.e. avoiding the burden, expenses, harassment, and lack of efficiency commonly associated with discovery in litigation.[184]

Examined case law illustrates judicial resistance towards permitting arbitrators to compel non-parties to attend depositions prior to the ultimate hearing on the matter. Such cases have uniformly held that arbitrators lack the authority under section 7 of the FAA to compel prehearing depositions.[185] Several other cases from federal district courts have also held that an arbitrator possessed the authority to compel non-parties to be deposed prior to the arbitration.[186]

In *Stanton v Paine Webber Jackson & Curtis, Inc.*[187] the District of Florida held that section 7 of the FAA 1925 permits arbitrators, drawing form their power to order and conduct such discovery as they find necessary, to compel non-parties to appear for depositions prior to the hearing. In *Amgen Inc. v Kidney Center of Delaware County, Ltd.*,[188] the Northern District of Illinois enforced a subpoena issued by a panel against a non-party to produce documents and testify at a deposition for use in arbitration.[189] However, there are also cases where the federal circuit courts that addressed the powers of arbitrators to compel non-party discovery—under section 7 of the FAA—have found, at least implicitly, that an arbitration panel lacked the authority to order non-parties to appear for prehearing depositions.[190]

In *COMSAT Corp. v National Science Foundation*[191] that an arbitrator may not compel a third party to comply with an arbitral subpoena for prehearing discovery absent a showing of special need or hardship. The court did not define the exact meaning of the term special need, except to say that at a minimum, a party must demonstrate that the information it seeks is otherwise unavailable.[192] Fundamental to the court's decision was the fact that parties who agree to arbitrate their disputes forego certain procedural rights attendant to formal litigation in return for a more

[183] FAA 9 U.S.C.A. § 7.

[184] DiUbaldo (2008), p. 90.

[185] *Hay Group v E.B.S. Acquisition Group*, 360 F.3d 404, 407 (3d Cir. 2004) noting that nothing in the text of section7 of the FAA 1925 empowers an arbitrator to compel prehearing depositions; DiUbaldo (2008), p. 94.

[186] *Amgen Inc. v Kidney Ctr. of Del. County, Ltd.*, 879 F. Supp. 878, (N.D. Ill. 1995); DiUbaldo (2008), p. 94.

[187] *Stanton v Paine Webber Jackson & Curtis, Inc.*, 685 F. Supp. 1241, (S.D. Fla. 1988).

[188] *Amgen Inc. v Kidney Ctr. of Del. County, Ltd.*, 879 F. Supp. 878, (N.D. Ill. 1995).

[189] *Amgen Inc. v Kidney Ctr. of Del. County, Ltd.*, 879 F. Supp. 878, 882 (N.D. Ill. 1995).

[190] DiUbaldo (2008), p. 95.

[191] *COMSAT Corp. v National Science Foundation* 190 F3d. (1999).

[192] *COMSAT Corp. v National Science Foundation* 190 F3d. at 276 (1999); DiUbaldo (2008), p. 95.

efficient and cost-effective resolution of their disputes. For this reason, the court found that a hallmark of arbitration, and a necessary precursor to its efficient operation, is a limited discovery process.

Similarly, in *Hay Group v E.B.S. Acquisition Corp.*[193] the Third Circuit found that pursuant to the unambiguous language of section 7 of the FAA, an arbitrator's subpoena power is limited to situations in which the non-party has been called to appear in the physical presence of the arbitrator and to hand over the documents at that time.

The Court noted that had the FAA intended to provide arbitrators with the authority to compel prehearing discovery, it would not have placed limitations on those situations in which a non-party can be compelled to produce documents and testimony. As such, the court held that an arbitrator lacks authority to compel prehearing discovery from non-parties, whether it be deposition testimony or document production.[194]

In *Odfjell ASA v Celanese AG*,[195] the court refused to enforce a subpoena issued by an arbitrator compelling a non-party to appear for a deposition and produce various documents requested by a party prior to the hearing.

The court stated that it would seem particularly inappropriate to subject parties who never agreed to participate in the arbitration in any way to the notorious burdens of prehearing discovery.

In *Atmel Corp. v LM Ericsson Telefon, AB*,[196] the court noted that the weight of judicial authority favours the view that the FAA does not authorise arbitrators to issue subpoenas for discovery depositions against third parties.

Other decisions from federal courts are in accord.[197] However, in a decision of the Northern District of Illinois, it was held that an arbitration panel had the authority to conduct non-party depositions prior to the hearing.[198] Relying on *Amgen Inc. v Kidney Center of Delaware County, Ltd.*,[199] the court found—as also justified under section 7 of the FAA 1925—implicit in the power to compel testimony and documents for purpose of a hearing, the lesser power to compel such testimony and documents for purposes prior to the hearing.[200]

Thus, while it appears that certain jurisdictions, particularly the Second and Third Circuits, are moving towards adopting a hard-line rule that arbitrators do not

[193] *Hay Group v E.B.S. Acquisition Corp.* 360 F3d (1999).

[194] DiUbaldo (2008), p. 95.

[195] *Odfjell ASA v Celanese AG* 328 F. Supp. 2d 505, 507 (S.D.N.Y. 2004).

[196] *Atmel Corp. v LM Ericsson Telefon, AB* 371 F. Supp. 2d 402, 403 (S.D.N.Y. 2005).

[197] *Gresham v. Norris*, 304 F. Supp. 2d 795, 796–797 (E.D. Va. 2004) noting that "a federal court may not compel a third party to comply with an arbitrator's subpoena for prehearing discovery, absent a showing of special need or hardship"; DiUbaldo (2008), p. 96.

[198] *Re Arbitration Between Scandinavian Reinsurance Co. Ltd. v Continental Cas. Co.*, No. 04-C-7020, (N.D. Ill. Dec. 10, 2004).

[199] *Amgen Inc. v Kidney Ctr. of Del. County, Ltd.*, 879 F. Supp. 878 (N.D. Ill. 1995).

[200] *Re Arbitration Between Scandinavian Reinsurance Co. Ltd. v Continental Cas. Co.*, No. 04-C-7020, at 3–4, (N.D. Ill. Dec. 10, 2004).

have the authority to compel a non-party to be deposed prior to a hearing, lower courts, namely in the Seventh Circuit and Eleventh Circuit have reached the opposite result.[201]

Two federal circuit courts directly limited the availability of non-party discovery in international arbitrations by holding that foreign and international arbitration panels may not invoke 28 U.S.C. § 1782 (part of the implementing legislation of the New York Convention on the Taking of Evidence Abroad in Civil or Commercial Matters) to obtain federal court assistance with discovery.

In the case of *In re Republic of Kazakhstan v Biederman Int'l* (*Kazakhstan*),[202] and in *NBC, Inc. v Bear Stearns & Co.*,[203] the Fifth and Second Circuits affirmed decisions quashing the subpoenas of foreign arbitration panels directly to American non-parties. In each case, the court rejected the plaintiff's contention that the foreign, private arbitration panel was a "proceeding" or "tribunal" within the meaning of 28 U.S.C. § 1782, and thus the subpoena should be enforced. The appellate courts reasoned instead that the statute contemplated only proceedings and tribunals of government entities, including administrative or investigative courts, acting as state instrumentalities or within the authority of the state.[204]

The *NBC*[205] and *Kazakhstan*[206] decisions leave open the question of whether a foreign arbitration panel's subpoena would be enforced if it were first converted into a judicial subpoena by a foreign court. That court could then seek assistance from the federal courts under 28 U.S.C. § 1782. Such a procedure may be available in certain foreign jurisdiction, including England.[207]

The Fourth Circuit, in *Comsat Corp. v. National Science Foundation*,[208] held that, in domestic cases arising under the FAA, the FAA does not authorize a federal court to compel a third party's compliance with an arbitrator's subpoena for pre-hearing discovery, absent a showing of special need or hardship. As the only appellate decision on point, the *Comsat* decision appears to tip the scales decidedly against non-party discovery.

Until then, district courts had allowed at least pre-hearing document discovery, but were split on compelling non-party depositions.[209] At least one district court had indicated a willingness not only to order non-party depositions, but to utilize the Federal Rules of Civil Procedure to extend the arbitration panel's subpoena powers to non-parties outside the federal district in which the panel sat.[210]

---

[201] DiUbaldo (2008), p. 97.

[202] *In re Republic of Kazakhstan v Biederman Int'l* (*Kazakhstan*), 168 F.3d 880 (5th Cir. 1999).

[203] *NBC, Inc. v Bear Stearns & Co.*, 165 F.3d 184 (2d Cir. 1999).

[204] Maloney et al. (2000), p. 479.

[205] *NBC, Inc. v Bear Stearns & Co.*, 165 F.3d 184 (2d Cir. 1999).

[206] In re Republic of Kazakhstan v Biederman Int'l (Kazakhstan), 168 F.3d 880 (5th Cir. 1999).

[207] Maloney et al. (2000), p. 480.

[208] *Comsat Corp. v National Science Found.*, 190 F.3d 269 (4th Cir. 1999).

[209] Permitting subpoenas requiring production of documents.

[210] Appeal filed, 95 F.3d 562 (7th Cir. 1996), *appeal dismissed on other grounds*, 101 F.3d 110 (7th Cir. 1996).

Notwithstanding *Comsat's*[211] reasoning that non-party discovery must be specifically authorized by statute, the court left a door open for discovery in a case of "special need." The decision did not address the "special need" standard, but it may approximate the "extraordinary circumstances" standard espoused by the Second Circuit. Those circumstances have arisen in the admiralty arbitration context when a vessel is preparing to leave port.[212] One factor considered is the "evanescent" nature of the evidence sought.

The *Comsat*[213] decision will be relevant in the international arbitration context because federal courts often rely upon case law interpreting the FAA when construing the international arbitration treaty, the New York Convention on the Recognition and Enforcement of Foreign Arbitral Awards. That reliance arises in part because the New York Convention on the Recognition and Enforcement of Foreign Arbitral Awards expressly applies the FAA insofar as its provisions do not conflict with the New York Convention on the Recognition and Enforcement of Foreign Arbitral Awards.

Potential arbitrants must be aware that significant third-party discovery may often not be available in arbitration. These three recent court of appeals decisions underscore U.S.A. courts' reluctance to allow wide-ranging, third-party discovery in arbitration.[214]

5.6.4 Other Discovery Issues

In *National Casualty Co. v First State Insurance Group*,[215] the First Circuit considered a challenge to an arbitration award based on the carrier's alleged improper discovery practices.

The plaintiff, National Casualty, served as a reinsurer to First State pursuant to a number of reinsurance agreements. Under the agreement of the parties, if First State settled its insureds' asbestos claims on a single-occurrence basis, National Casualty was obligated to reimburse First State to a greater degree than if the claims were settled on a multiple-occurrence basis. After First State settled a number of claims with its insureds, it represented to National Casualty that they had been settled on a single-occurrence basis. National Casualty demanded arbitration because it suspected that First State had misrepresented the bases on which the underlying claims had been settled in an effort to maximize the reinsurance reimbursement.[216]

---

[211] *Comsat Corp. v National Science Found.*, 190 F.3d 269 (4th Cir. 1999).

[212] *Koch Fuel Int'l Inc. v M/V South Star*, 118 F.R.D. 318 (E.D.N.Y. 1987).

[213] *Comsat Corp. v National Science Found.*, 190 F.3d 269 (4th Cir. 1999).

[214] Maloney et al. (2000), p. 480.

[215] *National Casualty Co. v First State Insurance Group*, 430 E3d 492 (1st Cir. 2005); Chiafullo et al. (2007), p. 462.

[216] *National Casualty Co. v First State Insurance Group*, 430 E3d 492 (1st Cir. 2005) at *495–496; Chiafullo et al. (2007), p. 462.

In the arbitration proceeding, National Casualty requested that First State provide documents regarding First State's internal assessment of the claims for which it was requesting reinsurance recovery. The arbitrators ordered First State to produce the documents, cautioning that if it refused to do so, the panel would draw whatever negative inferences it deemed appropriate.[217] Invoking the attorney-client privilege and work product doctrine, First State refused to produce the documents. National Casualty requested that the arbitration panel delay further proceedings until the parties could brief the prejudicial effect of the withholding of the documents, but the panel refused.[218] National Casualty then filed an action in federal court, seeking to enjoin further arbitration proceedings. While that claim was pending, the panel ruled in favour of First State, and National Casualty paid, the amount determined by the panel.[219] National Casualty then amended its federal court complaint to request the court overturn the arbitration award in light of First State's refusal to comply with the arbitration panel's order to produce the documents. National Casualty argued that this refusal constituted a breach of contract that voided the arbitration clause and terminated the panel's jurisdiction. It also sought to vacate the award based upon procedural deficiencies under sections 10(a)(1) and (3) of the FAA.[220]

The First Circuit affirmed, noting that under § 10(a)(3) there are three separate grounds for vacating an award. A vacatur is appropriate where the arbitrators were guilty of misconduct in refusing to postpone the hearing, upon sufficient cause shown, or in refusing to hear evidence pertinent and material to the controversy; or of any other misbehaviour by which the rights of any party have been prejudiced.[221] National Casualty claimed the second ground justified vacatur of the award, arguing that the arbitrators had refused to hear pertinent evidence. Rejecting that argument, the court held that they found no violation of the statute here, because any failure to hear evidence did not so affect the rights of a party that it may be said that he was deprived of a fair hearing.

The arbitrators ruled that as a result of First State's refusal to produce the requested documents, they would draw inferences against First State as to what those documents would show. This is a routine remedy, well within the arbitrator's powers. The drawing of an inference against First State in this case offset any unfairness to National Casualty that resulted from holding a hearing without giving National Casualty access to the actual documents it sought.[222]

---

[217] *National Casualty Co. v First State Insurance Group*, 430 E3d 492 (1st Cir. 2005) at *495–496; Chiafullo et al. (2007), p. 462.

[218] *National Casualty Co. v First State Insurance Group*, 430 E3d 492 (1st Cir. 2005) at *496; Chiafullo et al. (2007), p. 462.

[219] *National Casualty Co. v First State Insurance Group*, 430 E3d 492 (1st Cir. 2005) at *496; Chiafullo et al. (2007), p. 463.

[220] 9 U.S.C. § 10(a)(3) 2006); Chiafullo et al. (2007), p. 463.

[221] *National Casualty Co. v First State Insurance Group*, 430 E3d 492 (1st Cir. 2005) at *497; Chiafullo et al. (2007), p. 463.

[222] *National Casualty Co. v First State Insurance Group*, 430 E3d 492 (1st Cir. 2005) at *498 [quoting *Hoteles Condado Beach, La Concha & Convention Ctr. v Union de Tronquistas Local* 901, 763 E2d 34, 40 (1st Cir. 1985)]; Chiafullo et al. (2007), p. 463.

The court also rejected National Casualty's argument that the arbitrators could not have reached the results they reached if they had drawn the promised negative inference, noting that this was little more than an attack on the merits of the award and that courts do not generally review what weight arbitrators give to a single piece of evidence.[223] The court emphasized that arbitrators do not have to give specific reasons for the decisions they reach.[224]

5.7 Confidentiality

Arbitration has developed as a means, for providing dispute resolution that may be more efficient and flexible than litigation, because it is not subject to judicial strictures.

Moreover, western models of arbitration are generally private, in that only the parties to the arbitration agreements and their invitees may attend the proceedings. Arbitration is also private, to the extent that arbitrators do not publish reasoned opinions. Arbitration's private process, limits its transparency, by precluding the public's observation of and participation in the process. Arbitration is also private, to the extent that arbitral awards are, generally, not published.[225]

The right to privacy is recognised, in English law, as an implied right, which attaches to all agreements to arbitrate, as an incident of such a contract, unless it is expressly excluded by agreement of the parties.

Confidentiality, in arbitration, goes further than privacy, and connotes a certain amount of secrecy, which would preclude disclosure of any evidence, communication or other information about arbitration proceedings. In reality however, confidentiality is generally not guaranteed, as underlying information in arbitral proceedings may become public.

The Arbitration Act 1996 does not explicitly protect confidentiality. In the USA, the FAA 1925 does not address arbitral confidentiality, nor does USA law otherwise ensure secrecy of information disclosed in arbitration. In addition, many American courts permit discovery of arbitration materials in later cases.[226] As far as institutional rules are concerned, they generally preserve privacy, but do not ensure confidentiality of arbitration proceedings, as they often do not go further than requiring that arbitrators maintain limited levels of confidentiality in the process

[223] *National Casualty Co. v First State Insurance Group*, 430 F.3d 492 (1st Cir. 2005) at *498 [quoting *Hoteles Condado Beach, La Concha & Convention Ctr. v Union de Tronquistas Local* 901, 763 F.2d 34, 40 (1st Cir. 1985)]; Chiafullo et al. (2007), p. 463.

[224] *National Casualty Co. v First State Insurance Group*, 430 F.3d 492 (1st Cir. 2005) at *498 [quoting *Hoteles Condado Beach, La Concha & Convention Ctr. v Union de Tronquistas Local* 901, 763 F.2d 34, 40 (1st Cir. 1985)]; Chiafullo et al. (2007), p. 463.

[225] Schmitz (2006), pp. 1214–1216.

[226] *Princeton Ins. Co. v Vergano*, 883 A. 2d 44, 61–67 (Del. Ch. 2005); Schmitz (2006), pp. 1214–1218.

they administer.[227] Even when institutional rules or agreements require that arbitrations remain confidential, parties are often left wondering, whether courts will enforce the confidentiality provisions, and courts, have often found confidentiality provisions unconscionable,[228] or that parties have waived confidentiality requirements,[229] or that statutory mandates, public interest or governmental needs dictate the disclosure of information and material.[230]

The principle that arbitrations are private and confidential, as between the parties, would seem to be self-evident. After all, is this not one of the most important of the perceived advantages of arbitration, and one of the main reasons why business people around the world have made arbitration the forum of choice for the resolution of international commercial disputes? However, although often an explicit or implicit presumption of confidentiality exists, between the parties to an international commercial arbitration, at the same time, there is a disconnection between that presumption and the frequent realities of disclosure and publicity imposed by arbitrators, arbitral tribunal or the parties themselves.[231] Although common understandings of privacy, lull individuals into assuming that personal information revealed in arbitration may not become public, and that privacy and confidentiality are synonymous, in reality, the paradox is that, what is private in arbitration does not, necessarily, remain also confidential. This privacy paradox, connotes short-sighted contracting and simplistic assumptions about arbitral justice. Although the axiom of privacy in arbitration, i.e. the acceptance of the fact that, unless otherwise agreed, strangers are to be excluded from arbitration, would prompt to deduce, that parties should be also under an explicit duty not to disclose, to strangers, what has occurred in arbitrations, the stark reality is, that there exist, vast exceptions to the rule of privacy.[232]

---

[227] The AAA International Arbitration Rules, provide for a presumption that hearings remain private, but, that selected awards may be publicly available, unless the parties agree otherwise, and require the arbitrators, but not the parties, to maintain the confidentiality of arbitration proceedings and awards. The Internal Rules of the ICC, similarly require arbitrators and administrators, to maintain the confidential nature of their arbitral tribunal's internal operations, by refraining from disclosing evidence or information they learn through their participation in the arbitration; Schmitz (2006), pp. 1219–1220.

[228] *Plaskett v Bechtel Int'l*, 243 F. Supp. 2d 334, 340–345 (D.VI. 2003), finding arbitration agreements with a confidentiality provision unconscionable; Schmitz (2006), p. 1220.

[229] *AT&T Corp. v Pub. Serv Enters.*, Nos. CIV A. 99-4975, CIV A. 99-6099 2000 WL 387738, at *2 (E.D. Pa. Apr. 12, 2000), dismissing breach of a confidentiality contract claim, on grounds that, the claimant waived the confidentiality provision, to the extent it sought to use that provision in the same litigation; Schmitz (2006), p. 1220.

[230] *Omaha Indem. Co. v Royal Am. Managers, Inc.* 140 F.R.D. 398, 400 (W.D.Mo. 1991), finding that federal prosecutors could use arbitration testimony transcripts, subject to the arbitrating parties' stipulation of confidentiality for impeachment, in a criminal trial involving these parties; *City of Newark v Law Dep't*, 760 N.Y.S. 2d 431, 431–437 (N.Y. App. Div 2003), finding that an arbitration panel's confidentiality order was ineffectual, to the extent it conflicted with the public's access to such information, under the Freedom of Information Law; Schmitz (2006), p. 1220.

[231] Brown (2001), p. 975.

[232] For example, with regard to documents and information produced during the arbitration, a different approach may be warranted for different types of material and, consequently, the award

With regards to reinsurance arbitrations, as the latter have become more contentious, so too has the issue of whether such arbitrations should remain confidential. Many insurers, reinsurers, and other commercial entities do not want to risk the disclosure of sensitive business or proprietary information or potentially bind themselves to legal positions adopted by arbitration panels.

In the reinsurance context, problems arise when the contract is silent as to confidentiality, for example when the cedent and the reinsurer are engaged in multiple arbitrations involving similar contracts and issues, one party may oppose confidentiality so that it can use favourable awards, orders, or testimony from prior arbitrations, which are traditionally subject to a confidentiality agreement, against the other party in current and future arbitrations between them.

Furthermore, even if a confidential agreement is in place, a party may still attempt to unilaterally amend or even breach the agreement if the party believes it can influence an arbitration panel. Faced with this potential scenario, the party seeking the protections of confidentiality will look to the court for relief.

Notwithstanding the fact that the FAA 1925 and the Arbitration Act 1996 do not explicitly state whether arbitrations are required to be kept confidential or whether arbitrators have the authority to impose confidentiality, and the fact that the USA federal courts and the English courts have also failed to address whether there is a duty to maintain confidentiality in arbitrations, the situation remains blurred. Several commentators have argued that, even in the absence of a confidentiality agreement, it is customary for parties to arbitration to keep the proceeding confidential. Others have advocated for the position that arbitrations should not be confidential unless the parties have agreed to such terms.

The issue of confidentiality in arbitration can arise at various stages of the arbitration proceedings, i.e. in relation to the arbitral proceedings themselves, secondly in relation to discovery (disclosure) of documents and other evidence used during the arbitral process; and thirdly, in relation to the arbitral award.

With regards to confidentiality in arbitration in relation to the arbitral proceedings themselves, in the reinsurance context, the Privy Council case of *Associated Electric & Gas Insurance Services Ltd. (AEGIS) v European Reinsurance Company of Zurich (Bermuda)*,[233] involved two successive arbitrations between the same parties (AEGIS and European Re), arising out of two separate disputes under an automatic, facultative reinsurance agreement. Both disputes involved the obligation of European Re to indemnify AEGIS. The reinsurance agreement, required for the arbitration of disputes, before a three-member arbitration panel. The arbitrations were held in Bermuda before differently constituted panels of arbitrators.

---

and the reasons, underlying it, may be treated differently from the transcript of evidence taken during the hearing, witness statements, expert reports, written counsel summaries and legal arguments. Documents disclosed during the hearing, form another category, which calls for different treatment. The extent of any obligation of confidentiality, may depend upon the intended use of the material in question; Collins (1995), pp. 326–327.

[233] *Associated Electric & Gas Ins. Serv Ltd. v European Reinsurance Co. of Zurich (Bermuda)* [2003] UK PC 11 (Jan. 29, 2003) (AEGIS).

In the first arbitration, the parties had entered into a confidentiality agreement, which was included in agreed procedural directions issued by the arbitral panel. The agreement set out a general duty of confidentiality: "The parties, their lawyers, and the Court of Arbitration agree as a general principle to maintain the privacy and confidentiality of the arbitration. In particular they agree that the contents of the briefs or other documents prepared and filed in the course of this proceeding, as well as the contents of the underlying claim documents, testimony, affidavits, any transcripts, and the arbitration result will not be disclosed at any time to any individual or entity, in whole or in part, which is not a party to the arbitration between Aegis and European Re."

In the second arbitration, European Re sought to introduce the award from the first arbitration. Its purpose was to establish an estoppel defence, arguing that the findings in the earlier proceeding were binding on the parties and the arbitrators in the second proceeding.

AEGIS obtained an ex parte injunction, from a trial court in Bermuda, restraining European Re from introducing the first award, based on the confidentiality agreement. The Bermuda Court of Appeal, allowed European Re's appeal, and then vacated the injunction. AEGIS appealed to the Privy Council, arguing, in support of the injunction, that to disclose the award in the first arbitration to the panel in the second arbitration, would breach the principle of privacy associated with arbitration and, more specifically, the express confidentiality agreement reached in the first arbitration. It also argued that, European Re's estoppel defence, in the second arbitration, was so lacking in merit that it was an abuse of process to raise it.

The Privy Council recognised the need to preserve confidentiality and the lawyer-client privilege, but, in its analysis, appeared to place more importance on the essential purposes of arbitration to determine disputes between the parties, declare the rights and obligations of the parties, and bind them to that declaration, rather than on the principle of confidentiality. The Privy Council expressed reservations, about the desirability or merit of adopting a duty of confidentiality, as an implied term of arbitration and then formulating exceptions to which such a duty would be subject; and stated that, although commercial arbitrations are essentially private proceedings and, unlike litigation in the courts, do not place anything in the public domain, nevertheless, when it comes to the award, the same logic cannot be applied, since it might be necessary to refer to an award for an accounting or enforcement.

The case demonstrates that general principles of confidentiality are difficult to discern, and that confidentiality agreements will be evaluated having regard to the circumstances, in which they are made and the basic principles and purposes of arbitration. However, it is doubtful that any legislated solution would be effective to resolve the issue of confidentiality in all circumstances.[234]

[234] Thompson and Finn (2007), pp. 75–78.

It is concluded that arbitral tribunals have no power to consolidate proceedings, if parties have not expressly opted for it, except in cases where earlier awards of a competent court could be used to bind subsequent arbitrations. There are no set rules to determine such a usage or not, therefore general principles of law should be applied to determine the issue.[235]

In the USA, with regards to the treatment of arbitral confidentiality, as far as the proceedings *per se* are concerned, conversely to the position established by the majority of the case law in England, the predominant position, as this has been formulated by case law—such as *Compania Espanola de Petroleos SA v Nereus Shipping SA*[236]—has been that consolidation would be permitted and even encouraged in proper cases, in particular following US decisions such as *Volt Info. Sciences v Board of Trustees*,[237] whereby a construction contract between appellant and appellee contained an agreement to arbitrate all disputes arising out of the contract, and where the trial court denied appellant's motion to compel arbitration. However, USA courts have also ruled otherwise. In *Government of UK v Boeing Co*[238], the Second Circuit has held that the aspect of the decision in *Compania Espanola de Petroleos SA v Nereus Shipping SA*[239] decision is no good law and that, like in England, consolidation cannot be ordered in the absence of an agreement by the parties to arbitration.[240]

In *Weyerhaeuser Company v Western Seas Shipping Co*,[241] Weyerhaeuser appealed the district court's denial of its petition to compel the consolidation of two maritime arbitrations into a single arbitration before five arbitrators. Weyerhaeuser asserted that the court had the power to compel consolidation, under the United States Arbitration Act, 9 U.S.C., sections1–14, and under Fed.R. CivP. 81(a)(3) and 42(a). The principal authority relied upon, by Weyerhaeuser, for this proposition was *Compania Espanola de Petroleos, S.A. v Nereus Shipping, S. A.*[242] The case of *Compania Espanola de Petroleos, S.A. v Nereus Shipping, S.A.*[243] involved an appeal from a district court order consolidating two arbitration proceedings, one between the owner of a ship and the ship's charterer and one between the owner and the charterer's guarantor.

The Second Circuit affirmed the district court order, relying on two grounds. First, the court held that all three parties had consented to consolidation. All three had signed an addendum to the original charter party, to the effect that the guarantor would undertake all the charterer's duties in the event of the charterer's default. The

---

[235] Uff and Noussia (2009).

[236] *Compania Espanola de Petroleos SA v Nereus Shipping SA*, 527 F2d 966 (2d Cir. 1975).

[237] *Volt Info. Sciences v Board of Trustees* [489 US 468 (1989)].

[238] *Government of UK v Boeing Co*, 998 F2d 68 (2d. 1993).

[239] *Compania Espanola de Petroleos SA v Nereus Shipping SA*, 527 F2d 966 (2d Cir. 1975).

[240] *Government of UK v Boeing Co*, 998 F2d 68 (2d. 1993); Collins (1995), pp. 324–326.

[241] *Weyerhaeuser Company v Western Seas Shipping Co* 743 F.2d 635 (9th Circ. 1984).

[242] *Compania Espanola de Petroleos, S.A. v Nereus Shipping, S.A.*, 527 F.2d 966 (2d Cir.1975).

[243] *Compania Espanola de Petroleos, S.A. v Nereus Shipping, S.A.*, 527 F.2d 966 (2d Cir.1975).

court held that, since the original charter party imposed a duty to arbitrate, the addendum amounted to implicit consent to joint arbitration in the event of a dispute. Second, the Second Circuit stated that the liberal purposes of the FAA clearly require that this act be interpreted, so as to permit and even to encourage the consolidation of arbitration proceedings in proper cases.

The Ninth Circuit, insofar as *Compania Espanola de Petroleos, S.A. v Nereus Shipping, S.A.*[244] rested on the consent of the parties, distinguished it from *Weyerhaeuser Company v Western Seas Shipping Co*,[245] stated that it was clear that the parties in *Weyerhaeuser Company v Western Seas Shipping Co*[246] did not consent to joint arbitration and, insofar as *Compania Espanola de Petroleos, S.A. v Nereus Shipping, S.A.*[247] held that federal courts may order consolidation in the absence of consent, declined to follow it.

In *Baesler v Cont'tal Grain Co*,[248] the Eighth Circuit stated that consolidation of arbitral proceedings, absent relevant consent, is impossible, and agreed with the majority view that the FAA 1925 precludes federal courts from ordering consolidation of arbitration proceedings. It was also stated, that the Supreme court has explicitly rejected the assertion that the overriding goal of the Act is to promote the expeditious resolution of claims, and has recognised the passage of the Act as being motivated, first and foremost, by a congressional desire to enforce agreements into which parties had entered. In accordance with this purpose, the court read the FAA 1925, as requiring federal courts to enforce arbitration agreements as they are written, and, accordingly, held that, absent a provision in an arbitration agreement authorising consolidation, a district court is without power to consolidate arbitration proceedings.

In *Protective Life Ins. Corp. v Lincoln Nat'l Life Ins. Corp. v Lincoln Nat'l Life Ins. Corp.*,[249] Lincoln National Life Insurance Company appealed the district court's grant of summary judgment, and its order consolidating the arbitration of Lincoln's dispute with appellee Protective Life Insurance Company, and the arbitration of claims between Protective and a third party, Munich American Reassurance Company. On the issue whether a district court may consolidate arbitration proceedings, if the parties have not provided for consolidation in their arbitration agreements, the Eleventh Circuit ruled that it may not.

In *Government of the United Kingdom of Great Britain v Boeing Co*,[250] the Second Circuit reversed the district courts' order, for consolidation of arbitration proceedings arising from separate agreements to arbitrate, absent the parties'

[244] *Compania Espanola de Petroleos, S.A. v Nereus Shipping, S.A.*, 527 F.2d 966 (2d Cir.1975).

[245] *Weyerhaeuser Company v Western Seas Shipping Co*, 743 F.2d 635 (9th Circ. 1984).

[246] *Weyerhaeuser Company v Western Seas Shipping Co*, 743 F.2d 635 (9th Circ. 1984).

[247] *Compania Espanola de Petroleos, S.A. v Nereus Shipping, S.A.*, 527 F.2d 966 (2d Cir.1975).

[248] *Baesler v Cont'tal Grain Co*, 900 F2d. 1193 (8th Cir. 1990).

[249] *Protective Life Ins. Corp. v Lincoln Nat'l Life Ins. Corp. v Lincoln Nat'l Life Ins. Corp.*, 873 F.2d 281 (11th Cir. 1989).

[250] *Government of the United Kingdom of Great Britain v Boeing Co*, 998 F2d. 68 (2d Cir. 1993).

agreement to allow such consolidation, and stated that the courts need to enforce arbitration contracts, in accordance with the arbitration agreement terms.

In *American Centennial Ins Co v National Casualty Co,*[251] the Sixth Circuit concluded that, in the absence of a provision for consolidation, it was without authority to circumvent the mandate of the Act, that district courts are to direct parties "to proceed to arbitration in accordance with the terms of the agreement."[252]

To conclude, *Compania Espanola de Petroleos, S.A. v Nereus Shipping, S.A.*[253] is said to be the case that empowered federal courts to consolidate separate arbitral proceedings even absent an agreement by the parties. The Fourth and First Circuits, in cases like *Maxum Founds v Salus Corp.*[254] and *New England Energy Inc. v Keystone Shipping Co,*[255] are said to have followed the *Nereus Shipping*[256] ruling.

However, *Government of the United Kingdom of Great Britain v Boeing Co*[257] overruled *Compania Espanola de Petroleos, S.A. v Nereus Shipping, S.A.,*[258] and, generally speaking, since then the majority of the Circuits prohibit non consented consolidation, in an effort to support confidentiality in arbitration and, at the same time, promote the principle of party autonomy.

With regards to confidentiality in relation to discovery (disclosure) of documents and other evidence used during the arbitral process, the existence of the duty of confidentiality in such a case was judicially established in *Dolling-Baker v Merrett.*[259]

On this basis that the efficacy of a private arbitration will be damaged, even defeated, if proceedings in the arbitration are made public by the disclosure of documents relating to the arbitration, the court of Appeal, in *Dolling-Baker v Merrett,*[260] restrained a party to an arbitration from disclosing on discovery in a subsequent action documents relating to the arbitration.[261]

In *Dolling-Baker v Merrett,*[262] the plaintiff claimed against the defendants money due under a policy of reinsurance, under which the first defendant was one of the insurers and the second defendants were the placing brokers. On the plaintiff's application, the judge ordered that the first defendant make a list of all documents, relating to a similar policy disclosed in an arbitration, where the defendants were in the same position as insurer and placing broker. The first defendant applied for an

---

[251] *American Centennial Ins Co v National Casualty Co*, 951 F2d 107, (6th Cir. 1991).

[252] 9 U.S.C. § 4, 761 F. Supp. 472.

[253] *Compania Espanola de Petroleos, S.A. v Nereus Shipping, S.A.*, 527 F.2d 966 (2d Cir.1975).

[254] *Maxum Founds v Salus Corp.* 817 F2d. 1086 (4th Cir. 1987).

[255] *New England Energy Inc. v Keystone Shipping Co*, 855 F2d I, 4 (1st Cir. 1989).

[256] *Compania Espanola de Petroleos, S.A. v Nereus Shipping, S.A.*, 527 F.2d 966 (2d Cir.1975).

[257] *Government of the United Kingdom of Great Britain v Boeing Co*, 998 F2d. 68 (2d Cir. 1993).

[258] *Compania Espanola de Petroleos, S.A. v Nereus Shipping, S.A.*, 527 F.2d 966 (2d Cir.1975).

[259] *Dolling-Baker v Merrett* [1991] 2 All E.R. 890.

[260] *Dolling-Baker v Merrett* [1991] 2 All E.R. 890.

[261] Robb (2004).

[262] [1991] 2 All ER 891.

injunction, restraining the second defendants from disclosing the documents. The application was refused, but, on appeal, the court of Appeal held that, the documents ordered to be discovered were not relevant to the issues in the action, and that producing the documents was not necessary for disposing fairly of the case.

The court stated, obiter, that there existed an implied confidentiality element within the very nature of an arbitration agreement. The court did not define the extent of the obligation to preserve confidentiality, but implied that the implied duty to observe confidentiality covers all documents and materials used in the arbitration proceeding, and in the award rendered, and that it may be subject to certain exceptions, in cases where disclosure and inspection is necessary for the fair disposal of the action.[263]

Parker L.J. emphasised, that the obligation arose out of the nature of arbitration itself, and that the fact that a document is used in an arbitration does not confer on it any confidentiality or privilege which can be relied upon in subsequent proceedings but, in considering a question as to production of documents or discovery by list or affidavit, the court must nevertheless have regard to the obligation. However, Parker L.J. concluded that, if the court is satisfied that, despite the implied obligation, discovery and inspection are necessary for the fair disposal of the action, then discovery and inspection must take place, though other means of achieving a similar result should be taken into account.[264]

Following *Dolling-Baker v Merrett*,[265] the decisions in *Hassneh Insurance Co. of Israel v Mew*,[266] and in *Insurance Co v Lloyd's Syndicate*[267] reaffirmed the existence of an implied duty of confidentiality but recognised that it was subject to exceptions.

In *Insurance Co. v Lloyd's Syndicate*[268] it was stated that, although anyone acquiring confidential information, arising from the arbitration, would also be subject under English law to the same self-duties of confidentiality as the party to the arbitration, nevertheless such duties were not self-evident and English judicial authorities[269] had already demonstrated that the nature and the extent of the duty of confidentiality, in arbitration, is by no means fully chartered but subject to certain limitations and exceptions.

The court in *Hassneh Insurance Co of Israel v Stuart J Mew*[270] anticipated the policy, adopted by CPR r. 31.22, that any disclosed documents may not be used

---

[263] Brown (2001), p. 977; Uff and Noussia (2009).

[264] Robb (2004).

[265] *Dolling-Baker v Merrett* [1991] 2 All E.R. 890.

[266] *Hassneh Insurance Co. of Israel v Mew* [1993] 2 Lloyd's Rep. 243.

[267] *Insurance Co. v Lloyd's Syndicate* [1995]1 Lloyd's Rep. 272.

[268] *Insurance Company v Lloyd's Syndicate*, and in *Hyundai Engineering v Active Building & Civil Construction (Pte) Limited (in liquidation)*, unreported, Judgment of 9 March 1994.

[269] Such as *Oxford Shipping Co v Nippon Yesen Kaisha [The "Eastern Saga"]* [1984]2 Lloyd's Rep. 373 (QB)., *Dolling-Baker v Merrett* [1990]1 WLR 1205 and *Hassneh Insurance Co. of Israel v Mew* [1993] 2 Lloyd's Rep. 243.

[270] *Hassneh Insurance Co of Israel v Stuart J Mew* [1993]2 Lloyd's Rep 243.

except in the proceedings in which they are disclosed, subject to exceptions. In this case, the defendant was reinsured by the plaintiffs, under various reinsurance contracts between 1979 and 1984. When disputes arose, the defendant commenced an arbitration claiming to recover under the policies. An interim award was rendered, and the reassured wished to proceed against the placing broker for negligence and breach of duty as placing broker. The reassured wanted to disclose to the broker the interim award and the reasoning, and also to have other documents in the arbitration disclosed for possible future use. The plaintiffs agreed for the award and for the reasoning, insofar as it concerned the placing broker, to be disclosed, but they objected to the disclosure of the whole of the reasons or any other documents. The defendant asked for leave to disclose, and contended that the duty of confidence was lifted, in cases where disclosure to a third party was reasonable and necessary for a party's own interest. Colman J. held that, there was good reason for leave to disclose; firstly, if it was reasonably necessary to do so for the establishment by the defendant of his causes of action against the placing broker; secondly, if the documents, such as pleadings, witness statements, disclosed documents in the arbitration and transcripts were subject to a duty of confidentiality, as these documents were merely the materials which were used to give rise to the award which defined the rights and obligations of the parties to the arbitration; thus, accordingly, the qualification to the duty of confidentiality, based on the reasonable necessity for the protection of an arbitrating party's rights against a third party, could not be expected to apply to them, but, on the contrary, it would be the final determination of rights expressed in the award which was pertinent, as against third parties, and not the raw materials for that determination.[271] Hence, in *Hassneh Insurance Co. of Israel v Mew*,[272] the court went a step further, in recognising that exceptions to confidentiality may exist in order to facilitate subsequent proceedings.[273]

Another important aspect of arbitration is the extent to which an award is confidential. With regards to confidentiality in arbitration in relation to arbitral awards, in the reinsurance context, the qualification to implied undertaking, namely that an award and reasons might be disclosed as of right—if it was reasonably necessary for one party to disclose them for the purpose of the establishment of that party's rights against a third party, either in order to found a defence or as a basis for a cause of action[274]—was further considered in *Insurance Co v Lloyd's Syndicate*,[275] where the question which arose was whether it was open to a reassured, as of right, to disclose to reinsurers who constitute the following market, an arbitration award and reasons made in an arbitration award between the reassured and the leading reinsurance underwriter.

It was held, granting the injunction, that there was nothing in the reinsurance contracts, by which the following market agreed to be bound by the leading

[271] Robb (2004).

[272] *Hassneh Insurance Co. of Israel v Mew* [1993] 2 Lloyd's Rep. 243.

[273] Uff and Noussia (2009).

[274] *Hassneh Insurance Co of Israel v Stuart J Mew* [1993] 2 Lloyd's Rep. 243.

[275] *Insurance Co v Lloyd's Syndicate* [1995]1 Lloyd's Rep. 272.

underwriter's settlement; that there was an implied duty of confidence between Insurance and the Lloyd's Syndicate in respect of the award[276]; that the mere fact that the arbitration award would be persuasive on the following market did not bring the award within any exception entailed in *Hassneh Insurance Co of Israel v Mew*[277]; and that it was only necessary to disclose the award if the right in question could not be enforced or protected, unless the award and its reasons were disclosed to a stranger, that there was no justification for the implication of a wider qualification in the sphere of the reinsurance market, as the award and its reasons were not necessary elements in the establishment of Lloyd's Syndicate's claim; that where there was an implied negative covenant as to confidentiality; that it was not necessary to prove specific loss and damage in order to obtain an injunction, unless enforcement would impose severe hardship on the Lloyd's Syndicate; and, lastly, that there was no unconscionability on the facts sufficient to deprive Insurance of an injunction.

Unlike in *Hassneh Insurance Co of Israel v Mew*,[278] where the Court had taken the view that the disclosure of an award and reasons was allowed as "reasonably necessary",[279] in *Insurance Co v Lloyd's Syndicate*[280] the court took the view that

[276] *Hassneh Insurance Co of Israel v Stuart J Mew* [1993] 2 Lloyd's Rep. 243 applied.

[277] *Hassneh Insurance Co of Israel v Stuart J Mew* [1993] 2 Lloyd's Rep. 243.

[278] *Hassneh Insurance Co of Israel v Mew* [1993]2 Lloyd's Rep 243.

[279] In *Hassnesh v Mew* [1993]2 Lloyd's Rep 243 relying largely on *Dolling-Baker v Merrett* [1990] 1 WLR 1205 the court found that arbitration proceedings are subject to an implied duty of confidentiality and stated that if privacy is an inherent attitude of the arbitral process, then confidentiality must be as well, simply because privacy is meaningless without its confidentiality corollary. In addition, an exception to the confidentiality rule was found in *Hassnesh v Mew* [1993] 2 Lloyd's Rep 243 and it was held that disclosure of an arbitral award was permissible if necessary to establish causes of action in a subsequent proceeding. With regards to the circumstances under which an award can be disclosed in subsequent proceedings, Colman J held as follows: (1) if it was reasonably necessary for the establishment or protection of an arbitrating party's legal rights vis-à-vis a third party, that the award should be disclosed to that third party, in order to found a defence or as the basis for a cause of action, so to disclose it including its reasons would not be a breach of the duty of confidence. (2) if it was reasonably necessary for the establishment by the defendant of his causes of actions against Heath, that he should disclose or in his pleadings quote from the arbitration award, including the reasons of he should be entitled to do so without editing either the award or the reasons and without having to apply to the Court for leave to do. (3) it was to be implied as a matter of business efficacy in the agreement to arbitrate that, if it was reasonably necessary in order to run off the contracts to have access to the award including the reasons the defendant would be entitled to disclose that document to Heath. (4) the documents created by or in the course of an arbitration, to which an objection of confidence attached could not in principle have any different status from any other documents which were the subject of a duty of confidence. There was nothing to justify the voluntary disclosure to a third party of such arbitration documents, other than the award, in anticipation of the commencement of proceedings by or against that third party. And that to disclose such documents without the consent of the other arbitrating party would be a breach of the obligation of confidence. that, in so far as the injunction currently applied to the whole of the reasons as well as the award the order should to that extent be discharged; Robb (2004); Brown (2001), pp. 977–978.

[280] *Insurance Co v Lloyd's Syndicate* [1995]1 Lloyd's Rep. 272.

"reasonably necessary" covered only the case where the right in question could not be enforced or protected, unless the award and reasons were disclosed to a stranger to the arbitration, and that the making of an award must be a necessary element in the establishment of the party's legal rights against the stranger, as was also shown in *Ali Shipping Corp. v Shipyard Trogir*,[281] where Ali Shipping obtained an injunction to prevent Shipyard Trogir to rely on an award rendered between them, and where the court decided that Shipyard Trogir was unable to lift the confidentiality veil.

The decision of the English Court of Appeal in *Ali Shipping v Shipyard Trogir*,[282] signalled a revived moment toward a judicially enforceable duty of confidentiality; however, the question of confidentiality in international arbitral proceedings is far from settled,[283] parties expectations about the privacy and confidentiality of their arbitral proceedings are often disappointed or negated by courts, and nothing should be taken for granted with respect to confidentiality in international commercial arbitration.

The ruling in *Ali Shipping Corp v Shipyard Trogir*,[284] was extended in *Associated Electrics and Gas Insurance Ltd (Aegis) v European Reinsurance Co of Zurich*,[285] where the Privy Council held, that an award could be produced in

[281] *Ali Shipping Corp. v Shipyard Trogir* [1991]1 W.L.R. 314, C.A.

[282] *Ali Shipping v Shipyard Trogir* (1998)1 Lloyd's Rep. 643.

[283] In *Ali Shipping v Shipyard Trogir* [1998] 2 All ER 136, the Court of Appeal identified the following further circumstances, in which disclosure of an award would be allowed: "(1) "consent", i.e. where disclosure is made with the express or implied consent of the party who originally produced the material". Consent may in exceptional circumstances arise from the custom and practice of the relevant trade. (2) order of the court.(3) leave of the court. The practical scope of this exception i.e. the grounds on which such leave would be granted would give rise to some difficulty. However, on the analogy of the implied obligation of secrecy between banker and customer, leave would be given in respect of: (4) disclosure when, and to the extent to which, it is reasonably necessary for the protection of the legitimate interests of an arbitrating party. Potter LJ followed went on to note that the concept of reasonable necessity ought not to require the party seeking disclosure "*to prove necessity regardless of difficulty or expense*". Instead the court was to take a rounded view, "*taking account of the nature and purposes of the proceedings for which the material is required, the powers and procedures of the tribunal in which the proceedings are being conducted, the issues to which the evidence or information sought is being directed and the practicality and expense of obtaining such evidence or information elsewhere*" however, he held that "*it is not enough that an award or reasons might have a commercially persuasive impact*" (5) where the interests of justice require. This principle was derived from the judgment of Mance J in *London and Leeds Estates Ltd v Paribas Ltd (No 2)* [1995] 2 EG 134. Potter LJ held that this was not a wide ranging exception but rather a limited one based upon the importance of a judicial decision being reached upon the basis of truthful or accurate evidence of the witnesses concerned; Robb (2004); Brown (2001), pp. 970–971.

[284] *Ali Shipping Corporation v Shipyard Trogir* [1998] 1 Lloyd's Rep. 643.

[285] *Associated Electrics and Gas Insurance Ltd (Aegis) v European Reinsurance Co of Zurich* [2003] UKPC 11. [2003] 1 All E.R. (Comm) 253.

subsequent proceedings, as the documents to be used included material which could be useful to the public, and also, because it felt that the implied duty that all documents relating to arbitration are confidential, could be disregarded here in light of public interest considerations, and distinguished *Ali Shipping Corp v Shipyard Trogir*,[286] on the basis that the parties in it were not the same.

Furthermore, in *Lincoln National Life Insurance Co v Sun Life Assurance Co of Canada*,[287] where a party to the second of two arbitrations on a reinsurance dispute attempted to rely on the award of the first tribunal, to which they were not parties, in order to avoid certain reinsurance policies, on the grounds that the first award had held that one of the arbitration parties in the first arbitration, namely Cigna, had reinsured them, the High court held, that a third party should be allowed to rely on an award that they were not privy to, provided it was fair to do so, and the administration of justice would not be brought into disrepute.

The Court of Appeal reversed this finding and stated that, considerations of general justice were only applicable to litigation, and that the nature of arbitration may induce different rulings in arbitrations on closely related issues and that parties should be able to profit from the confidentiality and non-binding character of earlier awards.[288]

Prior cases to the *Lincoln National Life Insurance Co v Sun Life Assurance Co of Canada*[289] case, show that courts are reluctant to allow the use of an earlier award on subsequent arbitration between different parties.

The implications of the decision in *Lincoln National Life Insurance Co v Sun Life Assurance Co of Canada*[290] appear, *prima facie*, to be far reaching. The Lincoln arbitrators had to give not only persuasive consideration to the Cigna award, but they were held to be bound by it on an issue which had not been necessary for the determination of the Cigna arbitration. Sun/Phoenix argued, that the Lincoln arbitrators were not bound by the reasoning of the Cigna arbitrators nor by findings of fact which did not determine the ultimate position between Cigna and Sun/Phoenix. If the question related to litigation, *res judicata* would only apply to the answers from the previous litigation which are necessary to a decision and fundamental to it.

It is submitted that the ultimate result in *Lincoln National Life Insurance Co v Sun Life Assurance Co of Canada*,[291] was fair and just. Both, Cigna and Lincoln

[286] *Ali Shipping Corp v Shipyard Trogir* [1998] 1 Lloyd's Rep. 643.

[287] *Lincoln National Life Insurance Co v Sun Life Assurance Co of Canada* First Instance–[2004] EWHC 343. [2004] 1 Lloyd's Rep. 737, CA. [2004] EWCA 1660.

[288] Uff and Noussia (2009).

[289] *Lincoln National Life Insurance Co v Sun Life Assurance Co of Canada* First Instance–[2004] EWHC 343. [2004] 1 Lloyd's Rep. 737, CA. [2004] EWCA 1660.

[290] *Lincoln National Life Insurance Co v Sun Life Assurance Co of Canada* First Instance–[2004] EWHC 343. [2004] 1 Lloyd's Rep. 737, CA. [2004] EWCA 1660; Woolhouse (2004), pp. 150, 152–153.

[291] *Lincoln National Life Insurance Co v Sun Life Assurance Co of Canada* First Instance–[2004] EWHC 343. [2004] 1 Lloyd's Rep. 737, CA. [2004] EWCA 1660; Woolhouse (2004), pp. 150, 152–153.

contracts included arbitration clauses. The Lincoln arbitration depended partly upon the scope of the Cigna reinsurance. The issue, whether losses under the Unicover reinsurance would have been recoverable under the Cigna reinsurance, decided the applicability of the net retained lines clause of the Lincoln reinsurance, to losses under the Unicover whole account reinsurances. The question of the scope of Cigna reinsurance, was finally decided between Cigna and Sun Life, under the contractual machinery provided for dispute resolution. The findings should be equally binding in a subsequent arbitration between different parties, whether the decision on the scope of the Cigna reinsurance was made by a competent court or by an arbitral tribunal.

However, *Lincoln National Life Insurance Co v Sun Life Assurance Co of Canada*[292] is not an authority, for the general proposition that an award in an arbitration between A and B is always binding on the same issue in a subsequent arbitration between B and C. The general principle is still that an award has no effect, whatever upon non-parties to the arbitration; it cannot confer rights nor can it impose obligations upon third parties, unless they have expressly agreed to be bound by the outcome of the arbitration. An award is final and binding upon the parties and on any persons claiming through or under them. This is similar to the principle applicable to decisions of court *in personam*, which only operate as estoppel in favour of or against parties and those claiming through them, but not in favour of or against third parties and strangers.

The facts of each case will have to be examined, and considerations of justice and fairness will have to be applied thereto. Thus, the arbitrators in a subsequent arbitration have to examine, at the very least, the circumstances giving rise to the first arbitration, the issues referred to the first arbitration, the formal or otherwise nature of the first arbitration, the scope and extent of the arbitrators' enquiry and evidence in the first arbitration, the reasons in the award, etc. Considerations of confidentiality, will form the factors used, in order to decide whether the subsequent arbitrators have access to all the relevant materials in the first arbitration.[293]

In *Aegis* v *European Re*,[294] it was held that the confidentiality agreement was intended to prevent third parties, from relying on material generated during the arbitration against either of the two insurance companies, and that the legitimate use of an earlier award in a later arbitration between the same two parties was, therefore, not a breach of the confidentiality agreement.

While federal courts have yet to address whether arbitrators have the authority to impose confidentiality under the FAA, in *City of Newark v Law Department of*

[292] *Lincoln National Life Insurance Co v Sun Life Assurance Co of Canada* First Instance–[2004] EWHC 343. [2004] 1 Lloyd's Rep. 737, CA. [2004] EWCA 1660; Woolhouse (2004), pp. 150, 152–153.

[293] Woolhouse (2004), pp. 150, 152–153.

[294] *Associated Electric and Gas Insurance Services Ltd v European Reinsurance Co. of Zurich* UKPC 11, (2003)1 WLR 1041.

New York[295] it was held that an arbitration panel lacked the authority to prevent a non party to an arbitration agreement from obtaining certain documents pursuant to the Freedom of Information Law, despite the fact that the panel had issued a confidentiality order.

However, the precedential value of *City of Newark v Law Department of New York*[296] is limited with respect to the confidentiality of arbitrations under the FAA, since the underlying arbitration in that case did not arise under that statute. Moreover, it is arguable whether the issue of confidentiality is within the scope of procedural powers left for arbitrators.

Other decisions, relying on Supreme court precedent, have held that arbitrators, not courts, have the authority to decide procedural issues pursuant to the FAA.[297]

In addition, the ARIAS-US arbitration rules also dictate that arbitrations should be confidential and that arbitrators have the authority to impose confidentiality.[298] On the other hand, arbitration is a creature of contract, and there is some validity to the argument that parties should not be bound to confidentiality absent an express agreement to the contrary. Either way, this will be an interesting issue for arbitrators and parties to monitor going forward.[299]

5.8 Summary Adjudication

Another procedural issue that has been the subject of debate in recent years is whether arbitrators have the authority to decide a case by summary adjudication, absent an express agreement by the parties to do so. The FAA 1925 does not explicitly grant arbitrators the authority to decide a case by summary adjudication. Recent case law and industry commentary suggest, however, that courts and arbitrators may recognize this power on a more consistent basis going forward.[300]

In *Sheldon v Vermonty*[301] the Tenth Circuit affirmed a district court's denial of a motion to vacate an arbitration panel's award that was rendered prior to the ultimate

---

[295] *City of Newark v Law Department of New York* 760 N.Y.S.2d 431, 436 (App. Div. 2003).

[296] *City of Newark v Law Department of New York* 760 N.Y.S.2d 431, 436 (App. Div. 2003).

[297] *Green Tree Fin. Corp. v Bazzle*, 539 U.S. 444, 451–452 (2003).

[298] ARIAS-U.S. and ARIAS-U.S. (2004), p. 22; For example, the 2004 ARIAS-US procedures explicitly state that when parties disagree as to the scope of confidentiality, arbitrators should use their discretion in ordering whether and to what extent the arbitration should remain confidential; DiUbaldo (2008), pp. 103–104.

[299] DiUbaldo (2008), pp. 103–104.

[300] *Sphere Drake Ins. Ltd. v All Am. Life Ins. Co.*, No. 01-C-5226, 2004 WL 442640 (N.D. Ill. Mar. 8, 2004), denying a party's motion to vacate a panel's decision to award summary judgment based on the parties' position statements. *Sheldon v Vermonty*, 269F.3d 1202, 1206–1207 (10th Cir. 2001) affirming a district court's denial of a motion to vacate an arbitral award rendered by a panel based on a motion to dismiss filed prior to the hearing; DiUbaldo (2008), pp. 103–105.

[301] *Sheldon v Vermonty*, 269 F.3d 1202 (10th Cir. 2001).

hearing in a matter, after one of the parties moved for dismissal of the action, although it was noted that there is no express prohibition against such a procedure and that the arbitrators' actions did not deprive the party opposing the award of a fundamentally fair hearing.[302]

Similarly, in *Sphere Drake Ins. Ltd.*[303] the Seventh Circuit denied a party's motion to vacate an arbitration panel's decision to award summary judgment based on the parties' initial position statements filed in the matter.[304]

Additionally, several people in the reinsurance industry have touted the advantages that motions for summary adjudication can play in the arbitral process. These advantages include the elimination of costly and time-consuming discovery, the encouragement of settlements, and the promotion of the speedy and efficient resolution of disputes. While summary adjudication motions have been used somewhat infrequently and granted sparingly in reinsurance arbitration proceedings, there appears to be some movement towards the acceptance of these motions in the arbitral process.[305]

5.9 Hold Harmless Agreements

"Hold harmless" agreements are routinely executed in reinsurance and other commercial arbitrations and provide that the parties will not assert any claim, actions, or lawsuits against the arbitrators for matters arising out of or resulting from the arbitration. These types of agreements also provide that the parties will indemnify and hold the panel harmless against any and all expenses, costs, and fees that may be incurred, including their reasonable hourly fees, in connection with any action arising out of the arbitration.

In *Pacific Employers Insurance Co. v Moglia*,[306] one of the parties to the arbitration refused to sign the hold harmless agreement, and the panel declared that it could not proceed with the arbitration. After the case travelled through the court system for several years, the insurers filed an appeal with the Northern District of Illinois to end the stalemate. The Northern District of Illinois examined whether an arbitration panel could compel the parties to sign a "hold harmless" agreement in an arbitration conducted pursuant to the Commercial Arbitration Rules of the American Arbitration Association. The Court held that the arbitrators had the authority to require the parties to sign the hold harmless agreement and ordered the objecting party to sign that agreement, thus expending arbitral powers under the

[302] *Sheldon v Vermonty*, 269 F.3d 1202, 1206 (10th Cir. 2001).

[303] *Sphere Drake Ins. Ltd.*, 2004 WL 442640.

[304] *Sphere Drake Ins. Ltd.*, 2004 WL 442640, at *3; DiUbaldo (2008), p. 105.

[305] DiUbaldo (2008), p. 105.

[306] *Pacific Employers Insurance Co. v Moglia* No. 05 C 1366, 2007 U.S. Dist. LEXIS 21967 (N.D. Ill. Mar. 27, 2007).

FAA. The Court relied on the policy of the FAA favouring the enforcement of arbitration agreements, as well as other case law enunciating the strong policy in favour of a broad grant of arbitral immunity.

While the decision in *Pacific Employers Insurance Co. v Moglia*[307] is yet another example of the broad powers granted to arbitrators under the FAA, the enforcement of such agreements is a power arbitrators will in all likelihood rarely have to exercise, since most parties agree to sign the hold harmless agreements.[308] Overall, with regards to the powers of arbitrators in reinsurance arbitration, recent decisions illustrate that courts will show great deference to the authority conferred to arbitrators by statutes such as the FAA 1925. as far as many procedural issues are concerned. Nonetheless, a great deal of inconsistency remains in the judicial interpretation of certain arbitral powers.

The resolution of disputes between parties involving the power of arbitrators with respect to issues such as confidentiality and, especially, non-party discovery, can often impact whether parties will prevail in a current or future arbitration between them. Moreover, the determination of these issues, as well as consolidation, summary adjudication, and the enforceability of hold harmless agreements, can have a substantial effect on the cost-effectiveness and overall efficiency of arbitration, reasons that parties seek to arbitrate their commercial disputes in the first place.[309]

5.10 The Honorable Engagement Clause

Traditional reinsurance agreement arbitration provisions provide that the arbitrators shall interpret the contract as an "honorable engagement" rather than as a strict legal obligation. This honorable engagement clause affords arbitrators more flexibility in resolving a dispute and allows them to forbear from applying the strict rules of evidence and law of a particular state. Arbitrators are given broad discretion to base their decisions on fairness and on the custom and common practice in the reinsurance industry. Arbitrators are thus freed from the duty to follow a strict construction of the agreement's text. This freedom and flexibility can be extensive. The risk of including an honorable engagement clause in a reinsurance contract is twofold: It may lead to an interpretation of a reinsurance agreement that was not intended by the parties, and it may also lead to litigation over the extent of the discretion given to the arbitrators to depart from express contractual terms. Courts will not allow an arbitration panel to exceed its jurisdiction or vitiate the parties' contract rights because the reinsurance contract contains an honorable engagement

---

[307] *Pacific Employers Insurance Co. v Moglia* No. 05 C 1366, 2007 U.S. Dist. LEXIS 21967 (N.D. Ill. Mar. 27, 2007); DiUbaldo (2008), pp. 105–106.

[308] DiUbaldo (2008), p. 106.

[309] DiUbaldo (2008), p. 106.

provision in its arbitration clause. Clarity in the honorable engagement provision goes a long way toward avoiding litigation over the scope of the arbitration panel's power under that clause.

5.11 Conclusions

In reinsurance arbitrations parties commonly conduct proceedings in a form similar to a hearing before the state courts. Arbitrators are subject to a general to act fairly and impartially as between the parties. As the discussion has shown, there are several significant differences between reinsurance arbitration in England and reinsurance arbitration in the USA. For once, the panel's award is very difficult to overturn in the USA. In addition, USA reinsurance arbitration panels are not considering themselves bound to follow the law of a particular jurisdiction. Regarding consolidation of reinsurance arbitral proceedings case law illustrates that courts will show great deference to the authority conferred to arbitrators with respect to many procedural issues. The resolution of disputes between parties involving the power of arbitrators with respect to consolidation can often impact whether parties will prevail in a current or future arbitration between them. Moreover, the determination of issues such as consolidation and the enforceability of hold harmless agreements can have a substantial effect on the cost-effectiveness and overall efficiency of arbitration—reasons that parties seek to arbitrate their commercial disputes in the first place. The common adjudication of multi-party disputes prevents inconsistent findings, assists time management and allows for efficient utilisation of resources. Different from the case of litigation, where the mere lack of an agreement is no preclusion for consolidating disputes amongst all related parties, consolidation of arbitration proceedings is not as routinely possible as it is in litigation.

References

ARIAS-U.S., ARIAS-U.S. (2004) Practical guide to reinsurance arbitration procedure 22, UV, USA
Barlow Lyde and Gilbert LLP (2009) Reinsurance practice and the law. Informa, London
Brown AC (2001) Presumption meets reality: an exploration of the confidentiality obligation in international commercial arbitration. Am Univ Int Law Rev 16:969–1025
Chiafullo LA, Cruz-Brown KA, Rourke-Hugener J, Monahan JC, Rush DE (2007) Recent developments in excess insurance, surplus lines insurance and reinsurance law. Tort Trial Insur Pract Law J 42:435
Collins M (1995) Privacy and confidentiality in arbitration proceedings. Arb Int 11(3):321–336
DiUbaldo RW (2008) Evolving issues in reinsurance disputes: the power of arbitrators. Fordham Urban Law J 35:83–106
Dotseth K, Loynes K (2011) Consolidation of arbitration after Stolt-Nielsen. Def Couns J 78:362

Grais DJ (2007) Consolidation of arbitrations: courts have punted to arbitrators. Now what? Mealys Litig Rep Reinsur 18(5):1

Hammesfahr RW, Wright SW (1994) The law of reinsurance claims. Andrews Professional Books, Westtown

Holmes EM, Sutin LA (1996) Holmes' Appleman on insurance. Lexis, Los Angeles

Hosack G, Kline C (1998) Current title insurance issues in the U.S.A. Int ILR 6(4):106–109

Hummer P (1996) Reinsurance arbitrations from start to finish: a practitioner's guide. Def Couns 63:228–236

Kanefsky EP, Diubaldo RW (2009) Notable 2009 U.S. reinsurance arbitration decisions. Insur Reinsur Rev. www.edwardswildman.com/insights/PublicationDetail.aspx?publication=1914

King MS, Matosky JE (2011) Considering consolidation. Defense Counsel J 78:70

Ludwig B, Chester M (2008) The role of federal courts in consolidating reinsurance arbitrations: the latest cases – many questions still unanswered. New Appleman on insurance: current critical issues in insurance law. Lexis Nexis, Los Angeles

Maloney PT, Haddad JM, Kanefsky EP, Whelehan DD (2000) International insurance and reinsurance developments. Int Law 34:473

McDonald JJ (2001) Reinsurance arbitration 2001: will the new ways cripple arbitration? Def Couns J 68:328–338

Milligan-Wbyte J, Cannon Veed M (1989) Bermudian, English and American reinsurance arbitration law and practice and ADR methods. Tort Insur Law J 25:120

Monin LO, Brady MJ (1996) Updating reinsurance law developments: the gloves are beginning to come off. Def Couns J 63:219

Ostrager BR, Vyskocil MC (1996) Modern reinsurance law and practice. Glasser Legal Works, Little Falls

Robb A (2004) Confidentiality and arbitration, 39 Essex Street, 5 May 2004. http://www.39essex.com/docs/articles/ARO_Confidentiality_and_arbitration_talk_050504.pdf

Schmitz A (2006) Untangling the privacy paradox in arbitration. Univ Kan Law Rev 54:1211–1253

Ten Cate IM (2004) Multi-party and multi-contract arbitrations: procedural mechanisms and interpretation of arbitration agreements under US law. Am Rev Int Arb 15:133

Thomas JE et al (eds) (2011) New Appleman insurance law practice guide, vol 4, Separate lines of insurance. Lexis, Los Angeles

Thomas JE, Lyons S (eds) (2012) New Appleman on insurance law – library edition, vol 7, Property insurance (chapters 71–79 §§ 71.01–79.06). Lexis Nexis, Los Angeles

Thompson CR, Finn AMK (2007) Confidentiality in arbitration: a valid assumption? A proposed solution. Disp Resolut J 62:75–79

Tong Chun Fai E, Dewan N (2009) Drafting arbitration agreements with "Consolidation" in mind. AIAJ 5:70–94

Uff K, Noussia K (2009) On the protection of confidentiality of arbitral proceedings: a comparative approach of the position in England, Australia, U.S.A. and Canada. In: Klammaris K (ed) Fetschrift für Prof. K.D. Kerameus. Kluwer-Sakkoulas, Athens

Woolhouse SP (2004) The effect of an arbitration award on subsequent arbitration between different parties – an English law perspective. Int ALR 7(5):150–156

The Reinsurance Arbitration Award

A reinsurance arbitral tribunal may make a final award on the whole claim, or it may rule partially via an interim award, allowing the final award to be issued at a later stage and either reject or approve the relief sought. The award must also be in a form to allow it to be enforceable. The date of the award is significant for determining when time runs for purposes of enforcement proceedings. Once a valid award has been made, the arbitrators are divested of authority, except in the case of partial or provisional awards, or in the case of remission by the court of the award to the arbitrators. The successful party may bring an action on the award, or enforce it or challenge it. Subject to the unlikely circumstance that both parties agree in writing that an appeal should be brought, leave to appeal will only be given in exceptional circumstances entailed and detected by law. Court can vacate an award if it were procured by corruption, fraud, or undue means, or the arbitrators were corrupt and impartial, or guilty of refusing to postpone the hearing, upon sufficient cause shown or where the arbitrators exceeded their powers.

6.1. The Reinsurance Arbitration Award

6.1.1. The Arbitration Award

An arbitral tribunal may make a final award on the whole claim, or it may rule on a particular issue affecting the whole claim or a discrete part of that claim or any cross claim submitted for decision (section 47, Arbitration Act 1996). The arbitrators' power to make a final award[1] (whether complete or partial) is unfettered; by contrast, the arbitrators enjoy the power to order provisional measures only if that

[1] Barlow and Gilbert (2009), p. 24/3.

K. Noussia, *Reinsurance Arbitrations*, DOI 10.1007/978-3-642-45146-1_6,

power has been expressly conferred on them by the parties (section 39, Arbitration Act 1996).

If, during the arbitral proceedings, the parties settle their dispute, the tribunal may terminate the proceedings and record the settlement in an agreed award, which shall be treated as an ordinary award of the tribunal for purposes of the rules relating to formalities and the parties' respective liability or entitlement to costs (unless that issue has been settled as well), except that no reasons for the award need be given by the tribunal. Under section 58 of the Arbitration Act 1996, awards are expressed to be final and binding on the parties and persons claiming under them. The expression emphasises that third parties are not directly bound by any arbitral award. Moreover, section 58(2) of the Arbitration Act 1996 expressly reserves the right of an interested party to challenge the award by any available process of appeal or review.

6.1.2. Formalities

The Arbitration Act 1996 lays down, in sections 52–54, various formal requirements for awards, all of which apply in default of agreement by the parties. As a minimum requirement, the award must be in writing, signed by all the arbitrators or those who assented to it, it must contain reasons, and it must state the seat of the arbitration and the date on which the award was made. For the avoidance of doubt, an award is deemed to have been made at the seat of the arbitration, if that seat is in England, regardless of where the award was signed, despatched or delivered to any of the parties (section 53, Arbitration Act 1996).[2]

The date of the award is significant for determining the point from which time runs for purposes of enforcement proceedings (such proceedings must be brought within 6 years from the date on which the award was made) and for purposes of appeals or other challenges to the award, which must be commenced within 28 days from the date of the award. If the award is not dated, it will be deemed to have been dated when the last arbitrator signed it [section 54(2), Arbitration Act 1996]. In addition to the formalities listed above, various substantive requirements for a proper award may be inferred from the particular grounds defining "serious irregularity" for the purpose of a challenge to an award under section 68. In particular, the award should, on its face, resolve all issues referred to arbitration; should not show that the tribunal exceeded its powers; and it should not be uncertain or ambiguous as to its effect. Essentially, therefore, the parties, or any court, must be able to ascertain from the award precisely what decision has been reached and that all the issues have been finally determined by the arbitrators.

[2] This provision reverses the decision of the House of Lords in *Hiscox* v *Outhwaite* (*No. 1*) [1991] 2 Lloyd's Rep 435.

The award must also be in a form to allow it to be enforceable either by action at common law or under section 66 of the Arbitration Act 1996. Subject to any requirements which the parties may agree themselves as to notification, the award should be notified to the parties by sending them copies without delay (section 55, Arbitration Act 1996). The arbitrators, however, have a right to refuse to deliver an award to the parties unless and until their fees and expenses have been paid in full.[3]

6.1.3. Effect of a Valid Award

Once a valid award has been made, the arbitrators *become functus officio*, i.e. divested of authority, except in the case of: (a) partial or provisional awards; or (b) remission by the court of the award to the arbitrators. There is also the so-called "slip" rule. Section 57 of the English Arbitration Act gives power to correct clerical mistakes or errors arising from accidental slips or omissions.

A final award confers on the successful party a new right of action, since a submission to arbitration contains an implied promise to abide by the award and to implement its terms. It is this promise which can form the subject of an action at common law on the award. Generally, the award is a bar to further arbitral proceedings. In relation to awards of damages, the proper procedure is to take action to enforce the award, as opposed to further arbitration proceedings or fresh legal proceedings on the merits. If the award takes the form of a declaration, the parties are free to bring arbitral proceedings to enforce any monetary rights flowing from the declaration.

As a general rule, the exercise by arbitrators of their powers cannot affect third parties In the same way, therefore, their award cannot confer rights, or impose obligations on third parties. In certain instances, however, the decision of one arbitral tribunal may be taken as binding in other proceedings.

This point arose in *Lincoln National Life Insurance Company* v *Sun Life Assurance Company of Canada and Others*.[4] In that case, Lincoln had underwritten certain reinsurance contracts in respect of risks entered into by Sun Life. The agreement covered contracts known as the "Unicover whole account reinsurances" but included a net retained lines clause, the effect of which was to exclude cover for risks reinsured elsewhere. Sun Life also entered into an agreement with Cigna Reinsurance Company of Europe SA-NV whereby Cigna agreed to reinsure certain risks. Both agreements contained arbitration clauses. A dispute between Sun Life and Cigna was referred to arbitration. It was held that arbitration that the risks reinsured by Cigna included the Unicover whole account reinsurances but that

[3] Barlow and Gilbert (2009), pp. 26–25.

[4] *Lincoln National Life Insurance Company* v *Sun Life Assurance Company of Canada and Others* [2004] 1 Lloyd's Rep 737 (QB Com Ct).

Cigna had lawfully avoided its contracts of reinsurance. In the subsequent arbitration between Lincoln and Sun Life, Lincoln contended that it was not obliged to indemnify Sun Life in respect of the Unicover whole account reinsurances; Lincoln relied on the decision of the tribunal in the earlier Cigna arbitration, which had held that the Unicover whole account reinsurances were included in the Cigna reinsurance. Lincoln therefore argued that the Unicover whole account reinsurances were excluded from its reinsurance by virtue of the net retained lines clause. The question of whether the decision of a tribunal or court could be relied on in subsequent proceedings by a party who was not involved in the earlier proceedings against a party who was, and where the point in issue was the same in both disputes, had therefore to be considered by Toulson J. when the case came before him following an appeal by Lincoln against an award of the tribunal. In Toulson J.'s view the proper approach, which he considered reflected the modern tendency in cases of serial litigation involving common points but different parties, was to look at what was fair. In the present case, the balance of fairness was with Lincoln and on that basis the judge was willing to treat the relevant part of the award in the arbitration between Sun Life and Cigna as binding in the arbitration between Sun Life and Lincoln. Section 58 of the Arbitration Act 1996 provides, subject to contrary intention, that every arbitration award fc final and binding, not merely on the parties but also on those "claiming under them". Other parties, who have an interest in the subject matter of the reference and who may—if the parties to the reference agree—attend a hearing, run the risk of being found to have assented to or acquiesced in the reference, and should therefore protect themselves by reserving their position appropriately.

Unless otherwise stated in the applicable arbitration clause, an arbitration panel need not issue a decision or explain the rationale supporting its award.[5] This general principle is consistent with the strong policy favouring the finality of arbitration awards. Whether an arbitration award may include punitive damages depends upon the governing law and whether the FAA applies. When the FAA does apply—*i.e.*, the arbitration clause is contained in a contract involving interstate commerce or foreign entities—arbitrators may award punitive damages, even when the contract itself is governed by state law which prohibits punitive damages in arbitrations.[6] Where the FAA does not apply, a court must defer to state law on the issue of whether punitive damages are permissible.[7]

---

[5] *New York Stock Exchange Arbitration between Fahnestock & Co., Inc. v Waltman*, 935 F.2d 512, 516 (2d Cir.) cert. denied, 502 U.S. 942 (1991).

[6] *Mastrobuono v Shearson Lehman Hutton, Inc.*, 115 S. Ct. 1212 (1995). *Lee v Chica*, 983 F.2d 883 (8th Cir.), cert. denied, 114 S. Ct. 287 (1993). *Todd Sbipyards Corp. v Cunard Line*, 943 F.2d 1056 (9th Cir. 1991); *Raytheon Co. v Automated Business Sys.*, 882 F.2d 6 (Ist Cir. 1989); *Bonar v Dean Witter Reynolds, Inc.*, 835 F.2d 1378 (llth Cir. 1988).

[7] *New York Stock Exchange Arbitration Between Fahnestock & Co. v Waltman*, 935 F.2d at 518 (2d Cir.); Ostrager and Vyskocil (1996), pp. 14-41, 14-42.

6.1.3.1. Effect of a Valid Award: The Arbitrators

Once a valid award has been made, the arbitrators become *functus officio*, i.e. divested of authority, except in the case of: (a) partial or provisional awards; or (b) remission by the court of the award to the arbitrators. There is also the so-called "slip" rule. Section 57 of the Arbitration Act 1996 gives power to correct clerical mistakes or errors arising from accidental slips or omissions.

6.1.3.2. The Parties

A final award confers on the successful party a new right of action, since a submission to arbitration contains an implied promise to abide by the award and to implement its terms. It is this promise which can form the subject of an action at common law on the award.

Generally, the award is a bar to further arbitral proceedings. In relation to awards of damages, the proper procedure is to take action to enforce the award, as opposed to further arbitration proceedings or fresh legal proceedings on the merits. If the award takes the form of a declaration, the parties are free to bring arbitral proceedings to enforce any monetary rights flowing from the declaration.

6.1.4. Enforcement

The successful party may bring an action on the award. Alternatively, he may apply under section 66 of the Arbitration Act 1996 for leave to enforce an award.

6.1.4.1. Action on an Award

The action is based upon an implied promise in the arbitration agreement to perform a valid award, and a plaintiff in any such action must plead and prove both the arbitration agreement and the award.

6.1.4.2. Section 66 (of the Arbitration Act 1996) Application

The court may make an order giving leave to enforce the award in the same manner as a judgment or order of the court to the same effect and, in addition, give leave to enter a formal judgment in terms of the award. The latter may be important, for example, in order to serve a bankruptcy notice. The essential difference between section 66 of the Arbitration Act 1996 and the rather fuller action on the award is the relative speed and cheapness of the summary procedure under section 66 of the Arbitration Act 1996.

Any such order or judgment may include the costs awarded by the arbitrators (and the arbitrators' fees), together with the interest which an award usually carries as from its date.

The costs of the section 66 application cannot be included in any judgment in terms of the award but may well be included in the order giving leave to enter judgment which will also cater for the costs of signing judgment. One may enforce an award in a foreign currency, the relevant amount being converted into sterling pounds at the appropriate rate on the date when the court authorises execution.

6.1.4.3. Challenging an Award

Challenges to the award can be made under sections 67 or 68 of the Arbitration Act 1996, whereas an appeal on a point of law is made under section 69 of the Arbitration Act 1996. Under section 70(2), in the case of either a challenge under sections 67 or 68 or an appeal under section 69, the applicant or appellant must have first exhausted any available arbitral process or review and any available recourse under section 57 for the correction of the award or additional award.

Section 70(3) of the Arbitration Act 1996 sets out the time limit for making an application or appeal, which normally must be within 28 days of the date of the award. Although the court has the power to hear the application in private [CPR 62.10(1)], the hearing of an appeal on a question of law under section 69 (Arbitration Act 1996) will generally be heard in public—CPR 62.10(3) (a). However, by CPR 62.10(4) this provision does not apply to the application for leave to appeal under section 69(2) (b). There will therefore be confidentiality implications for any material used in the hearing of any appeal under section 69 of the Arbitration Act 1996.

6.1.4.3.1. Challenging the Award: Lack of Substantive Jurisdiction or Serious Irregularity

A party to arbitral proceedings may, upon notice to the other parties and to the tribunal, make an application to court to vary or set aside an award, either on the basis that the tribunal lacked substantive jurisdiction (section 67, Arbitration Act 1996) or that the proceedings were affected by "serious irregularity" (section 68, Arbitration Act 1996). A party may lose the right to challenge an award by continuing to take part in the proceedings without raising any objection either at all or within the time allowed by the arbitration agreement or by the tribunal. Before making any such application, the party must have first exhausted any available arbitral process of appeal or review. The application must be brought within 28 days of the date of the award, or the date on which the applicant was notified of the result of any applicable arbitral process of appeal or review. Pending an application under section 67, the arbitral tribunal may continue the proceedings and make any further award which may be relevant.

In *Azov Shipping Co.* v. *Balde Shipping Co.* (*No. 1*)[8] an application was made under section 67 of the Arbitration Act 1996 because it was uncertain whether the identity of the parties to the dispute was the same as that of the parties to the arbitration agreement, following the break-up of the former USSR and the restructuring of former Soviet shipping companies. The arbitrator had held that Azov was a party to the arbitration agreement and that he had jurisdiction to determine the dispute.

Azov challenged this decision and sought directions for there to be oral evidence and cross-examination on the issue. The court acceded to Azov's application, holding that although some prejudice to the expeditious and economical disposal of the matter might be caused, justice required the admission of oral evidence because the resolution of the jurisdiction issue involved substantial questions of fact and the court, on a challenge to an arbitrator's decision, should not be placed in a worse position than the arbitrator for the purpose of determining that challenge (*a fortiori* where, as in this case, the arbitrator acknowledged that he had come to his decision with some uncertainty). "Serious irregularity" is a new term. Its focus is the award, although it is clear from section 68 that irregularity may also affect the tribunal or the conduct of the proceedings. If a serious irregularity becomes apparent during arbitral proceedings, the proper course for a party to adopt is to make an objection forthwith. This is particularly important as under section 73 of the Arbitration Act 1996 the applicant making a challenge under sections 67 or 68 can lose the right to object later if he takes part or continues to take part in the arbitral proceedings without making an objection "forthwith or within such time as is allowed by the arbitration agreement or the tribunal or by any Provision of the Act". There is an exception to this provision if the applicant can show that he did not know and could not with reasonable diligence have discovered the grounds for the objection at the time. Nonetheless, an objection should be made as soon as it is reasonably possible if the party envisages making a challenge under either section. If there is shown to be serious irregularity affecting the tribunal, the proceedings, or the award, the court may remit the award to the tribunal for reconsideration, set the award aside in whole or in part, or declare the award to be of no effect, either in whole or in part. The court should, however, always remit the award to the tribunal unless satisfied that it would be inappropriate to do so in the circumstances.

The general approach of the courts to the issue of serious irregularity (or "misconduct" prior to the introduction of the Arbitration Act 1996), has been largely non-interventionist.

This approach was summarised by Bingham J. in *Zermalt Holdings SA* v. *Nu-Life Upholstery Repairs Ltd*[9] "As a matter of general approach, the courts strive to uphold arbitration awards. They do not approach them with a meticulous legal eye

---

[8] *Azov Shipping Co.* v. *Balde Shipping Co.* (*No. 1*) [1999] 1 Lloyd's Rep 68 (QB Com Ct).

[9] *Zermalt Holdings SA* v. *Nu-Life Upholstery Repairs Ltd* [1985] 2 EGLR 14 (QB Com Ct).

endeavouring to pick holes, inconsistencies and faults in awards and with the objective of upsetting or frustrating the process of arbitration. The approach is to read an arbitration award in a reasonable and commercial way expecting, as is usually the case, that there will be no substantial fault that can be found with it." Various heads of serious irregularity are listed in section 68(2) of the Arbitration Act 1996, which also provides that an irregularity will only be "serious" if it has caused or will cause substantial injustice to the applicant. The grounds of serious irregularity listed range from the failure by the tribunal to comply with its general duties of fairness, impartiality and the adoption of suitable procedures, through failure to deal with all issues put to it and uncertainty or ambiguity as to the effect of the award, to the award's being obtained by fraud or in a manner contrary to public policy.

In the USA Courts continued to struggle in 2009 with whether the doctrine of manifest disregard of the law remains a valid basis for challenging arbitration awards arising under the FAA, in light of the US Supreme Court's decision in *Hall Street Associates L.L.C. v Mattel Inc.*.[10]

In *Hall Street Associates L.L.C. v Mattel Inc.*[11] the Supreme Court held that the statutory grounds for vacating and modifying arbitration awards are "exclusive" under the FAA, and thus cannot be expanded, even if expressly agreed upon by the arbitrating parties.

Subsequent to that decision, federal courts have reached varied conclusions as to whether that decision eliminated the judicially created doctrine of manifest disregard of the law as a basis for challenging arbitration awards. For example, while Courts in the Second, Sixth and Ninth Circuits have continued to find that manifest disregard of the law survived the decision in *Hall Street Associates L.L.C. v Mattel Inc.*,[12] the Fifth Circuit held that this doctrine has been abrogated by this decision.

The U.S.A. Supreme Court has yet to clarify whether it intended that in *Hall Street Associates L.L.C. v Mattel Inc.*[13] be interpreted to eliminate the doctrine of manifest disregard of the law as grounds for challenging awards. Moreover, it does not appear that the Supreme Court is in a hurry to do so, having recently denied writs of certiorari in three cases which examined whether manifest disregard of the law remains valid, including the decisions from the Sixth and Ninth Circuits

---

[10] *Hall Street Associates L.L.C. v Mattel Inc.* 128 S.Ct. 1396 (2008).

[11] *Hall Street Associates L.L.C. v Mattel Inc.* 128 S.Ct. 1396 (2008).

[12] *Hall Street Associates L.L.C. v Mattel Inc.* 128 S.Ct. 1396 (2008). *Comedy Club, Inc. v Improv. West. Assoc.*, 553 F.3d 1277, 1290 (9th Cir. 2009); *Coffee Beanery Ltd. v WW L.L.C.*, 300 Fed. Appx. 415, 418–419 (6th Cir. 2008). *Idea Nuova Inc. v GM Licensing Group, Inc.* No 08-civ.-8595 (S.D.N.Y., Aug. 19, 2009). *Global Reinsurance Corp. of America v Argonaut Ins. Co.*, 2009 WL 928014 (S.D.N.Y., Mar. 3, 2009); Kanefsky and Diubaldo (2009), p. 8.

[13] *Hall Street Associates L.L.C. v Mattel Inc.* 128 S.Ct. 1396 (2008). *Comedy Club, Inc. v Improv. West. Assoc.*, 553 F.3d 1277, 1290 (9th Cir. 2009). *Coffee Beanery Ltd. v WW L.L.C.*, 300 Fed. Appx. 415, 418–419 (6th Cir. 2008); *Idea Nuova Inc. v GM Licensing Group, Inc.* No 08-civ.-8595 (S.D.N.Y., Aug. 19, 2009). *Global Reinsurance Corp. of America v Argonaut Ins. Co.*, 2009 WL 928014 (S.D.N.Y., Mar. 3, 2009).; Kanefsky and Diubaldo (2009), p. 8.

referenced above.[14] Insurers, reinsurers and practitioners should stay tuned for developments in this area of the law, including whether jurisdictions continue to treat manifest disregard of the law differently going forward.[15]

6.1.4.4. Appeals

The Arbitration Act 1996 clarifies the previous Statute law and court practice, and continues the doctrine of allowing appeals from arbitral awards only on questions of English law, and only with the leave of the court.

6.1.4.4.1. Leave to Appeal

Subject to the unlikely circumstance that both parties agree in writing that an appeal should be brought, leave to appeal will only be given if the court is satisfied [section 69(2) of the Arbitration Act 1996]: "(a) that the determination of the question will substantially affect the rights of one or more of the parties; (b) that the question is one which the tribunal was asked to determine; (c) that, on the basis of the findings of fact in the award; (i) the decision of the tribunal on the question is obviously wrong, or (ii) the question is one of general public importance and the decision of the tribunal is at least open to serious doubt, and (d) that, despite the agreement of the parties to resolve the matter by arbitration, it is just and proper in all the circumstances for the courts to determine the question."

Some of the provisions of section 69(2) of the Arbitration Act 1996 mirror the judgments of the House of Lords in what were previously the two principal cases on the question of whether leave to appeal should be granted, namely *The Nema*[16] and *The Antaios*.[17]

In *The Nema*,[18] a distinction was drawn between the construction of contracts involving standard contract terms and contracts not involving Standard terms.

In the former, leave should be granted when "such terms apply upon the occurrence of events of a kind that it is not unlikely may reproduce themselves in similar transactions between other parties engaged in the same trade" so that a decision "would add significantly to the clarity and certainty of English commercial law".

---

[14] *Improv West Assoc., v Comedy Club Inc.*, 2009 WL 1648924 (Oct. 5, 2009). *Coffee Beanery, Ltd. v WW, LLC*, 2009 WL 1342336 (Oct. 5, 2009). *Grain v Trinity Health*, 2009 WL 1421117 (Oct. 5, 2009); Kanefsky and Diubaldo (2009), p. 8.

[15] Kanefsky and Diubaldo (2009), p. 8.

[16] *The Nema* [1981] 2 Lloyd's Rep 239.

[17] *The Antaios* [1984] 2 Lloyd's Rep 235.

[18] *The Nema* [1981] 2 Lloyd's Rep 239.

Even then leave should be granted only when the judge considers "that a strong prima facie case had been made out that the arbitrator had been wrong in his construction".

These criteria were confirmed in *The Antaios*[19] in which Lord Diplock added that where there are conflicting decisions involving contracts and standard terms, leave to appeal from the arbitrators' construction of the contract should be granted and, in appropriate cases, leave to appeal further to the Court of Appeal should be granted, so as to help attain a "desirable degree of certainty in English commercial law".

From the above two decisions, it is apparent that a much stronger case for saying that the award was wrong will be required where the issues of law are limited to the circumstances of a particular dispute than where they are of general practical or theoretical importance. The additional requirement of section 69(3)(d) of the Arbitration Act 1996, that it be just and proper for the court to determine the question notwithstanding the arbitration agreement, underlines the fact that the court will be minded to reconsider the merits of an arbitral award only in exceptional circumstances.

In *CMA CGM SA* v *Beteiligangs-Kommanditgeselhchafi MS "Northern Pioneer" Schiffahrtgesellschaft GmbH & Co.*,[20] the charterers of a ship sought leave to appeal from an award made by an arbitral tribunal in favour of the owners. At first instance, Tomlinson J had refused leave to appeal, but had then granted the charterers leave to appeal against his refusal, in order that the Court of Appeal might consider whether or not he had applied the statutory criteria correctly.

The Court of Appeal observed that the criteria laid down by section 69(3) of the Arbitration Act 1996 were clearly strongly influenced by the guidelines in *The Nema*,[21] but did not follow these guidelines entirely. The words in section 69 (3) (c) (ii) referring to the decision of the tribunal as being "at least open to serious doubt" imposed a test which was broader than the House of Lords' requirement that permission to appeal should not be given "unless the Judge considered that a strong prima facie case had been made out that the arbitrator had been wrong".

Subject to this consideration, however, if a judge hearing an application for permission to appeal from an arbitral award decided that the statutory criteria for granting such permission were not satisfied, he should refuse leave to appeal and should not grant leave for a further appeal against that refusal. His decision on the merits of the application for leave to appeal should be final. Section 69(5) of the English Arbitration Act 1996 provides that the court shall determine an application for leave to appeal without a hearing, unless it appears that a hearing is required. This constitutes a departure from the previous practice, under which it was normal for there to be an oral hearing, albeit usually only a brief one.

---

[19] *The Antaios* [1984] 2 Lloyd's Rep 235.

[20] *CMA CGM SA v Beteiligangs-Kommanditgeselhchafi MS "Northern Pioneer" Schiffahrtgesellschaft GmbH & Co.* [2003] 1 Lloyd's Rep 212 (CA).

[21] *The Nema* [1981] 2 Lloyd's Rep 239.

It is axiomatic that an arbitral award must be reasoned if there is to be any possibility of an appeal from it. Section 52(4) of the Arbitration Act 1996 provides that an award shall contain reasons for it, unless the parties have agreed to dispense with reasons. Failure to state reasons for an award could be a ground of "serious irregularity" under section 68(2) (h).

6.1.4.5. Exclusion Agreements

The right of appeal is available "unless otherwise agreed". The Arbitration Act 1996 provides that an agreement to dispense with reasons for the tribunal's award shall be taken as an agreement to exclude the court's jurisdiction to hear any appeal. Moreover, if the parties express an intention to have their dispute decided by reference to considerations other than English law (as permitted by section 46) it is possible that the award will not throw up any question of English law which could form the basis of an appeal. Under section 87 of the Arbitration Act 1996 in the case of a domestic arbitration, any agreement to exclude the court's[22] jurisdiction to hear an appeal is not effective unless made after the commencement of the proceedings in which the award appealed from has been delivered.

6.1.4.6. Appeal to the Court of Appeal

No further appeal lies from the High Court to the Court of Appeal unless a High Court judge grants leave. Section 69(8) of the Arbitration Act 1996 provides that such leave shall not be given unless the judge considers that the question of law is one of general importance or one which for some other special reason ought to be considered by the Court of Appeal.

In *Henry Boot Construction (UK) Limited* v *Malmaison Hotel (Manchester) Limited*[23] a single judge hearing an appeal from the award of an arbitral tribunal had refused leave for a further appeal to the Court of Appeal. The disappointed party nevertheless applied to the Court of Appeal for leave to appeal against that refusal. The Court of Appeal held that it did not have jurisdiction to grant such leave under section 69(8): the judge's decision on leave to appeal was final.[24]

[22] Barlow and Gilbert (2009), pp. 26-30, 26-32.

[23] *Henry Boot Construction (UK) Limited* v *Malmaison Hotel (Manchester) Limited* [2000] 2 Lloyd's Rep 625 (CA).

[24] Barlow and Gilbert (2009), pp. 26-30–26-33.

6.1.5. Confidentiality of Awards

It is generally accepted that arbitration proceedings are confidential. The general rule, therefore, is that documents which have come into existence pursuant to arbitration proceedings may not be used for any other purpose. *Hassneh Insurance Company of Israel v Mew*[25] states an important exception to this principle.

In *Hassneh Insurance Company of Israel v Mew*,[26] the reinsured (Mr Mew) had commenced arbitration proceedings against the reinsurer (Hassneh) to recover sums claimed under various reinsurance contracts. In the arbitration proceedings, Hassneh raised a number of defences, including non-disclosure and misrepresentation. Mew wished to make a claim against his reinsurance brokers in the event that (as indeed happened) his claim against the reinsurers failed. There was no arbitration agreement between Mew and his brokers, so the brokers had to be sued in separate proceedings in court. In the court proceedings, Mew wished to disclose the interim award made in the arbitration and the reasons for the award, and it was envisaged that at some future stage in the action against the brokers, Mew might wish also to disclose transcripts of witness statements, pleadings and other documents from the arbitration. Hassneh were content for Mew to disclose to the brokers the award and part of the reasons therefore. They objected, however, to the disclosure of the whole of the reasons and to the disclosure of any other documents, and sought an injunction to restrain such disclosure on the basis that it would be a breach of confidence by Mew.

Colman J. held that the scope of the duty of confidence which attaches to an arbitration award must be limited by certain practical considerations, such as the purpose for which awards may be expected to be used in the ordinary course of commerce. For example, a reinsurer may have to prove his liability to a reinsured for purposes of claiming against his retrocessionaire. If that liability has been established in arbitration proceedings, then the most obvious means of proof is a reference to the arbitration award. The judge remarked that any Suggestion that the duty of confidentiality precluded the use of arbitration awards in such circumstances "would be unlikely to be enthusiastically received by the commercial community".

He held further that if it was reasonably necessary, for the establishment or protection of an arbitrating party's legal rights vis-à-vis a third party, that the arbitration award should be disclosed to the third party, either because it formed the basis of the arbitrating party's cause of action against the third party or because the arbitrating party wished to found a defence on the award against a claim which might be made against him by the third party, then in such circumstances disclosure of the award, including the reasons for it, would not be a breach of any duty of confidence.

[25] *Hassneh Insurance Company of Israel v Mew* [1993] 2 Lloyd's Rep 243 (QB Com Ct).

[26] *Hassneh Insurance Company of Israel v Mew* [1993] 2 Lloyd's Rep 243 (QB Com Ct).

Accordingly, the judge made a declaration to the effect that Mew was entitled to disclose to the brokers the award and the full reasons, without any editing, if, as was asserted, this was reasonably necessary for him to establish his cause of action against the brokers.

So far as other documents were concerned, however, Colman J. ruled that pleadings, witness statements, documents disclosed on discovery and transcripts of evidence given during the arbitration were subject to a duty of confidence. Such documents were merely the materials used in arriving at the award which defined the rights and obligations of the parties to the arbitration; and it was the final determination of the rights expressed in the award which was pertinent as against third parties, not the raw materials which had been considered in reaching that determination.

In a further judgment, Colman J. has emphasised that disclosure of an arbitration award and the reasons for the award may be made to a stranger to the arbitration only if such disclosure is necessary to enforce or protect the legal rights of the party wishing to disclose the award.

The judge so held in a decision given in chambers and released for publication only on condition that the names of the parties should be changed to keep their identities secret: the case has therefore appeared under the title *Insurance Company's Lloyd's Syndicate*.[27] The syndicate, having been successful in arbitration proceedings against the Company, which was the lead reinsurer on an excess of loss contract to which five other reinsurers subscribed, sought to send the findings of the arbitrators to the co-reinsurers who, despite the award, continued to refuse to pay their proportion of the sums claimed by the syndicate. The Company successfully applied for an interlocutory injunction against disclosure of the award and reasons to the co-reinsurers.

Colman J. held that the mere fact that an arbitration award and reasons might have a commercially persuasive impact on third parties with whom the reinsured had contracted did not bring the award within any exception to the general rule that it was to be treated as confidential by the parties to the arbitration. For the purposes of coming within the qualification to the duty of confidentiality established in *Hassneh Insurance Company of Israel v Mew*[28] disclosure of the award must be the only way in which the party wishing to make the disclosure could enforce or protect his rights. The making of the award must, therefore, be a necessary element in the establishment of that party's legal rights against the stranger to whom the award was intended to be disclosed.

In *Ali Shipping Corporation* v *Shipyard Trogir*,[29] the Court of Appeal granted Ali Shipping a final injunction preventing the defendant shipyard from disclosing, in arbitrations between the shipyard and third parties, material generated in an earlier arbitration between Ali Shipping and the shipyard. The court recognised that

---

[27] *Insurance Company's Lloyd's Syndicate* [1995] 1 Lloyd's Rep 272 (QB Com Ct).

[28] *Hassneh Insurance Company of Israel v Mew* [1993] 2 Lloyd's Rep 243 (QB Com Ct).

[29] *Ali Shipping Corporation* v. *Shipyard Trogir* [1998] 1 Lloyd's Rep 643 (CA).

there were limitations or exceptions to the general principle that an obligation of confidentiality was to be implied into arbitration agreements and that the boundaries of such obligation have yet to be delineated. The court restated the exceptions to the general principle, namely: (1) consent; (2) order of the court; and (3) leave of the court where disclosure is reasonably necessary to establish or protect the legal rights of one of the parties vis-à-vis a third party. On the facts of this case, the court did not consider that a case of "reasonable necessity" could be made out. The court did, however, observe that to date the exception had been applied only to the award itself and the reasons for the award. In the opinion of Potter L.J., it was clear "...that the principle covers also pleadings, written submissions, and the proofs of witnesses as well as transcripts and notes of the evidence given in the arbitration". In *Associated Electronic & Gas Insurance Services Limited* v *European Reinsurance Company of Zürich*,[30] on appeal from the Court of Appeal of Bermuda, the Privy Council considered the position where Aegis (the Appellant) had obtained an injunction preventing European Re (the Respondent) from disclosing in a second arbitration an award made in an earlier arbitration between the same parties. The court at first instance had granted the injunction but the Court of Appeal allowed European Re's appeal and discharged the injunction.

The Privy Council held that the confidentiality agreement between the two parties should not be construed so as to prevent one party from relying upon an award as having given that party rights against the other. The Privy Council therefore agreed with the Court of Appeal that the injunction should be discharged and dismissed the appeal.[31]

6.1.6. Enforceability of Reinsurance Arbitral Awards: The US Approach

Another noteworthy issue development for reinsurers and cedents alike is the affirmation of the enforceability of arbitration awards, absent manifest abuse of discretion. This issue is crucial within reinsurance, since virtually all disputes are resolved through arbitration. Thus, a losing party can expect little recourse from American courts to overturn an arbitration award.

An illustration of this concept is reflected in the recent Ninth Circuit decision, *Michigan Mutual Insurance Co. and Others v Unigard Security Insurance Co.*,[32] ("*Michigan Mutual*") where a reinsurance arbitration award was upheld that granted certain retrocessionaires a relief beyond what they requested in the

---

[30] *Associated Electronic & Gas Insurance Services Limited v European Reinsurance Company of Zürich* [2003] UKPC 11.

[31] Barlow and Gilbert (2009), pp. 26-33–26-35.

[32] *Michigan Mutual Insurance Co. and Others v Unigard Security Insurance Co.*, 44 F.3d 826 (9th Cir. 1995).

underlying arbitration. The *Michigan Mutual*[33] case reaffirms the legal trend within the United States to uphold arbitration awards.

In *Michigan Mutual*,[34] Unigard Insurance Co. ('Unigard') acting as a reinsurer retroceded its liability to Michigan Mutual Insurance Co. and other companies ('retrocessionaires') under a quota share retrocessional contract. Previously, Unigard had entered into a reinsurance agreement with International Surplus Lines Insurance Co. ('ISLIC') where Unigard reinsured ISLIC and was in turn reinsured for its obligation by retrocessionaires under the quota share contract. A dispute arose between Unigard and ISLIC concerning the terms of this agreement, which resulted in an arbitration award against Unigard in favour of ISLIC for $1.5 million. In its arbitration with retrocessionaires, Unigard refused to divulge any information concerning its dispute with ISLIC, notwithstanding Unigard's claim against retrocessionaires for reimbursement of the $1.5 million claim and for future obligations under that agreement. The arbitration panel found Unigard in breach of the quota share contract and concluded that the lack of information by Unigard precluded Unigard from asserting any obligation toward retrocessionaires for the ISLIC claims. In its decision, the Ninth Circuit noted the anomaly of the panel's award: In this case, the arbitration award is somewhat surprising because its effect is to put retrocessionaires in a better position than that which they would have been had the panel awarded the contract recision requested by retrocessionaires. We cannot conclude, that the arbitrator's award was either completely irrational or a manifest disregard of the law.

In another part of its ruling, the *Michigan Mutual*[35] court determined that the arbitration clause of the quota share retrocessional agreement gave the panel wide latitude to resolve disputes between the parties. The court noted that the contract provided that the parties had to submit 'any' dispute to arbitration with no limitation placed on the panel. The *Michigan Mutual*[36] court determined that when arbitrators are not limited by the terms of an arbitration agreement, they are normally 'empowered to grant a relief reasonably fitting and necessary to the final determination of the matter presented to them'.[37]

The *Michigan Mutual*[38] decision demonstrates the extent to which a court will go to reaffirm an arbitration award. It has telling lessons for parties who are involved in arbitration proceedings. Once the parties are in arbitration, there is

---

[33] *Michigan Mutual Insurance Co. and Others v Unigard Security Insurance Co.*, 44 F.3d 826 (9th Cir. 1995).

[34] *Michigan Mutual Insurance Co. and Others v Unigard Security Insurance Co.*, 44 F.3d 826 (9th Cir. 1995).

[35] *Michigan Mutual Insurance Co. and Others v Unigard Security Insurance Co.*, 44 F.3d 826 (9th Cir. 1995).

[36] *Michigan Mutual Insurance Co. and Others v Unigard Security Insurance Co.*, 44 F.3d 826 (9th Cir. 1995).

[37] Kline (1995), p. 417.

[38] *Michigan Mutual Insurance Co. and Others v Unigard Security Insurance Co.*, 44 F.3d 826 (9th Cir. 1995).

little or no opportunity to overturn a panel award.[39] In arbitrations, no record is kept and the parties' appellate rights are severely limited. Parenthetically, the panel award within *Michigan Mutual* may have been triggered by Unigard's recalcitrance. Unigard's refusal to divulge information concerning ISLIC while at the same time asserting claims against the retrocessionaires in excess of $1.5 million may have been a significant factor in the Ninth Circuit's affirmation of the arbitration award.[40]

6.1.6.1. Appeal of an Arbitral Award in the USA

Traditionally, in the USA reinsurance arbitral awards typically constitute of a very short document, sometimes even one page, most times simply stating which party prevailed either by ordering one party to pay the other a sum certain or by denying the claim for payment. There will usually also exist a statement that all other requests for relief are denied, and some provision for arbitration related costs. The parties may ask jointly a panel to issue a reason award but in most cases at least one of the parties has no desire for that and the panel will seldom draft one unless it must.[41]

An arbitral award is exceedingly difficult to overturn in the USA, and this is even more true of reinsurance arbitral awards which typically have very little content that could be claimed in courts (findings of facts, conclusions of law etc.). Under the FAA[42] a court may not vacate an award unless (1) where the award was produced by corruption or fraud, (2) where there was evident partiality or corruption in the arbitrators, (3) where the arbitrators were guilty of misconduct in refusing to postpone the hearing upon sufficient cause shown or refusing to hear evidence material to the controversy or (4) where the arbitrators exceeded their powers or so imperfectly executed them that a mutual, final and definite award upon the subject matter submitted is not made.

The foregoing bases for vacatur under the FAA have generally been construed narrowly by the courts. Accordingly, even if a court were to disagree with the arbitration panel's findings of fact, conclusions of law, logic or any other aspect of the award, the court could not vacate the award on the basis of that disagreement.

In 2008 the USA Supreme Court ruled that parties may not contractually expand the federal court's scope of review of an arbitral award.

In *Hull Street Associates L.l.C. v Mattel Inc.*[43] the Supreme Court rejected the attempt by private parties to provide in their arbitration clause that the court could vacate an arbitral award if the panel had misconstrued the law or made unsupported

[39] Kline (1995), p. 417.

[40] Kline (1995), p. 418.

[41] Barlow and Gilbert (2009), p. 50-31.

[42] 9 U.S.C. §10.

[43] *Hull Street Associates L.l.C. v Mattel Inc.*552. U.S. (2008).

factual findings. The Supreme Court held that the Congress had set forth the statutory grounds upon which a court could vacate an arbitral award under the FAA and those grounds could not be altered by parties seeking more expansive judicial review.[44]

6.1.6.2. Post-Hearing Challenges to Arbitration Awards

Following an arbitration proceeding, the FAA permits a losing party to seek to have the award vacated. Section 10 specifies that awards may be vacated where: (1) the award was procured by corruption, fraud or undue means; (2) there was evident partiality or corruption on the part of the arbitrators; (3) the arbitrators were guilty of misconduct in refusing to postpone a hearing or in refusing to hear material evidence or of any other misbehavior by which the rights of a party were prejudiced; or (4) the arbitrators exceeded their powers. There also is support for vacating awards if they are in manifest disregard of the law or otherwise contrary to public policy.

Notwithstanding the various bases for overturning an award, a reviewing court has a limited scope. The U.S. Supreme Court has followed the line that as long as the arbitrator is even arguably construing or applying the contract and acting within the scope of his authority, that a court is convinced he committed serious error does not suffice to overturn his decision.[45]

Notwithstanding also the various bases for overturning an award, a reviewing court has a limited scope. The U.S.A. Supreme Court has stated that as long as the "arbitrator is even arguably construing or applying the contract and acting within the scope of his authority", that a court is convinced he committed serious error does not suffice to overturn his decision.[46] In practice, courts have demonstrated a reluctance to vacate arbitration awards.

In *Merit Insurance Co. v Leatherby Insurance Co.*[47] the Seventh Circuit expressed the prevailing judicial philosophy when it stated that the "standards for judicial intervention are therefore narrowly drawn to assure the basic integrity of the arbitration process without meddling in it."

In *International Surplus Lines Insurance Co. v People's Insurance Co. of China*,[48] the District Court for the Northern District of Illinois affirmed an award in excess of $23 million, noting that: (1) "a court cannot disturb an award based on

---

[44] Barlow and Gilbert (2009), pp. 50-40–50-44.

[45] *United Paperworkers Int'l Union v Misco Inc.*, 484 U.S. 29 (1987) (contrary to public policy); Hummer (1996), p. 236.

[46] *United Paperworkers Int'l Union v Misco Inc.*, 484 U.S. 29 (1987) at 38; Hummer (1996), p. 236.

[47] *Merit Insurance Co. v Leatherby Insurance Co.* 714 F.2d 673, 681 (7th Cir. 1983), cert. denied; Hummer (1996), p. 236.

[48] *International Surplus Lines Insurance Co. v People's Insurance Co. of China*, No. 94 C 2838, 1994 WL 502015 at *2–4 (N.D. Ill. Sept. 12, 1994); Hummer (1996), p. 236.

alleged lack or insufficiency of the evidence"; (2) a court may not vacate an award where the treaty has been misinterpreted because "so long as the panel interpreted the reinsurance treaties, the award stands"; and (3) the failure to receive evidence does not justify vacating an award "even if the reviewing court might have decided that issue differently had it been before the court in the first instance or if the arbitrators erred in interpreting the law."[49]

A federal district court in New Jersey described its function in reviewing an arbitration award as "extremely limited," noting that "in reviewing an award, the court should not consider whether the arbitrators committed an error of law."[50] Thus, one of the principal differences between arbitration and a trial is the lack of any meaningful review of an adverse decision. Courts frequently have declined to overturn awards in reinsurance arbitrations, even when the awards are subject to serious challenge.[51]

For example, in *Executive Life Insurance Co. v Alexander Insurance Ltd.*[52] the Eighth Circuit upheld an award that, by the arbitrators' own admission, granted a form of relief not provided for in the reinsurance agreement and not based on custom and practice in the industry. Rather, the award was simply a remedy fashioned by the arbitrators to achieve an "equitable disposition [that] serious and determined negotiating efforts of the parties might have produced."[53]

6.1.6.3. Motion to Vacate an Arbitration Award

Section 10 of the FAA narrowly limits the bases on which a court can vacate an arbitration award. Section 10(a) provides that the federal district court for the district "wherein the award was made" may vacate an award: (1) Where the award was procured by corruption, fraud, or undue means; (2) Where there was evident partiality or corruption in the arbitrators, or either of them; (3) Where the arbitrators were guilty of misconduct in refusing to postpone the hearing, upon sufficient cause shown, or in refusing to hear evidence pertinent and material to the controversy; or any misbehaviour by which the rights of any party have been prejudiced; (4) Where the arbitrators exceeded their powers, or so imperfectly

[49] Hummer (1996), p. 236.

[50] *Employers Reins. Corp. v Admiral Ins. Co.*, No. CIV. A. 90-3147, 1990 WL 169756 (D. N.J. Oct. 30, 1990); Hummer (1996), p. 236.

[51] *La Reunion Francaise v Martin*, No. 93 CIV. 7165 (MBM), 1995 WL 338291 (S.D. N.Y. May 31, 1995) (rejecting claim that arbitrator modified rather than clarified award on remand from district court); *Northwestern Nat'l Ins. Co. v Allstate Ins. Co.*, 832 F.Supp. 1280 (E.D. Wis. 1993) (rejecting claim that a neutral arbitrator had undisclosed "reputational" interest in outcome because he had established reinsurance program similar to one at issue for his former employer); Hummer (1996), p. 236.

[52] *Executive Life Insurance Co. v Alexander Insurance Ltd.* 999 F.2d 318, 319 (8th Cir. 1993); Hummer (1996), p. 236.

[53] Hummer (1996), p. 236.

executed them that a mutual, final, and definite award upon the subject matter was not made.[54] The burden rests on the party seeking to vacate the award.[55]

Broadly stated, Section 10 of the FAA permits vacatur of arbitration awards for egregious departures form the parties' agreed-upon arbitration.[56] Courts do not and will not review arbitral awards for legal or factual error.[57] Grounds for vacatur are extremely limited in order to avoid frustrating the basic purposes of arbitration, i.e. to dispose of disputes efficiently and to avoid the expense and delay or protracted court proceedings.[58] Thus, it should be noted that it is well established that the standard of review for an arbitration award is "extremely narrow."[59] The stringent standard for vacating awards is a necessary corollary to the federal policy favouring arbitration.

As the Fourth Circuit has noted in *Remmey v PaineWebber, Inc.*,[60] a policy favouring arbitration would mean little, of course, if arbitration were merely the prologue to prolonged litigation. In *Transit Casualty Co. v Trenwick Reinsurance Co.*,[61] the court denied a motion to vacate an arbitration award under § 10(c) based on two evidentiary rulings by the panel. First, the panel refused to admit a letter addressed to the cedent's party-arbitrator which the panel ruled had not been timely submitted. Second, the panel admitted an exhibit from the cedent had been tampered with. The court held that such evidentiary rulings fall within a panel's broad discretion and that the cedent had, in any event, not been prejudiced, since it had fully addressed the issues relating to the excluded letter in a post-hearing brief.

In *International Surplus Lines Insurance Co. v People's Insurance Co. of China*,[62] People's Insurance Company of China ("PICC") sought to vacate an

---

[54] 9 U.S.C. § 10(a) (1990); Ostrager and Vyskocil (1996) §§ 14.05, 14-44, 14-45.

[55] *Transit Cos. Co. v Trenwick Reins. Co., 659* F. Supp. 1346, 1351 (S.D.N.Y. 1987), *affd mem.*, 841 E2d 1117 (2d Cir. 1988).

[56] *Hall Street Assocs., LLC v Mattel, Inc.*, 552 U.S. 576, 583 (2008); Thomas and Lyons (2012), §§ 77.04[13][a], 77-137.

[57] *Certain Underwriters at Lloyd's, London v Argonaut Ins. Co.*, No. 04 C 5852, 2009 U.S. Dist. LEXIS 87827, at *9 (N.D. 111. Sept. 24, 2009) (internal quotation marks omitted); *AT&T Mobility LLC v Concepcion*, 131 S. Ct. 1740, 1752 (2011) ("Review under § 10 focuses on misconduct rather than mistake."); *Century Indem. Co. v Fencourt Reinsurance Co., Ltd.*, 640 F. Supp. 2d 626 (E.D. Pa. 2009) ("Courts do not have the authority to overturn an award even if the panel was mistaken in fact, misinterpreted the contract, or made erroneous legal conclusions."); Thomas and Lyons (2012), §§ 77.04[13][a], 77-137.

[58] *Scandinavian Reinsurance Co. Ltd. v St. Paul Fire & Marine Ins. Co.*, 668 F.3d n 71 (2d Cir. 2012); *Liberty Re (Berm.) Ltd. v DH Blair & Co. v Transamerica Occidental Life Ins. Co.*, No. 04 Civ. 5044 (NRB), 2005 U.S. Dist. LEXIS 9774 (S.D.N.Y. May 23, 2005) ("Arbitration awards are subject to a very limited review in order to avoid undermining the twin goals of arbitration, namely settling disputes efficiently and avoiding long and expensive litigation."); *Transit Cas. Co. v Trenwick Reinsurance Co. Ltd.*, 659 F. Supp. 1346, 1351 (S.D.N.Y. 1987); Thomas and Lyons (2012), §§ 77.04[13][a], 77-137.

[59] *Transit Cas. Co. v Trenwick Reins. Co.*, 659 F. Supp. at 1351.

[60] *Remmey v PaineWebber, Inc.*, 32 F.3d 143, 146 (4th Cir. 1994).

[61] *Transit Casualty Co. v Trenwick Reinsurance Co.* 659 F. Supp. at 1346.

[62] *International Surplus Lines Insurance Co. v People's Insurance Co. of China*, No. 94 C 2838 (N.D. 111. Sept. 12, 1994).

arbitration award for International Surplus Lines Insurance Company ("ISLIC") in a dispute involving a number of reinsurance treaties. The court rejected PICC's three-pronged motion under the FAA § 10(a)(4). First, the court noted that insufficiency of the evidence accepted by the arbitrators is not grounds for vacatur. Second, the court rejected PICC's claim that the award was ambiguous and, therefore not final, stating that an award is final and definite so long as it indicates what each party is required to do. Third, PICC's contention that the arbitration panel exceeded its powers by refusing to enforce the reinsurance treaties' Access to Records provisions was rejected because it was within the panel's discretion to allow ISUC to withhold certain documents even if the reviewing court would have acted differently in ordering discovery.

Another issue is whether an interim order rendered in an arbitration is reviewable on a motion to vacate. One court has determined that an interim order which precluded a party from sharing information regarding the arbitration with co-reinsurers who were concurrently involved in separate arbitrations was not an "award" reviewable by a court, but merely a "procedural and largely (though not entirely) discovery-oriented ruling."[63]

In *Yasuda Fire & Marine Ins. Co. of Europe, Ltd. v Continental Cas.* Co.,[64] the court also held that an interim order that a party post a letter of credit, to which the other party to the arbitration had no access, was merely a security measure, and not an "award" but even if considered an award, it was justified under the terms of the reinsurance agreement.[65]

The grounds enumerated in FAA Sections 10 and 11 represent the exclusive bases for vacating or modifying an award. Parties cannot expand by agreement the grounds upon which courts can vacate or modify awards, beyond the bases set forth in FAA Sections 10 and 11.[66]

Some courts have concluded, however, that—notwithstanding U.S. Supreme Court decision in *Hall Street Assocs., LLC v Mattel, Inc.*[67] arbitral awards may be vacated where they are in "manifest disregard of the law."[68] In order to vacate an

---

[63] *Yasuda Fire & Marine Ins. Co. of Europe, Ltd. v Continental Cas. Co.*, 890 F. Supp. 578 (1993).

[64] *Yasuda Fire & Marine Ins. Co. of Europe, Ltd. v Continental Cas. Co.*, 890 F. Supp. 578 (1993).

[65] Ostrager and Vyskocil (1996), pp. 14-46, 14-50.

[66] Thomas and Lyons (2012), §§ 77.04[13][b]–77.04[14], 77-139, 77-166.

[67] *Hall Street Assocs., LLC v Mattel, Inc.*, 552 U.S. 576, 585 (2008).

[68] *Comedy Club, Inc. v Improv W. Assocs.*, 553 F.3d 1277, 1290 (9th Cir. 2009); *Coffee Beanery, Ltd. v WW*, LLC, 300 F. App'x 415, 418–419 (6th Cir. 2008); *Schwartz v Merrill Lynch & Co.*, 665 F.3d 444, 451–452 (2d Cir. 2011); *T.Co Metals LLC v Dempsey Pipe & Supply, Inc.*, 592 F.3d 329, 339 (2d Cir. 2010); *Am. Centennial Ins. Co. v Global Int'l Reinsurance Co.*, No. 12 Civ. 1400 (PKC), 2012 U.S. Dist. LEXIS 94754 (S.D.N.Y. July 9, 2012) ("As a 'judicial gloss' on section 10 (a), the Second Circuit recognizes two additional bases for vacatur: where the award is in 'manifest disregard' of the law or of the terms of the parties' agreement."); *Century Indem. Co. v Fencourt Reinsurance Co., Ltd.*, 640 F. Supp. 2d 626, 628 (E.D. Pa. 2009) ("The court may only revise the arbitration award if it was completely irrational, [or] if the panel's award does not draw its essence from the agreement and the arbitrator is dispensing his own brand of industrial justice, or if there is a manifest disregard of the agreement.") (internal quotation marks omitted); *Wachovia Sec, LLC v*

award under the "manifest disregard" standard, the court must find that: "(1) the arbitrators knew of a governing legal principle yet refused to apply it or ignored it altogether, and (2) the law ignored by the arbitrators was well defined, explicit, and clearly applicable to the case."[69] Courts will vacate awards under the "manifest disregard" standard only in "exceedingly rare" cases, such as instances of "egregious impropriety" or "affirmative misconduct."[70] By contrast, several other courts have concluded that "manifest disregard" is not a separate ground for vacatur, in the wake of *Hall Street Assocs., LLC v Mattel, Inc.*[71] Finally, a number of courts have not yet decided the question.[72]

Brand, No. 10-2111, 2012 U.S. App. LEXIS 3047, at *20 (4th Cir. Feb. 16, 2012) (concluding that manifest disregard survived *Hall Street* as an independent ground for vacating an arbitration award); Thomas and Lyons (2012), §§ 77.04[13][b]–77.04[14], 77-139, 77-166.

[69] *British Ins. Co. of Cayman v Water St. Ins. Co. Ltd.*, 93 F. Supp. 2d 506, 515 (S.D.N.Y. 2000); *Saipem Am., Inc. v Wellington Underwriting Agencies Ltd.*, No. H-07-3080, 2008 U.S. Dist. LEXIS 108267, at *31 (S.D. Tex. Mar. 18, 2008) ("To prove that an arbitrator manifestly disregarded the law, a plaintiff must show 1) the arbitrator made an obvious error, one that was capable of being readily and instantly perceived by the average person qualified to serve as an arbitrator and 2) the award resulted in significant injustice.. . . The term "disregard" implies the arbitrator appreciates the existence of a clearly governing principle but decides to ignore or pay no attention to it. The governing law must be well-defined, explicit and clearly applicable."); Thomas and Lyons (2012), §§ 77.04[13][b]–77.04[14], 77-139, 77-166.

[70] *General Sec. Nat'l Ins. Co. v Aequicap Program Administrators*, 785 F. Supp. 2d 411, 417 (S.D.N.Y. 2011) (awards can be vacated on the grounds of manifest disregard of the law only in "those exceedingly rare instances where some egregious impropriety on the part of the arbitrators is apparent") [quoting *Duferco Int'l Steel Trading v T. Klaveness Shipping A/S*, 333 F.3d 383, 389 (2d Cir. 2003)]; *New York Newspaper Printing Pressman's Union No. 2 v The New York Times Co.*, No. 91 Civ. 4677, 1992 U.S. Dist. LEXIS 7624 (S.D.N.Y. May 22, 1992) (courts will only vacate awards "in the very rare instances when an arbitrator's procedural aberrations rise to the level of affirmative misconduct" causing prejudice) [quoting United Paperworkers Int'l Union v. Misco, 484 U.S. 29, 40 (1987)]; Thomas and Lyons (2012), §§ 77.04[13][b]–77.04[14], 77-139, 77-166.

[71] *Hall Street Assocs., LLC v Mattel, Inc.*, 552 U.S. 576, 585 (2008); *Frazier v CitiFinancial Corp.*, 604 F.3d 1313, 1324 (11th Cir. 2010) [concluding that judicially created grounds for vacating an arbitration award did not survive *Hall Street Assocs., LLC v Mattel, Inc.*, 552 U.S. 576, 585 (2008)]; *Affymax, Inc. v Ortho-McNeil-Janssen Pharms., Inc.*, 660 F.3d 281, 285 (7th Cir. 2011); *Air Line Pilots Ass'n, Int'l v Trans States Airlines, LLC*, 638 F.3d 572, 578 (8th Cir. 2011); *Citigroup Global Mkts., Inc. v Bacon*, 562 F.3d 349, 358 (5th Cir. 2009) ("Manifest disregard of the law as an independent, non-statutory ground for setting aside an award must be abandoned and rejected."); *Ramos-Santiago v UPS*, 524 F.3d 120, 124 n.3 (1st Cir. 2008) (*dicta*); Thomas and Lyons (2012), §§ 77.04[13][b]–77.04[14], 77-139, 77-166.

[72] *Regnery Publ'g, Inc. v Miniter*, 368 F. App'x 148, 149 (D.C. Cir. 2010); *Kashner Davidson Sec. Corp. v Mscisz*, 601 F.3d 19, 22 (1st Cir. 2010); *Paul Green Sen. of Rock Music Franchising, LLC v Smith*, 389 F. App'x 172, 176-777 (3d Cir. 2010); *Abbott v Law Office of Patrick J. Mulligan*, No. 10-4113, 2011 U.S. App. LEXIS 19468, at *19 (10th Cir. Sept. 21, 2011); Thomas and Lyons (2012), §§ 77.04[13][b]–77.04[14], 77-139, 77-166.

FAA Section 10(a)(1) applies to deliberate efforts to deceive the panel and opposing party about material issues. Courts will vacate awards on grounds of fraud or undue means when a party can: "(1) establish the existence of the alleged fraud or undue means by clear and convincing evidence, (2) demonstrate due diligence in attempting to discover the fraud before entry of the award, and (3) demonstrate that the fraud was material to the arbitrator's decision."

Fraud is invoked most commonly in cases of perjured testimony or falsified evidence. Courts have vacated arbitral awards based on fraud where an expert witness presented false testimony,[73] and where a party sought arbitration expenses relating to a treaty under which the parties agreed to bear their own costs.[74] Courts have generally interpreted "undue means" as conduct equivalent in gravity to corruption or fraud.[75] An arbitrator's failure to disclose a relationship with a party may constitute "undue means." An award will not be vacated for fraud or undue means if the complaining party "had an opportunity to rebut his opponent's claims at the arbitration hearing."[76]

Arbitral awards can also be vacated if there was evident partiality or corruption in the arbitrators, or either of them. Evident partiality "may be found only where a reasonable person would have to conclude that an arbitrator was partial to one party

[73] *Bonar v Dean Witter Reynolds, Inc.*, 835 F.2d 1378 (11th Cir. 1988) (vacating award where an expert witness lied about all of his credentials—where he went to school, what degrees he had, and what jobs he had held); Thomas and Lyons (2012), Chapters 71–79 §§ 71.01–79.06, §§ 77.04[13][b]–77.04[14], 77-139, 77-166).

[74] *Virginia Sur. Co., Inc. v Certain Underwriters at Lloyd's, London*, No. 1-10-1753, 2011 111. App. Unpub. LEXIS 647 (111. App. Ct. Apr. 20, 2011) (vacating arbitration award, concluding that reinsurer committed fraud by seeking arbitration expenses relating to treaty as to which the parties agreed to bear their own costs, where the parties submitted expenses to the panel in camera); Thomas and Lyons (2012), §§ 77.04[13][b]–77.04[14], 77-139, 77-166.

[75] *American Postal Workers Union, AFL-CIO v United States Postal Serv.*, 52 F.3d 359, 362 (D.C. Cir. 1995) ("undue means" refers to "equivalent in gravity to corruption or fraud, such as physical threat to an arbitrator"); *National Cas. Co. v First State Ins. Group*, 430 F.3d 492, 499 (1st Cir. 2005) ("The best reading of the term 'undue means' under the maxim noscitur a sociis is that it describes underhanded or conniving ways of procuring an award that are similar to corruption or fraud, but do not precisely constitute either."); *S&B Eng'rs & Constructors, LTD v Alstom Power, Inc.*, No. 3:04-CV-0150-L, 2006 U.S. Dist. LEXIS 73749, at *8 (N.D. Tex. Oct. 2, 2006) ("with respect to 'undue means,' this term connotes behavior that is immoral if not illegal, or otherwise in bad faith.") [quoting *In re Arbitration Between Trans. Chem. Ltd. and China Nat'l Mach. Im. and Exp. Corp.*, 978 F. Supp. 266, 304 (S.D.Tex. 1997)]; Thomas and Lyons (2012), §§ §§ 77.04[13][b]–77.04[14], 77-139, 77-166.

[76] *Biotronik Mess-und Therapiegeraete GmbH & Co. v Medford Medical Instrument Co.*, 415 F. Supp. 133, 137 (D.N.J. 1976); *Virginia Sur. Co., Inc. v Certain Underwriters at Lloyd's, London*, No. 1-10-1753, 2011 111. App. Unpub. LEXIS 647 (111. App. Ct. Apr. 20, 2011) (affirming order vacating arbitration award in part, concluding that cedent could not have discovered reinsurer's fraud in seeking expenses which the reinsured had agreed to bear because fees were submitted to the panel in camera on grounds of privilege); Thomas and Lyons (2012), §§ 77.04[13][b]–77.04[14], 77-139, 77-166.

to the arbitration."[77] The alleged partiality must be direct, definite, capable of demonstration, and the party asserting it must establish specific facts that indicate improper motives on the part of the arbitrator.[78] Arbitrators must disclose to the parties any dealings that might create an impression of possible bias. In reviewing claims of bias, courts consider various factors, including: (1) the extent and character of the personal interest, pecuniary or otherwise, of the arbitrator in the proceedings; (2) the directness of the relationship between the arbitrator and the party he is alleged to favor; (3) the connection of that relationship to the arbitrator; and (4) the proximity in time between the relationship and the arbitration proceeding.[79] "Evident partiality" determinations are highly fact-specific and context-specific. Challenges to arbitrators on grounds of evident partiality frequently involve the following issues:

- *Personal Involvement in the Dispute.* An arbitrator's personal involvement in the dispute at issue can constitute evident partiality.
- *Financial Interest in the Outcome of the Arbitration.* Arbitrators may be deemed impermissibly partial where they have a financial interest in the outcome of the arbitration. However, courts have refused to vacate awards where arbitrators failed to disclose a "trivial" financial interest in a party.[80]
- *Arbitrator's Reputational Interest in Award.* An arbitrator's reputational interest in the arbitration award does not constitute evident partiality.
- *Relationship with Party or Counsel.* Courts have vacated arbitral awards where an arbitrator had close personal or business relationships with a party to the arbitration.[81]
- *Failure to Disclose Relationship with Party or Counsel.* Courts have declined to vacate awards where arbitrators failed to disclose relationships with parties or their counsel that were not close personal or business relationships.[82] In

[77] *Scandinavian Reinsurance Co. Ltd. v St. Paul Fire & Marine Ins. Co.*, 668 F.3d 60, 64 (2d Cir. 2012); Thomas and Lyons (2012), §§ 77.04[13][b]–77.04[14], 77-139, 77-166.

[78] Thomas and Lyons (2012), §§ 77.04[13][b]–77.04[14], 77-139, 77-166.

[79] *Scandinavian Reinsurance Co. Ltd. v St. Paul Fire & Marine Ins. Co.*, 668 F.3d 60, 64 (2d Cir. 2012); Thomas and Lyons (2012), §§ 77.04[13][b]–77.04[14], 77-139, 77-166.

[80] *Transit Cas. Co. v Trenwick Reinsurance Co. Ltd.*, 659 F. Supp. 1346 (S.D.N.Y. 1987) (umpire not evidently partial where he failed to disclose that he owned stock in corporation that had an equity interest in one party, concluding that the financial interest was "trivial and carries with it no reasonable suggestion that [the umpire] would be biased against Transit"); *Scandinavian Reinsurance Co. Ltd. v St. Paul Fire & Marine Ins. Co.*, 668 F.3d 60, 64 (2d Cir. 2012); Thomas and Lyons (2012), §§ 77.04[13][b]–77.04[14], 77-139, 77-166.

[81] Thomas and Lyons (2012), Chapters 71–79 §§ 71.01–79.06, §§ 77.04[13][b]–77.04[14], 77-139, 77-166.

[82] *U.S. Care, Inc. v Pioneer Life Ins. Co. of 111.*, 244 F. Supp. 2d 1057, 1063 (CD. Cal. 2002) (party-appointed arbitrator did not display evident partiality by failing to disclose that his company had 41-year old reinsurance contract with corporate affiliate of party that appointed him, where he had no personal involvement with the contract; the court concluded that he was not "disinterested": "The alleged relationship ... is simply too tenuous to support a 'reasonable impression of partiality.. . . [The arbitrator's] affiliation with a company doing business with a sister company

particular, several courts have rejected assertions that an arbitrator's involvement in professional organizations compromises his or her impartiality. Courts generally acknowledge that arbitrators are often drawn from small, specialized communities and that some degree of professional association among them and certain arbitrating parties is inevitable.[83]

- *Participation in Arbitration Involving Similar Issues.* Arbitrators were partial where they failed to disclose their involvement in an arbitration involving related parties and similar issues.
- *Repeated Appointments by One Party.* Courts have frequently rejected challenges that arbitrators were biased because one party repeatedly appointed them to arbitration panels.[84]
- *Assistance in Appointing Other Arbitrators to Other Panels.* An arbitrator's assistance in appointing fellow arbitrators to other arbitration panels does not evince evident partiality.
- *Opinion on Disputed Issues.* Courts have held that an arbitrator's previous expression of an opinion on an issue disputed in the subject arbitration does not demonstrate evident partiality.[85]
- *Disagreements with Party or Counsel.* Disagreements with counsel do not by themselves demonstrate evident partiality affecting his or her client.[86] Arbitrators do not display evident partiality by ruling consistently in favour of one party.[87]

---

to a party to the arbitration does not establish—or create an inference—that [he] was 'clearly not disinterested.'"); Thomas and Lyons (2012), §§ 77.04[13][b]–77.04[14], 77-139, 77-166.

[83] *Morelite Constr. Corp. v New York City Dist. Council Carpenters Benefit Funds*, 748 F.2d 79, 83 (2d Cir. 1984) ("[T]o disqualify any arbitrator who had professional dealings with one of the parties (to say nothing of a social acquaintanceship) would make it impossible, in some circumstances, to find a qualified arbitrator at all."); Hunt v. Mobil Oil Corp., 654 F. Supp. 1487, 1502 (S.D.N.Y. 1987); Thomas and Lyons (2012), §§ 77.04[13][b]–77.04[14], 77-139, 77-166.

[84] *Arrowood Indem. Co. v Trustmark Ins. Co.*, No. 3:03-CV-1000 (PCD), 2010 U.S. Dist. LEXIS 109782 (D. Conn. Feb. 2, 2010) (rejecting claim that an umpire was partial where, following his appointment, the cedent selected the arbitrator six times as its party-appointed arbitrator, and that the cedent's appointments represented 12–17.5 % of the arbitrator's income over the preceding three years); Thomas and Lyons (2012), §§ 77.04[13][b]-77.04[14], 77-139, 77-166.

[85] *Nationwide Mut. Ins. Co. v First State Ins. Co.*, 213 F. Supp. 2d 10 (D. Mass. 2002) (party-appointed arbitrator did not display evident partiality where 18 years earlier she expressed an opinion on an issue in the case, had *ex parte* communications with one party when such communications were permitted, and the panel denied one party discovery after the panel's interim award); Thomas and Lyons (2012), §§ 77.04[13][b]–77.04[14], 77-139, 77-166.

[86] *LLT Int'l, Inc. v MCI Telecomms. Corp.*, 18 F. Supp. 2d 349 (S.D.N.Y. 1998); Cook Chocolate Co. v. Salomon, Inc., 748 F. Supp. 122 (S.D.N.Y. 1990) (disagreements between arbitrator and one party's counsel did not demonstrate bias); Thomas and Lyons (2012), §§ 77.04[13][b]–77.04[14], 77-139, 77-166.

[87] *Sheet Metals Workers v Jesse Mfg., Inc.*, 900 F.2d 1392 (9th Cir. 1990) (procedural rulings in one party's favor were not evidence of bias); Thomas and Lyons (2012), §§ 77.04[13][b]–77.04 [14], 77-139, 77-166.

- *Procedural or Evidentiary Errors*. Procedural or evidentiary errors do not demonstrate evident partiality on the part of arbitrators.[88]
- *Deliberations by Incomplete Panel*. Courts have declined to vacate awards on grounds of evident partiality based on claims that an arbitrator was excluded from the panel's deliberations.[89]
- *Interim Relief Awards*. Ordering interim relief in favor of one party does not demonstrate evident partiality.[90]
- *Damages Awards*. Arbitrators do not display evident partiality by awarding damages deemed insufficient by one party to the arbitration. A party with an objection to a panel member based on partiality must raise it with the arbitrators, or else the party waives the objection.

Arbitral awards can also be vacated where the arbitrators were guilty of misconduct in refusing to hear evidence pertinent and material to the controversy. Such misconduct must amount to a denial of fundamental fairness of the arbitration proceeding.[91] A hearing is fundamentally fair if there was adequate notice, a hearing on the evidence, and an impartial decision by the arbitrators. Parties are not entitled to the same evidentiary and procedural safeguards employed by courts, and a panel's failure to comply with such standards does not by itself deprive parties of a fundamentally fair hearing. A party bears a higher burden of showing that it was deprived of a fair hearing, if the arbitration clause in the relevant reinsurance contract provision contains an honorable engagement clause, which expressly relieves the panel of judicial formalities.[92]

[88] *Areca, Inc. v Oppenheimer & Co., Inc.*, 960 F. Supp. 52, 56 (S.D.N.Y. 1997) (panel did not display partiality by precluding party's CFO from testifying where it presented several other witnesses and exhibits, and it "repeatedly failed to articulate what important testimony could be elicited from" the CFO, concluding that "evident partiality may not be shown by alleged procedural or evidentiary errors, by legitimate efforts to move the case along, or by failure to follow the rules of evidence."); *P.T. Reasuransi Umum Indonesia v Evanston Ins. Co.*, No. 92 Civ. 4623 (MGC), 1992 U.S. Dist. LEXIS 19753, at *5 (S.D.N.Y. Dec. 23, 1992) (refusing to vacate arbitration award, concluding that panel was not partial where it refused reinsurer's request to postpone hearing made 4 days in advance of the hearing and without justification); *Transit Cas. Co. v Trenwick Reinsurance Co.*, 659 F. Supp. 1346, 1351 (S.D.N.Y. 1987) (denying motion to vacate arbitral award under § 10(c) where panel's evidentiary rulings, in admitting one document and refusing to admit another document into evidence, did not prejudice the cedent since the cedent addressed issues relating to the excluded letter in its post-hearing brief).

[89] *Petition of Fertilizantes Fosfatados Mexicanos, S.A.*, 751 F. Supp. 467, 468 (S.D.N.Y. 1990) (confirming award, concluding that arbitrators were not biased where dissenting arbitrator claimed that he was excluded from panel's deliberations; the court concluded that the dissenter's claims were unsubstantiated and that he was simply "frustrat[ed] in failing to convince the majority of his position").

[90] *Certain Underwriters at Lloyd's, London v Argonaut Ins. Co.*, 264 F. Supp. 2d 926 (N.D. Cal. 2003) (umpire was not evidently partial to cedent by ordering interim payment to cedent, concluding that the reinsurer failed to adduce specific facts indicating improper motives).

[91] Thomas and Lyons (2012), §§ 77.04[13][b]–77.04[14], 77-139, 77-166.

[92] Thomas and Lyons (2012), §§ 77.04[13][b]–77.04[14], 77-139, 77-166.

Such challenges to awards—under Section 10(a)(3) of the FAA—have involved the following issues:

- *New Claims.* Arbitrators have wide discretion over the submission of new claims.
- *Scheduling.* Arbitrators have discretion over scheduling issues.
- *Procedure.* Panels enjoy wide discretion in rendering procedural rulings.
- *Discovery.* However, a panel's decision to limit discovery in areas of material dispute does not necessarily constitute misconduct.[93]
- *Evidence.* Arbitrators have substantial discretion over evidentiary matters, and their awards are rarely vacated on grounds that they improperly received evidence.
- *Granting Judgment Without Holding an Evidentiary Hearing.* Arbitrators need not hold an evidentiary hearing in order to: grant interim relief; grant summary judgment; rule on the preclusive effect of prior litigation; rule on the pleadings; or rule based on stipulations. Finally, they can rule without holding a hearing if the parties do not request a hearing.
- *Consideration of Matters Outside the Record.* Arbitrators are not held to have committed misconduct by considering evidence outside the record.
- *Limited Deliberations.* Courts generally will not vacate arbitration awards based on limited deliberations by panel members issuing an award.
- *Attorneys' Fees Awards.* Arbitrators do not commit misconduct or exceed their powers by awarding attorneys' fees.

A court can also vacate an arbitration award "where the arbitrators exceeded their powers, or so imperfectly executed them that a mutual, final, and definite award upon the subject matter was not made."[94] To establish that a panel exceeded its powers under Section 10(a)(4) of the FAA, a party must establish that the arbitration panel lacked the authority, based on the parties' arbitration agreement, to address a certain issue. It is only when an arbitrator strays from interpretation and application of the agreement and effectively dispenses his own brand of industrial justice that his decision may be unenforceable. Arbitrators are held to have exceeded their powers in the following situations: (a) where the panel was not constituted in accordance with the parties' agreement, (b) where a panel requires interim security as a condition of a merits hearing, (c) where the arbitrators panel has ruled on matters not submitted to them, (d) where the arbitrators have notified key contract provisions, (e) where a panel has awarded a relief to a non-party to the arbitral agreement, (f) where a panel has awarded a relief enjoined by a court order, (g) where a panel has refused to hear certain evidence, (h) where the panel orders remedies not expressly permitted by contract and not resolving issues submitted to

---

93 *Nat'l Union Fire Ins. Co. v Odyssey Am. Reinsurance Corp.*, No. 05 Civ. 7539 (DAB), 2009 U.S. Dist. LEXIS 108318 (S.D.N.Y. Nov. 18, 2009); Thomas and Lyons (2012), §§ 77.04[13][b]–77.04[14], 77-139, 77-166.

94 US—9 U.S.C. § 10(a)(4).

the panel, (i) where the panel issued a non-reasoned award contrary to the parties' agreement.[95]

6.1.6.4. Preclusive Effect of an Arbitration Award

Arbitration awards generally have preclusive effect.[96] After an award has been judicially confirmed, it becomes a judgment of the court, and that judgment has preclusive effect. U.S.A. courts have generally concluded that unconfirmed arbitration awards also have preclusive effect, as well as that preclusion doctrines bar parties from litigating in court issues previously decided in arbitration.[97] A prior arbitration decision is given issue-preclusive effect when: (1) [T]he identical issue was raised in a previous proceeding; (2) the issue was actually litigated and decided in the previous proceeding; (3) the party [against whom the doctrine is being used] had a full and fair opportunity to litigate the issue; and (4) the resolution of the issue was necessary to support a valid and final judgment on the merits.[98]

As a practical matter, asserting preclusion based on an arbitration award may be difficult, because the award at issue may lack specific findings of fact and conclusions of law.

Arbitration awards are generally not entitled to preclusive effects where they have been vacated, or where they do not clearly decide a particular issue.[99] Arbitrators rather than courts have the power to decide the preclusive effects, if any, of prior arbitration awards.[100]

[95] Thomas and Lyons (2012), §§ 77.04[13][b]–77.04[14], 77-139, 77-166.

[96] *Hoeft v MVL Group, Inc.*, 343 F.3d 57, 68 (2d Cir. 2003) ("cases are legion in which courts have refused to permit parties to depose arbitrators. . . regarding the thought processes underlying their decisions."); Thomas and Lyons (2012), §§ 77.04[13][b]–77.04[14], 77-139, 77-169.

[97] *Union America Ins. Co. v Allstate Ins. Co.*, 302 F. Supp. 2d 865, 868 (N.D. Ill. 2004) (enjoining retrocedent from re-arbitrating issues decided in earlier arbitration, concluding that "[forcing a party to relitigate a case which has already been decided once can constitute irreparable injury justifying an injunction"); *Stulberg v Intermedics Orthopedics*, 997 F. Supp. 1060, 1068 (N.D. 111. 1998) ("the court finds that the previously issued unconfirmed arbitration award has preclusive effect on the subsequent proceedings before this court."); Thomas and Lyons (2012), §§ 77.04[13][b]–77.04[14], 77-139, 77-169.

[98] *Bear, Stearns & Co., Inc. v 1109580 Ontario, Inc.*, 409 F.3d 87, 91 (2d Cir. 2005). The issue-preclusive effect of a prior arbitration depends on whether the party against whom the doctrine is asserted was a party to the prior arbitration, or in privity with such a party; Thomas and Lyons (2012), §§ 77.04[13][b]–77.04[14], 77-139, 77-169.

[99] *Brownco Int'l, Inc. v Ogden Steel Co.*, 585 F. Supp. 1432, 1435 (S.D.N.Y. 1983) ("Where a previous arbitration award is ambiguous in respect of what issues were decided, it necessarily has limited value in subsequent litigation."); Thomas and Lyons (2012), §§ 77.04[13][b]–77.04[14], 77-139, 77-169.

[100] *Hotel Ass'n v Hotel & Restaurant Employees Union*, Local 25,963 F.2d 388 (D.C. Cir. 1992); *Weaver v Florida Power & Light Co.*, 172 F.3d 771, 774 (11th Cir. 1999); *Blue Cross Blue Shield of Mass., Inc. v BCS Ins. Co.*, Nos. 11-2343, 11-2757, 2011 U.S. App. LEXIS 25304, at *9 (7th Cir. Dec. 16, 2011); Thomas and Lyons (2012), §§ 77.04[13][b]–77.04[14], 77-139, 77-169.

Arbitrators similarly have the authority to determine the preclusive effect of prior court judgments on issues committed to their discretion.[101] Some courts have noted that arbitration awards are entitled to the same preclusive effect, in a subsequent arbitration, that they enjoy in later litigation.[102]

Arbitrators' application of preclusion doctrines is subject to deferential standards of review.[103]

6.1.6.4.1. Applicability of *Res Judicata* and Collateral Estoppel

Consistent with the strong federal public policy favouring arbitration as an efficient and effective means of dispute resolution, courts have uniformly held that the doctrines of *res judicata* and collateral estoppel apply to arbitration awards to bar subsequent consideration of previously considered claims and issues.[104]

6.1.6.4.2. Requirement that the Award Be Confirmed

The few cases to address the issue of whether an arbitration award must be confirmed in order for *res judicata* or collateral estoppel to apply are divided. Most of the reported cases addressing the preclusive effect of an arbitration award do not reach this issue at all either because the award under consideration was confirmed or none of the parties raised the issue. Some USA jurisdictions (including New York) require that the award be confirmed, while others treat the arbitration award as a final judgment without more.

6.1.6.4.2.1. Majority of Inconclusive Cases

There are a significant number of cases in which courts apply *res judicata* or collateral estoppel to arbitration awards which were confirmed by a court and upon which judgment had been entered, but there is no discussion of whether

---

[101] *Sphere Drake Ins. Ltd. v The Lincoln Nat'l Life Ins. Co.*, No. 05 C 6411, 2006 U.S. Dist. LEXIS 70533, at *14 (N.D. 111. Sep. 13, 2006) ("Deciding the issue of the collateral estoppel effect of the English Judgment was within the scope of the parties' arbitration agreement."); Thomas and Lyons (2012), §§ 77.04[13][b]–77.04[14], 77-139, 77-169.

[102] *American Ins. Co. v Messinger*, 371 N.E.2d 798, 801 (N.Y. App. Div. 1977) ("Fundamental to our consideration of the present appeal is recognition that in general the doctrines of claim preclusion" (fel.8A-12/2012 Pub.60087); Thomas and Lyons (2012), §§ 77.04[13][b]–77.04[14], 77-139, 77-169.

[103] Thomas and Lyons (2012), §§ 77.04[13][b]–77.04[14], 77-139, 77-169.

[104] *Dean Witter Reynolds v Byrd*, 470 U.S. 213 (1985). *Clark v Bear Stearns & Co.*, 966 F.2d 1318 (9th Cir. 1992). *Benjamin v Traffic Executive Ass'n Mastern Rattroads*, 869 E2d 107 (2d Cir. 1989). *American Ins. Co. v Messinger*, 43 N.Y.2d 184 (1977).

confirmation was essential to the outcome.[105] Indeed, a number of these cases contain language which can reasonably be read

as not requiring confirmation of an award.[106] On the other hand, some cases contain language which appears to require confirmation of arbitration awards as a condition for preclusive effect.[107] There are also a number of cases which never mention whether the arbitration award upon which preclusive effect is sought has been judicially confirmed.[108]

6.1.6.4.2.2. Cases Requiring Confirmation

In *Wurttembergishe Fire Insurance Co. v Republic Insurance Co.*,[109] the court concluded that an unconfirmed arbitration award, not reduced to judgment, could not, as a matter of law, be the basis for the application of *res judicata* or collateral estoppel.

In *Wurttembergishe Fire Insurance Co. v. Republic Insurance Co.*,[110] cross-motions to confirm and vacate an arbitration award were filed and then withdrawn because of settlement by the parties. Although the terms of the settlement were not part of the record, it appeared that the losing party had paid the full amount awarded in the arbitration. The court analogized this scenario to litigated cases which settle during trial or after verdict, but before entry or judgment. The court concluded that the requisite finality was not present and that preclusive doctrines did not apply to the award.

In *Pompano Windy City Partners, Ltd. v Bear Stearns & Co.*,[111] the court stated that the doctrines of *res judicata* and collateral estoppel would not apply where the arbitration award had been confirmed, but judgment had not been entered. Even though the award had been confirmed, the court refused to apply the preclusion doctrine until judgment was entered.

---

[105] *Schweitzer Aircraft Corp. v Local 1752, Int'l Union, United Auto. Aerospace & Agricultural Implement Workers of Amer., 29* F.3d 83, 87 (2d Cir. 1994). *Universal Am. Bärge Corp. v J-Chem., Inc., 946E2 n560.*

[106] *American Renaissance Lines v Saxis S.S., Co.*, 502 E2d at 678 (2d Cir. 1974).

[107] *Ufbeil Construction Co. v New Windsor*, 478 F. Supp. 766 (S.D.N.Y. 1979), *aff'd*, 636 E2d 1204 (2d Cir. 1980).

[108] *Clark v Bear Stearns & Co.*, 966 F.2d 1318 (9th Cir. 1992). *O'Neill v Merrill Lynch Pierce Fenner & Smith*, 654 F. Supp. 347 (N.D. 111. 1987).

[109] *Wurttembergishe Fire Insurance Co. v Republic Insurance Co.*, No. 86 Civ. 2696 (S.D.N.Y Oct. 28, 1987).

[110] *Wurttembergishe Fire Insurance Co. v Republic Insurance Co.*, No. 86 Civ. 2696 (S.D.N.Y Oct. 28, 1987).

[111] *Pompano Windy City Partners, Ltd. v Bear Stearns & Co.*, Nos. 87 Civ. 7560, 88 Civ. 7159 (S.D.N.Y. Feb. 17, 1993).

6.1.6.4.2.3. Cases Holding That Confirmation Is Not Required

In *Wellons, Inc. v T.E. Ibberson Co.*,[112] the Eighth Circuit the prevailing party moved to confirm an arbitration award which the other party moved to vacate. Before the award had been confirmed, the parties settled their dispute. The district court found that the settlement agreement, pursuant to which the full amount of the award was paid, adopted the arbitration award, thus making it "final" for collateral estoppel purposes. On appeal, the Eighth Circuit found that the fact that the award in the present case was not confirmed by a court and was modified by a subsequent settlement "does not vitiate the finality of the award."[113] The Eighth Circuit held that collateral estoppel applies when the issues have been fully adjudicated regardless of a subsequent settlement agreement.[114]

6.1.6.4.2.4. Deciding the Preclusive Effect of an Award in a Subsequent Arbitration

Often, the issue of the preclusive effect of an award arises in the context of a subsequent arbitration under the same or similar contract. In those circumstances, a procedural question arises as to whether the party seeking preclusion may petition a court to determine the preclusive effect and bar the subsequent arbitration or whether the determination of the preclusive effect of the prior award must itself be arbitrated in the subsequent proceeding.

The federal circuit courts are divided on this procedural issue. Five circuits have held that the preclusive effect is for a court to decide because the issue addresses whether a dispute exists to refer to arbitration in the first instance.[115] In contrast, three circuits have determined that defences based upon *res judicata* and collateral estoppel, like defences such as laches and waiver, should be referred to the arbitrators.[116]

6.2. Reinsurance Arbitrations and the Issue of the Application of Strict Rules of Law

On the whole, courts which operate within the civil law system of continental European countries have tended to approve of the inclusion of "equity clauses" in commercial arbitration agreements and have been willing to ensure the enforcement of such clauses.[117]

---

[112] *Wellons, Inc. v T.E. Ibberson Co.*, 869 E2d 1166 (8th Cir. 1989).

[113] 869 F.2d at 1169.

[114] 869 F.2d at 1169.

[115] *Kelly v Merrill Lynch, Pierce, Fenner & Smith, Inc.*, 985 F.2d 1067, 1069 (11th Cir.), cert. denied, 114 S. Ct. 600 (1993).

[116] *Chicago Typographical Union No. 16 v Chicago Sun-Times, Inc.*, 860 E2d 1420, 1424 (7th Cir. 1988). Ostrager and Vyskocil (1996) §§ 14-06, 14-46, 14-51–14-59.

[117] Kodwo (1992), p. 29. This has been so, even though there may have been theoretical problems involving the application of equity clauses in various commercial arbitration agreements.

For instance, in its decision in the relatively recent case of *Société Intrafor Coloret Subtec Middle East Co. M. M. Gagnant Guilbert et al.*,[118] the Paris Court of Appeal (*Cour d'Appel de Paris*) had occasion to rule that commercial arbitrators were entitled to avoid the strict application not only of the provisions of law, but also of a contractual clause, so long as they did not infringe rules of public policy (*ordre publique*).[119]

In contrast, common law courts have tended to frown upon and to discourage the inclusion of equity clauses in commercial arbitration agreements and have sought to strike them down. The judgment of Megaw J.,[120] sitting in the Commercial Court, in *Orion Compania Espanola de Seguros* v. *Belfort Maatschappij Voor Algemene Verzekgringen*,[121] ("*Orion Compania Espanola de Seguros*") may be said to have exemplified that.[122]

In that case, a dispute between the parties to a quota share non-marine reinsurance treaty was referred to arbitration, under an equity clause which provided, inter alia, that arbitrators and an umpire were relieved from all judicial formalities and might abstain from following the strict rules of law, and that they should settle any dispute referred to them according to an equitable, rather than a strict legal, interpretation of its terms.

However, the then Commercial Court judge ruled that arbitrators must, in general, apply a fixed and recognizable system of law, and that the parties to a commercial arbitration agreement could not make a question of law any less a question of law by purporting to agree that it should be decided by some extra-legal criterion. Indeed, the relevant equity clause was held to be contrary to public policy and, therefore, deemed to be invalid.

Apparently, a similar approach was adopted by the judiciary in the common law jurisdiction of Australia.[123] However, since the ruling of the Commercial Court in the English case of *Orion Compania Espanola de Seguros*,[124] the English Court of Appeal has on two occasions had to rule on the validity and the enforceability of particular equity clauses in reinsurance contracts.

It is, therefore, necessary to examine the relevant jurisprudence of the Court of Appeal. But before doing so, it should be noted that, even though equity clauses have not tended to feature prominently in other areas of English commercial

---

[118] *Société Intrafor Coloret Subtec Middle East Co. M. M. Gagnant Guilbert et al.*, Revue de l'Arbitrage (1985), No. 2, 300.

[119] Kodwo (1992), p. 29.

[120] As he then was.

[121] *Orion Compania Espanola de Seguros* v. *Belfort Maatschappij Voor Algemene Verzekgringen*, [1962] 2 Lloyd's Rep. 257.

[122] Kodwo (1992), p. 30.

[123] Rogers (1989), p. 156.

[124] *Orion Compania Espanola de Seguros* v. *Belfort Maatschappij Voor Algemene Verzekgringen*, [1962] 2 Lloyd's Rep. 257.

arbitration law and practice, nevertheless, they have tended to feature prominently in reinsurance contracts or treaties.

It has been contended that the prevalence of equity clauses in reinsurance contracts or treaties, over the years, stems "more from a wish to evade certain inconvenient provisions of the then Stamp Acts,[125] rather than from a decision to subject this particular sort of contract to a system of abstract justice." The paucity of English judicial decisions in respect of the inclusion of equity clauses in commercial arbitration agreements generally is, therefore, hardly surprising.

6.2.1. Relevant Jurisprudence of the Court of Appeal

The ruling of the Court of Appeal in *Eagle Star Insurance Co. Ltd. v Yuval Insurance Co. Ltd.*[126] and that of the same court in the case of *Home and Overseas Insurance Co. Ltd.* v. *Mentor Insurance Co.* (*U.K.*) *Ltd.* (*In Liquidation*)[127] may be deemed to be the only two English judicial rulings of note in this area of arbitration law and practice.[128]

In the *Eagle Star Insurance Co. Ltd.* case,[129] the plaintiffs insured big firms of contractors against the risks incurred by them in carrying out their contract works.[130] A treaty or a contract of reinsurance was concluded between the plaintiffs and the defendants in respect of contractors' all risk policies. The contract or treaty of reinsurance contained an arbitration clause which provided, inter alia, that arbitrators and an umpire were not to be bound by strict rules or principles of law, but were to settle a dispute referred to them according to an equitable, rather that the situation was that a strict legal interpretation of the provisions of the reinsurance contract or treaty.

Evidently, this type of equity clause in a commercial arbitration agreement would be likely to be deemed less obtrusive even by the most ardent advocate of judicial review of commercial arbitration proceedings and awards. *A fortiori*, the adoption of a judicial policy of restraint, since the coming into force of the Arbitration Act 1979, would seem to render such an equity clause less objectionable or unobjectionable. After all, the freedom of action allowed commercial arbitrators, in that regard, relates merely to the operation of the interpretative process.

---

[125] Now repealed.

[126] *Eagle Star Insurance Co. Ltd.* v. *Yuval Insurance Co. Ltd.*, [1978] 1 Lloyd's Rep. 357, C.A.

[127] *Home and Overseas Insurance Co. Ltd.* v. *Mentor Insurance Co.* (*U.K.*) *Ltd.* (*In Liquidation*), [1989] 1 Lloyd's Rep. 473. [1990] 1 W.L.R. 153, C.A.

[128] Kodwo (1992), p. 30.

[129] *Eagle Star Insurance Co. Ltd.* v. *Yuval Insurance Co. Ltd.*, [1978] 1 Lloyd's Rep. 357, C.A.

[130] Kodwo (1992), p. 31.

Appropriately, therefore, in delivering the main judgment in the Court of Appeal in the *Eagle Star Insurance Co. Ltd.* case,[131] with which Goff L.J.[132] and Shaw L.J. agreed, Lord Denning M.R. stressed out that earlier on in time the courts used to be very jealous of arbitrations and, thus, would find all sorts of reasons for interfering with arbitrators and their awards; however the approach to arbitration has changed in modern days and courts welcome arbitrations in commercial disputes, encourage reference to arbitration and do not lightly interfere with their awards.[133]

Moreover, in considering whether the Court of Appeal needed to exercise its discretionary power of granting a stay of the proceedings involved so as to allow the dispute to go to arbitration, Goff L.J. maintained that, in view of the fact that the arbitrators and the umpire, by the express terms of the equity clause, would be able to consider the matter more leniently and have regard, more generally, to commercial considerations than would be done if the matter were heard in a court of law, a stay of the relevant judicial proceedings was highly warranted.

Incidentally, the Court of Appeal rejected the view expressed by Megaw J. in the earlier case of *Orion Compania Espanola de Seguros*[134] as to the invalidity and the non-enforceability of equity clauses contained in commercial arbitration agreements. The legal and practical significance of the decision of the Court of Appeal in the *Eagle Star Insurance Co. Ltd.* case,[135] could hardly be underestimated, for, it has heralded a "sea of changes" in this area of the common law approach to the inclusion of equity clauses in commercial arbitration agreements.[136]

Like the *Eagle Star Insurance Co. Ltd.* case,[137] the case of *Home and Overseas Insurance Co. Ltd.*[138] also involved an assessment of the validity and enforceability of an equity clause contained in a reinsurance arbitration agreement. The plaintiffs in the latter case were reinsurers who entered into numerous contracts of reinsurance with the defendants, between the period 1973 and 1981. All the contracts were in standard form of which one clause provided that the reinsurance was only to pay the excess of an ultimate net loss to the defendants. Another clause required disputes, arising between the parties to be referred to arbitration and sought to direct the arbitrators to "interpret this reinsurance as an honourable engagement and to make their award with a view to effecting the general purpose of this reinsurance

[131] *Eagle Star Insurance Co. Ltd.* v. *Yuval Insurance Co. Ltd.*, [1978] 1 Lloyd's Rep. 357, C.A.

[132] As he then was.

[133] Bearing in mind that the latter observation was made just before the enactment of the Arbitration Act 1979, its juridical and practical significance could hardly be underestimated.

[134] *Orion Compania Espanola de Seguros* v. *Belfort Maatschappij Voor Algemene Verzekgringen*, [1962] 2 Lloyd's Rep. 257.

[135] *Eagle Star Insurance Co. Ltd.* v. *Yuval Insurance Co. Ltd.*, [1978] 1 Lloyd's Rep. 357, C.A.

[136] Kodwo (1992), p. 32.

[137] *Eagle Star Insurance Co. Ltd.* v. *Yuval Insurance Co. Ltd.*, [1978] 1 Lloyd's Rep. 357, C.A.

[138] *Home and Overseas Insurance Co. Ltd.* v. *Mentor Insurance Co. (U.K.) Ltd. (In Liquidation)*, [1989] 1 Lloyd's Rep. 473. [1990] 1 W.L.R. 153, C.A.

in a reasonable manner rather than in accordance with a literal interpretation of the language." In 1985, the defendants went into voluntary liquidation, with a number of valid claims by their insurers outstanding. The plaintiffs applied to the High Court for summary judgment under R.S.C., Order 14, seeking a declaration that the reinsurance agreements or treaties permitted recovery, by the defendants from the plaintiffs, in respect of those sums only that had been paid by the defendants to their insurers and reinsurers.[139]

Hirst J., sitting in chambers in the Commercial Court, dismissed the plaintiffs' application for summary judgment and ordered that their action against the defendants be stayed under section 4 of the Arbitration Act 1950, so as to allow the case to go to arbitration. It should be noted that the defendants, indeed, made an application for such a stay of the proceedings, in reliance on the relevant arbitration clause contained in each reinsurance agreement.

In so dismissing the application of the plaintiffs, Hirst J. held, *inter alia*: (1) that the "honourable engagement" clause in the reinsurance contracts did entitle arbitrators to view matters of construction of the terms of those contracts more leniently and with regard, more generally, to commercial considerations than would be permissible in a court of law; (2) that the parties had freely chosen arbitration as the forum for the resolution of their disputes and had freely chosen the relaxed criteria provided by the relevant clause, and that, consequently, it would be unjust to deprive the defendants of their chosen forum and those chosen criteria; and (3) that there was an overwhelming case for granting a stay of the proceedings.

But the plaintiffs appealed to the Court of Appeal against the decision of Hirst J. on the grounds, *inter alia*: (1) that an arbitration clause which conferred on arbitrators a jurisdiction to determine questions of construction of the terms of the reinsurance contracts, other than in accordance with the principles of construction determined by the courts of law, was not an arbitration agreement, within the meaning of the Arbitration Acts of 1950, 1975 and 1979; (2) that the criteria by which the arbitrators were to determine questions of construction of the terms of the relevant reinsurance contracts were irrelevant in deciding whether or not the action should be stayed by the courts; and (3) that, in the circumstances, the action should not have been stayed by Hirst J. However, the Court of Appeal dismissed the appeal and affirmed the decision of Hirst J.Lloyd L.J., maintained that it was implicit in the decision of the Court of Appeal in the latter case that arbitrators, appointed under a clause which entitled them to look to the general purpose of a contract, rather than to the literal interpretation of the language of such contract, might properly reach a result which would not be the same, or not necessarily the same, as would be reached by a court of law, in the absence of such a clause. He pointed out that he did not mean that the arbitrators could rewrite the contract or ignore the language altogether or be a law unto themselves. He conceded that, on most questions of construction, two views were possible. Consequently, he saw no reason why the

[139] Kodwo (1992), pp. 32–33.

parties to an arbitration agreement should not be able to require arbitrators to adopt the more lenient view, even if a court would be likely to adopt a stricter view.[140]

There is no doubt that, in its decision in *Eagle Star Insurance Co. Ltd.*,[141] a unanimous Court of Appeal viewed the inclusion of an equity clause in a commercial arbitration agreement as legally unobjectionable and enforceable, albeit the relevant equity clause related simply to the interpretation of the terms of a contract.[142]

The pronouncement of Parker L.J. in *Home and Overseas Insurance Co. Ltd.*,[143] that he had no hesitation in accepting the submission that a clause which purported to authorise commercial arbitrators to settle a dispute referred to them according to what they deemed to be fair and reasonable, rather than in accordance with settled principles of law, would be legally invalid and unenforceable, may be deemed to be at odds or to be inconsistent with the relevant ruling of a unanimous Court of Appeal in *Eagle Star Insurance Co. Ltd.*[144]

In an attempt to justify his pronouncement, Parker L.J. sought to distinguish the equity clause involved in the *Eagle Star Insurance Co. Ltd.* case[145] from that involved in the *Home and Overseas Insurance Co. Ltd.* case,[146] by maintaining that there was a difference between the two. Yet a look at the two respective equity clauses hardly reveals a difference between them. Nor is it to be overlooked that, in his judgment in *Home and Overseas Insurance Co. Ltd.*,[147] Lloyd L.J. expressed a view on the issue which was diametrically opposed to that of Parker L.J.

Moreover, an apparent conflict or inconsistency between the attitude of Parker L.J. and that of Lloyd L.J. to the propriety and enforceability of an equity clause of the kind involved in that case is discernible.

Unless, therefore, the relevant pronouncement of Parker L.J. in the *Home and Overseas Insurance Co. Ltd.* case[148] is treated as just a dictum, it would tend to undermine the cogent and highly desirable ruling of a strong and unanimous Court of Appeal in the *Eagle Star Insurance Co. Ltd.* case.[149] This would tend to be so,

---

[140] *Home and Overseas Insurance Co. Ltd.* v. *Mentor Insurance Co.* (*U.K.*) *Ltd.* (*In Liquidation*), [1989] 1 Lloyd's Rep. at p. 487. [1990] 1 W.L.R. at p. 164.

[141] *Eagle Star Insurance Co. Ltd.* v. *Yuval Insurance Co. Ltd.*, [1978] 1 Lloyd's Rep. 357, C.A.

[142] Kodwo (1992), p. 34.

[143] *Home and Overseas Insurance Co. Ltd.* v. *Mentor Insurance Co.* (*U.K.*) *Ltd.* (*In Liquidation*), [1989] 1 Lloyd's Rep. 473; [1990] 1 W.L.R. 153, C.A.

[144] *Eagle Star Insurance Co. Ltd.* v. *Yuval Insurance Co. Ltd.*, [1978] 1 Lloyd's Rep. 357; Kodwo (1992), p. 35.

[145] *Eagle Star Insurance Co. Ltd.* v. *Yuval Insurance Co. Ltd.*, [1978] 1 Lloyd's Rep. 357, C.A.

[146] *Home and Overseas Insurance Co. Ltd.* v. *Mentor Insurance Co.* (*U.K.*) *Ltd.* (*In Liquidation*), [1989] 1 Lloyd's Rep. 473. [1990] 1 W.L.R. 153, C.A.

[147] *Home and Overseas Insurance Co. Ltd.* v. *Mentor Insurance Co.* (*U.K.*) *Ltd.* (*In Liquidation*), [1989] 1 Lloyd's Rep. 473. [1990] 1 W.L.R. 153, C.A.

[148] *Home and Overseas Insurance Co. Ltd.* v. *Mentor Insurance Co.* (*U.K.*) *Ltd.* (*In Liquidation*), [1989] 1 Lloyd's Rep. 473.[1990] 1 W.L.R. 153, C.A.

[149] *Eagle Star Insurance Co. Ltd.* v. *Yuval Insurance Co. Ltd.*, [1978] 1 Lloyd's Rep. 357, C.A.

even though Lloyd L.J. appears to have expressed a different view from that expressed by Parker L.J. in the *Home and Overseas Insurance Co. Ltd.* case.[150]

Besides, Balcombe L.J. agreed with the views of Parker and Lloyd L.JJ. in the latter case. In other words, the views of an evenly-divided Court of Appeal in the latter case would not seem to leave the unanimous ruling of a strong Court of Appeal in the *Eagle Star Insurance Co. Ltd.* case[151] entirely intact. On the basis that the relevant pronouncement of Parker L.J. in the *Home and Overseas Insurance Co. Ltd.* case[152] is not treated as a mere dictum, it is arguable that an element of uncertainty may have come to be introduced into this area of English arbitration law and practice.

Nor is it to be overlooked that the apparent conflict or inconsistency between Parker L.J.'s pronouncement in the latter case and the ruling of a unanimous strong Court of Appeal in the *Eagle Star Insurance Co. Ltd.* case,[153] as well as the apparent inconsistency between that pronouncement of Parker L.J. and the view expressed by Lloyd L.J. in the *Home and Overseas Insurance Co. Ltd.* case,[154] would be likely to cause a great deal of uncertainty in the operations of the reinsurance industry.

On the other hand, there seems to be some justification for saying that the relevant ruling of the Court of Appeal in the *Eagle Star Insurance Co. Ltd.* case[155] still represents the binding judicial precedent in this area of English arbitration law and practice. After all, it was a unanimous and a strong Court of Appeal that made that ruling. Moreover, that ruling certainly accords with the principle of the autonomy of the wills or wishes of the parties to an arbitration agreement.[156]

The traditional aversion of the English judiciary to the inclusion of equity clauses in commercial arbitration agreements may be said to have been overcome when the Court of Appeal unanimously came to treat a clause of that nature as legally valid and enforceable, in its decision in the *Eagle Star Insurance Co. Ltd.* case[157] considered above.

However, the pronouncement of Parker L.J. in the *Home and Overseas Insurance Co. Ltd.* case,[158] also considered above, as to the invalidity and

[150] *Home and Overseas Insurance Co. Ltd.* v. *Mentor Insurance Co.* (*U.K.*) *Ltd.* (*In Liquidation*), [1989] 1 Lloyd's Rep. 473. [1990] 1 W.L.R. 153, C.A.

[151] *Eagle Star Insurance Co. Ltd.* v. *Yuval Insurance Co. Ltd.*, [1978] 1 Lloyd's Rep. 357, C.A.

[152] *Home and Overseas Insurance Co. Ltd.* v. *Mentor Insurance Co.* (*U.K.*) *Ltd.* (*In Liquidation*), [1989] 1 Lloyd's Rep. 473. [1990] 1 W.L.R. 153, C.A.

[153] *Eagle Star Insurance Co. Ltd.* v. *Yuval Insurance Co. Ltd.*, [1978] 1 Lloyd's Rep. 357, C.A.

[154] *Home and Overseas Insurance Co. Ltd.* v. *Mentor Insurance Co.* (*U.K.*) *Ltd.* (*In Liquidation*), [1989] 1 Lloyd's Rep. 473. [1990] 1 W.L.R. 153, C.A.

[155] *Eagle Star Insurance Co. Ltd.* v. *Yuval Insurance Co. Ltd.*, [1978] 1 Lloyd's Rep. 357, C.A.

[156] Kodwo (1992), p. 35.

[157] *Eagle Star Insurance Co. Ltd.* v. *Yuval Insurance Co. Ltd.*, [1978] 1 Lloyd's Rep. 357, C.A.

[158] *Home and Overseas Insurance Co. Ltd.* v. *Mentor Insurance Co.* (*U.K.*) *Ltd.* (*In Liquidation*), [1989] 1 Lloyd's Rep. 473. [1990] 1 W.L.R. 153, C.A.

unenforceability of a clause of that nature,[159] may be deemed to have undermined the relevant ruling of a unanimous and strong Court of Appeal in former case may have also—to a certain extent—deterred users of the commercial arbitral process generally, and business or commercial enterprises within the reinsurance industry in particular, which tend to incorporate equity clauses in their contracts with other parties in choosing to arbitrate their reinsurance disputes in England.[160]

In the U.S.A. the position followed in *Hartford Fire Ins. v. Lloyd's Syndicate*,[161] where an arbitration clause purported all disputes to be arbitrated and permitted the arbitrators to disregard all judicial formalities and abstain from following strict rules of law and where no choice-of-law provision existed and where, due to the fact that some of the parties to these contracts were domiciled outside the United States, the arbitration proceedings were governed by the New York Convention, the Court confirmed the arbitration award and held in the first place that the Reinsurers could properly move to vacate the confirmation of the arbitration award based on public policy grounds, because the New York Convention expressly permitted such ground to be a basis for a motion to vacate; however, in disposing of Reinsurers' state public policy argument, however, the Court held that the Convention, as a treaty of the United States, clearly pre-empts any state law or state public policy defences unless the parties have contracted otherwise, which was not done in this case.

Finally, noting that many jurisdictions permit the indemnification of punitive damages while many other jurisdictions prohibit such indemnification, the Court disposed of Reinsurers' national public policy argument, holding that there can exist no national public policy against the contractual indemnification of punitive damage awards.

Further, the court can find no federal authority concluding that such indemnification is against our national public policy.

Hartford Fire Ins. v. Lloyd's Syndicate[162] indicates that an arbitration award of ECO/punitive damages (with respect to reinsurance agreements not containing a choice of law provision) will not be disturbed if the arbitration is governed by the Convention, in spite of the public policy against indemnification for such damages in the forum state or the states in which the relevant claims arose. *Hartford Fire Ins. v. Lloyd's Syndicate*[163] further suggests, however, that a different result would be reached if the reinsurance agreements under examination had included a choice of law provision. Accordingly, insurers and reinsurers may wish to re-examine the

[159] Kodwo (1992), p. 37.

[160] Kodwo (1992), p. 38.

[161] *Hartford Fire Ins. v. Lloyd's Syndicate*, No. 3:97CV00009 (AVC), 1997 U.S. Dist. LEXIS 10858 (D. Conn. July 2, 1997).

[162] *Hartford Fire Ins. v. Lloyd's Syndicate*, No. 3:97CV00009 (AVC), 1997 U.S. Dist. LEXIS 10858 (D. Conn. July 2, 1997).

[163] *Hartford Fire Ins. v. Lloyd's Syndicate*, No. 3:97CV00009 (AVC), 1997 U.S. Dist. LEXIS 10858 (D. Conn. July 2, 1997).

arbitration provisions in their reinsurance agreements to determine, in the event the New York Convention applies, whether it is advantageous to include or exclude a choice of law provision.

It should also be noted that *Hartford Fire Ins. v. Lloyd's Syndicate*,[164] sheds no light on the likely judicial treatment of a similar arbitration award (involving two United States companies) which is governed, not by the Convention, but by the FAA.[165]

Following an arbitration proceeding, the FAA permits a losing party to seek to have the award vacated. Section 10 specifies that awards may be vacated where: (1) the award was procured by corruption, fraud or undue means; (2) there was evident partiality or corruption on the part of the arbitrators; (3) the arbitrators were guilty of misconduct in refusing to postpone a hearing or in refusing to hear material evidence or of any other misbehaviour by which the rights of a party were prejudiced; or (4) the arbitrators exceeded their powers. There also is support for vacating awards if they are in manifest disregard of the law or otherwise contrary to public policy.[166]

Notwithstanding the various bases for overturning an award, a reviewing court has a limited scope. However, courts are reluctant to vacate arbitration awards.[167]

6.3. The Effect of an Arbitration Award on a Subsequent Arbitration Between Different Parties

Generally, an arbitration award is final and binding only upon the parties to the arbitration and those claiming under or through them. The parties, by submitting their dispute to arbitration, undertake to be bound by the award. In what circumstances are the findings in an award binding upon arbitrators in a subsequent arbitration between different parties?[168]

As a general rule, the exercise by arbitrators of their powers cannot affect third parties. In the same way, therefore, their award cannot confer rights, or impose obligations on third parties. In certain instances, however, the decision of one arbitral tribunal may be taken as binding in other proceedings.

This point arose in *Lincoln National Life Insurance Company* v. *Sun Life Assurance Company of Canada and Others* [2004] 1 Lloyd's Rep 737 (QB Com Ct). The question of whether the decision of a tribunal or court could be relied on in subsequent proceedings by a party who was not involved in the earlier proceedings

[164] *Hartford Fire Ins. v. Lloyd's Syndicate*, No. 3:97CV00009 (AVC), 1997 U.S. Dist. LEXIS 10858 (D. Conn. July 2, 1997).

[165] *Hartford Fire Ins. v. Lloyd's Syndicate*, Int. I.L.R. 1998, 6(1), N8-10 Page 2.

[166] Hummer (1996), pp. 235–236.

[167] Hummer (1996), pp. 235–236.

[168] Woolhouse (2004), p. 150.

against a party who was, and where the point in issue was the same in both disputes, had therefore to be considered by Toulson J. when the case came before him following an appeal by Lincoln against an award of the tribunal. In Toulson J.'s view the proper approach, which he considered reflected the modern tendency in cases of serial litigation involving common points but different parties, was to look at what was fair. In the case concerned, the balance of fairness was with Lincoln and on that basis the judge was willing to treat the relevant part of the award in the arbitration between Sun Life and Cigna as binding in the arbitration between Sun Life and Lincoln. Section 58 of the Arbitration Act 1996 provides, subject to contrary intention, that every arbitration award fc final and binding, not merely on the parties but also on those claiming under them. Other parties who have an interest in the subject matter of the reference and who may—if the parties to the reference agree—attend a hearing, run the risk of being found to have assented to or acquiesced in the reference, and should therefore protect themselves by reserving their position appropriately.

6.4. The Facts and Arbitral Holding in *Lincoln National Life Insurance Co v Sun Life Assurance Co of Canada*

Lincoln underwrote one layer of reinsurance for Sun/Phoenix including the Unicover whole account reinsurance. In effect, Lincoln had underwritten certain reinsurance contracts in respect of risks entered into by Sun Life. The agreement covered contracts known as the "Unicover whole account reinsurances" but included a net retained lines clause, the effect of which was to exclude cover for risks reinsured elsewhere. Subsequently Sun/Phoenix attempted to obtain reinsurances from Cigna in terms which were intended to be broad enough to include the Unicover reinsurances. Sun Life also entered into an agreement with Cigna Reinsurance Company of Europe SA-NV whereby Cigna agreed to reinsure certain risks. The scope of the cover under the Lincoln reinsurance was defined in part by the net retained clause; it excluded whatever risks were insured under the Cigna reinsurance. Sun/Phoenix claimed indemnity from Cigna in respect of the Unicover risks. The issue whether the Unicover whole account reinsurances were reinsured by Cigna was an issue directly between Sun/Phoenix and Cigna, but had a secondary impact on the scope of the Lincoln reinsurance. The Lincoln and Cigna reinsurances both contained arbitration clauses.

The dispute which arose between Sun Life and Cigna was referred to arbitration. It was held in that arbitration that the risks reinsured by Cigna included the Unicover whole account reinsurances but that Cigna had lawfully avoided its contracts of reinsurance. In the subsequent arbitration between Lincoln and Sun Life, Lincoln contended that it was not obliged to indemnify Sun Life in respect of the Unicover whole account reinsurances; Lincoln relied on the decision of the tribunal in the earlier Cigna arbitration, which had held that the Unicover whole account reinsurances were included in the Cigna reinsurance. Lincoln therefore argued that the Unicover whole account reinsurances were excluded from its reinsurance by virtue of the net retained lines clause.

6.4.1. The Cigna *Award*

The Cigna arbitrators, after a full hearing and in a reasoned award, decided that the Unicover whole account reinsurances were reinsured by Cigna, but that the policy had been validly avoided. Their award determined the position between Sun/Phoenix and Cigna. It was not necessary for the Cigna arbitrators to decide whether the Unicover whole account reinsurances were reinsured by Cigna, in view of their determination that the Cigna reinsurances had been lawfully avoided. However, it was a point which had been raised before then, and they decided it after they had heard all relevant evidence.[169]

6.4.2. Were the Arbitrators in the Lincoln *Arbitration Bound by the Award in Cigna?*

The Lincoln arbitrators held that the tribunal had to decide what was the effect of that decision and how far did it take the claimant in the Lincoln arbitration. The tribunal then reluctantly came to the view that it had to look beyond the award and reasons for the award rather than simply seek to interpret the decision of the tribunal in the Cigna arbitration.

It did so on the grounds that the tribunal in the Cigna arbitration were not focusing on the issues that had arisen in the Lincoln arbitration and were not concerned with analysing the evidence before them with a view to providing any insight into the issues that had to be decided in the Lincoln arbitration.

The tribunal in the Lincoln arbitration therefore concluded that Cigna never agreed to cover the Unicover reinsurances and could never have been required to pay losses arising from the Unicover reinsurances. This finding was contrary to that arrived by the Cigna arbitrators.

Had the issue arisen in a subsequent arbitration between the same parties, the principle of issue estoppel would have applied. An award can be enforced by way of issue estoppel if a party to an arbitration tries to reopen an issue finally decided in an earlier arbitration award.[170] However, issue estoppel did not apply to Lincoln v Sun

---

[169] Woolhouse (2004), p. 150.

[170] *Associated Electric and Gas Insurance Services Ltd v European Reinsurance Company of Zurich* [2003] UKPC 11.

Life because there was no identity of parties; Lincoln had not been a party to the Cigna arbitration.[171]

Toulson J. had to decide whether the Lincoln arbitrators were free to depart from the determination of rights and obligations between Sun/Phoenix and Cigna as set out in the Cigna award.

Having found that the Cigna arbitrators had addressed the issue of the scope of Cigna reinsurance and reached an unambiguous decision on it, Toulson J. held that the Lincoln arbitrators were bound by the Cigna award and that they were not free to conclude that the Unicover whole account reinsurances were not covered by Cigna.[172]

Toulson J. held that the result was not unfair. Sun/Phoenix had the opportunity of putting their case on the scope of the Cigna cover fully and fairly before the Cigna arbitrators and there was no suggestion that the Cigna arbitrators' decision was in any way perverse.

This was a case in which an award between A and B was held to be binding on B in an arbitration between B and C, and B was stopped from reagitating the issue which had been decided in the award between A and B. In arriving at the decision that the Cigna award was binding on the Lincoln arbitrators, Toulson J. referred to various cases-both where an earlier award was relied upon by or against a stranger to that arbitration. Three of these are discussed below.

6.4.3. Previous Cases on the Effect of an Earlier Award on Subsequent Arbitration Between Different Parties

6.4.3.1. *Sacor Maritima SA v Repsol Petroleo SA*

In *Sacor Maritima SA v Repsol Petroleo SA*[173] disputes arising out of the head charter and the sub-charter were referred to two separate arbitrations. The vessel was chartered by Sacor from her owners Kosan under a time charter (the head charter). Under a contract of affreightment ("COA") Sacor undertook to provide Repsol as charterers a vessel to carry chemical cargoes. At the conclusion of the voyage the cargo was found to have been contaminated with carbon dioxide because the vessel's tanks had not been purged with nitrogen prior to loading. Kosan settled the cargo receivers' claim and commenced arbitration against Sacor under the head charter. The sole arbitrator found that Sacor was liable to Kosan for the acts or omissions of the SGS surveyor appointed by Repsol.

Sacor commenced arbitration proceedings against Repsol and claimed indemnity. The arbitrators found that acts or omissions of both the parties led to the

[171] Woolhouse (2004), p. 150.

[172] Woolhouse (2004), p. 151.

[173] *Sacor Maritima SA v Repsol Petroleo SA* [1998] 1 Lloyd's Rep. 518 [QBD (Comm)].

ultimate loss. Sacor argued that the finding of the sole arbitrator in the arbitration under the head charter that Sacor was liable to Kosan by virtue of acts or omissions of the SGS surveyor should have been treated as binding in the arbitration between Sacor and Repsol.

It was held that there was no principle on which the sole arbitrator's findings of fact or conclusion on causation on the evidence before him in the arbitration under the head charter could be regarded as binding in the context of a different arbitration involving different evidence between Sacor and Repsol under the COA. If Sacor had established in the COA arbitration Repsol's liability to indemnify them, Sacor might have been able to measure their loss by reference to the award in the arbitration under the head charter. But as between Sacor and Repsol, Repsol was entitled to take any point open to them on liability.

Lord Mance noted that the two tribunals, despite their overlapping constitution, had arrived at inconsistent factual findings, but that they did so in disputes between different parties under different contracts and on different evidence. This was a risk inherent in separate arbitrations, where in the absence of consent there is no procedure (as there is in civil litigation) for consolidation of proceedings.

In this case there was no dispute about Sacor's liability to Kosan. What was sought was to take findings of fact and conclusions of causations made in the first arbitration and transpose them onto the second arbitration on the question whether Repsol incurred any liability to indemnify Sacor in respect of Sacor's unquestioned liability to Kosan; that was a matter for determination by the second tribunal.[174] This was different from *Lincoln National Life Insurance Co v Sun Life Assurance Co of Canada*[175] in which the issue in the Lincoln arbitration was precisely the same as in the Cigna arbitration, namely, what was the scope of the Cigna reinsurance.

6.4.3.2. *The Sargasso*

Toulson J. also referred to the decision of the Court of Appeal in *Stargas S.P.A. v. Petredec Ltd (The Sargasso)*[176] in which Stargas chartered a vessel from Petredec as disponent owner under a time charter. Neste chartered the same vessel from Stargas for the carriage of a cargo of propylene under a voyage charter. The cargo of propylene was contaminated with the chemical carried by the vessel on her previous two voyages. Neste claimed against Stargas for breach of the voyage charter in an arbitration proceeding and was awarded damages against Stargas. Stargas claimed an indemnity from Petredec. Clarke J. held that Stargas was

[174] *Sacor Maritima SA v Repsol Petroleo SA* [1998] 1 Lloyd's Rep. 518 [QBD (Comm)] at para. 73.

[175] *Lincoln National Life Insurance Co v Sun Life Assurance Co of Canada* [2004] EWHC 343 (Comm).

[176] *Stargas S.P.A. v. Petredec Ltd (The Sargasso)* [1994] 1 Lloyd's Rep. 412.

entitled to recover damages in the amount of the award together with interest and costs unless Petredec pleaded and proved that Stargas failed to take reasonable steps to mitigate their loss or that the award was such that no reasonable arbitrators could reach on the evidence or was in some other respect perverse.

Clarke J. observed that the position would be different if it was not reasonably foreseeable that the liability of the charterer to the sub-charterer would be ascertained in a particular way or if the terms of the two charterparties were different.[177] Clarke J. noted that (a) in the case of a guarantee of the due performance of all obligations of the principal debtor, the surety is not bound by an arbitration award in an arbitration between the principal debtor and the creditor; (b) as a matter of construction, the guarantee containing general words, although applicable generally to obligations of the principal debtor arising under the relevant agreement, does not apply to an obligation to honour an arbitration award; and (c) the position under an ordinary contract of reinsurance or retrocession, in the absence of agreement, is the same as under a contract of guarantee.

Clarke J. treated the matter as a question of causation of loss and observed: "It seems to me that where the breach of the two charterparties is proved to be the same and the arbitrators have held the charterer under a charterparty liable to a sub-charterer in a particular amount the better view as a matter of principle is to say that the cause of the liability so determined was the breach of the charter-party. Any other conclusion would or might cause injustice to the charterer because the charterer may not have available evidence, which is available to the owner or a deponent owner. On the other hand the conclusion which I have reached does not seem to be unjust to the owner or (in this case) the deponent owner because if he had available relevant evidence which will assist the charterer in his defence to the sub-charter's claim he can make it available to him. If for some reason he does not and the charterers act reasonably throughout, the charterer should in my judgement be able to pass his liability to the owner. That is in my judgment so even if it can later be shown that the arbitrator made an error of fact or law...."

In *Stargas S.P.A. v. Petredec Ltd* (*The Sargasso*),[178] a party to a previous award was relying on the award against a stranger rather than the other way round, as was the case in *Lincoln National Life Insurance Co v Sun Life Assurance Co of Canada.*[179]

6.4.3.3. *Drake Insurance Plc v Provident Insurance Plc*

In this case K was driving a car belonging to her husband, S, when she hit a motorcyclist, causing him serious injuries. S was insured under a policy with

---

[177] Woolhouse (2004), p. 151.

[178] *Stargas S.P.A. v. Petredec Ltd* (*The Sargasso*) [1994] 1 Lloyd's Rep. 412.

[179] *Lincoln National Life Insurance Co v Sun Life Assurance Co of Canada* [2004] EWHC 343 (Comm); Woolhouse (2004), p. 152.

Provident in respect of the car which K was driving and K was a named driver on the policy. K was herself insured under a policy with Drake. Drake's policy contained a rateable proportion clause so that it was not liable to pay or contribute more than its rateable proportion of the claim if there was other existing insurance to cover the same loss.

S made a claim on K's behalf under the Provident policy. After investigation Provident purported to avoid the policy for non-disclosure of (a) a previous speeding conviction for S, and (b) the acceptance of liability by a third party for an accident in which K's car had been hit from behind. S referred his claim against Provident to arbitration under an informal scheme and the arbitrator held that Provident was entitled to avoid the policy on ground of non-disclosure, although under Provident's underwriting criteria the effect of S's speeding conviction would have been offset by the establishment that the previous accident had not been K's fault and the normal premium would have been charged on renewal.

K then claimed under the Drake policy. Drake believed that Provident had been wrong to avoid. Drake then met the motorcyclist's claim and brought proceedings against Provident for equitable contribution. Provident claimed that they had avoided the policy and were not co-insurers and that Drake's own liability would have been half of the claim under the rateable proportion clause so that in paying more than half it had acted as a volunteer. It was common ground that it was for the court to decide whether Provident had been entitled to avoid its policy.

Rix L.J. then described the problem Drake faced as follows: "... in order to show that it was a co-insurer, Drake must rely on the fact (which is common ground) that it is not bound by the arbitration award between Provident and [S]; whereas in order to show that it was not a volunteer and was bound to indemnify [K] against a hundred per cent of her liability, Drake must rely on the fact (which is not common ground) that she would be defeated by the same arbitration award. It escapes being a volunteer on the ground that it is not a co-insurer and claims contribution on the ground that it is a co-insurer."

Clark L.J. held that it was necessary to consider whether, if Drake had advanced the rateable proportion clause as a partial defence to K's claim, she would have recovered against Drake on a 100 % basis or only a 50 % basis. Clark L.J. therefore concluded that when Drake discharged the liability on a 100 % basis by way of a settlement it was not paying 50 % as a volunteer. Rix L.J. described the award as "fact of the world" binding as between K and Provident, to which K would have been entitled to point on the issue whether there was another existing insurer.

Toulson J. referred to Drake Insurance v Provident Insurance to derive the two points set out below[180]:

(a) The recognition that if there had been proceedings between K and Provident, K could have relied upon the arbitrator's decision as determining that there was no cover (whether that decision was right or wrong). This could have led to double

---

[180] *Lincoln National Life Insurance Co v Sun Life Assurance Co of Canada* [2004] EWHC 343 paras. [90]–[91].

injustice to K; first, the failure of the claim for indemnity against Provident, and second, if she had then recovered only half an indemnity from Drake.

(b) The court was clearly concerned to reach a result which reflected the justice of the case and this influenced its reasoning. It could have held that as between the two insurers Drake could not be heard to assert that they were co-insurers for one purpose but to deny it for another. This was clear from Clark, LJ's observation[181] that "...for the reasons given earlier ... Provident was not in fact entitled to avoid. Yet by its argument that Drake paid [K] as a volunteer, it hopes to achieve a result by which Drake remains liable for the whole claim, which in equity should be shared between them."[182]

6.4.3.4. What Is the Effect of an Earlier Determination if It's in a Judgment or a Settlement Agreement?

It should not make any difference to the applicable principles if the earlier determination was in an arbitration award or a judgment.

Had the scope of the Cigna reinsurances been decided by a judgment of the High Court or by the judgment of a foreign court, that would have been binding on the Lincoln tribunal on the question of the scope of Cigna reinsurance so long as the court was a court of competent jurisdiction.

What would be the position if the High Court made obiter observations on the question and did not need to dccide it?

The answer has to be that such observations of the High Court would have carried persuasive weight alone and that the arbitrators would not be bound by such determination.

If the dispute between the parties to the Cigna arbitration had been settled by the parties, rather than by an award, would that have been binding on the tribunal in the Lincoln arbitration?

It is submitted that the settlement, if *prima facie* reasonable, would certainly not have irrelevant in the Lincoln arbitration: the original Cigna policy could have been put into evidence in the Lincoln arbitration to show the scope of that reinsurance and the settlement of a dispute about the interpretation of that policy would have been in a similar position. However, the question of the effect of a settlement upon a subsequent tribunal is not as straightforward as the effect of an award or a judgment.[183]

If and to the extent that an unreasonable settlement has been entered into, the loss has been caused not by the breach but by the plaintiff's voluntary assumption of liability under the settlement. Proving the existence of the settlement thus goes only

[181] *Lincoln National Life Insurance Co v Sun Life Assurance Co of Canada* [2004] EWHC 343 para. [155].

[182] Woolhouse (2004), p. 152.

[183] *Biggin & Co LD v Permanite* LD [1951] 2 K.B. 314; *General Feeds v Slobodna* [1999] 1 Lloyd's Rep. 688; Woolhouse (2004), p. 152.

part of the way to proving the recoverable loss. It would also be consistent with the duty to mitigate a loss to hold that if and to the extent that a plaintiff is unable to establish that the settlement on which he founds his claim has been reasonably entered into, he has to that extent failed to mitigate his loss.

Unless the claim is of sufficient strength reasonably to justify a settlement and the amount paid in settlement is reasonable having regard to the strength of the claim, it cannot be shown that the loss has been caused by the relevant eventuality or breach of contract.[184]

6.4.3.5. The Implications of Lincoln v Sun Life

The implications of the decision in *Lincoln National Life Insurance Co v Sun Life Assurance Co of Canada*[185] appear, *prima facie*, to be far reaching. The Lincoln arbitrators had to give not only persuasive consideration to the Cigna award, but they were held to be bound by it on an issue which had not been necessary for the determination of the Cigna arbitration.

Sun/Phoenix argued that the Lincoln arbitrators were not bound by the reasoning of the Cigna arbitrators nor by findings of fact which did not determine the ultimate position between Cigna and Sun/Phoenix. If the question related to litigation, *res judicata* would only apply to the answers from the previous litigation, necessary to a decision and fundamental to it.

However, the ultimate result in *Lincoln National Life Insurance Co v Sun Life Assurance Co of Canada*,[186] it is submitted, was fair and just. The general principle is still that an award has no effect whatever upon non-parties to the arbitration; it cannot confer rights nor can it impose obligations upon third parties unless they have expressly agreed to be bound by the outcome of the arbitration.

An award is final and binding upon the parties and on "any persons claiming through or under them." This is similar to the principle applicable to decisions of court in personam which only operate as estoppel in favour of or against parties and those claiming through them, but not in favour of or against third parties and strangers.

The facts of each case will have to be examined and considerations of justice and fairness applied thereto. Thus, the arbitrators in a subsequent arbitration have to examine, at the very least, the circumstances giving rise to the first arbitration, the issues referred to the first arbitration, the formal or otherwise nature of the first arbitration, the scope and extent of the arbitrators' enquiry and evidence in the first arbitration, the reasons in the award, etc. Considerations of confidentiality will decide whether the subsequent arbitrators have access to all the relevant materials in the first arbitration.[187]

---

[184] Woolhouse (2004), p. 154.

[185] *Lincoln National Life Insurance Co v Sun Life Assurance Co of Canada* [2004] EWHC 343.

[186] *Lincoln National Life Insurance Co v Sun Life Assurance Co of Canada* [2004] EWHC 343.

[187] Woolhouse (2004), p. 154.

Modern international business transactions typically involve complex webs of interwoven agreements, multi-layered legal obligations and the interposition of numerous corporates and other entities.

In the event of a dispute, the problem of conflicting decisions on the same or related disputes arising from the interrelated contracts can raise its head. The risk can be partially acute in the arbitration arena and, as arbitration becomes an increasingly popular form of dispute resolution and probably the most preferred way of dispute resolution in reinsurance, the question of the extent of the application of *res judicata* and issue estoppel with respect to arbitrations involving multiple parties and multiple contracts has gained prominence in the last years.[188]

The case of *Sun Life Assurance Company of Canada & Ors v The Lincoln National Life Insurance Co*[189] is a case where the English Court of Appeal had to confront this very issue. In *Sun Life Assurance Company of Canada & Ors v The Lincoln National Life Insurance Co*[190] three insurance companies ("Sun Life"/ "Phoenix") had entered into separate reinsurance contracts with two reinsurance companies, Cigna and Lincoln.

Both reinsurance contracts contained arbitration clauses and disputes subsequently arose with respect to both contracts. The arbitration between Sun Life/ Phoenix and Cigna ("Cigna arbitration") took place first and the Cigna arbitration tribunal held that Cigna had been entitled to avoid the reinsurance contracts on the grounds of misrepresentation and non-disclosure.

However, the tribunal also opined that certain reinsurances, then referred to as the Unicover reinsurances, were among the risks that were covered by the Cigna reinsurance.[191]

The arbitration between Sun Life/Phoenix and Lincoln ("Lincoln arbitration") took place subsequently. Among other things, the Lincoln arbitration tribunal had to consider and decide whether the Lincoln reinsurance covered the Unicover reinsurances. It was common ground that, due to a clause in the Lincoln reinsurance contract, whether this exposure was covered depended on whether the Unicover reinsurances were covered by the Cigna reinsurance, apart from avoidance of the same. If it did, the effect of the clause would have meant that the Unicover reinsurances were not covered by the Lincoln reinsurance. Lincoln therefore argued that the decision of the Cigna arbitration tribunal bound Sun Life/Phoenix as against Lincoln, and that they therefore could not re-raise the issue. The tribunal decided this issue against Lincoln and the matter eventually went on appeal before the English Court of Appeal.[192]

---

[188] Mohan and Teck (2005), p. 161.

[189] *Sun Life Assurance Company of Canada & Ors v The Lincoln National Life Insurance Co* [2004] EWCA Civ 1660.

[190] *Sun Life Assurance Company of Canada & Ors v The Lincoln National Life Insurance Co* [2004] EWCA Civ 1660.

[191] Mohan and Teck (2005), p. 162.

[192] Mohan and Teck (2005), pp. 161–162.

In its decision the Court of Appeal found on the facts that the decision of the Cigna arbitration tribunal as to whether the Unicover reinsurances were covered by the Cigna reinsurance had not been necessary or fundamental to its award. This was because the award had been based on the wholly separate issue of whether there had been misrepresentation. Accordingly,[193] an issue estoppel on this point could not apply. This much, however, is straightforward law.

However, the Court of Appeal indicated that even if it had been prepared to find that the decision of the Cigna arbitration as to the Unicover reinsurances had been fundamental and hence binding as between Cigna and Sun Life/Phoenix, this would not have availed Lincoln.

The problem faced by Lincoln was that issue estoppel, strictly understood, applies only as between the two parties or their privies to a decision and does not normally extend to third parties. Lincoln sought to establish that a third party to an arbitral award, in this case Lincoln, is entitled to rely on that award to the extent that it favours him. This principle that had been asserted by Lincoln was rejected by the Court of Appeal.

The Court noted that an award by an arbitrator would only be effective as against a third party stranger to the arbitration, in the following cases, i.e. (a) where the award could be regarded as a relevant fact for the purpose of the second dispute and (b) where the third party stranger had agreed to be bound by the decision of the earlier arbitration tribunal.

Accordingly, the Court of Appeal made it clear that an earlier arbitral award would not bind a party to the award in any later proceedings against a third party and hence it would be free to contradict the finding in an award.[194] This of course, might well practically mean that a party involved in related arbitrations involving multiple parties and multiple contracts but in relation to the same matrix of facts and factual issues could well find himself caught in between inconsistent awards.[195]

It follows from the above that unlike in the case of litigation proceedings where by the problem of proceedings between separate parties in relation to the same matrix of facts and factual issues is resolved either via the use of provisions for joinder of parties or consolidation of proceedings or through the application by the courts of the principle of abuse of process, in arbitral proceedings the same problem cannot be easily solved as there is no automatic mechanism for joinder or consolidation.

Yet, the practical effect is that parties in contractual arrangements involving multiple contracts and multiple parties may well find themselves hamstrung by inconsistent arbitral awards.[196]

One solution would be for parties to rely on consolidation provisions. However, in practice such provisions are lacking in many arbitral rules and legislation dealing

[193] Even as between Sun Life/Phoenix and Cigna.

[194] Mohan and Teck (2005), p. 163.

[195] Mohan and Teck (2005), p. 164.

[196] Mohan and Teck (2005), p. 164.

with arbitration. And even where they exist, the third party must agree to be joined. As a creature of contract, the arbitral tribunal cannot force an unwilling third party to be part of the arbitral process. And while it is possible for parties, in the interests of efficiency, costs and obviating inconsistent awards, to contractually provide for consolidation and joinder in their agreements, yet this may well not be the most appropriate option for the following reasons: firstly, any costs savings may not be evenly distributed between the parties.

Secondly, joining parties to an existing on-going arbitration, or commencing arbitration proceedings with multiple parties raises significant issues as to appointment of arbitrators and the composition of the tribunal.

Finally, where the arbitration involves confidential information that may be relevant only to issues between some of the parties and not all, its disclosure to parties who would not otherwise have access to the information and to whom access is not strictly necessary, would pose problems.[197]

A second solution might seem that parties provide for a single common arbitrator to sit on the different arbitral proceedings and either act as a single arbitrator in all the proceedings or act as one of the arbitrators in each of the differently constituted tribunals in the different proceedings.[198] The appointment of a single arbitrator can however raise issues. The principal issue that may arise is the reliance of the common arbitrator on documents and information on one arbitration to decide issues in the other arbitration where these documents and information have not been rendered as evidence.

Another issue is that the arbitrator may find himself confronted with a charge of bias based on the view that he already had made up his mind in the first arbitration and accordingly failed to exercise his duty to decide the dispute before him in the second arbitration.[199]

A third solution is that parties may wish to provide for issue estoppel in the arbitration agreement. However, this solution also bears pitfalls. For once, arbitration are commonly conducted on a rough and ready basis with more relaxed rules of evidence and procedure whereby issue estoppel may well be inappropriate. Secondly, because issue estoppel can work both predictably where a decision on any one issue can be discerned and because arbitrators usually merely issue a single encompassing award, it will be difficult to apply as any later arbitral tribunal can only imply from the initial award what the decision on any particular issue was.[200]

[197] Mohan and Teck (2005), p. 165.

[198] *Abu Dhabi Gas Liquefaction Co Ltd v Eastern Bechtel Corp.* [1982] 2 Lloyd's Rep. 42; Mohan and Teck (2005), p. 166.

[199] Mohan and Teck (2005), p. 166.

[200] Mohan and Teck (2005), p. 167.

6.4.3.6. Critique

In an ideal world interdependent disputes would be decided by a single tribunal in a consolidated arbitration. However, a tribunal has no power to consolidate proceedings unless the parties agree to confer such a power. In most cases, the decision of an arbitral tribunal would be binding only on the parties to the arbitration and those claiming through them.

The exceptions when an earlier award is held to be binding on a subsequent arbitration tribunal appear to have been made in the following cases:

(a) when the earlier award, under a contractual machinery for dispute resolution, determined the rights and obligations of the parties to a contract A and B, so that the award can be treated as part of the contract and thus proved in the same way as any contract can be proved; and
(b) when the breach of a charter-party and sub-charter is proved to be the same and where the arbitrators have held the charterer under a charter-party liable to a sub-charterer in a particular amount the better view as a matter of principle is to say that the cause of the liability so determined was the breach of the charter-party. By analogy in cases involving re-sale of goods similar principle should apply.

If the earlier determination were in a judgment of a competent court, it would be binding on the subsequent arbitral tribunal in similar circumstances. However, a settlement of an earlier dispute between A and B, unless incorporated into a consent award, might not necessarily have the same effect as an award or a judgment of a competent court. The subsequent tribunal will have to consider whether the settlement was a reasonable one.

There are no hard and fast rules for deciding when the earlier award would be binding in a subsequent arbitration between different parties and indeed, it will be difficult to set out rules which will be applicable to every conceivable set of facts. Broad considerations of what is fair and just should lead to the right answer in each case.[201]

6.4.3.7. German Case Law—OLG Düsseldorf, Beschluss vom 14. August 2007: I-4-Sch-02-06

In an arbitration between the parties in respect of disputes arising out of reinsurance agreements, the arbitral tribunal (consisting of three arbitrators), following an oral hearing on 18 and 19 January 2005, had issued an arbitral award dated 9 May 2005, dismissing the claim. Counsel for claimant received a copy of the award, signed by one arbitrator only, on 11 May 2005.

---

[201] Woolhouse (2004), p. 156.

Claimant requested that the proceedings be reopened and argued that the award was void because it was signed by one arbitrator only. Furthermore it requested correction, interpretation and supplementation of the award, since the tribunal had not ruled on a subsidiary claim raised by it. On 28 July 2005, the arbitral tribunal transmitted to the parties an award signed by all three arbitrators, still dated 9 May 2005 and which was identical in content to the award transmitted to the parties on 11 May 2005.

Claimant requested that the proceedings be reopened and argued that the award was void because it was signed by one arbitrator only. Furthermore it requested correction, interpretation and supplementation of the award, since the tribunal had not ruled on a subsidiary claim raised by it. On 28 July 2005, the arbitral tribunal transmitted to the parties an award signed by all three arbitrators, still dated 9 May 2005 and which was identical in content to the award transmitted to the parties on 11 May 2005. The proceeding to supplement the award is not yet concluded.

The Düsseldorf Higher Regional Court (OLG) set aside the award transmitted on 28 July 2005. It held that the fact that the procedure to supplement the award was not yet concluded did not preclude a request to set aside the award. The claimant had a legally recognized interest in having a detrimental and procedurally defective decision reviewed. This applied in any event if the time-limit provided for the procedure to supplement the award (Sec. 1058 sub. 3 Code of Civil Procedure—ZPO) was substantially exceeded.

The court held that an arbitral award pursuant to Sec. 1054 sub. 4 ZPO required the signature of all arbitrators. Until the award carried the signature of all arbitrators, the award—for lack of formal issuance—was not binding. In the present case, the award was therefore formally issued by the arbitral tribunal on 28 July 2005.

The court held furthermore that the arbitral tribunal had violated the principle of due process. In transmitting the award without deciding on the requests of the claimant for interpretation and supplementation, the arbitral tribunal had not given due consideration to the claimant's arguments. The tribunal had also not decided on the subsidiary request of the claimant. This violation of the due process affected the decision of the arbitral tribunal.

The tribunal's decision could not be rendered in the form of a partial award, because it could not be excluded that the decision to be rendered in respect of the supplementary award would also affect the partial decision already issued by the arbitral tribunal. The court referred the matter back to the arbitral tribunal for a renewed decision.

6.5. Conclusions

Following the arbitral award, a party to arbitral proceedings may, upon notice to the other parties and to the tribunal, make an application to court to vary or set aside an award, either on the basis that the tribunal lacked substantive jurisdiction or due to the proceedings serious irregularity. The grounds of serious irregularity range from the failure by the tribunal to comply with its general duties of fairness, impartiality and the adoption of suitable procedures, through failure to deal with all issues put to it and uncertainty or ambiguity as to the effect of the award, to the award's being obtained by fraud or in a manner contrary to public policy. In the reinsurance industry another issue for reinsurers and cedents alike is the affirmation of the enforceability of arbitration awards, absent manifest abuse of discretion. The *Michigan Mutual*[202] decision demonstrates the extent to which a court will go to reaffirm an arbitration award.

References

Barlow L, Gilbert LLP (2009) Reinsurance practice and the law. Informa, London
Hummer PM (1996) Reinsurance arbitrations from start to Finish: a practitioner's guide. Def Couns J 63:228
Kanefsky EP, Diubaldo RW (2009) Notable 2009 U.S. reinsurance arbitration decisions. Insur Reinsur Rev. www.edwardswildman.com/insights/PublicationDetail.aspx?publication=1914
Kline CG (1995) Recent US direct insurance and reinsurance decisions: their impact on Europe. Int ILR 3(12):414–418
Kodwo BJ (1992) Commercial arbitrators authorised not to apply strict rules of law and judicial review. J Bus Law 4:26–38
Mohan RC, Teck LW (2005) Some contractual approaches to the problem of inconsistent awards in multi-party, multi-contract arbitration proceedings. Asian Int Arbitration J 1(2):161–162
Ostrager BR, Vyskocil MC (1996) Modern reinsurance law and practice. Glasser Legal Works, Little Falls
Rogers AJ (1989) Contemporary problems in international commercial arbitration. Int Bus Lawyer 17:156
Thomas JE, Lyons S (eds) (2012) New Appleman on insurance law – library edition, vol 7, Property insurance (chapters 71–79 §§ 71.01–79.06). Lexis Nexis, Los Angeles
Woolhouse SP (2004) The effect of an arbitration award on subsequent arbitration between different parties – an English law perspective. Int ALR 7(5):150–156

[202] *Michigan Mutual Insurance Co. and Others v Unigard Security Insurance Co.*, 44 F.3d 826 (9th Cir. 1995).

Discussion

Fair, efficient and reliable dispute resolution procedures are vital to protect the rights and clarify the duties of parties arising under reinsurance contracts. Reinsurance dispute resolution practices, and especially arbitration, enable parties to enforce their rights under reinsurance contracts. Party autonomy allows parties to make certain decisions relating to the conduct of the reinsurance arbitration. Hence parties may choose the rules to govern their arbitration proceedings. Also, courts will enforce the parties' agreements with respect to arbitrator selection, and arbitration award enforcement.

7.1 General Remarks

Industry custom and practice play a role in connection with both how a reinsurance relationship comes into being and how reinsurance contract is interpreted. Notwithstanding that reinsurance contracts often involve substantial exposures, such contracts can—consistent with industry custom and practice—be based on a single page "slip" outlining only the basic details of the parties' relationship. Standard and manuscript terms are used in reinsurance contracts.

In facultative reinsurance contracts, it is common to incorporate standard terms from the insurance policy issued by the cedent to the underlying insured. In treaty reinsurance contracts, the parties may employ standard terms, manuscript terms, or some combination of both. A reinsurer's acceptance of a placement slip creates a binding reinsurance contract. A slip usually contains just the essential elements of parties' contract, such as the type of risk, the sum and the limit to be reinsured as well as the cedent's retention and the premium to be paid to the reinsurer. The effect of formal reinsurance wording and the interaction between such wording and between a slip to which the parties agreed originally, does not exclude and amendments agreed by the parties through an endorsement or rider.

Regarding the construction and interpretation of reinsurance contracts, any interpretation should begin with the application of general contract principles. If

K. Noussia, *Reinsurance Arbitrations*, DOI 10.1007/978-3-642-45146-1_7,

the language of the contract is ambiguous, one should thereafter look into extrinsic evidence, such as the drafting history or the industry custom and practice, the intent of the parties and the purpose of the contractual relationship. Certain presumptions apply in the reinsurance context, such as the fact that, as with any commercial contract, most courts will apply a standard of good faith and fair dealing to all parties to the reinsurance contract. However, there are also instances where a tribunal might apply a higher standard of utmost good faith to the reinsurance relationship. In addition, custom and practice play pivotally important roles in the reinsurance context. The slip plays a central role in constructing and interpreting the reinsurance contract. The slip may be the only written document establishing the reinsurance relationship, or there may also be a written document following the slip, in which case the terms of the slip might be used to aid in the interpretation if the terms of the final written document are ambiguous.

Regarding the incorporation of terms, specific considerations might apply in relation to the incorporation of underlying documents and terms. In *HIH Casualty & General Insurance v New Hampshire Insurance Company*[1] the London appellate tribunal laid out the considerations for determining whether a specific term should be incorporated into the reinsurance contract.

One of the critical steps in reaching a proper legal interpretation of any reinsurance contract is accurately determining which jurisdiction's law will govern the resolution of any legal dispute. If a reinsurance contract has an express choice of law provision, providing for the application of a particular jurisdiction's law to any disputes arising under the reinsurance contract, this provision will virtually always be enforced by courts and arbitral tribunals. However, in determining the appropriate choice of law resolution, one must first confirm the nature of the legal dispute in which the potential choice of law dispute arises. If the choice of law issue concerns a matter of substantive law, there are different issues which need to be considered than if the issue concerns a matter of procedural law. In any event, in the context of arbitration, arbitrators sometimes view themselves as not bound by the strict rules of law and elect not to make any formal choice of law determination.

There are some key provisions which are common to reinsurance contracts and which collectively define and delineate the nature and scope of the indemnification obligations assumed by the reinsurer and the corresponding duties of the reinsured and reinsurer which are of critical importance to their relationship. Most notably, the terms addressed include the terms relating to the duties of the parties in the event of a loss or claim under the reinsurance (e.g. "Follow the Settlements", "Follow the Fortunes").

The express provisions found in reinsurance contracts apart, some of the more significant duties and responsibilities of a reinsurance contract may actually be implied. Of the most frequently discussed implied terms arising from reinsurance contracts are the doctrines of "Follow the Settlements" and "Follow the Fortunes".

[1] *HIH Casualty and General Insurance Ltd* v *New Hampshire Insurance Co* [2001] 2 Lloyd's Rep 161.

A majority of courts have considered that absent specific custom and practice evidence showing otherwise, these concepts are not implied as a matter of law. However, it has also been suggested that the doctrines of "Follow the Settlements" and "Follow the Fortunes" can be implied in a reinsurance contract, where an express "Follow the Settlements" or "Follow the Fortunes" clause is not explicitly present and where there is sufficient evidence of an industry custom and practice or a particular course of dealing between the contracting parties.[2]

7.2 Overall Conclusions in Relation to Arbitration

7.2.1 An Overview

Adequate, fast and trustworthy dispute resolution procedures are vital to protect the rights and clarify the duties of parties arising under reinsurance contracts. Prior to the case where a reinsurance dispute has arisen, the duty of utmost good faith binds both cedents and reinsurers.

In relation to the parties' choice of forum in reinsurance disputes, the reinsurance industry—due to the certain advantages of arbitration—has historically favoured it over litigation.

In effect, arbitration is deemed to provide more expert, expeditious, cost-effective, and private and confidential proceedings. Not least, courts routinely enforce agreements to arbitrate. They have held that the words "arbitration" or "arbitration clause" can constitute an enforceable arbitration agreement, especially when supplemented by reinsurance industry custom and practice.

In general, arbitral panels enforce parties' agreement relating to the substantive law governing their reinsurance contracts. Parties are also free to agree on the procedures to govern their arbitrations.

Like other, reinsurance arbitrations are private and confidential. Re the awards, arbitrators may issue interim awards, if the parties agree, prior to issuing the final one granting or denying the relief requested. Finally, arbitral awards have a preclusive effect.

7.2.2 General Observations in Relation to Reinsurance Arbitrations

Reinsurance dispute resolution practices, and especially arbitration, enable parties to enforce their rights under reinsurance contracts.

[2] Thomas and Lyons (2012), Abstract, 72-2.

The duty of utmost good faith binds both cedents and reinsurers.

Regarding discoverability of reinsurance information, courts disagree whether reinsurance information is discoverable. On the one hand discovery is permitted, especially when reinsurance information furnished evidence relating to bad faith, late notice, lost policies, policy interpretation, reasonableness of the settlement, or rescission. On the other hand reinsurance information and files are held not to be discoverable, because they are irrelevant or protected by confidentiality, attorney-client privilege, work product, or by the common interest doctrine. The golden line lies somewhere in between. Several courts have also concluded that as far as a reinsurer's right to access records of a cedent under an "access to records" clause in the reinsurance contract, the act of requiring cedents to provide factual information relevant to the underlying claim or its handling does not necessarily also entitle a reinsurer to discover a cedent's privileged documents.

The reinsurance industry has historically been a strong supporter of arbitration, due to the fact that arbitration entails in its nature a concise, precise and confidential nature. Notwithstanding the above advantages, it should also be mentioned that litigation also offers some other advantages such as a greater power to obtain provisional relief, a far more extensive discovery, the ability to join related parties, the value of the existence of precedent and the uniformity of the result reached. It is to be noted that litigation is used more often in relation to facultative reinsurance certificates than in the case of reinsurance treaties.[3]

As far as enforceability of reinsurance arbitrations clauses is concerned, courts decide whether parties are bound by an arbitration clause, as well as the scope of the issues to be arbitrated. Courts also will routinely enforce agreements to arbitrate. Courts in the USA and in England have held that even a simple wording purporting to arbitration is enough to constitute a valid and enforceable arbitration agreement when supplemented by reinsurance industry custom and practice, and have compelled arbitration against non-signatories under theories of agency, estoppel, incorporation, third-party beneficiary and veil-piercing. Although parties can waive their rights to arbitrate claims, courts do not readily find waiver, not least because of the strong federal policy in the USA and the analogous position in favour of arbitration in England. If the parties' agreement contains an arbitration provision, courts generally compel arbitration of claims that a party breached the reinsurance contract. In addition, contract formation issues, such as claims of fraudulent inducement, rescission and reformation, are arbitrable where the arbitration clause is broad, unless the fraud was directed at the arbitration clause itself. Extra-contractual claims are also generally arbitrable when the arbitration clause is broad and the relevant claims arise from the parties' contract. In general, arbitration panels enforce parties' agreements relating to the substantive law governing their reinsurance contracts.[4]

---

[3] Thomas and Lyons (2012), Abstract, 77-2.

[4] Thomas and Lyons (2012), Abstract, 77-4.

Courts will also enforce parties' agreements with respect to arbitrator selection of arbitrators. To varying degrees and depending also on the dispute at issue, parties and courts seek in reinsurance arbitrators the following attributes: industry experience, arbitration experience, legal experience, competence, integrity, impartiality, persuasive ability and availability. Arbitrators should make full disclosures at the start of an arbitration and should continue to disclose pertinent information throughout the proceedings as necessary. All arbitrators, whether party-appointed or neutral, must remain open-minded and participate in the arbitration process in a fair, honest and good faith manner. Although a neutral must be impartial, it is generally understood in the reinsurance industry that party-appointed arbitrators may be predisposed initially to the party that appointed them. Most courts do not permit challenges to arbitrators on grounds of bias before a panel issues its award. Nonetheless a few courts have disqualified arbitrators pre-award i.e. if the arbitrator's appointment breaches the contract, or if the arbitrator's bas is blatant, or if the arbitrator committed "over misconduct".[5]

Arbitrators have the authority to order interim relief in aid of arbitration proceedings, absent contrary agreement of the parties. Courts have the concurrent authority to order also provisional relief in connection with arbitration proceedings, absent contrary agreement of the parties.

Parties are free to agree to the procedures that will govern their arbitrations. In general—under the FAA, U.S.A. state legislation, the Arbitration Act 1996, the UNCITRAL Model Law and the rules of various trade organizations, arbitrators have the power to decide issues relating to provisional remedies, consolidation, choice of forum, choice of law, scheduling, evidence-taking and disclosure, bifurcation, appointment of experts, and granting judgment without an evidentiary hearing. Courts generally hold that arbitrators may decide to consolidate arbitral proceedings. Reinsurance arbitral panels also have broad discretion over disclosure and evidence-taking, limited only by the requirement that they afford parties fundamental fairness. Arbitrators have also broad discretion over the conduct of an evidentiary hearing, including authority with respect to the location of the hearing, bifurcation of proceedings, admissions, evidence, taking adverse inferences, granting judgment without a hearing, and deciding defenses such as waiver and estoppel. Confidentiality is also an important element of arbitration proceedings and awards. Arbitration proceedings themselves are private and third parties are not admitted. However, the confidentiality of arbitration materials may be undermined by a party's failure to adhere to confidentiality requirements, subsequent court proceedings to confirm, modify or vacate an arbitration award, or regulatory inquiries.[6]

Re arbitration awards, arbitrators have the authority to issue interim awards, absent contrary agreement of the parties, and later on a final award granting or denying the relief requested. In addition, arbitrators have the authority to rule on

[5] Thomas and Lyons (2012), Abstract, 77-4.

[6] Thomas and Lyons (2012), Abstract, 77-5.

summary adjudication in appropriate cases, absent agreement to the contrary. Arbitrators have also wide discretion to award remedies when the arbitration clause is broad, including the powers to award: declaratory relief; equitable relief such as rescission and reformation; damages; disgorgement; interest; attorney's fees and costs as well as punitive damages.[7] Arbitral awards have a preclusive effect. In relation to the enforcement of arbitration awards, parties seeking court confirmation of reinsurance awards must establish subject-matter jurisdiction. Courts can also enforce interim awards. In relation to vacatur of arbitral awards, courts may vacate arbitral awards only for egregious departures from the parties' agreed-upon arbitration.[8]

7.3 More Specific Observations: Critique

Reinsurance is a transaction in which the primary insurer cedes all or part of a risk of loss to the reinsurer and the latter, in return for agreeing to indemnify the reinsured for losses that may occur, receives a premiums from the reinsured. Reinsurance contracts often contain an arbitration clause stipulating that should a dispute arise, it will be resolved via arbitration.

Although fundamentally there is no real difference between litigation and arbitration, as both are proceedings where a neutral third party decides the dispute between the parties and issues a binding decision, nevertheless there are dramatic practical differences to be noted between litigation and arbitration, the biggest difference being the decider of the dispute which, in arbitration, is an arbitrator or a panel of arbitrators, often experts from the reinsurance industry sector. Parties in arbitration, contrary to state court litigation, are also free to decide on the rules to govern their dispute. Such rules may come from arbitral bodies or parties may agree to form them on an *ad hoc* basis. Flexibility of the process is also another significant advantage of arbitration over litigation, as parties may liberally agree for the place of the hearing or that the documents to be procured for the conduct of the case. This is justified due to the private, confidential, and consensual character of the arbitral proceedings.

The above apart, there are also other reasons for the reinsurance industry's preference for arbitration. This preference is justified by the very nature of reinsurance contracts, for treaties are special commercial contracts, usually drafted by knowledgeable lawyers and cover numerous contingencies. Arbitrations are much more amicable as a process, if compared to litigation, and discovery is more restrictive, hence less extensive as well as predicated on confidentiality. Most arbitration awards remain known only to the parties involved, i.e. they are not published, and do not serve as precedent. Reinsurance arbitrations are also very

[7] Thomas and Lyons (2012), Abstract, 77-5.

[8] Thomas and Lyons (2012), Abstracts, 77-5, 77-6.

flexible, in terms of procedure and are conducted often on an informal *ad hoc* basis that the parties elect and are characterised *inter alia* by speed, flexibility and efficiency. In that sense also, reinsurance arbitrations embrace the use of expert adjudication. This together with the fact that reinsurance arbitrations provide adjudication by industry experts offers parties a system of alternative resolution of business disputes, tempered by industry custom and practice, rather than strictly legal decisions. In effect, parties result in having much more trust and confidence in the ultimate awards rendered by expert adjudicators, not least also because—the arbitrators being industry experts—will have more flexibility in arriving at an award, for they will apply the customs and practices of the industry in fashioning their decision. Parties may also prefer arbitration over litigation in the context of international reinsurance disputes as arbitration agreements and awards are generally more easily enforced.

Notwithstanding the above advantages, there are also some disadvantages often cited: the finality of the award of the arbitral tribunal is often cited as a disadvantage, since no appeals process exists for arbitration proceedings. In addition, the character of arbitration proceedings with lack of precedent or uniformity in decisions, is also at time disadvantageous, especially in cases where the same exact issue is being decided by an arbitral panel in an entirely different way than by another panel. Another often cited disadvantage is the arbitration's virtual unassailability, as there is virtually no recourse for a losing party in arbitration and there is also little or no recourse to overturn an award on appeal, as this has also been reflected in the reflected in the USA decision of the Ninth Circuit in *Michigan Mutual Insurance Company and Others v Unigard Security Insurance Company.*[9]

Perhaps a solution to the above would be for parties to include an as much detailed as possible arbitration clause in the reinsurance agreement, covering as many issues as possible. Notwithstanding the above factors, still most of the reinsurance disputes continue to be resolved through settlement or arbitration.

Cedent companies and reinsurers may draft arbitration clauses as they desire. English courts have held that general words of incorporation are not sufficient to incorporate an arbitration clause as demonstrated in the ruling in *Excess Insurance Company v Mander.*[10] A narrowly drawn arbitration clause will render only the specific issues within its scope as arbitrable[11] ones, hence parties should pay extra attention in broadly drafting such clauses as in this way the arbitration clauses may also encompass extra-contractual claims.[12]

[9] *Michigan Mutual Insurance Company and Others v Unigard Security Insurance Company*, 44 F.3d 826 (9th Cir. 1995).

[10] *Excess Insurance Company v Mander* [1995] L.R.L.R. 385.

[11] *McDonnell Douglas Finance Corp. v Pennsylvania Power & Light Co.*, 858 E2d 825,832 (2d Cir. 1988). *Associated Brich Mason Contractors of Greater N.Y, Inc. v Harrington*, 820 F.2d 31,35 (2d Cir. 1987). *Prudential Lines, Inc. v Exxon Corp., Associated Indemnity Corp. v Home Insurance Co.*, 19 F.3d 1432 (6th Cir. 1994)704 F.2d 59, 64 (2d Cir. 1983); Ostrager and Vyskocil (1996), §§ 14-01, 14-6, 14-7.

[12] *Prima Paint Corp. v Flood & Conklin Manufacturing Co.*, 388 U.S. 395.

Serious problems may arise if the parties' have not clearly expressed their intentions regarding the scope of arbitration. In the case law, the predominant position is that any doubt concerning the scope of arbitrable issues should be resolved in favour of arbitration and there is also a clearly expressed tendency to support the conclusion of the existence of the intent to arbitrate in simple phrases entailing arbitration.[13] However, one extra reason why arbitration clauses need to be clearly and broadly drawn is the need to avoid any doubts.

As one of the reasons why parties opt for arbitration in reinsurance is the fact that the dispute will be resolved by a panel of industry experts, there is great importance placed in the reinsurance arbitration panel's qualifications and the process of selecting an arbitrator and umpire. The arbitrator's qualifications and appointment may be challenged.

The compelling reason for opting for reinsurance arbitration being the efficiency and cost-effective nature of it, consolidated arbitration proceedings are generally favoured. Case law has not always been supportive of consolidation in arbitration. The decision in *Compania Espanola de Petroleos S.A. v Nereus Shipping S.A.*[14] not accepting the argument for consolidation was overturned in *Wyerhaeuser Co v Western Seas Shipping Co.*[15] Since *Howsam v Dean Witer Reynolds Inc.*[16] and *Green Tree Financial Corp v Bazzle*,[17] the established tendency is for courts to leave consolidation matters to arbitral tribunals.

The nature and extent of discovery available in reinsurance arbitrations varies and to a certain extent also depends on the parties wishes and stipulations. Confidentiality is also a strong element for the parties' choice to arbitrate. In reality however, it is generally not guaranteed. The Arbitration Act 1996 does not explicitly protect confidentiality. In the USA, the FAA does not address arbitral confidentiality, nor does USA law otherwise ensure secrecy of information disclosed in arbitration.

Regarding the governing law in reinsurance arbitrations, in England, the Arbitration Act 1996 redefines the relationship between arbitrators and the courts and supports arbitration by reflecting the view that reflects the view that the decision of the parties to choose a private tribunal rather than the courts to resolve their dispute must be respected (section 1, Arbitration Act 1996). In the USA, the FAA is the primary source of arbitration law and promotes a policy in favour of arbitration. In Germany, arbitration is widely used and regulated in the Tenth Book of the ZPO. In addition, there is a strong policy in promoting and favouring arbitration.

All of the legal instruments, i.e. the Arbitration Act 1996, the FAA and the ZPO, as well as the New York Convention, provide for the enforcement of arbitration

---

[13] *Hartford Accident and Indemnity Co. v Swiss Reinsurance*: *Security Life Insurance Co. of America v Hannover Life Reinsurance Co. of America*, 2001 WL 392412 (D. Minn.).

[14] *Compania Espanola de Petroleos S.A. v Nereus Shipping S.A.*, 527 F2d 966 (2d Cir. 1975).

[15] *Wyerhaeuser Co v Western Seas Shipping Co* 743 F.2d 635 (9th Cir. 1984).

[16] *Howsam v Dean Witer Reynolds Inc.*537 US 79 (2002).

[17] *Green Tree Financial Corp v Bazzle* 539 US 444 (2003).

agreements. A reinsurance arbitral tribunal issues either a final award or a partial and interim award, allowing the final award to be issued at a later stage. The arbitration award must also be in a form to allow it to be enforceable. Following the arbitral award, a party to arbitral proceedings may make an application to court to vary or set aside an award. In the reinsurance industry, courts will recognize and enforce arbitral awards, absent manifest abuse of discretion.[18] Hence, courts will vacate an award if it were procured by corruption, fraud, or undue means, or the arbitrators were corrupt and impartial, or guilty of refusing to postpone the hearing, upon sufficient cause shown or where the arbitrators exceeded their powers, or on the basis that the tribunal lacked substantive jurisdiction or due to the proceedings serious irregularity.

References

Ostrager BR, Vyskocil MC (1996) Modern reinsurance law and practice. Glasser Legal Works, Lexis Nexis, Little Falls

Thomas JE, Lyons S (eds) (2012) New Appleman on insurance law – library edition, vol 7, Property insurance (chapters 71–79 §§ 71.01–79.06). Lexis Nexis, Los Angeles

[18] As shown in the *Michigan Mutual Insurance Co. and Others v Unigard Security Insurance Co.*, 44 F.3d 826 (9th Cir. 1995) ruling.

Table of Cases

A. England

Abrahams v Med. Re [1991]1 Lloyd's Rep. 216 . . . 50
AIG Europe SA v *QBE International Insurance Ltd* [2001]2 Lloyd's Rep. 268 . . . 70
Ali Shipping Corp. v Shipyard Trogir [1991]1 W.L.R. 314 C.A . . . 238, 284, 307
Anonymous Greek Co of General Insurances ("*The Ethniki*") *v AIG Europe (UK) & Ors*, [2000] Lloyd's Rep. 34 . . . 81
Associated Electric & Gas Insurance Services Ltd v European Reinsurance Co of Zurich [2003]1 All ER (Comm) 253 . . . 257, 284
Australia Widows Fund Life Assurance Society Ltd v National Mutual Life Association of Australia Ltd [1914] AC 634 . . . 57
Azov Shipping Co. v. *Balde Shipping Co. (No. 1)* [1999]l Lloyd's Rep 68 (QB Com Ct) *Axa* v *Ace Global Markets* [2006] Lloyd's Rep IR 683 . . . 75
Cigna Life Insurance Co of Europe SA-NV & Ors v Intercaser SA de Seguros y Reaseguros [2001] CLC 1356. . . 80
CGU International Insurance v *AstraZeneca Insurance Co.*, [2006] Lloyd's Rep IR 409. . . 63
Dolling-Baker v Merrett [1991]2 All E.R. 890 . . . 279, 280, 281
Eagle Star Insurance Co. Ltd v Yuval Insurance Co. Ltd [1978]1 Lloyd's Rep. 357 . . .23, 326, 329, 330, 331
Ethiopian Oil Sea Pulses Export Corporation v Rio del Mar Foods Incorporated (1990)1 Lloyd's Rep. 86. . . 156
Excess Insurance Co Ltd & Anor v Mander [1995] CLC 838 . . . 76, 77, 93, 220
Excess Insurance Co Ltd v Mander [1997]1 Lloyd's Rep. 119.
Fenton Insurance Co. Ltd v Gothaer Versicherungsbank VVaG [1997]1 Lloyd's Rep. 172. . . 61
General Reinsurance Corp. v Fennia Patria (1983) 2 Lloyd's Rep 287 (CA). . . 51, 53

K. Noussia, *Reinsurance Arbitrations*, DOI 10.1007/978-3-642-45146-1,

Harbour Assurance Co (UK) Ltd v Kansa General International Insurance Co Ltd [1993] QB 701 . . . 145
Hassneh Insurance Co. of Israel v Mew [1993]2 Lloyd's Rep. 293 . . . 152, 281, 282, 283, 305, 307
Heyman v Darwins [1942] AC 356 . . . 144, 145
Hiscox UnderwntingLtd v Dickson Manchester & Co Ltd [2004] EWHC 479 (Comm) . . . 212, 228
Hobbs Padgett & Co. (Reinsurance) Ltd v J CKirkland Ltd [1969] 2 Lloyd's Rep 547 (CA)
Home and Overseas Insurance Company Ltd v Unione Italiana Anglo Saxon Reinsurance Company [1978]1 Lloyd's Rep. 476 . . . 326, 329, 330
Home Insurance Co v Administratia Asigurarilor De Stat [1983]2 Lloyd's Rep. 674 . . . 22
Hume v AA Mutual International Insurance Company Ltd [1996] LRLR 19 (QB Com Ct) . . . 231
Insurance Co. v Lloyd's Syndicate [1995]1 Lloyd's Rep. 272 . . . 25, 281, 283
Insurance Co of Africa v *SCOR (UK) Reinsurance Co* Ltd [1985] 1 Lloyd's Rep 312 . . . 62
Lincoln National Life Insurance Co v Sun Life Assurance Co of Canada [2005] 1 Lloyd's Rep 606 . . . 284, 285, 338, 341, 342
Mackenderv. Feidia AG [1967] 2 QB 590 . . . 145
Orion Compania Espanola de Seguros v Belford Maatschappij Voor Algemene Verzekringeen [1962]2 Lloyd's Rep. 257 . . . 23
Orion Insurance Co. plc v Sphere Drake Insurance plc [1990]1 Lloyd's Rep. 465 . . . 50, 327
Pacific & General Insurance Co. Ltd v Hazell [1997] LRLR 65 . . . 61
Pine Top Insurance Co Ltd v Unione Italiana Anglo Saxon Reinsurance Co Ltd [1987] 1 Lloyd's Rep 476 . . . 58, 74, 75, 77
Sacor Maritima SA v Repsol Petroleo SA [1998] 1 Lloyd's Rep. 518 (QBD (Comm)) . . . 336
Scott v Avery (1856) 5 HL Gas 811 . . . 230
Stargas S.P.A. v. Petredec Ltd (The Sargasso) [1994] 1 Lloyd's Rep. 412 . . . 337, 338
Toomey v *Eagle Star Insurance Co Ltd (No 1)* [1994] 1 Lloyd's Rep 516 . . . 67
Trygg Hansa Insurance Co Ltd v Equitas Ltd [1998]2 loyd's Rep. 439 . . . 77, 91
Youell v Bland Welch & Co. (1990)2 Lloyd's Rep 423 (QB) . . . 51
Zermalt Holdings SA v. *Nu-Life Upholstery Repairs Ltd* [1985] 2 EGLR 14 (QB Com Ct) . . . 300

B. USA

Aegis Security Insurance Co. v Philadelphia Contributionship, 416 F. Supp.2d 303 (M.D. Pa. 2005) 263
Affiliated FM Ins. Co v Constitution Reins,. Corp., 416 Mass. 839 N.E.2d 878 (1994) 56
Allianz Life Ins. Co. of N. Am. v American Phoenix Life & Reinsurance Co., No. 99-802, 2000 U.S. Dist. LEXIS 7216 (D. Minn. Mar. 28, 2000) 167, 243, 244
American Centennial Ins Co v National Casualty Co, 951 F2d 107, (6th Cir. 1991) 279
American Home Assur. Co. v American Fidelity & Cas. Co., 356 F.2d 690 (2nd Cir. 1966) 161
Apperson v Fleet Carrier Corp. 879 E2d 1344 (6th Cir. 1989) 192
Arthur Andersen LLP, et al. v. Carlisle, et al., 129 S.Ct. 1896 (2009) 238
Associated Indemnity Corp. v Home Insurance Co., 19 F.3d 1432 (6th Cir. 1994) 143
Atlantica Ins. Co., Ltd v Pan Atlantic Group, Inc. No 86-6363 (S.D.N.Y. June 24, 1987) 174
Atmel Corp. v LM Ericsson Telefon, AB 371 F. Supp. 2d 402 (S.D.N.Y. 2005).
CNA Reinsurance Co. v Trustmark Ins. Co., No. 01 C 1652, 2001 U.S. Dist. LEXIS 7523 (N.D. 111. June 5, 2001) 158
Del Webb Construction v Richardson Hospital Authority. 823 F.2d 145 (5th Cir. 1987) 256
Dorinco Reinsurance Co. v Ace American Insurance Co, 2008 US Dist. LEXIS 4593 (ED. Mich. Mar. 5, 2008) 178, 263
Employers Insurance Co. of Wausau v Century Indemnity Co., 443 E3d 573 (7th Cir. 2006) 165, 259
Employers Insurance of Wausau v *Certain Underwriters at Lloyd's*, No. 91-CV-529 (Wis. Cir. Ct., Marathon County, October 14, 1992) 187
Employers Ins. Co of Wasau v Century Ind. Co., 443 F.3d 573 (7th Cir. 2006) 165, 259
Evanston Ins. Co. v Kansa Gen. Int'l Ins. Co., No. 94C4957 (N.D. Ill. Oct. 17, 1994 and Jan. 13, 1995) 181
Exchange Mut. Fire Ins. Co. v Mutual Fire Ins. Co., (1915) 59 Pa Super 240 49
First Option of Chi. Ins. v Kaplan, 514 US 938 (1995) 165
Frank B. Hall In24c. v Colorado School Districts Self-Insurance Pool No. 92-CV-225 (Colo. Dist. Ct. March 26, 1993) 168, 170, 245
Green Tree Financial Corp v Bazzle 539 US 444 (2003) 179, 251, 258, 261, 358
Goshawk Dedicated Lmtd. v Portsmouth Settlement Co 466 F. Supp. 2d 1293 (N.D. Ga. 2006) 100, 101, 105, 107, 110, 113, 114

Government of U.K. of Gr. Brit. v Boeing Co., 998 F.2d 68 (2d Cir. 1993). 253, 277, 279
Hall Street Assocs., LLC v Mattel, Inc., 552 U.S. 576 (2008) 301, 310, 314, 315
Hamilton Life Ins. Co v Republic Nat. Life Ins. Co., (1969, CA2 NY) 408 F2d 606 162
Hartford Accident and Indemnity Co. v Swiss Reinsurance Co. of America, 246 F.3d 219 (2d Cir. 2001) 168, 247
Hastie v *De Peyster* 3 Cai R. 190, NY Sup. 1805 63
Howsam v Dean Witer Reynolds Inc.537 US 79 (2002) 251, 257, 258, 259, 261, 358
In Re Republic of Kazakhstan v Biederman Int'l (Kazakhstan), 168 F.3d 880 (5th Cir. 1999) 269
Lavino Shipping Co. v Santa Cecilia Co. No 72 Civ. 3097, 1972 AMC 2454 (SDNY 1972). 257
Lincoln National Life Insurance Company v *Sun Life Assurance Company of Canada and Others* [2004] 1 Lloyd's Rep 737 (QB Com Ct). 296, 333
Matter of the Arbitration between Argonaut Midwest Insurance Co. v General Reinsurance Corp. 1998 U.S. Dist. LEXIS 12497 (N.D. Ill. 1998) 198, 199
Manhattan Life Ins. Co v Prussian Life Ins. Co (1924, CA2 NY) 296 F 39 61
Medical Insurance Exchange of California v Certain Underwriters at Lloyds, London, No. C 05-2609 PJH, 2006 WL 463531 (N.D. Cal. Feb. 24, 2006) 163
Michigan Mutual Insurance Company and Others v Unigard Security Insurance Company, 44 F.3d 826 (9th Cir. 1995). 29, 30, 237, 238, 308, 309, 357
Milliken v Pratt, 125 Mass. 374 (1878). 111, 112
Mitsubishi Motors Corp. v Soler Chrysler-Plymouth, Inc., 473 U.S. 614 (1985) 114
Moses H. Cone Memorial Hosp. v Mercury Constr. Corp., 460 U.S.1. (1983) 142, 166
Nationwide Gen. Ins. Co. v Investors Ins. Co. of Am., 332 N.E.2d 333, 336 (N.Y. 1975) 162
Nationwide Mut. Ins. Co. v First State Ins. Co., 213 F. Supp. 2d 10 (D. Mass. 2002) 191
NBC, Inc. v Bear Stearns & Co., 165 F.3d 184 (2d Cir. 1999) 269
NECA Ins. Ltd. v National Union Fire Ins. Co., 595 F. Supp. 955 (S.D.N.Y. 1984).
New England Reinsurance Corporation v Tennessee Ins. Comp., 780 F. Supp. 73 (D. Mass 1991) 181
New York State Marine Ins Co v *Protection Ins Co* 18 F.Cas 160 (CC Mass 1841). 63
North Carolina League of Municipalities v Clarendon Nat'l Ins. Co., 733 F.Supp. 1009 /E.D.N.C. 1990) 158, 67, 242

North River Ins Co v *CIGNA Reinsurance Co* 52 F.3d 1194 (3rd Cir. (NJ) Apr 13, 1995) 59, 69, 70, 73
Odfjell ASA v Celanese AG 328 F. Supp. 2d 505, (S.D.N.Y. 2004) 268
Ott v *AllStar Ins Corp* 99 Wis.2d 635, (Wis. Jan 06, 1981) 68
Pacific Employers Insurance Co. v Moglia No. 05 C 1366, 2007 U.S. Dist. LEXIS 21967 (N.D. Ill. Mar. 27, 2007) 288
P.B. Hall Company of Colorado v Colorado School Districts Self Insurance Pool, No 92 CV 225 (Col Dist. Ct. March 21, 1993), 3 Mealey's Reins.Rep. No 24 166
Pedcor Management Co. Inc. v Nations Personnel of Texas, 343 F.3d (4th Cir. 2003) 179
Pompano Windy City Partners, Ltd. v Bear Stearns & Co., Nos. 87 Civ. 7560, 88 Civ. 7159 (S.D.N.Y. Feb. 17, 1993) 233
Progressive Casualty Ins. Co. v Reaseguradora Nacional de Venezuela (1992, SD NY) 802 F Supp 1069 . . . . . 48, 78
Re Matter of Arbitration between Chilean Nitrate & Iodine Sales and Intermarine Corp. No. 71 Civ. 2348 HRT 1972 AMC 2460 (SDNY 1971) 257
Remmey v PaineWebber, Inc., 32 F.3d 143 (4th Cir. 1994) 313
Security Life Insurance Co. of America v Hannover Life Reinsurance Co. of America, 2001 WL 392412 (D. Minn.) 168, 247
Selcke v New England Insurance Co., 995 F.2d 688 (7th Cir. 1993) 143
Shaw's Supermarkets Inc. v United Food and Commercial Workers Union, Local 791, 321 F.3d 258
Sheldon v Vermonty, 269 F.3d 1202 (10th Cir. 2001) 287
Société Intrafor Coloret Subtec Middle East Co. M. M. Gagnant Guilbert et al., Revue de l'Arbitrage (1985), No. 2, 300 324
Sphere Drake Ins. Ltd. v The Lincoln Nat'l Life Ins. Co., No. 05 C 6411, 2006 U.S. Dist. LEXIS 70533 (N.D. 111. Sep. 13, 2006) 287
Stanton v Paine Webber Jackson & Curtis, Inc., 685 F. Supp. 1241, (S.D. Fla. 1988) 267
Stoh-Nielson SA v Ammal Feeds Intern, Corp., 548 FJd 85 (2008) 178, 255
The Bremen v Zapata Off-Shore Co, 407 U.S. 1 (1972) 111, 112
Trustmark Ins. Co. v. John Hancock Life Ins. Co., 631 F.3d 869 (7th Cir. 2011), cert. denied, 79 U.S.L.W. 3641 (U.S. May 16, 2011) (No. 10-1213) 202, 207, 208, 209, 210, 211
Tumey v. State, 273 U.S. 510 (1927) 206
United States v South-Eastern Underwriters Ass'n, 322 U.S. 533 (1944) 193
Utopia Studios Ltd. v. Earth Tech Inc., No. 08-cv-3515 (E.D.N.Y. April 20, 2009) 293
Volt Info. Sciences, Inc. v Bored of Trustees of Leland Stanford Junior Univ., 489 U.S. 468 (1989) 258, 277
Wellons, Inc. v T.E. Ibberson Co., 869 E2d 1166 (8th Cir. 1989) 323
Weyerhaeuser Co v Western Seas Shipping Co., 743 F2d 635 (9th Cir, 1984) 250, 258, 277, 278, 358

Wetherell v Sentry Reinsurance, Inc., (1990, ED Pa)743 F Supp 1157 51
Wurttembergishe Fire Insurance Co. v Republic Insurance Co.,
No. 86 Civ. 2696 (S.D.N.Y Oct. 28, 1987) 323
Yasuda Fire & Marine Ins. Co. of Europe v Continental Casualty Co.,
37 F3dd 345 (7th Cir. Ill. 1994). 314
Zenith Insurance Co. v Employers Insurance of Wasau, 141 F3d 300
(7th Cir. 1998) 83

C. Germany

BayObLG, decision of 11. 8. 2000, 4 Z Sch 05/00 346
BGH, decision of 17. 8. 2000, III ZB 43/99 . . . . 346, 347, 348
BGH, decision of 1. 2. 2001.III ZR 332/99 . . . . 346, 347, 348
BGH, decision of 30. 1. 2003, III ZB 6/02 . . . . 346, 347, 348
OLG Köln, decision of 27. 3. 2001, 9 Sch 06/01 . . . . 346, 347, 348
OLG Stuttgart, judgment of 27. 7. 01, 4 U 251/00 . . . . 346, 347, 348
VG Frankfurt, decision of 12. 11. 2001, 9 E 5148/00(1) 346, 347, 348

Table of Statutes

A. International

Guidon de la Mer 8
New York Convention on the Recognition and Enforcement
of Foreign Arbitral Awards. 26, 27, 72, 358, 99, 10, 101, 102, 103, 104, 105, 107, 108, 109, 110, 112, 113, 114, 128, 129, 155, 167, 193, 194, 236, 239, 331, 358
Regulation (EC) No 593/2008 of the European Parliament and of
the Council of 17 June 2008 on the law applicable to contractual
obligations (Rome I Regulation) 219
UNCITRAL Model Law on International Commercial
Arbitration . . . 73, 354, 88, 117, 120, 123, 124, 125, 126, 127, 129, 132, 136, 138
Vienna New York Convention on the Law of Treaties (VCLT). 103, 104

B. England

Act of the Parliament of 1745. 9
Allied Control Council Act No. 47 of March 1947 14
Arbitration Act 1950. 87
Arbitration Act 1975. 87
Arbitration Act 1979. 87
Arbitration Act 1996. . . . . 18, 72, 85, 88, 89, 90, 92, 93, 154, 171, 184, 185, 189, 190, 191, 194, 195, 211, 215, 218, 219, 227, 228, 229, 273, 275, 293, 294, 295, 298, 299, 300, 302, 303, 304, 328, 354, 358.
Civil Procedure Rules (CPR) 89, 151, 281, 299
Insurance Companies Act 1982. 4
Limitation Act 1980 87
Marine Insurance Act 1906. 49

K. Noussia, *Reinsurance Arbitrations*, DOI 10.1007/978-3-642-45146-1,

C. USA

Federal Arbitration Act. . . . . . . 72, 85, 97, 98, 99, 100, 138, 141, 155, 167, 172, 174, 188, 189, 192, 193, 194, 195, 197, 198, 199, 200, 205, 206, 212, 214, 235, 238, 239, 240, 241, 246, 247, 250, 251, 254, 256, 257, 265, 266, 267, 268, 270, 273, 275, 278, 286, 288, 297, 310, 312, 315, 320, 332, 354, 358.
Federal Rules of Civil Procedure (Fed. R.Civ.P.) 189
McCarran-Ferguson Act 99, 100, 101, 102, 103, 107, 108, 109, 110, 113, 214

D. Germany

Allgemeine Landesrecht für die Preussischen Staaten 1794. 8
Civil Code (BGB). 124
Code of Civil Procedure (ZPO). 358, 85, 123, 124, 125, 126, 127, 129, 131, 138, 347
Commercial Code (HGB) 124
Hamburger Assekuranz- und Havarie-Ordnung 1731 9
Insurance Law (VVG) 124
German Arbitration Act 123, 124, 125, 126, 127, 132, 135

About the Author

Dr. Kyriaki Noussia is an attorney at law admitted to the Athens Bar as a Greek Barrister and is licensed to appear before the Supreme Court and the Conseil d'État. She specialises in arbitration and in international commercial law. She has an extensive and wide-ranging experience *inter alia* in insurance, reinsurance, marine insurance, arbitration and mediation, banking and finance, energy, oil and gas, investment and environmental law. Since 2011 she has set up her own legal practice and is able to advise in the above areas both in a stand-alone and in a transactional context as well as on the contentious side. Prior to that she has held numerous academic positions abroad, such as at the University of Hamburg Faculty of Law and the Max Planck Institute for Comparative and international Private Law in Hamburg, Germany, where she was an Alexander von Humboldt Research Fellow (2007–2010). Prior to that she has been a C.S.E.T. Lecturer in Common Law at the University of Birmingham, UK (Birmingham Law School). In 2013 she was a Fulbright (Greece) Visiting Scholar at Columbia Law School, USA. She is also a member of various associations and committees in the fields of international commercial law, arbitration, international procedural law, insurance and reinsurance law, transportation law and private international law.

K. Noussia, *Reinsurance Arbitrations*, DOI 10.1007/978-3-642-45146-1,

About the Author

Index

A
Agreed award, 266
Agreement to arbitrate, 19
Alternative dispute resolution, 28, 29
Applicable law, 18, 196
Arbitrability, 62, 85, 144–147, 150, 225
Arbitrable, 151, 156
  disputes, 86
  issues, 198
Arbitral agreements, 78, 94
Arbitral awards, 113, 211, 266, 274, 275, 280, 281, 283, 284, 286, 289, 312, 315, 322, 325
Arbitral panels, 321
Arbitral proceedings, 152, 173, 204, 251, 252, 267, 269–271
Arbitral rules, 312
Arbitral tribunals, 16, 17, 134, 207, 267, 271
Arbitrations, 2, 20–24, 31, 32, 76, 130, 132, 135, 198, 268, 292, 304, 319, 321–323
  agreements, 17, 22, 34, 61, 69, 73, 77, 80, 81, 85–89, 91, 94, 95, 108, 124, 125, 127, 129, 133, 136, 140, 141, 147, 150, 153, 163–166, 169, 170, 173, 175, 178, 191–193, 195, 198, 207, 208, 216, 239, 251–253, 269–271, 274, 276, 279, 290, 295–300, 313, 319, 320, 323
  award, 18, 22, 51, 62, 132, 136, 185, 213, 268, 271, 272, 277–279, 282, 290–294, 301, 302, 309, 316, 321, 322, 325
  clauses, 16, 19, 21, 24, 31, 32, 41, 42, 61–66, 69, 73, 74, 78–80, 82, 83, 86, 120, 124, 126–128, 130, 132, 136, 139, 141, 142, 144, 145, 147, 149, 150, 153, 157, 160, 161, 166, 167, 174, 179, 182, 183, 191, 196–198, 206, 208, 215, 217, 218, 220, 238, 267, 279, 296, 298, 311, 323, 324
  decision, 291
  dispute, 216
  panels, 24, 80, 203, 212, 224, 248
  proceedings, 16, 23, 36, 67, 74, 118, 120, 125, 135, 136, 160, 186, 211, 229, 248, 251, 253, 262, 267, 276, 277, 279, 281, 302, 305, 313, 321
  provisions, 85, 149, 177, 191, 207
  treaty, 23
  tribunal, 312
Arbitrators, 77, 287, 292, 322
Awards, 17–19, 22, 65, 76, 108, 184, 187, 245, 248, 254, 255, 257, 258, 265–272, 274, 276, 277, 281, 282, 286, 287, 289, 290, 293, 302, 304, 309, 313–315, 325

C
Cedents, 70, 74, 81, 120, 124, 145, 157, 158, 160, 225, 227, 228, 248, 283, 316
Collateral estoppel, 292, 294
Confidentiality, 23, 246–250, 252–254, 256, 258, 259, 261
Consolidated arbitration, 225
Consolidation, 221, 225–228, 230, 231, 233–236, 238, 251, 252, 261, 262, 312
Contra proferentem, 47, 209
Costs of the award, 18
Court proceedings, 276

K. Noussia, *Reinsurance Arbitrations*, DOI 10.1007/978-3-642-45146-1,

D
Disclosure, 76
Discovery, 21, 22, 62, 115, 210, 238, 239, 241, 243, 244, 284, 290
Dispute resolution, 2, 34, 113, 124, 131, 160, 164, 292, 319
  method, 27

E
Enforcement, 88
Estoppel, 154
Excess of loss ratio non-proportional reinsurance treaties, 5
Excess of loss reinsurance, 59
Excess of loss treaties, 60
Exchange of the statements, 18
Expert evidence, 115

F
Facultative, 40
Facultative non-proportional reinsurance, 4
Facultative obligatory treaty, 58
Facultative proportional reinsurance, 4
Facultative reinsurance, 4, 41, 59, 317
  agreement, 41
  contracts, 55–57
Federal circuit courts, 294
Federal courts, 212
Federal law, 93
Final award, 265
Follow the forms, 53
Follow the fortunes, 53, 55, 318, 319
Follow the settlements, 53, 54, 56, 61, 318, 319
Formal treaties, 5
Fronting agreements, 56
Full reinsurance clause, 57, 61

G
Good faith, 133

H
Hold harmless agreements, 226, 260–262
Honourable engagement, 19, 21, 32, 43, 78, 81, 140, 297, 298
  clauses, 19, 261

I
Insurance
  companies, 11
  industry, 10
Interim awards, 63
International arbitration, 114, 119
International disputes, 23
International reinsurance business, 10
Issue estoppel, 311, 312

J
Jurisdictions, 119
  clause, 65

L
Lex mercatoria, 196
Litigation, 2, 20, 22–24, 31, 35, 36, 118, 130, 132, 135, 159, 198, 319, 320, 322

M
Marine insurance, 6, 10
Marine reinsurance, 7, 8
  contracts, 140

N
Non-obligatory treaty, 58
Non-proportional reinsurance, 4
  contracts, 55, 56
  treaties, 5
Notice of arbitration, 16

O
Obligatory treaties, 58

P
Party-appointed arbitrators, 17
Party autonomy, 15, 107, 195, 252
Placement slip, 5, 14, 26
Policy, 45
Premiums, 40, 57, 59, 60
Privacy, 23, 249
Proceedings, 266, 268
Proportional facultative, 56, 57
  reinsurance, 60, 61

Proportional reinsurance, 4, 56
  treaties, 5
Proportional treaties, 5, 57
Provisional measures, 265
Public policy, 301
Punitive damages, 268, 301

Q
Quota share non-marine reinsurance treaty, 295
Quota share proportional reinsurance treaty, 5
Quota share reinsurance, 59
Quota share treaty, 42

R
Reaty reinsurance, 4
Reinsurance, 6, 8, 19, 80, 322
  agreements, 7, 51, 67, 68, 81, 86, 87, 129, 141, 147, 159, 166, 191, 193, 197, 198, 248, 261, 298, 302, 314
  arbitral awards, 280
  arbitral proceedings, 262
  arbitral tribunal, 325
  arrangements, 47
  business, 11, 14
  clauses, 36, 87
  company, 9
  contracts, 6, 7, 11, 12, 19, 24, 34, 35, 39, 40, 42–45, 47–51, 54, 56, 57, 61, 65, 70, 77, 79–83, 87, 88, 95, 120, 126, 128, 132, 141, 154, 157, 160, 162, 163, 166, 175, 196, 255, 276, 295, 296, 298, 311, 317–320, 322
  cover, 6, 9, 11
  disputes, 12, 23, 24, 33–36, 61, 73, 77, 78, 81, 82, 121, 129, 132–135, 143, 151, 163, 167, 198, 227, 257, 301, 319, 323
  disputes resolution, 319
  engagement, 21
  industry, 12, 13, 23, 26, 31, 45, 73, 74, 149, 151, 163, 260, 301, 319–321, 325
  information, 320
  issues, 28
  markets, 34, 35, 46, 82, 101, 102, 134, 255
  mediation, 33
  policies, 100, 145
  relationship, 14, 15, 23, 317, 318
  slip, 69
  transactions, 71
  treaties, 2, 19, 20, 26, 30, 35, 53, 60, 77, 78, 82, 149, 151, 214
  wording, 317
Reinsurance arbitrations, 3, 22–24, 34–36, 62, 76, 101, 124, 130, 132, 139, 169, 175, 191, 201, 248, 261, 262, 319, 320, 322–324
  agreement, 297
  award, 36
  clause, 74
  clauses, 133, 186, 187
  panels, 76, 212
Reinsurers, 12
Res judicata, 221, 292, 294, 311
Retrocession, 64
  agreement, 64
Retrocessionaires, 25, 41, 64, 213, 218, 276, 279, 280

S
Seat, 17
  of the arbitration, 77
Separability, 15, 127, 129, 157, 194
Situs, 32
Slips, 39, 43, 44, 61, 77, 78, 140, 147, 217, 218, 317
Standard terms, 274
Stop loss
  excess, 5
  treaties, 57
Summary adjudication, 259
Surance agreement, 14
Surance contract, 36
Surplus proportional reinsurance treaty, 5
Surplus treaties, 57

T
Treaties, 30, 93, 296
  reinsurance, 26, 41, 317
Tribunal, 18, 19, 268

U
Usages, 45, 46
Utmost good faith, 44, 70, 71

V
Vacatur, 245, 280, 283–285

W
Warranties, 45

MIX
Papier aus verantwortungsvollen Quellen
Paper from responsible sources
FSC® C105338

If you have any concerns about our products,
you can contact us on
ProductSafety@springernature.com

In case Publisher is established outside the EU,
the EU authorized representative is:
Springer Nature Customer Service Center GmbH
Europaplatz 3, 69115 Heidelberg, Germany

Printed by Libri Plureos GmbH
in Hamburg, Germany